A

CONTEMPORARY

READER

Essays for Today and Tomorrow

Edited by

HARRY W. RUDMAN   and   IRVING ROSENTHAL
ASSOCIATE PROFESSOR OF ENGLISH   ASSISTANT PROFESSOR OF ENGLISH
THE CITY COLLEGE OF NEW YORK   THE CITY COLLEGE OF NEW YORK

THE RONALD PRESS COMPANY • NEW YORK

4

Library of Congress Catalog Card Number: 61–6148

PREFACE

We have brought together this collection of essays to acquaint the student in freshman English and in composition with representative samples of good current writing on contemporary issues. The selections, many anthologized here for the first time, constitute models of effective, functional writing. Their subjects are well suited to the student's interests and abilities; their range extends from the immediate, lesser concerns of fraternity life and campus athletics to the weightier problems of present-day culture and world affairs. They include lively discussions of such varied matters as the state of the popular arts, the nature of our business civilization, the promise and the menace of automation, the debate on television as a teaching device, and the controversy over the testing of weapons powerful enough to threaten the existence of life on our planet. We believe that these vital materials afford the most critical means of encouraging individual thought and expression and for teaching the requisite vocabulary, comprehension, and writing skills.

We have made every effort to achieve a diversity of interest that should appeal to all students regardless of their fields of specialization; at the same time we have included groups of selections that have special interest for those in the liberal arts and for those in the more specialized areas of science, technology, business, and education. The instructor will, therefore, have ample opportunity to make a choice of material best suited to the interests and capacities of his class. Most of the selections are self-contained units. Many of them present varying aspects, if not opposite sides, of some fundamental questions of our times.

Selections in an anthology are used in different ways—for discussion, testing reading comprehension, developing vocabulary, explaining rhetorical devices, and stimulating writing by the student. It has been our experience that many instructors pay little attention to the editorial apparatus to be found in some collections of essays; they prefer, instead, the freedom to bring to their teaching a degree of freshness, individual emphasis, and flexibility that is often restricted by conventional pedagogic devices. For that reason we have included only brief biographical summaries and suggested theme topics intended to serve as springboards for further thought and exploration by the student.

We are indebted to the many authors and their publishers who have granted permission to reproduce their publications. To our wives, Judith E. Rudman and Ruth Rosenthal, we express our gratitude for their forbearance, suggestions, and willingness to be our first and most critical readers.

Harry W. Rudman
Irving Rosenthal

New York, N. Y.
January, 1961

CONTENTS

EDUCATION: AIMS AND PROBLEMS

COLLEGE LIFE

THE WORLD OF BOOKS

WRITING AND THE POWER OF LANGUAGE

THE POPULAR ARTS

THE WORLD OF BUSINESS

WAYS OF SCIENCE

PARENTS AND CHILDREN

PEOPLE AND PLACES

OUR UNEASY WORLD

THE AMERICAN SCENE

EDUCATION: AIMS
AND PROBLEMS

EDUCATION IN DEMOCRATIC
SOCIETY

David Daiches

> Educated at Edinburgh University and Oxford, David Daiches
> now teaches at Cambridge University. In this country he taught
> at the University of Chicago and at Cornell. An eminent critic
> and a prolific writer, he is the author of such works as *Virginia
> Woolf* (1942), *Robert Louis Stevenson* (1947), *Robert Burns*
> (1951), and *Willa Cather* (1951), biographies; *The Novel and
> the Modern World* (1939), a critical study; *Two Worlds* (1956),
> an autobiography; and *A Critical History of English Literature*
> (1960).

The other day I heard a professor of education at an important
Midwestern university give a talk to a group of his colleagues on his
experiences in Thailand, where he had been for over a year advising
on education. In shocked tones he told his audience that in Thai
schools the pupils have to pass an examination before they can be
moved up from one grade into the next. He added that the American
team out there were trying to remove this dangerously undemocratic
practice, and so enable a much higher percentage of pupils to move
up each year and complete their schooling. Thus everybody would be
educated, not only a tiny few, with the happy consequence that the
people would be fortified against the seductions of Communism. At

another point in his talk he said that Thai education was too "intellectual" and not sufficiently practical and vocational: no garage
mechanic in Thailand was really competent to do automobile repairs.
(Whether the kind of technical education which the professor advocated, a kind of education in which Soviet Russia, if the statistics published in the Western press are accurate, leads the world, was also a
defense against Communism, he did not say.) In general, he seemed
to regard education as either (a) the moving up a ladder to the top,
regardless of what was done or learned in the process of moving, or
(b) training to do a particular job of work, which will be the pupil's
means of livelihood in afterlife.

Educators in Britain and America would agree that education must
be democratic and it must be useful. Of course these are sensible ideas;
few would claim that education ought to be undemocratic and useless.
The difference between the British and the American approach lies
in their respective definitions, or at least implicit definitions, of democracy and usefulness as applied to education. A democracy, in British
eyes, has the duty of providing free education to every child according
to his "age, ability, and aptitude" (in the words of the Education Act
of 1944). The more democratic the educational system, the more the
schools will strive to give to each pupil, whatever his class or economic
background, that education which encourages and makes full use of
whatever abilities he possesses.

As for the *usefulness* of education, there is still much general feeling
in England that the function of education is to teach the pupil how to
spend money, not how to make it. That is one reason why the British
are having such difficulty in persuading youngsters to go in for the
sciences rather than the humanities; the latter are concerned with the
art of living, with books and music and good conversation, with the
training of "a gentleman or noble person in virtuous and gentle discipline" (as Spenser put it in explaining the object of his *Faerie
Queene*). A surprising number of British middle-class parents still consider that kind of education the "best," and they want their children
to have it. So if—to oversimplify—the American definition of the
democratic and the useful in education leads to the contradictory ideals
of equality of curriculum and of promotion on the one hand, and
vocational training according to a future job on the other, the British
definition of the same terms leads to the equally contradictory ideals
of training according to individual abilities and aptitude on the one
hand, and on the other to a general preference for the "arts side" over
the "science side."

This, of course, applies to secondary education rather than to the
colleges and universities, and each attitude is rooted in history in a
complex manner. (The Harvard report on *General Education in a*

Free Society discusses the historical background of the American situation with considerable insight.) I begin with a reference to secondary education deliberately, because the whole pattern of differences between the British and American academic scenes derives from basic differences in their attitudes to secondary education. The British have always put far more emphasis on secondary education; the large majority of the educational reforms of the last hundred years in England have been concerned with elementary or secondary education, and in the last quarter-century and more all concern about the curriculum, about "general education in a free society," about distinguishing between pupils of different abilities within the same age group, about language teaching, aptitude testing, teaching methods, and so on, has been concentrated on education at the secondary level.

The schools, not the colleges and universities, have been the main object of controversy between humanists and scientists and between all other opposed or professedly opposed schools of thought about education. On the whole, the universities have gone quietly on training the relatively few people sent up to them from the top forms of the secondary schools. My impression is that in America many more of these problems have been discussed with reference to the colleges (e.g., the question of "freshman English" and of basic literature courses) and there has been more excitement among serious and responsible educators about the college curriculum than about earlier educational levels (e.g., the Hutchins experiment in Chicago, the Harvard report, the continuous experimentation in so many liberal arts colleges).

The reason for this appears to me to be that while in America the ideal is that everybody should move right up to the top of the educational ladder—that is, right up to the university—the British ideal is that it is the object of secondary education, going ideally up to the age of seventeen or eighteen, to train the complete man, or as much of him as is available in any given individual, and that education beyond that level is for a minority with special gifts or special purposes. American secondary education is in some respects committed by its interpretation of the democratic doctrine to going at the pace of the slowest, and thus the high school curriculum is watered, leaving much basic knowledge to be acquired at college. British secondary education, which has chosen the other horn of the dilemma and tends to go at the pace of the quickest, being geared really to the needs of the brightest pupils and giving them every kind of special treatment and "forcing," puts the main burden of education onto the secondary level. The British schoolboy who is at all bright will work harder between the ages of, say, thirteen and eighteen than he will ever need to work at the university.

I remember myself with what immense relief I left school at Edin-

burgh to proceed to the university. Now at last I was free to do only
the subjects that really interested me, and no longer hard hours of
homework every evening on a great variety of subjects. I had had five
years each of mathematics, physics and chemistry, and Greek; and six
years each of English, history, and Latin, together with three years of
French and two of German. (In recent years there has been an increasing tendency to specialize in the last two years of school, and concentrate on two or three subjects in preparation for university scholarship
examinations.) And these subjects were all learned cumulatively, building each year on what was learned the year before, not taken in isolated units as is so often done in American high schools. I am not
saying that my education was ideal—it was fiercely competitive, and it
did very little for the large number of pupils who could not keep up
with the competitive pace set by the bright pupils at the top, and it
also was sometimes too formal and mechanical—but it was *solid*. It
told me nothing about how to be a good citizen, but it taught me some
basic skills, including several languages and more mathematics and
sciences than is generally taught in the first and sometimes the second
year of American colleges. It also taught me how to write essays, one
of the most stressed features of British secondary education.

There is a good case against this kind of secondary education.
American educators would say that it penalized heavily the non-academic type of pupil, and that the whole curriculum was conceived in
too narrowly academic terms. The first charge is certainly justified;
the second can be debated. The Education Act of 1944 tried to meet
the first charge by distinguishing between different types of schools,
or of curricula within a single "comprehensive" school, at which a
child was entitled to a free education. There was the academic "grammar school" for those who showed an aptitude for it, and "modern"
schools or technical schools for the others. The sifting is done by the
now famous—or notorious—"eleven plus" examination.[1] Thus the
non-academic students are taken care of in a much more general and
flexible kind of education, but not at the expense of the progress of
the traditional "bright boy." The trouble is that the "grammar
school" (which alone leads to the university) still enjoys the highest
social prestige, and middle-class parents want to send their children
there whether they qualify for a free place or not. The Education Act
promised "parity of esteem" between the different types of school and
of teacher; but it has not worked out that way. The British know very
well that the grammar school type of education is for the brightest
pupils—in the traditional sense of that term—and it is they who are

[1] An examination (in English and arithmetic, together with intelligence and aptitude tests) taken as a rule when the child is eleven years old or a little over.

being trained as an elite to do the most responsible of the nation's jobs. And, naturally, they want their children to be among the elite.

All this is by way of explanation of the often noted fact that the British student generally knows more when he comes up to the university than the American college freshman does. If going to college is a democratic right, then education must be spread out in order to leave something for the college to do for those who have no aptitude for higher learning. At Indiana University, where I am at the moment, the freshman and even sophomore courses in language and literature represent, in both content and level of teaching, what is taught in Britain two or even three years before the end of secondary education. And yet this is not altogether true. For the American freshman and sophomore has often a kind of curiosity, a provocative, uninformed but insistent "show me" attitude, an insistence on pitting his own limited experience against his teacher's knowledge, that makes the American college classroom at these levels very different indeed from the classroom of either the British grammar school or the British university.

"Why did Ulysses spend all that time in getting home to his wife after he left Troy?" a freshman asked one of my colleagues here the other day, during a lesson on the Odyssey. "If he'd really wanted to get home quickly, he would have managed it. I think he was kidding himself when he said he was so anxious to get back." This is naive, but it is not stupid, and it is not the kind of thing an English schoolboy would ask. The bright English schoolboy would mug up the standard works on the Homeric world and turn out a sophisticated essay on "Homer and the Heroic Age" based on a conflation of half a dozen books he had read in the school library; but it would never occur to him to ask whether Ulysses was kidding himself when he expressed his anxiety to return home quickly. The English schoolboy tends to relate knowledge to other knowledge, in order to form an elegant pattern (the bright essay being always the standard of achievement in the humanities); the American freshman wants to relate everything he reads or is told to his own experience. The latter as a rule has no sense of history or of form or of the *otherness* of different times and places; the former often lacks a sense of personal implication in what he studies.

To British—and indeed European—eyes, American education seems to waste some of the best learning years, at least for the brighter pupils, and to postpone until an unnecessarily late stage the essential core of education. But there is another side to the picture. The better American students are less blasé and work harder than their British opposite numbers, and by the end of their four undergraduate years have often achieved a kind of sophistication in terms of their subject which is at the opposite pole from the attitude revealed by the fresh-man's question about Ulysses. That kind of sophistication, which is particularly noticeable among the brighter students of literature, is consciously won by hard effort; it is (and I am talking of the best students) often the prelude to the use of specialized techniques in graduate work. The English student, building on his school training, will develop his accustomed skills with a kind of leisurely elegance and often, by the time he gets his degree, is not fundamentally any better educated than when he left school. He is likely to be less am-bitious, more skeptical, less fundamentally serious than the American.

In such fields as literature, philosophy, and history, at least, the bright British student will most appreciate the lecturer who plays with ideas cleverly and suggestively, but the bright American student re-sents that: he wants the truth, or the right methods, and no nonsense. "Do you believe in that view of literature you were developing in your lecture this morning?" a Cornell student once asked me. I said that I did not, but I thought it was interesting to play with the idea a little and see where it led us. He replied, almost angrily, that if I did not believe the theory to be true I should not waste my own and the class's time discussing it at such length; it was sheer verbal gym-nastics, and the students were there to *learn,* not to be played with. "Is C. S. Lewis's book on sixteenth-century literature a book to be read?" a graduate student asked me the other day at Indiana. I replied that it was a fresh and sometimes brilliant reading of the texts of the period, and though I quarreled sharply with some of the views expressed in it, I thought it a most stimulating book, well worth read-ing. "But will it give me a proper view of the period?" she persisted. "I don't know," I replied. "I'm not sure what the 'proper' view of the period is. Read it and make up your own mind about it." This answer was not regarded as satisfactory.

I often have the feeling that the American student, who works hard and learns fast, never has time to enjoy his work. I am thinking espe-cially of those who go on to graduate study. They have learned an immense amount by the time they enter graduate school and have often surpassed in knowledge and in methodological skill their British counterparts, but they have the air of never having lived long enough with their subject. A graduate student in English literature will rush on to do research on Marvell's imagery before he is really at home in English literature and really inward with its traditions and achieve-ments. And there will be even less likelihood of his having any true sense of European culture as a whole. The reason for this is partly, of course, that he is American and not English or European, and to this extent it is unfair to take a European literature as an example. But there is another reason, too: his whole education—his *real* education, that is, which began with college—has been too rushed. No one, I might suggest in passing, ought ever to take a course in such a subject as "Masterpieces of World Literature," for one can only become acquainted with the great tradition in world literature by leisurely reading over a long period of time. It is true, as modern educational psychologists so often point out, that adults learn faster than children and that there is no point in pushing youngsters to learn over a long period of time what concentrated effort can teach them later in life. But I think there is something to be said for spreading things out,[2] for slow and cumulative learning. The hard-working, conscientious, somewhat puritanical American graduate student often outstrips his British opposite number at surprising speed; but in the process he grows old faster, too, and he also learns to regard his subject as a field to be covered rather than as a body of knowledge to be explored and relished.

The dangers on the British side are, however, just as great, though different. They differ not only from the American dangers I have described but also among different British universities. For there are three main types of British universities, as distinct from each other in methods, organization, and traditions as British universities as a whole are from American universities. The three groups are: Oxford and Cambridge; the four Scottish universities; and the English universities other than Oxford and Cambridge—the so-called "provincial" universities. Oxford and Cambridge are unique in that the tutorial system rather than lecture courses provides the essential teaching, and although, at least in Cambridge, the complex relationship between the colleges and the university is showing signs of strain in some quarters, the main business of these universities remains the cultivation of the student's mind through regular discussion with a tutor or supervisor. This of course leaves the student at the mercy of the particular tutor he is landed with, and the student often has no contact at all with the most distinguished teachers of his subject in the university. The dangers of the Oxford and Cambridge system are dilettantism, a tendency, at least in arts subjects, to value a superficial "brilliance" above knowledge and deep understanding, and a disparity in tutorial possibilities. But the advantages are enormous, and my own conviction—having studied and taught at Edinburgh and Oxford, and taught at Chicago, Cornell, and Cambridge—is that it is still the best system that has been worked out.

It should be realized that the large majority of present-day students at Oxford and Cambridge as well as at other British universities have

---

[2] This may appear to contradict what I said earlier about the excessive spreading in American high school teaching, but that spreading is not the result of steady, cumulative study but of scattered and fragmented study.

their fees and maintenance paid for by grants or scholarships of one kind or another. No one who can enter a university is now prevented by lack of means from going there. But no one who has not had the grammar school type of education can qualify for university entrance, and a pupil who has just missed qualifying for a free grammar school education at eleven plus, and whose parents are too poor to send him to a fee-paying grammar school or boarding school, may in this way be deprived of a university education. But, apart from this problem (and it is a serious one), it is true to say that the economic factor in sending one's children to a university is today less of a worry to British parents than it is to Americans.

The shifting social patterns at Oxford and Cambridge have had some interesting results. Before the war it was the regular thing for the good student to do the bulk of his reading in the vacations, and to spend his terms discussing what he had read or amusing himself. But now more and more students take jobs during vacations (not during term time, which would be unthinkable, for the whole concept of university education demands that during term the student remain free to respond to all the currents flowing in a university community, of which formal teaching is only one). This means that they have not the time to do vast amounts of reading between terms, and this is shifting the whole pattern of teaching. The tendency to get by on a minimum of reading, often that done at school, and to compensate by wit and elegance for lack of knowledge, presents a real danger. To avoid that, tutors and supervisors (they are "tutors" at Oxford and "supervisors" at Cambridge) are growing more inclined to give out weekly reading assignments in the American manner.

The Scottish universities are in general organized more like the American. Teaching is done in formal lecture courses, and there is an air of serious professionalism about it. The student who takes an honors degree in English at a Scottish university is expected to plough through the whole of English literature. There is a great deal of reading of factual lectures to large classes, and a general conservatism in the form and content of the teaching. A degree in English literature at Cambridge is intended to produce a cultivated young man who has read and thought enough about a selected number of literary works to have an understanding and an appreciation of the values and varieties of literature. In Edinburgh, the objective is to train a future teacher of English, and a thorough, solid training is provided. The Cambridge degree in an arts subject is not designed primarily as a professional qualification, but at a Scottish university it is so designed.

Too much teaching at Scottish universities is plain dull. And even if the professor himself (there is only one person with the title of professor in each subject at British universities, and in Scotland and the provincial universities he runs the department) gives the large survey course to first-year students, the advantages of contact with the great man are often nullified by the routine way in which he fulfills his task. Here the liveliness and informality of American college teaching would be a welcome innovation.

The English provincial universities suffer from the fact that the best students still tend to be siphoned off to Oxford or Cambridge, and also from certain confusions about the nature and function of the teaching they provide. They fall sometimes between the two stools of Scottish professionalism and Oxford amateurism. But they have some of the best men in the country—particularly the younger men—on their staffs and, in spite of the large formal lecture course which carries much of the burden of teaching, there is often liveliness and experiment as well as a very high level of academic competence, notably in certain scientific subjects. But the shadow of Oxford and Cambridge still hangs over these universities, making both staff and students uncertain of themselves and sometimes restless and discontented. Kingsley Amis's novel *Lucky Jim* is set in a provincial university, and the masochistic clowning through which Amis reveals that the graces of the older universities are not for him betrays an almost spiteful withdrawal from "culture" that is a disturbing symptom.

Finally, a word about administration. Britain has always resisted the notion that university administrators should form a separate class from scholars and teachers, and has almost always drawn its heads of universities from the world of scholarship. In Oxford and Cambridge, the vice-chancellor, who is the administrative head of the university, is drawn from the heads of colleges, each one serving only for a few years. The real work of administration on the academic policy level is done by committees of members of the faculty. Details of financial administration and the execution of policy as it affects the daily routine of university life are alone in the hands of permanent administrators. No single person in any British university has the power that a college dean has in America: such power is vested in the hands of faculty boards. There is no such thing as a board of trustees. Government money comes to the universities through the University Grants Committee, which consists of vice chancellors of the various universities, and whose function is to get government money without government control. The device works well, and the British universities, which are extremely jealous of their independence, are proud of the machinery they have set up for getting money from the Treasury without strings. No questions about universities can be asked in Parliament because no minister is responsible for them (the Minister of Education has no responsibility for or control over the universities).

But administration by committees has some serious drawbacks. It is a heart-breaking job to carry an organizational reform through, especially in Oxford or Cambridge, because the agreement of so many diverse persons must first be secured. A few older members of committees can successfully postpone any innovation almost indefinitely. No one in Britain could possibly do the sort of thing that, say, Hutchins did at the University of Chicago. The result is that traditions are maintained and continuity preserved, but often at the price of the indefinite postponement of needed reforms and the minimizing of profitable experimentation.

The American tendency to put non-academic administrators at the head of universities seems to me dangerous, though the sheer size of many of the American universities makes some aspects at least of administration a highly technical problem. And then there is the fund-raising aspect. But most of all it seems to me that the vitality and flexibility of American universities, which are their greatest assets, are seriously threatened by the I.B.M. machine. I am astonished at the degree to which procedures are *gleichgeschaltet* in a large state university and the human element ignored in order that the machines may be kept rolling.

The chief glory of the American university lies in the fact that it is not really a university in the British sense at all, but a vast collection of educational machinery, good and bad, elementary and advanced, in which the most exciting and fruitful educational activities can go on, as well as the silliest and most useless. To it come students of every degree of ability and with all kinds of interests, and amidst all the proliferating courses and degrees each, if he is lucky, can find something to help him in one way or another. A British university, on the other hand, is an institution of higher learning intended for the minority of citizens who are interested in and can profit by higher learning. That, at least, is the ideal. Now the American system, which results from the belief that ideally every citizen should go to a university and that the university should therefore have something to offer in every sphere and at every level, needs a rigid administrative machinery to hold it together. If in the British system the high objectives of the universities are often found to be in contradiction with professional needs on the one hand, and with ideals of urbane gentlemanly culture on the other, in the American system the freedom and variety which its very lack of discrimination makes possible are threatened by growing administrative rigidity.

Underlying the many differences between the educational systems of the two countries are some significant differences in social philosophy. The British believe that the function of higher education is to train an elite who will perform the most responsible and demanding tasks of the nation. The more democratic you are the more you will strive to make sure that you will choose this elite on the basis of innate ability and aptitude alone, regardless of any other consideration, economic, social, or personal. Equalitarianism is preached by a large section of the British Labor party, and it is in fact being rapidly achieved. But it is *economic* equalitarianism: Britain today is probably the country with the most economic equality in the world. You train the best people to do the most important jobs—but you mustn't pay them any more than you pay people with a less academic education doing more routine jobs.

In spite of the well-meant efforts of left-wing politicians and educators, some kind of social snobbery is bound to continue in England, for it is bound up with the whole concept of different education for different abilities. But this snobbery will be a matter of kind of job, kind of accent (which in England largely depends on where you are educated), and level of intellectual interest, rather than of birth, ancestry, or income. How far an elite of this kind can maintain its dominance without economic superiority or stability of social background remains to be seen.

In America, where the paradox of equality and individualism has long existed (equality demands that everybody get the same education, which is anti-individualistic, but it also demands that each person get ahead in a free enterprise economy, which produces extreme economic individualism), the relation between education and prestige is much more complicated. Suspicion of the intellectual in politics, which strikes a European as such a characteristic feature of the American scene, is bound up with the traditional national refusal to regard differences in quality of education as necessary or desirable. But as America becomes more and more the leader of the democratic world, the problem of training informed and responsible citizens to fill the crucial jobs in domestic and international affairs may well force American educators into accepting in both theory and practice greater differences in education than have hitherto been regarded as desirable.

Suspicion of the intellectual in politics is a feature of a self-contained and more or less isolated country; it may well be that America's role in world affairs today will have a greater long-term effect on the pattern of American education than any of the democratic theorists have had. It was Britain's need for an elite to run a vast empire in the nineteenth century that produced the basic pattern of modern British education, and America, which has taken over so many international responsibilities from the older powers, may have to modify its own educational system in order to fulfill them adequately.

Suggested Topics

1. American and British concepts of the "usefulness" of education
2. Are American secondary school students underworked?
3. The tutorial system, "still the best . . ."
4. Should students work at jobs while going to college?
5. Should everyone be permitted to go to college?
6. The need for enlarging the American intellectual elite

THE SERVICE OF THE UNIVERSITY
Howard Mumford Jones

A distinguished scholar, writer, and educational statesman, Howard Mumford Jones has taught at a number of leading American universities and is now Professor of English at Harvard University. In 1955 he was Chairman of the American Council of Learned Societies.

Philosophically speaking, a university is defined as a congregation of scholars engaged in the discovery, preservation, and inculcation of truth. Scholars, of course, include scientific investigators. Those who desire to learn are supposed to attend upon this congregation and, through an apprenticeship system descending from the Middle Ages, master the mysteries of the art and practice of some branch of learning. They commence scholar, to use the archaic phrase, when they win the first degree in the arts, but their real initiation into the priesthood of learning comes only when they have achieved an advanced degree. On this formal theory the congregation of scholars creates its own corporation, owns its own assets, elects its own administrative head, assesses its own fees, makes its own rules, and lives its own life within, yet apart from, the community in which it is housed. The institution, in this definition, can exist as well under one form of the nation-state as under any other; and the theory ignores

This paper was originally delivered on November 8, 1956, at the University of North Dakota Faculty Conference on The Role of the University in Intellectual Leadership. Reprinted from the ACLS *Newsletter*, Winter, 1956-57. By permission of the American Council of Learned Societies and the University of North Dakota.

time and space, government, religion, business, war and peace, depression and prosperity. It is directed to the pure pursuit of truth.

Whatever the merit of this great ideal—and that it has greatness is clearly proved by our perpetual debate over the principles of academic freedom—it is probable that no such university ever existed. When theology was the queen of the sciences and all secular knowledge was subsumed under theology, the European university was protected by the aegis of the church; its faculty was dominated by the doctors of sacred theology; the knowledge it pursued was not, and could not be, heretical; and its ultimate head was the head of the Christian faith. This theory and system still constitute the framework of the Roman Catholic college and universities.   .

With the growth of humanism, the coming of the Protestant Reformation, and the rise of modern science the founders or patrons of universities, especially in the north of Europe, came to alter in type and to be drawn not from predominantly religious figures but from secular authorities, such as kings, princes, noblemen, and in some cases even cities. Medieval forms continued, of course, and continue to this day, as any commencement ceremony evidences. But from the Renaissance through the Age of Enlightenment, there was a slow drift toward acceptance of the place of secular government in the organization of the university, without, however, ever wholly destroying recognition of the university as a corporation. Thus Oxford and Cambridge long sent representatives to the British Parliament; the kingdom of Prussia established the great University of Berlin during the Napoleonic Wars; and, for that matter, Napoleon himself, in modernizing France, created an entire educational system under the title and theoretical control of the University of France, a system echoed in this country in the creation and legal powers of the Regents of the University of the State of New York.

In Europe, however, or at least in Europe north of the Pyrenees and west of the Vistula, governmental creation or support did not extinguish the independent life of the university. An ancient tradition struggled against the concept of the efficient state; and though government might, and frequently did, deplore the uselessness of university learning or deprecate the views expressed from various university chairs, government usually found it wiser not to interfere. Government commonly confined its activities to the formal confirmation of university appointments when that was necessary and to making such grants from government funds as might be needed to sustain the life of the institution. It took years for the British Parliament to carry through reforms necessary to modernize Oxford and Cambridge; and, though this tolerance of obsolescent education does no credit to the academic mind, the reluctance of Parliament to alter ancient customs shows how firmly entrenched in Europe was (and is) the tradition of university autonomy.

In the Latin countries of the New World—that is, in the territory south of Texas and, in some small measure, in Quebec—the developing structure of universities more nearly parallels Renaissance tradition than it does the formula we are more familiar with in the United States. A typical case is the University of Guatemala, the history of which, charmingly set forth by Professor John Tate Lanning in a recent book, will seem to administrators in the United States a perfect example of how not to manage an institution of learning.

Here, in the United States, our concept of the university has been our own. It has developed on its own lines, and, it seems to me at least, has differentiated itself more and more sharply from the formula for universities elsewhere in the world.

Take the differences first, since to list them may sharpen our sense of the uniqueness of the American situation. We have, to begin with, no clear and consistent concept of the difference between a university and a college. Norwich University in Vermont is not a university but a military school, whereas Bryn Mawr College performs many of the functions of a university. Yale University colleges are living quarters, but I have known state teachers colleges that referred to the first-string football team as the varsity. We do not in this country, as they do at Oxford and Edinburgh, elect an honorary head of the institution, called the "Chancellor," leaving to a Vice-Chancellor the actual conduct of administration, although I see some symptoms that this distinction is developing among us. We do not even elect an annual head, or "Rector," as they do at Munich. Our presidents are chosen for an indefinite tenure, and are not elected by scholars but put over us by a quite non-academic body known as "Regents" or "Trustees"; it is, we say, their "responsibility" to do so. Again, the whole colorful life of the American undergraduate campus is unknown in Europe, barring an occasional spring festival like that in Oslo; and the responsibility which an American institution feels for housing, feeding, and looking after its customers is virtually non-existent in Europe, where the university is conceived as an institution for the adult, not for the adolescent. Finally, let us remember that in point of law the American professor is nothing more than the hired employee of a corporate body over which he has no control, whereas in Europe and in other continents the professor is *ex officio* a member of the corporate body called the university. This arises in large part because in Europe the university, in the medieval sense of the word, preceded the corporation in our sense of the word, just as it preceded the modern nation-state. But in this country the situation is far otherwise.

In this republic we differentiate between the privately endowed institutions and those that are publicly supported, between the ivy league and the state universities and colleges. The difference between the two groups has become a real difference, but it is not a difference in origins. With us the beginnings of the state preceded the beginnings of the university. The first university was as much the creation of the state as is the University of North Dakota. The public corporation known as the Massachusetts Bay Colony anteceded the President and Fellows of Harvard College, who were in fact their legal constructs; and in Virginia the colony gained and lost a charter prior to the creation of William and Mary in 1693. The same type of historical development holds true for the other colonial colleges. They were the creations of the state; and to this day, though there are colleges supported from private funds rather than from tax money, no college, no university, no degree-granting institution of any kind can exist without the prior consent of government, state, or federal, or in certain cases territorial. You can in many commonwealths start a tutoring school, or a kindergarten, or a college of embalming, or a school of commercial art without the consent of the state, even though you may eventually have for one reason or another to submit to inspection by a state agency; but nowhere in the United States can you lawfully confer a recognized academic degree without the approbation of government. Academic institutions have uniformly been the legal creatures of the government, not of the church, and not of scholars spontaneously meeting and declaring their intention of teaching. Meet they may as much as they wish, but they cannot confer degrees without the state's consent.

To this general rule there is one type of apparent and fleeting exception, but the exception is only apparent. Harvard College was intended to perpetuate a learned ministry; William and Mary in Virginia and King's College in New York had their associations with the Anglican faith, then the state church in those colonies; Yale and Princeton also had their religious sanctions and purposes. Not until Benjamin Franklin started the school that eventually became the University of Pennsylvania do we have an institution of higher learning in America wholly secular in its purposes. But true though this is, it is also true that the state, not the church, possessed the legal authority to create a degree-granting college, just as it is true that the gradual legal secularization of these more ancient colleges sprang from the authority of the state.

I suggest that this fact is of tremendous significance. It means that from the earliest times American higher education has been both the creation and the responsibility of the state; that any church or any association of private persons desiring to create a degree-granting school must comply with the laws of the state before it can even begin; and that the state may, for cause, step into any situation where, in the judgment of competent opinion, the charter granted an institution is being used to conceal fraud, and may insist upon amendment, as has been done in the case of certain fraudulent medical schools. It is not too whimsical to say that long before we had a pure food and drug act, we had a pure degree act; and even though in most cases the matter is a mere formality, the important fact is that the formality exists and is demanded and guaranteed by *government*, not by scholars, not by priests, not by commercial persons operating schools for private gain.

The fundamental fact that in American history the state precedes the university and that the university is the creature of the state and can have no foundation for its legal being other than public law, explains our unique problem in governing and controlling our universities. In the typical American situation the college secures a charter, but the charter, or in the case of publicly supported institutions, the constitutional provision or the public law proceeding from the constitution, does *not* create the college. It merely creates a corporation or a board that is authorized to create a college. In law, therefore, the university as an autonomous congregation of scholars engaged in the discovery, preservation, and inculcation of truth does not exist. All that exists is a board of trustees or regents charged with the duty of hiring persons by contract to do certain acts. The chief among these persons is commonly called the president. In the case of charters granted to private institutions he may sometimes also be the president of the board, but even as president of the board he is as much legally subject to dismissal for being an unprofitable servant as any instructor or teaching fellow of low degree. The American concept is in no way (except as an after-thought) the concept of a congregation of scholars engaged in discovering and preserving truth; it is, instead, the concept of an arm of the state intended to get things done or authorizing other persons, in the case of charters granted to private colleges, to hire certain persons to get things done. In no case do the charter and the privilege go directly to the scholars who are theoretically the institution.

As our population spreads westward, it is interesting to see how persons thus authorized go about the creation of universities. The board is created, it meets, it elects a chairman, but, once it has determined where the university is to be, it does not send out invitations to scholars to apply or to attend, it does not announce that it is prepared to receive proposals for a professorship in chemistry, a professorship in internal medicine, a professorship in Latin, and so on. Rather, its next step is to select an agent to secure the services of such employees as in his judgment he can hire. By implication, the board declares its technical incompetence, and delegates its powers to an agent. This agent is the president, who, as the representative of the board, becomes not merely the general manager of the nascent enterprise but also the only channel of communication between the members of the board, who in most cases have no professional academic competence, and the body of scholars which alone, in any intellectual sense, constitute the desired university.

If the formal definition of a university as a congregation of scholars accumulating and disseminating truth is accepted, this development is obviously an arresting anomaly. Goodwill is the only thread connecting the premise with the conclusion. If this good will is lacking, all goes awry, as in the case of a state institution, the president of which flatly informed a professor of biology that he was hired to teach so many classes of so many students and if he didn't like it, he could jolly well get out. The American Association of University Professors struggles with the anomalies of the American theory of university creation and university management, and from time to time presents us with a melodrama from academic life, in which the professor is commonly cast as Eliza, the president appears as Simon Legree, and the board of regents are the baffled bloodhounds.

These abuses in the American system often arise from innocence. The trustees or the regents or the president, who is sometimes imported into the situation because he has name value in the political or business world, is unable to understand that the professor, though he is legally only a hired man, is a very special sort of hired hand, from whom the legal theory underlying his hiring should be gracefully concealed. But although there are, I suppose, annually many violations of the rules of the American Association of University Professors—certainly there must be more than ever get reported in their *Bulletin*—the astonishing thing is not that these violations occur, but that they are few. The American pattern for creating and administering a university makes no great amount of sense if you consider the example of more experienced parts of the world as paramount, but inasmuch as our pattern is one under which a score or so of American universities have risen in a very few decades to world influence, it is just possible that the example of other parts of the world need not be paramount. I have spoken of good will as the chief nexus between the governing board and the congregation of scholars. This good will is, I think, commonly underestimated. Hundreds of busy men acting as regents and trustees have been willing to give of their time to institutions, the necessity of which they see but the operations of which they do not always comprehend, but by humbling themselves to learn, they have tried to grasp the nature of the university. If American universities, public and private, are today sought out by scholars from all parts of the world, surely some credit is due to the trustees and regents who have helped shape these institutions. The foolish or cowardly behavior of a small fraction of these trustees should not blind us to the notable achievement of the vast majority of them over the years.

That the American pattern for creating and governing a university is anomalous seems clear. The philosophic concept of the university moves in one direction; the actual legal doctrine moves in precisely the opposite direction. The first exemplifies democracy on a high plane, the second administrative autocracy. This conflict has troubled a good many critics, among them men as varied in their points of view as Thorstein Veblen, Upton Sinclair, and Simon Flexner. In moments of crisis, moreover, the university administrator or the university trustees are commonly charged with being dictatorial; and sometimes, in fact, they are.

Yet is it not that our anomalous American pattern for governing universities is of a piece with our inconsistent but workable democratic culture? The shortcomings of political democracy as a form of government have been the occasion of despairing comment from the Federalist days of John Adams to the time of Walter Lippmann. No one can reasonably deny that our political democracy, from the Congress to the town meeting, could be improved. We do not vote in the numbers we should, we frequently do not vote on any ascertainable principle of rational choice, we frequently vote in haste and amend at leisure. Yet perhaps the true index of our democratic culture is to be found not in the weakness of our political system, but the strength of our system outside politics—in the clubs, the societies, the groups, national, state, and local, that diversify our national life. Whatever the group we join, whether it be the Modern Language Association or the Wednesday afternoon sewing club, International Rotary, or the vestry of the local Episcopal church, it is almost invariably run on the lines of a Greek democracy. We meet and organize, so to speak, under Robert's Rules of Order; we adopt a constitution giving everybody a voice in the affairs of the society, electing officers for limited terms, protecting the minority in its right, and excluding or expelling dissident or unwanted members only after ample opportunity has been given them to alter their ways, the expulsion coming in accordance with clear and simple rules, if it has to come at all. Even the most impromptu gathering in America commonly proceeds upon tacit assumptions of fair play; if it does not, we distrust it. Nothing is more damning to a labor union, a patriotic society, the board of local charities, or any other American gathering, formal or informal, than the suspicion that the meeting has been rigged, that a steam roller has been run over dissent. On the mere probability of such a charge, associations and clubs have perforce been split. Indeed, is not our whole objection to Communist methods that, though they keep the forms of democracy, they violate its meaning?

In spite of the inconsistency between the legal theory of its management and the philosophical theory of its function, the American university operates, and operates successfully, because it is staffed by Americans reared on that simplest of all formulas for getting men to work together, the democratic formula, and is itself in the great current of the national life which flows according to these formulas. Even the most arbitrary president of a university cannot get along without that most ubiquitous of democratic inventions, the committee. In the long run the majority faculty opinion wins out and the tyrannical dean or the reactionary board of trustees is defeated because he or they are struggling vainly to stifle a deep, ethical instinct in the American people.

The American university as the creation of the American people is fundamentally an expression of this popular instinct for equality and use. Most Americans give at least lip service to the famous proposition set forth in the North-West Ordinance of 1787: "Religion, morality, and knowledge, being necessary to good government, and the happiness of mankind, schools and the means of education shall forever be encouraged." Most Americans have done more. They wanted education and set out to get it. They felt that the instruments of the government they were improvising or creating offered the quickest means by which to spread education over a vast territory; and on pragmatical grounds of need and immediate experience rather than after a study of European precedent, they brought the unique American system into being—the local schoolboard, the state-wide board of regents, the charter for the trustees of the privately endowed institution.

The great virtue of this remarkable invention is that it rests upon a particular theory of education, including higher education, as a form of public service. The great reproach brought against the ivy colleges in the old days was, indeed, that they did not recognize this doctrine, but were on the contrary expressive of snobbery. The eventual response of the ivy colleges to this reproach is, I think, illuminating. They did not defend the necessity, perhaps even the duty, of creating an intellectual elite in a world so specialized that half the physicists do not know what the other half are talking about; on the contrary, they demonstrated that they are just as public and popular as anybody else. With us, in truth, the popular theory has triumphed over the concept that the nation needs an intellectual elite, and the notion of the university as a service institution prevails in the United States to a degree that astonishes the foreign scholar.

When a state law compels the state university to admit to its beginning class any graduate of a state high school simply because he or she is a graduate and regardless of his or her qualifications for the intellectual life, this result of the doctrine that the primary duty of the university is to serve the state must either delight or depress the observer, all depending upon his philosophy of education and his concept of democratic culture. This is perhaps the doctrine of service in an extreme form, but it should not be cited as evidence that the doctrine is itself wrong-headed. On the contrary, the concept of the state university in the service of the state has very great merits, as can be swiftly demonstrated. Cut off, in your imagination, the vast complex of university activities arising from this idea, reduce the university to its primary form as a congregation of scholars engaged in the passionless pursuit of truth, and see how much is altered. We abandon the extension division, correspondence courses, adult education, the short courses for farmers and other groups, the use of the university campus for all sorts of meetings not directly connected with higher education, the state-wide tours of the university band, the university orchestra and the university debaters, the reference services of the library, inter-library loans, the university radio, the accrediting system for secondary schools (at least in many commonwealths), the municipal reference bureau, the legislative reference bureau, the going out of faculty members to lecture and lead discussions in cities, towns, and villages, the informal relations between the university and religious denominations in the state, the easy access of puzzled citizens to scholar and scientist, the alumni association, the friends of the university library, teacher-training in all probability, the university as a center for state-wide activities in music, the theater, public speaking, and the graphic arts—these and a hundred other activities which we take for granted, disappear, and the university, in monastic seclusion, has no other concern for the life of the people than to secure its annual grant and to hope that by its mere existence it will do them good. In this catalogue I say nothing of athletics, for as regards university football I agree with ex-President Hutchins that it would be cheaper and more profitable to buy a string of horses and race them for a good-size purse.

But this great concept of service to the state has also its characteristic weakness, and I am not sure we are always aware of its dangers. This weakness does not lurk in the administrative and legal anomaly of a congregation of scholars run like an industrial corporation under a general manager hired and retired by the board. As I have indicated, I think good will and a deep national instinct for democratic behavior offset the difficulty here; and although cases of violating academic freedom continue to occur, no one familiar with the situation as it was, say, in 1890, and the situation as it is today but must feel that academic tenure, academic freedom, and academic responsibility are better understood and more generally accepted now than they were when Johns Hopkins was founded in 1876. I do not mean that all is rosy; I do mean that the firm insistence upon a set of principles by the American Association of University Professors, coupled with the ancient and healthy competition for men and prestige, have softened the asperities of the administrative-faculty tug of war.

It is elsewhere, I think, that we must look for our characteristic institutional weakness; and I suggest that that weakness lies not in the assumption that the dean or the president, the regent or the trustee is the natural enemy of the professor, but rather in the common failure of both administration and faculty to distinguish between the university as a service institution and the university as an institution in the service of the state.

You will recall how in Voltaire's *Candide* Dr. Pangloss demonstrates that noses were made to wear spectacles and therefore we have spectacles, that legs were made to wear breeches and therefore we have trousers. About half a century after that book appeared, the Rev. William Paley seized upon this tempting argument, and in his famous *Natural Theology* demonstrated that, with one notable exception, everything had a use and place in the world and so made for happiness. The one exception lay in the animal kingdom. His mind went willingly along with that of the Creator until he came to snakes, but there, he said regretfully, the provision of poison for venomous snakes seemed to him over-done. I think that in our enthusiasm for the university as a service institution, we may have rather over-done the notion of service.

I have been mildly critical of the philosophic concept of the university as a congregation of scholars pursuing truth for its own sake, although, as I also said, we would be poor indeed if we lost this great concept. A university is, or should be, a place dedicated to the adult pursuit of learning. It is not, or at least it should not be, an advanced high school; it is not a junior college; it is not an academy; it is not even synonymous with a college of liberal arts, though a college of liberal arts may properly be a constituent part of the American university. Above all, a university is not, or ought not to be, a place for the inculcation of the rudiments of intelligence and culture merely because, under our somewhat invertebrate system of public education, youth is earlier permitted to neglect these rudiments.

I do not believe the proper function of a university is to teach boys and girls the elements of spelling, punctuation, grammar, and the writing of simple sentences; yet I suppose the greater part of the time and energy of the largest single fraction of the staff of the American university is spent in doing, not what the high school should have done, but what the grade school should have done for the high school. I do not believe the university is the place to begin studying a foreign language; yet another large section of the faculty is engaged in this absurdity. Like the daughters of Danaus, they yearly pour the elements of Spanish, French, or German into leaky buckets, the water running out of the buckets at the end of the year. The young have been so often assured that the English they have not mastered is the universal language of all mankind that they do not bother to learn any other— in shocking contrast to European and Asiatic youth. I do not believe the university is the place to teach the rudiments of arithmetic, algebra, and plane geometry, though such teaching, or something like it, occupies the time of most persons teaching mathematics in the American university. In fact I do not believe the university is the proper place to teach the elements of reading, or the elements of physics, or the elements of chemistry, or the elements of botany, or the elements of any other subject commonly supposed to be made available in the secondary schools. The American university, however, has taken on all these chores in the name of service and because, popular opinion to the contrary, the American university staff is too good-natured to refuse this service to the state.

One of the two wisest persons I have ever known—the other was Jane Addams of Hull House—was the late Alfred North Whitehead. Mr. Whitehead, I think, once uttered the cryptic remark that the characteristic weakness of the American university is good teaching. He had in mind the tendency to sacrifice the true function of a university to a secondary task. The true concern of a university is with learning, not with teaching. Teaching is but a secondary, even a misleading, function in this context. It is a misleading function when the concept of learning is, as is too often the case, sacrificed to the concept of teaching; when, for example, adolescents are solemnly asked to rate mature scholars in terms of their entertainment value in the classroom, and an administration in turn seriously accepts these callow judgments as a factor in the keeping and promoting of scholars. I wonder how Thoreau, Nietzsche, Veblen, Spinoza, Kierkegaard, or Aristotle would have fared in such a system.

I think the common misapprehension of the true nature of a university is demonstrated every spring and every fall when the representatives of the textbook industry swarm over our campuses, offering their wares for adoption, suggesting that a desk copy of such and such a book will improve everything, and persuading professors that the best way to get their views into circulation is to write something for freshmen. Imagine an interview between an American textbook sales-man and the historian of the decline and fall of the Roman empire! And picture Gibbon's bewilderment at being told that a poll of sopho-more classes showed that his work was too long, too learned and too literary, and that, to be published, it must be reduced to a single, short, snappy volume suitable for the adolescent mind and making constant references to social parallels between ancient Rome and modern America!

As it is a matter of common report that fundamental ideas in science and philosophy still originate for the most part in foreign countries because the Americans, with all their cleverness, all their equipment, all their admirable concern for human betterment, do not have opportunity for fundamental thinking in their universities but must withdraw from them and enter an Institute for Advanced Study or secure a Guggenheim Fellowship to take them away from institu-tions that are supposed to exist for furthering fundamental thought, I wonder if we may not be overplaying our hand in this matter of service. Extreme busyness in the name of service, of teaching, of com-mittee work, of laudable outside activities first threatens, then curtails, and finally overwhelms many conscientious and able specialists who might in other circumstances have devoted themselves to thought.

The university, without abandoning its admirable relation to the state, must remain the capital and fortress of thought. Emerson's definition of the scholar still holds; it is man thinking. As we exhaust our natural resources, as our wonderful machines pile leisure like an embarrassment around us, as the tensions and perplexities of the world increase about us, as the life span lengthens and the population grows, we have need of man thinking—thinking fundamentally, thinking philosophically, thinking morally; for without thought the people perish. It is good to serve, but if I may alter a familiar line, they also serve who only stand and think. Our noisy and pleasant activities on the campus fill the ear with sound, but at the heart of the university there should always be a zone of silence, a quiet and protected place away from the market and the Rotary Club, where our best men can discover truth, preserve it, and diffuse it, not as service but as idea. That is the core of the university concept, and if we lose it, we lose everything. Can we somehow at once combine and separate the two aspects of American university life—the day-to-day serviceability to the state that public universities so admirably have developed, and the protection of man thinking in the light of time and eternity? To protect that man is the quintessential service of the university to the state, and the continuing problem of the American institution is how to fuse into a single whole these two excellent but opposed ideas of university life.

Suggested Topics

1. Universities and the "pure pursuit of truth"
2. American higher education: the state's creation and responsibility
3. The "pure degree act"
4. The university: a service institution performing *too* much service
5. The function of a university—learning or teaching?

MUST THE TV TECHNICIANS TAKE OVER THE COLLEGES?

Ernest Earnest

Chairman of the Department of English at Temple University, Ernest Earnest has written on English romantic poetry and American literature. He is also the author of *Academic Procession, An Informal History of the American College, 1636-1953.*

I

There is a note of panic in much of the discussion about mounting college enrollments. One might think that the prospect of twice the present college population ten years hence might seem good news to educators who have long deplored the cultural limitations of the American people. Instead, the almost unrelieved gloom of the prophets can only be matched by the prophesies of disaster at the time of the first G. I. Bill following World War II. Then, as now, the educational journals and the public prints were filled with discussions of the shortage of instructors, of the lack of facilities, and the baleful effects of overcrowding.

In this atmosphere of alarm, all sorts of panaceas are being suggested by administrators and foundations. Americans tend to assume that any problem can be solved by a new pill, serum, or ingenious gadget. Thus, closed circuit television for the classroom has been seized upon as the most hopeful solution for the expected shortage of teachers. The Fund for the Advancement of Education has financed experiments with TV at several universities. At least 80 colleges are trying it out.

Reprinted from the *AAUP Bulletin*, September, 1958. By permission of the American Association of University Professors and the author.

The danger of educational TV is twofold. On the one hand, it may lead education into unexpected and undesirable channels; on the other, this seemingly easy solution of the teacher shortage may prevent a genuine re-examination of our system of higher education.

I for one believe that our present methods waste trained manpower on the one hand, and on the other provide a lot of poor instruction. Even without the impending deluge of students, the colleges need to overhaul their academic structure and methods. Later on, I shall outline some possible improvements.

II

First, however, let us look at some of the changes in academic organization which are likely to result from any extensive use of closed circuit TV. Too often TV instruction is evaluated merely in terms of the test scores of the guinea-pig students as compared to the scores made by their fellows in conventional classrooms. If, as seems to be the case in some subjects, the TV students do as well on an examination as those who faced a live instructor, this is taken to prove the success of classroom TV. The alleged value of the meeting of minds does not always show up in the test scores.

Even at this early date, it seems probable that for certain kinds of instruction TV works as well as live teaching. This, of course, may be less a proof of the value of TV than of the failure or misdirection of much conventional teaching. The acquisition of factual knowledge may not be what the student should get in class. Too often the American student uses the classroom as a substitute for study. If the classroom has a function, it is the place for testing ideas and skills, for the interchange of ideas.

Like the conventional lecture system, classroom TV lends itself to the sausage-stuffing concept of education. But perhaps its greatest danger to higher education is not something that can be measured by testing students; the threat lies in its effect upon the professional status of the teacher. It is not difficult to foresee in a faculty the development of a small group of TV "personalities" and a proletariat of section hands and paper graders. To some degree the lecture-quiz section method develops these hierarchies, but TV would intensify the division. On any faculty, the most successful TV performers are not necessarily the ablest scholars. And the less prosperous institutions, having invested large sums to install TV, would find an irresistible temptation to use filmed lectures by skilled performers at other universities.

At first glance, it might seem desirable for students at run-of-the-mill institutions to hear and see on the screen the outstanding classroom performers in the nation. In like fashion, it once seemed as if the motion picture and the radio would bring the outstanding actors and musicians to the general public. But the outstanding actors wound up by playing sentimental or spectacular drivel, and except for a few FM stations, radio music is largely juke box. What passes for a cultural program on TV is a policeman answering questions on Shakespeare or a grandmother demonstrating her knowledge of baseball.

One might argue that universities would keep up the cultural and scholarly level of TV lectures and demonstrations. One may argue about as effectively against Gresham's law that bad money drives out good money. But probably most universities which have introduced courses to teach the techniques of TV can match programs such as one conducted by one head of a Department of Speech and Radio, who put on a funny cap and ran a comedy quiz show for the kids. This same man argued that Milton Berle made a cultural contribution.

III

People who talk about classroom TV tend to overlook the problem of control. Who runs the show? As dozens of books and plays about Hollywood demonstrate, the quality of the movies is determined, not by writers and actors, but by producers, a managerial class not noted for culture, or even literacy. Shakespeare on TV is cut to the size determined by advertisers and program directors.

Well, who would eventually control classroom TV—the professors or the technical experts in the Audio-Visual Department? Perhaps the question answers itself, but let us look at the way college machinery operates. Obviously, TV courses are adaptable only to large groups. There is no point in using it for a course elected by fifteen or twenty students. As every faculty member knows, there is always administrative pressure to limit the number of courses chosen by few students. This limitation is not always an evil—professors left to themselves would proliferate courses as the French spawn political parties. It is probably not necessary to a sound liberal arts program to offer separate undergraduate courses in Wordsworth and Coleridge. But a course in Greek may be a must, even if only five students enroll.

Today, every college and university worth its salt offers some small, unpopular courses along with the many large required courses—often even more unpopular. How would TV change the picture? First of all, there is a tremendous financial investment. To justify it, the equipment must be used as much of the time as possible. At once the pressure for courses of mass enrollment becomes even more powerful. At present, scholarly Professor Vinson may be able to persuade the administration to let him offer *Chaucer* to twenty-five students in the place of *The Modern American Novel* to seventy-five. But what about the

Billy Phelps type, who can attract half the student body to his humorous, anecdotal lectures on *The Novel*—meaning of course popular novels? Professorial humor being what it is, the popular lecturer could well use another standard TV device—the laughs supplied on tape.

At present, the showmen in every department are subject to some control by the other members of the department. Most departments require a good proportion of solid, scholarly courses for their majors. But to a considerable extent TV could take control away from scholars and department heads. The most popular hours would almost certainly go to the mass TV courses. So would the better classrooms. In an era when political bosses give serious attention to the TV personalities of aspirants to the Presidency of the United States, it is not too fantastic to imagine candidates for professorships being given screen tests.

Worse still, the "personalities" could use economic arguments to justify much higher salaries than those paid to less popular professors. With a huge investment in TV equipment, a university could not afford to lose its chief attractions. Again, we need only see how the multimillion dollar investments of the movie makers produced the star system. And what would happen if a departmental chairman was unwilling to promote a TV glamour boy on his staff, but the director of the Audio-Visual department contended that the man was essential? This is another question which answers itself. It all adds up to the fact that college TV would be run not by the scholars, but by the more cynical symbol manipulators.

With classroom TV, one man could easily deliver all the lectures in a large course. In history or political science, for instance, this means that all students would get the subject from a single point of view. Standardization is a fine thing for piston rings, but not for brains. Yet the economic pressure of a large investment in TV equipment might well carry standardization beyond the walls of a single college. If a lecture is piped into a dozen classrooms, why not into a dozen colleges?

The essential fact is that the introduction of the machine into any cultural area always forces the adaptation of the cultural medium to the machine. One of the invariable steps in this process is the shift of control to the technicians and the manipulators. The movies, radio, and commercial TV are only extreme examples. The men running televised political campaigns have learned to play down issues, in favor of "selling a product." Already the professors have learned to design their examinations for scoring on IBM machines. And as every teacher knows, the nature of the examination determines how and what the student will study. The machine has even lowered the quality of cheating. The student no longer copies the date 1066 onto a crib; he makes a note to mark the third pair of lines on question 9.

IV

All this leaves unanswered the question of what to do about the impending flood of students. If not mass lectures or TV, then what? Well, two needs are obvious: more teachers and better teaching. TV or no TV, someone must grade themes, someone conduct quiz sections, someone hold student conferences. Whether or not we must preserve the present faculty-student ratio, there will still be a need for many more teachers.

Some of these are already available. When the flood of veterans appeared after World War II, many former teachers—married women and retired persons—came back to the classroom—frequently on a part-time basis. When the emergency was over, most colleges returned to a reliance on full-time staff members. But this reservoir of qualified people still exists. It is possible that mandatory retirement of faculty members at 65 or so is motivated to a considerable degree by the desire of administrators to replace top-salary professors with inexpensive younger people. Lawyers, doctors, Senators, and Supreme Court Justices often continue to perform distinguished service long beyond the compulsory retirement age for professors.

Most important of all, the colleges need to develop more efficient uses of manpower. In perhaps no other important civilian activity is there so much waste of professorial training and experience. In most institutions it is taken for granted that faculty members should do a lot of routine chores: taking roll, proctoring examinations, compiling grades, keeping their own files, etc.

At institutions with graduate schools, graduate assistants do some of these chores, but not all of them. Why should Professor X, aged 60, rummage through the card catalogue, fill out slips, and wait in line for books—then three weeks later climb stairs with an armful to return them to the desk? Yet how many faculty members can command the services of an assistant for such chores? Just last fall I asked an elderly professor of physics if he had had a good vacation. No, he said; he had been in the hospital with a hernia acquired while lifting a heavy box of apparatus. It is unlikely that the surgeon who operated on him ever encountered a similar occupational hazard.

Most faculty members need more secretarial help—and better help. Secretarial salaries in colleges are usually so low that office girls are green, poor at shorthand, typing, and filing, and completely incapable of handling routine business on their own. They must consult the professor about files, about minor problems; they cannot be expected to answer routine correspondence. When a departmental secretary becomes expert at these things, she is likely to be translated to the office of a dean or the registrar. Faculty members who are not departmental chairmen usually have little or no secretarial help. They become accustomed to typing their own letters, answering the telephone, delivering messages, and keeping their own files. Even with present low academic salaries, this is high-priced office work. In no other business or profession are people in the upper echelons expected to do the kind of chores most professors take for granted.

The combination of menial labor and low salaries to which most faculty members are condemned helps to explain why so many psychologists and sociologists are whoring on Madison Avenue. This trend to moonlighting among psychologists, social scientists, and communications experts is attracting into the teaching profession a type of faculty member who is not primarily interested in education. A university is simply a good address for their extra-curricular activities. As Vance Packard has shown in *The Hidden Persuaders,* an unholy number are devoting their "scholarship" to preying on the consumer's hidden fears and sex drives in order to sell beer and cigarettes. Anyone who has tried to get a psychologist to attend a committee meeting on educational problems has discovered how little time the college is getting for its money. Like some labor unions, the colleges might well examine the activities of their highest paid staff.

V

In addition to demanding that faculty members have some interest in education, there are other ways of using man-power more effectively. Experienced faculty members might be thought of less as platform performers than as supervisors of the work of others. Graduate assistants and new instructors need much more guidance than they usually get. The English Department at one large institution found that the grading of a set of mimeographed themes followed by a discussion with experienced staff members was an excellent way of training graduate assistants to grade themes. But the experienced people had to do this on their own time.

This next point is heresy, but it may be that faculty members should get over the notion that the classroom is an instructor's castle. Inexperienced people need observation and help from experienced teachers. And obviously the colleges are going to use a lot of inexperienced teachers during the next ten years.

Opposed to this need for the use of experienced people as supervisors is the need to let students come in contact with the ablest people on the faculty. Freshmen, especially, need to find out that learning can be an exciting thing.

These two apparently conflicting needs might both be met by introducing more flexibility into the educational process. If the able scholars and experienced teachers were freed from a regular classroom routine, they could be asked to supervise the work of junior staff members and also deliver a limited number of lectures and possibly to conduct an occasional quiz section. If a freshman met a Kittredge or a Trilling only a half dozen times a year, he would be better off than his fellow condemned to two unrelieved semesters with Mr. Drudge. And there would be fewer Mr. Drudges if instructors got more supervision from top notch people. The groping section hand could be helped to find his way; the hopeless pedant would be more quickly discovered and dismissed.

Equally important would be the effect on the morale of the young teacher. Most of the time he would be in charge of a class; he would not be a mere roll taker and paper grader. It is equally true that young instructors have an enthusiasm which carries over to students and that they make egregious errors. A system which combined responsibility with supervision and counsel would preserve the enthusiasm and minimize the mistakes.

The pattern here suggested is similar to that in the industrial world. As a man moves up the ladder, he does less routine work; he is provided with expert assistants and secretaries. His job becomes increasingly one of planning, policy making, and supervision. At the same time, promising younger people are being trained for the supervisory posts.

In the academic world a real difficulty would be to develop a tradition of supervisory responsibility. Professor X, freed from a rigid classroom schedule, would be prone to bury himself in the stacks or even disappear to the golf course. Having kept his own files for thirty years, and typed his own letters, he would have to learn how to use expert help. But once Professor X learned to delegate routine chores and formed the habit of meeting frequently with graduate assistants and instructors, he might find that his scholarship and teaching skills were more effective than ever. Certainly the give-and-take of discussions with younger members of the staff might bring new life into the routine of college teaching.

It is also reasonable to hope that a system involving frequent discussion between young instructors and older professors would produce a climate healthful to scholarship. Unlike the TV performer, who would of necessity learn the tricks of the showman, the faculty member accustomed to meeting with his peers would know that his scholarship counted more than his profile. Section hands for TV personalities would quickly develop a class consciousness; they would spend their time in bars making fun of the glamour boys. In contrast, young in-

structors meeting regularly with older professors might even learn to
like and respect them. The profession might become so attractive that
the teacher shortage would solve itself.

Suggested Topics

1. "Automation" in higher education
2. A "showman" type of teacher I have known
3. Screen tests for professors
4. The sausage-stuffing concept of education
5. Standardization—fine for piston rings, but not for brains
6. Needed: more teachers and better teaching

TWENTIETH CENTURY
APPROACHES TO   *Robert F. Schenkkan*
TWENTIETH CENTURY PROBLEMS

A Reply to Ernest Earnest

> Director of radio and television at the University of Texas,
> Robert F. Schenkkan has been associated with the National
> Demonstration Project of the College Closed-Circuit Television
> Network as project director. He studied at the Universities of
> Virginia and North Carolina.

I

There appeared in a recent issue of the *AAUP Bulletin* an article
by Professor Ernest Earnest entitled, "Must the TV Technicians Take
Over the Colleges?" There was a note of panic in Professor's Earnest's
discussion of the use of television for instruction, although he admitted, "it seems probable that for certain kinds of instruction TV
works as well as live teaching." This statement was immediately qualified by the observation that this may be "less a proof of the value of
TV than of the failure or misdirection of much conventional teaching."

Professor Earnest is obviously exercised about many things besides

Reprinted from the *AAUP Bulletin*, March, 1959. By permission of the *AAUP
Bulletin* and the author.

classroom television, and, for the reader's amusement, I have drawn up a partial list of these:

Commercial radio—"Except for a few FM stations . . . largely juke box."

Television—"What passes for a cultural program is a policeman answering questions on Shakespeare."

Motion pictures—(see Television).

Americans—"They tend to assume that any problem can be solved by a new pill, serum, or ingenious gadget."

The conventional lecture system—"It lends itself to the sausage-stuffing concept."

The lecture-quiz section method—"It develops hierarchies."

Professorial humor—it "could use . . . laughs on tapes."

Audio-Visual departments—"cynical symbol manipulators."

Psychologists, social scientists, and communications experts—"an unholy number are devoting their scholarship to preying on the consumer's hidden fears and sex drives in order to sell beer and cigarettes."

Educational TV producers—TV technicians.

On the surface this is all good professorial humor (see professorial humor above), but there is a note of purpose in it that indicates perhaps that the author is a pretty fair country sort of cynical symbol manipulator himself. After all, the manipulators operate by means of loaded words and slanted phrases and through the juxtaposition of the product with emotion-charged terms, whether these are relevant or not. This seems a reasonably accurate description of Professor Earnest's method.

II

Whether the approach is that of humor, demagoguery, or naiveté, however, the matters treated are of some real importance to American education and deserve consideration on their merits. Perhaps the most significant of these is the notion that "the acquisition of factual knowledge may not be what the student should get in class. It is, instead, a place . . . for the interchange of ideas." Is it? Are the ideas which the freshman has about chemistry or Shakespeare really worth the class time required for the "interchange"? If he has ideas (and let us be frank, many of the graduates of our high schools have barely encountered, let alone created, any ideas), the discipline of presenting these in an organized way, on paper, is probably far more valuable to his development than this vaunted interchange. This might even be true of some sophomores (has he encountered the word "sophomoric"?), some juniors, and, in very rare cases, seniors. Most professors really do know more than their students. The kind of "togetherness" learning, fashionable in some educational circles, has been successfully resisted at the university level so far. It is true that often the classroom is used as a substitute for study, but it does not follow from this that its function is "testing ideas and skills." What ideas? What skills?

Even more to the point is the question: what classrooms? Professor Earnest appears to view all classrooms as derived from a single stereotype, no matter what the subject or the level of instruction. This, of course, is arrant nonsense. In some courses it is necessary to demonstrate certain objects, materials, or processes; in some it is not necessary but it helps to illuminate the subject; in others it would be impossible. In some classrooms one needs discussion; in others discussion is a waste of time.

If we are to re-examine some educational practices (and let us hope we do), another relevant question is: What portion of class time in each course ought to be given over to what kind of teaching?

It is obvious that we need to extend both the creative time *and* the teaching time of our finest minds. Professor Earnest would solve this problem by making administrators of all our senior professors. Secretarial help and the assistance of filing clerks would be most welcome, and these are needed, but administrative duties are something else again. Disregarding the question of taste and talent for administration, is it much of a solution to require those already wearing the two hats of teacher and research scholar to don a third? Already we may be losing too many of our finest teachers and researchers to administrative duties because of the growing complexity of our institutions. It is likely to be much less damaging to add "TV teacher" to teacher and scholar. In fact, many teachers maintain that the challenge of television teaching has given them a fresh interest in re-examining their own teaching and that they have learned much which is directly applicable to the classroom.

III

Re-examination seems to be the watchword wherever instruction by television is attempted. And out of this re-examination, here and there have come some genuine improvements. To cite a simple illustration from our own institution, the demonstrations of laboratory work provided to our freshmen by television are unquestionably superior to the classroom method previously used. This is evidenced by the virtual cessation of laboratory accidents, the cutting down of laboratory time for the completion of the same work, the freeing of faculty time for more direct contact with the students, the increased usefulness of laboratory assistants, and the acceptance by both faculty and students of the superiority of the new method. This is not because of the "failure or misdirection of conventional teaching" in the sense that any blame should attach to prior faculty efforts. The simple fact of the matter is that no really satisfactory solution to the teaching problem could be found until television presented the opportunity. There is a large and growing literature available to Professor Earnest on the subject of instruction by television which makes it clear that ours is not an isolated phenomenon.

Professor Earnest makes much of the "tremendous financial investment" in TV equipment. "In order to justify" such investment, administrators and departmental chairmen (and budget councils, I presume) will insist on academically ruinous uses of TV. Professor Earnest is obviously not acquainted with the facts of university and college economics or with the cost of television equipment. Such equipment may cost from $25,000 to about $125,000. It can be bought for less than the low figure but is then of lesser usefulness. More can be spent than the high figure, but this is probably gilding the lily. On the other hand, classrooms (average, 30 feet by 40 feet) may cost from $13 to $22 a square foot. Television equipment, then, can be bought at the cost of a single classroom. I have not noticed any frantic pressure, nationwide, to make curriculum or course content conform to the dictates of classroom usage. With college building programs running into the millions, TV equipment is not, comparatively speaking, a tremendous investment. The argument is utterly fallacious.

Professor Earnest points out that "the most successful TV performers are not necessarily the ablest scholars." This may be true. It is also true, as hosts of college graduates will testify, that the ablest scholars are not always the best teachers of undergraduates. The experience of educational television producers is that the *good* classroom teachers are almost always good TV teachers.

IV

Perhaps in our re-examination of American education we ought to be looking at the problem from the student's point of view. Perhaps, at least in his first years, the student wants and needs to be inspired to learn, to read, to study. He is not always wholly ready for the rarefied atmosphere of true scholarship the moment he comes to us, and, alas! sometimes he never quite makes it. But few of us have ever met the college student who could not be moved, however briefly, by a great teacher. And perhaps it would be good experience for the "section hands" (as Professor Earnest prefers to term the graduate assistants) to watch a great teacher at work. Perhaps the inexperienced teachers Professor Earnest foresees (correctly, I believe) using in such great numbers in the next ten years would learn something, too.

What of the question of television and the numbers crisis? Let us

begin by saying that, as in any activity, there are a few extreme enthusiasts connected with educational television who really feel that it
will provide the solution to everything. The vast majority, however,
consider it only one solution, and a partial one. What are some of the
problems it may partially solve?

We are prone to think of the coming crisis in numbers as just that:
too many students for the teachers. It is not, of course, going to be that
at all. It is simply going to be too many students for instruction of
quality in some instances. We can take on the retreads, as Professor
Earnest suggests, and the ill-qualified, and meet the crisis of the numbers themselves, but the competition for genuinely qualified teaching
personnel is already savage, and the process is hardly under way.
Smaller institutions, in particular, are going to find themselves virtually unable to offer certain kinds of instruction even if they deliberately restrict enrollment, as many of them are already doing. Larger
institutions are going to find it increasingly difficult to hold enrollments within reasonable limits, and so will be stretching a point here
and a point there to permit teaching by persons really not qualified.
Is it better to have physics taught by TV than to have it not taught at
all, or taught very badly? One thing television can do is to supply the
expert personnel otherwise not available.

Professor Earnest tells us that "if a freshman met a Kittredge or a
Trilling only half a dozen times a year, he would be better off than his
fellow condemned to two unrelieved semesters with Mr. Drudge." In
this connection, "met" is an interesting word. If he means that word
and not some other, I assume he is talking about the average-sized
college section. In this case, his thesis is sound, but his arithmetic is
appalling. If an institution has 2500 freshmen and the section-size is
thirty, a Kittredge would have to meet eighty-three sections half a
dozen times for a total of freshman class meetings of 249 a semester.

I would like to be present when this idea is presented to the proposed victim. On the other hand, if a Kittredge or a Trilling made
half a dozen television appearances, all 2500 students could at least
see and hear him. They could also see and hear him in a way which
appears to provide a greater sense of intimate contact under some
circumstances than the actual classroom contact itself. The power of
the close-up on television is very considerable. It is curious, too, that
the camera appears to magnify the real qualities an individual possesses. Sincerity, humility, understanding of, and feeling for, the subject
matter come across with greatly increased force. Professor Earnest is
wrong in his fears regarding the "showmen"; they do not, in the
experience of those who work with the medium, make the best TV
teachers. The best teachers do. Thus Professor Earnest inadvertently
has aligned himself with educational television as it continues to

realize one of its more obvious and efficacious functions—that of delivering the student into the presence of the great teacher and out of the toils of Mr. Drudge.

V

Another way in which TV can help is by relieving teachers of the responsibility for the preparation of elaborate demonstrations for a single class group. This is applicable in many fields of science, social science, and even, though not so obviously, in many fields of the humanities. It seems hardly worth while, sometimes, to present a complex demonstration for a class of thirty-five students, particularly if one has to repeat the whole process two hours later. It is sometimes impossible to do so because such demonstrations are often the product of group effort.

The attempt has been made in many institutions, over a considerable period of time, to make various types of audio-visual aids available to instructors for enrichment purposes. This has met with varying degrees of success, depending on the institution, but, by and large, it cannot be said that the movement has been a spectacular success. The principal reason is that it often seems to the instructor to be more trouble than it may be worth; projectors are notoriously cranky and professors are not uniformly handy with equipment. On the other hand, even those of us who teach can turn on a television set with comparative ease. We do not have to darken rooms, thread projectors, or manipulate tape recorders; we do not even have to drop the needle on a record without scratching the record or breaking the needle.

Television is acceptable from other points of view. Professor Earnest tells us "faculty members should get over the notion that the classroom is an instructor's castle." He is likely to find this a difficult doctrine to promulgate. But most of us welcome a guest lecturer, and television can be that guest. For those who really have something to contribute to the education of the young, the opportunity to reach more of them more effectively is obviously attractive.

Professor Earnest is concerned lest TV be used to provide all classroom materials at many institutions at once. This is a reasonable fear if one can suppose that institutional sovereignty, along with the Soviet state, is going to wither away. To anyone experienced in dealing with this problem such fears seem groundless. Of course, some materials are going to be used on more than one campus. Recently, there has been filmed a series of interviews with Dr. Jung. Because we cannot all have Dr. Jung on our psychology faculties, should we be deprived of these? Robert Frost makes an annual tour of a group of university campuses. These visits are memorable for students and faculty alike. But Mr.

Frost is getting old. The tour is bound to cease soon. Should we no longer have the privilege of seeing and hearing him? Will Professor Earnest read the poetry of Robert Frost to his class instead? Will this be an improvement?

VI

Professor Earnest unfortunately knows a number of things that are not so: "The essential fact is that the introduction of the machine into a cultural area *invariably* shifts control to the technicians and manipulators." I refer him to the invention of movable type and the development of the printed book. As he clearly knows, this destroyed educational control of the universities and put us all at the mercy of the typesetters. Its effect on the Church has been even more marked and one can hardly find a bishop these days who is not a member of the International Typographical Union.

What is most unfortunate, though, about the Earnest approach, is that it plays upon a fear that is not real. The invention of the mechanical jenny let loose upon England a storm of violence as a result of the fear that spinners would no longer be needed. Professor Earnest clearly equates the intelligence of college professors with that of eighteenth century English peasants. I do not think he expects us to tear down the universities as the spinners did the mills, but his whole concept is unworthy. If TV is not useful, let's reject it, but let's do it for the right reasons.

Television in education is in use; it is going to be used more widely. Faculties are not going to yield authority over course content or curricula because of it. They are going to experiment with television until they know what it can do best for their students. In their efforts to do this, they are going to be aided by educational broadcasters, people who are making a profession of using the mass media, broadcast and closed circuit, for educational purposes. They are, for the most part, dedicated people who believe that radio and television have uses other than the juke-box ones; so Professor Earnest ought to be their ally. The "few FM stations" he mentions number 681, and of these, 165 are manned by educational broadcasters. Educational broadcasters operate thirty-three ETV stations as well, with at least a dozen more shortly to go on the air. And there is not a commercial to be seen. Some 115 colleges and universities are now offering regular instruction on television. They do not do this in order to make profiles more important than scholarship, or to develop class-conscious TV showmen. They are perceptive enough to know that this would destroy them. But—more important—their interest in education is as real as Professor Earnest's. To have come to terms with the Twentieth Century need not argue that twenty centuries of prior thought and ethics have been left out of the calculations. It does indicate a recognition that today's problems will not yield invariably to yesterday's solutions.

VII

I suppose I have more faith than Professor Earnest in America, in higher education—instructors, professors, *and* administrators. I know something of the effort that is going into experimentation with this medium all over the country and something of the results obtained. I know, too, that in an era when the demands upon the educational schedule are growing in astronomical fashion, it is providential to have at hand a device which promises a substantial measure of aid.

Suggested Topics

1. The importance of discussion in the classroom
2. The shortage of qualified college teachers
3. What makes a great teacher?
4. The values of audio-visual aids
5. Not all subjects can be taught by television
6. The need for experimentation in education

PUBLIC SCHOOLS ARE BETTER
THAN YOU THINK   *Sloan Wilson*

Author of the popular novel *The Man in the Gray Flannel Suit*, Sloan Wilson taught English at the University of Buffalo, was a director of the 1955 White House Conference on Education, and has been a member of the Board of Education in New Canaan, Connecticut.

Ever since the war, I've put up with about as much debate concerning the public schools as I can stand quietly, and I'm going to get into the act. Of course, I'm no great expert on the technical aspects of the thing, but I need only to inspect the torrent of recent

Reprinted from *Harper's Magazine*, September, 1955. By permission of the author.

books and articles attacking or defending the schools to realize that this is a subject which offers marvelous opportunities to a writer tired of research. Here is a field in which uninformed opinions are at a premium. A truly ignorant man can easily work himself up into a feverish fury about the public schools, and in a brief article or book can unburden himself of enough righteous indignation to heat a summer hotel in January.

On the other hand, a person who has really learned something about the schools is almost hopelessly crippled when it comes to writing genuinely dramatic books and articles. He finds he has to qualify his generalities, and all kinds of awkward facts keep getting in the way of rich, rolling prose and sweeping accusations. For a man who seeks to say something startling about the public schools, a little knowledge is a dangerous thing, and a lot of it is almost an insuperable handicap. It's impossible for an informed person to give easy answers to the hard questions besetting the public schools, yet how can hard answers compete in the literary market place with easy ones? One reason why true educational savants are such notably dull writers is simply that they know too much.

The verbal splendor resulting from recent charges that the schools are not teaching reading right, and older charges that they aren't teaching *anything* right, is undeniably exhilarating. Abraham Lincoln is supposed to have said that a man should preach as though he were fighting bees, and I can't help admiring the way critics of the schools have transferred his advice to their line of endeavor. We haven't heard much lately about the evils of Progressive Education—in fact, the very phrase has acquired a nostalgic ring—but there are still a few people around who seem convinced that the public schools are promoting socialism of some kind, or worse. The schools have been called Godless, and their administrators have been widely described as just plain cotton-headed. A good argument can be started almost anywhere over the question of whether there should be federal aid to education. Businessmen voice pathetic complaints that the high-school graduates they hire as secretaries just can't spell, and college professors snort about the qualifications of entering freshmen. The phrase "crisis in education" has become a cliché, used by some to mean that the schools are incredibly inept, and by others to mean that they are woefully short of money. A visitor to this country would almost inevitably deduce from the headlines that things have never been so tough. As a rather bewildered friend of mine said recently at a PTA meeting, what's going on around here, anyway?

I have an uneasy answer. In the last fifty years, and especially in the last ten years, our nation has gone humanitarian to a great and wonderful degree, but it doesn't yet want to pay for it. The schools have never been anywhere near as good as they are today, but the gap between what they are and what the people want is greater than ever before. Nobody really wants to provide the money, time, and thought necessary for closing that gap—the hope is that it can just be argued away. Most of the controversy over public education stems from a strong desire to get something for nothing.

To understand the truth of this, it is necessary to have a clear, unsentimental picture of the way the schools were in the past. The idea that we once had marvelous public schools in this nation, and that modern philosophies of education have ruined them, is the most obvious kind of nonsense. As a matter of fact, no nation through all history has ever had good public schools for all its people, or seriously tried to. Really good education for every child is a startling new concept, one of which the United States can be justifiably proud.

Anyone who dosn't believe this should go to the trouble of consulting records to find just what kind of public schools existed in his own town fifty years ago. What most people would discover is that fifty years ago, city schools were dull and dingy buildings, with classes of forty or more pupils common. Country schools were usually one-room affairs, with children of widely varying age and ability taught at the same time. Few of the teachers fifty years ago had anywhere near as much education of any kind as most teachers today. The elementary school curriculum was pretty much limited to the Three Rs, and the high schools confined themselves to a college-preparatory program. As someone has said, the subjects were optional: the pupil could take them or stay home. The vast majority of the students never went to high school.

Admittedly, there was a certain clarity about the school situation fifty years ago that is lacking today. Most high-school graduates could spell quite well, because it was usual for only brilliant students to go.to high school at all. There were no remedial reading classes, because those who couldn't read were simply dropped. It was also undeniably true that the great majority of all American children got very little education of any kind. Apparently, people didn't care about that much fifty years ago—there was far less talk about an educational crisis then than there is today. Throughout all history most people of the world had got very little education, so why get excited about it? Of course the public schools were threadbare, and the classes crowded, and the teachers little educated, but they were, after all, charity schools, and it was pretty good to have any free schools at all. Most people who could afford it sent their children to private schools as a matter of course, and they supplemented straight classical programs of education with tutors:

the dancing master, the music teacher, the tennis instructor, and all the rest of them. The children of working men got their vocational education by dropping out of school early and becoming apprentices, and no one brooded about their lack of general education. There was no crisis—most people saw nothing whatsoever to worry about.

The extraordinary thing is that the revolution against this age-old concept has been so quiet, and so invisible that many people today aren't aware that it took place. It all happened very simply. Every year more and more pupils sought admittance to the high schools. A high-school education was part of the American dream, and people in those days dreamed hard and fruitfully. High schools which dropped too many pupils began to get a bad reputation. Public schools are, after all, managed by politically selected school boards, and are designedly sensitive to public pressure. The theories of professional educators did not instigate the great change in public education—it was the demand of the public, insistently voiced through every school board in the land. And what the public wanted was perfectly clear: a high-school education for every American child.

But all children aren't capable of a straight classical program, plenty of educators objected. Well all right, the answer came: most children are capable of acquiring *some* education, aren't they? Give each child as much as you can. Don't kick them out of school. It's a disgrace to be kicked out of school, and schools shouldn't be in the business of disgracing children. Just keep all the children, and give them as much as possible.

No one voice, no one proclamation, gave this answer. It was worked out gradually by thousands of day-to-day decisions at count-less school-board meetings throughout the country. Professional educators tried to find a way to obey the command. They devised new programs for those who were unable or unwilling to take the col-lege-preparatory work. The sound of the hammer was heard in the land as courses in manual training and mechanics proliferated. For the girls there were "domestic arts," a new phrase for cooking, sew-ing, and other housewifely chores. And of course, the traditional subjects were still taught—they were taught to more people than ever before. The educators did their best to provide something useful for the slow without handicapping the gifted.

As school enrollments increased, the demand of the public proved insatiable. At school-board meetings, wistful parents kept showing up to ask for something new. Why not courses in dancing and music and tennis—it didn't seem fair that the children of the poor should be entirely cut off from such things. Shrewd managers of factories appeared to ask that vocational education be tailored to meet their immediate employment needs. People worried about safety asked why courses in driving automobiles couldn't be instituted to help cut down the terrible death toll on highways. Others requested courses in family life to help reduce the divorce rate, and instruction about alcoholic beverages to help reduce alcoholism. The schools were asked to encourage good citizenship, patriotism, and international understanding. And how about moral and spiritual values? Sure, the schools can't teach sectarian religion, but moral and spiritual values can't be entirely left out, can they?

Everybody wanted to add something, and nobody wanted to cut anything out. Certainly no one has ever suggested that the Three Rs are less important than they ever were—in fact, shrill proofs have been offered that in this highly technical age, they are *more* important, and the schools should emphasize them more. More of everything has been the cry—more and yet more!

Well, we'll try, the educators said. Educators I've met are a remarkably cheerful and resilient crowd. They had to say they'd try, for school administrators are paid to carry out the educational programs voted for by school-board members. They didn't, of course, always succeed. All kinds of new problems loomed before them.

Say that a town which fifty years ago had a hundred high-school pupils now has a thousand—that's a conservative amount of growth in this nation. How do you find which of those thousand pupils are capable of college-preparatory work, and how do you give it to them without splitting them off from all the others and creating a socially dangerous kind of elite group within each school system? How do you teach a hundred subjects as efficiently as you once taught a dozen?

The answers usually involved requests for more money. The public was demanding more of the schools, and inevitably, the schools had to demand more of the public. Here, of course, the controversy began, for the people who asked new courses were under the impression that public education is free. What do you mean, it costs money? What's getting into the schools, anyway? They're spending more and more every year, they're going hog wild! Taxes are going up. Somebody must be getting something out of this. It's socialism, that's what it is. The two great American ideals of good universal education and low taxation collided with a bang—or more accurately, with a long series of bangs which continues to deafen our ears today.

The people also found that the addition of millions of new high-school students and hundreds of new courses had somehow changed things. Bewildered complaints about the schools mounted. A high-school diploma didn't mean what it used to—it meant simply that the schools had done all they could for the recipient during the prescribed number of years. That, after all, was what the public had asked, wasn't it?

Yes, but the able children are getting as good an education as they ever did, and millions more of them are getting an opportunity for it, the educators said soothingly. But was it true? Sometimes not. The intent of neither the public nor the educators had changed, but immediate realities sometimes forced the dilution of college-preparatory courses. It takes a lot of money to run a top-notch college-preparatory program in the midst of all the other duties the schools have been called upon to perform. In some schools—indeed, in many schools—children who wish to prepare for college are a real minority group. All kinds of unpredictable things happen. Recently a great many Negroes moved to a large Midwestern city from a rural part of the South where the Negro children had had woefully inadequate schools. The schools in the Midwestern city had to help the Negro children to make up for years of poor preparation, and there was no special appropriation to meet the emergency. No one should be much surprised to find that for a while, the general level of education offered by those schools sank.

What's the matter with public education, people want to know. And at the same time they say, too many American children have bad teeth. Can't the schools provide free dental inspection, and free dental care for those who can't afford treatment? Sure, that's public health, not public education, but few towns have public-health agencies capable of providing free dental inspection or care for so many children. It would be cheaper to do it through the schools than to create special agencies. After all, we can't let the children's teeth rot, can we? Look at the great number of young men rejected by the draft boards during the last war because they had poor teeth.

What it all amounts to is that the American people rather suddenly subscribed to the ideal of public schools which will do all they possibly can to help each child become as healthy, wealthy, and wise as native endowments permit. It's perhaps a logical ideal for this country—it tends to set a sort of one-generation limit on class barriers, and it certainly glorifies the holiness of the individual, be he poor or rich. I rather doubt that the public thought of such fancy theories. Somehow it just didn't seem fair to allow a child to go to hell in a basket because his parents wouldn't or couldn't get his teeth examined, or because he couldn't learn French. There must be some good in every child, the feeling was—let's do what we can to develop it. So the decision was made, without any real recognition of the fact that something new was being conceived. Having set the goal, the people have apparently forgotten that enormous effort and expense are needed to reach it. They seem to expect the great change in the schools to take place smoothly, without any bother or confusion at all, and certainly without more expense.

In spite of that, an extraordinary amount of progress has been made. In the past seventy-five years or so, high-school enrollments have been multiplied by about ninety. More education is being passed on to more children than ever before in history, as well as more health care, entertainment, and all the rest of it. The advance is perfectly measurable: the average scholastic attainments of soldiers in World War II were tested and found to be much higher than those of the soldiers in World War I. Most suburban schools in America are incredibly good, compared to any sort of school in the past. Many centralized rural schools give the children of farmers an education as good as anyone in the nation can get. The people seem to vacillate between complacency at these gains and exaggerated horror at weaknesses which have not yet been overcome.

There are still plenty of one-room schools where the wood stoves glow with no sign of progress. What is worse, from the point of view of the number of children involved, big city schools have shown perhaps the least improvement of all. In the big cities, those who can afford it still send their children to private schools, and the middle-class people are rushing to the suburbs. The result is that many big-city schools exist almost exclusively for the children of the very poor. Those are the children who need the best schools, and all too often, they get the worst. Not much is being done about their plight.

The natural vacillation of the public between complacency and outrage is encouraged by books, news stories, and magazine articles. Books like *The Blackboard Jungle* give a picture of the worst big-city schools, and everybody gets into a tizzy. Articles about Utopian suburban schools, protected by the suburb's own brand of economic segregation, calm things down. Then a book charging that the schools are using the wrong method to teach reading whips things up again. Halfway measures are apparently no good in books of this kind—the one I'm thinking of gives the impression of assuming that *no* children are learning to read properly these days. To parents like myself, whose children learned to read beautifully in the public schools, this sort of thing can be confusing, but there is a wonderful authority in the printed word—I sometimes catch myself wondering if my daughters really can read, even while they're contentedly curled up with books which I at their age found incomprehensible. Critics of this kind have one thing in common: they lead the reader to believe that if one relatively inexpensive step were taken, like the use of more phonics to teach reading, everything would be just dandy in the schools.

This is a perfect example of what I mean by an easy answer to a hard question. Here we have slum schools, with miserable buildings, swollen classes, and disturbed children in need of special care. Here we have an increasing birth rate which demands more and more facilities just to keep the quality of education where it is. Here we have a shortage of teachers resulting from the fact that the birth rate was lowest twenty-five years ago when young teachers were born, and from increasing industrial competition for capable young adults. Here we have more and more demands placed upon the schools every day, and a constantly proliferating list of school duties, with no clear system of priorities governing either the expenditure of money or the pupil's time. And here also we have a book which attracts more public attention than any other book on education recently published, and it appears to give a very simple answer: teach more phonics, and everything will be all right.

Maybe there is an easy answer, after all—easy to say, if not easy to do. Maybe everything would be all right if the public just realized the nobility of the goal it has set for the schools, and also realized the enormous amount of money, time, and thought needed to achieve it. Maybe everything would be all right if everyone realized that the goal of schools capable of wasting no human talent is eminently worth pursuing, and that a nation with the economic power of this one could for the first time in history achieve it.

The common realization of those things would be the first step. The second step would be for thoughtful people in every state and community to sit down and examine the facts about their schools, hear all relevant opinions, and chart their own course. Programs like that of the National Citizens Commission for the Public Schools and the White House Conference on Education have been designed to encourage that process. The business of getting together to look at facts isn't very dramatic, and often it's downright dull, but it probably is the only way the bright dream of good schools for everyone can be made a reality.

The job of figuring out how righteous indignation about weaknesses of the schools can be converted into constructive action will not be done by people who wave their arms while criticizing the schools as though they were fighting bees. It will be done by serious-minded people calmly appraising the schools in their own community. It will be done by people who have learned to be patient of differing points of view, and who know how to enlarge areas of agreement, rather than capitalizing on controversy. Somehow an ancient fallacy will have to be righted. *The schools are no good,* many people are saying nowadays, and they imply, *therefore, do not support them.* I certainly agree that many schools are pretty poor now, as they have been always, and I believe that they therefore should be supported doubly. The job of creating schools capable of developing all the abilities of all American children will never be easy, but without any doubt the American people are in their own curious way plodding toward it. There is certainly hope in the fact that for the past fifty years, they have plodded with the speed of hares.

Suggested Topics

1. Federal aid to education
2. How to recruit teachers
3. Is there a "crisis in education"?
4. Good education costs money.
5. The average American is better educated now.
6. An evaluation of my early school training

COLLEGE LIFE

ARE FRATERNITIES NECESSARY? *Stephen Birmingham*

The author of two novels, *Young Mr. Keefe* (1958) and *Barbara Greer* (1959), Stephen Birmingham graduated from Williams College in 1950 after spending his junior year at Oxford. He is a frequent contributor to a number of popular magazines.

"Neither a borrower nor a lender be" was one of the canons of my fraternity. Still, from that great grab bag of communal living that was my fraternity house, I emerged, upon graduation, with several articles of dubious ownership—a single white athletic sock, a pitch pipe, a size seventeen-and-a-half shirt, an ash tray monogrammed *H,* two towels, one marked Gymnasium and the other marked Hotel Meurice, Paris, and a copy of the official fraternity pledge training book marked DO NOT REMOVE FROM LIBRARY.

I rediscovered this little volume the other day and read, "Your fraternity chapter will be your home; for four years it will take the place of parents, and, as its mysteries and ideals are unfolded to you, it will come to occupy a place of unequaled importance in your heart." I was swept back into the world of seal and ritual, songs, badges, official flowers, colors, calls and whistles, flags and mottoes, secret vows and handshakes. And I decided to visit this world again to see what had happened to it since I left it.

The house that was my home for four years at Williams College, and that took the place of my parents during that time, was a square, solid, unpretentious red-brick building. It had two and a half floors in varying states of disrepair caused by the fifty-odd pairs of feet that tramped in and out each day. On the first floor there was a living room, a library, a sun porch, dining room, kitchen and a telephone room. The walls of the last were inscribed with the names and telephone numbers of young ladies from Smith, Vassar, Wellesley and Mount Holyoke, along with pertinent statistics, comments, warnings and endorsements. The upper two floors contained perhaps a dozen sleeping rooms, accommodating about two dozen members of the upper two classes. The décor of the house would best be described as Early Alumni.

Most of the furniture was massive, unmovable and donated. Some of the larger, more permanent pieces bore bronze plaques, engraved with their donors' names, their class numerals, and scraps of poetry in their praise. On the living-room mantel was a collection of silver cups and trophies, usually unpolished, representing athletic or scholarship awards our house had won. In a special library cabinet was a file of old exams, maintained in the wistful hope that through some fluke, Physics 12 would be given the same exam in 1949 that it had been given in 1948.

Downstairs, in the dark and secret bowels of the house, was our Chapter Room or "Goat Room." In some fraternity houses the location of this *sanctum sanctorum* can be spotted from the outside—wherever you see a long and windowless expanse of wall. But in our house the Goat Room's location was less apparent, since it was carved out of the subsoil and was approached through a long, twisting cellar passageway. The door to the Goat Room was always locked, and no one but an initiated member was permitted inside. As pledges we used to speculate wildly on what it contained; only hard wooden benches, jammed against concrete walls, we later discovered. The walls were painted, for dramatic effect, with lamp-black, and in cold weather when they sweated, we often emerged from meetings weirdly streaked with black. The room was unventilated, and sometimes held a faintly noxious odor caused, we thought, by a plumbing defect. Filing out of this room, sweating, soiled and gasping for air, our appearance suggested far more fiendish goings-on than voting to hire a jazz combo for House-party weekend.

Although keeping house in this building had many of the problems and much of the excitement of an all-male camping trip—the peccadilloes of the coal-burning furnace, the mysteries of the fuse box, the arbitrary appearance of ceiling leaks—it is not always thus in a college fraternity. In my recent study of the fraternity world I discovered that perhaps the greatest single truth about college fraternity houses is that if you have seen one, you have *not* seen them all. Most chapter houses are owned by alumni corporations, and the size and splendor of each house is governed by the state of its alumni pocket-books. At Penn State several fraternity houses look like low, sprawling country clubs. At the University of Pennsylvania they are mostly trim, elegant town houses. At Purdue you will see a tall Gothic castle with crenelated walls and gargoyles; at Tulane, a bungalow. At the University of Oklahoma one fraternity house looks far grander than the United States Supreme Court building. At U.C.L.A. there is one that resembles, appropriately, a huge motel. There are fraternity houses with billiard rooms, music rooms, conservatories, gymnasiums, bowling alleys and Turkish baths. A Dartmouth fraternity excavated for an indoor swimming pool, but when the college objected on grounds of safety the hole was turned into an underground night club.

Precisely how these pleasure domes of youth came to college campuses from Brunswick, Maine, to San Jose, California—and even sent colonies northward into Canada—is an American phenomenon. Certain English public schools in the early 18th Century may have contained secret societies with Greek letters, grips, vows and passwords, but the first college fraternity was formed at the second oldest American college—William and Mary—in 1776. This was Phi Beta Kappa and, though it is now a nonsecret scholastic honorary society that takes in both men and women, it was, in the beginning, a men's social fraternity. It even had a well-heeled alumnus, Elisha Parmele, who, through a bequest, established other chapters at Harvard and Yale.

The idea caught on, and Phi Beta Kappa spread to Dartmouth, Union and Bowdoin. At Union, three more fraternities were started—Kappa Alpha, Sigma Phi and Delta Phi—the so-called Union Triad. From then on there was no stopping fraternities. Through the 19th Century they blossomed like wild-flowers. They spread across the Allegheny Mountains, across the Mississippi River, across the plains, over the Rockies, the Sierras and into California. They are still spreading.

Despite its size, this world is highly organized. Every national fraternity has a headquarters, usually with a permanent office and paid staff. Each headquarters collects dues from its members and, with this often sizable income, makes cautious loans to individual chapters for building and repairs, helps establish new chapters, finances a traveling secretary (a sort of brotherly inspector general whose job it is to visit every chapter once or twice a year to see whether fraternity policies are being carried out), publishes a fraternity newsletter or magazine, and otherwise keeps track of its scattered chickens. And, like a huge tent over the national fraternities, is an organization called the National Interfraternity Conference.

The figures change so rapidly that it is hard to get an accurate count but, at this writing, there are sixty-one national fraternities in the N.I.C. called by combinations of every letter in the Greek alphabet from Alpha to Omega (except Eta, Iota and Omicron, which nobody seems to want), and several of these fraternities have over a hundred chapters. Among the largest are Alpha Tau Omega, Beta Theta Pi, Delta Tau Delta, Kappa Sigma, Lambda Chi Alpha, Phi Delta Theta, Pi Kappa Alpha and Sigma Alpha Epsilon. Perhaps the most famous is Sigma Chi, because of its *Sweetheart* song.

Altogether, these fraternities have over 3250 student chapters in the United States and Canada, and their undergraduate population is close to two hundred thousand men. These figures do not include scores of single-chapter "local" fraternities, nor do they include the "satellite" fraternities which serve specific professions—law, medicine, science, journalism and so on.

Although the N.I.C. is technically powerless, actually it is vastly influential. It is, as one N.I.C. delegate put it, the "conscience" of American fraternities. It cannot dictate fraternity policy, but it can suggest and advise. It cannot punish, but it can scold. It is run by fraternity men who receive no salary but who through their dedication to fraternity affairs long after college have earned widespread respect.

The N.I.C. fills a complicated role. It has committees working to improve relations between fraternities and their colleges, to study ways of improving undergraduate scholarships, to find causes of and cures for cheating in classrooms, to study fraternity manners and morals. The Conference has long opposed hazing and takes credit for the fact that fraternity pledges no longer are paddled with cricket bats or subjected to treatment that is brutal, humiliating or silly. (The N.I.C. stands, I am sure, foursquare against goldfish swallowing, pillow fighting and panty raids.) Its aims are loftly and its successes, in many cases, have been noteworthy.

On the touchy matter of discrimination, however, the N.I.C.'s stand has been something less than foursquare. Somewhat hesitantly, back in 1922, the Conference declared that it "did not favor fraternities founded upon denominational or racial lines." But since that time it is hard to see that the N.I.C. has taken much of a position on the subject one way or the other. One of the N.I.C.'s great fears is "bad press," and, as a result, almost any statement on the question comes cushioned with qualifications, double negatives, even contradictions.

At the local level, many fraternities exclude Negroes and Jews—by "gentlemen's agreements" if not by written rules; many others pay no attention to what, in the quaint language of fraternityland, are called "exoteric requirements." (*Exoteric* means "outside"; I had to look it up too.) In the N.I.C. itself are ten or eleven fraternities—one is Zeta

Beta Tau—that are considered "essentially Jewish." As yet, however, no Negro fraternities are represented in the Conference, although at least one, Alpha Phi Alpha, has over a hundred chapters. The reason the N.I.C. gives for this is that too large a proportion of the Negro fraternity chapters are established at nonaccredited colleges.

Oddly enough, the N.I.C. shyly states that it has "no available figure" concerning how many of its members have specific restrictive clauses in their constitutions, though one would think that a simple head count would not be hard to make. Still, over the years, white-Christian clauses have been disappearing from fraternity constitutions. How the N.I.C. feels about this can best be seen, perhaps, in this rather wistful sentence from a recent N.I.C. *Yearbook:* "The picture is discouraging . . . when one realizes that a large majority of N.I.C. members currently have no exoteric requirements; each succeeding year sees first one then another fraternity delete membership requirements from its constitution."

In explaining its sentiments on the subject, the N.I.C. frequently uses that wonderful and pesky old word, "freedom." It wants its members to have freedom—presumably freedom to discriminate, if they so wish.

In the academic world, I discovered, the N.I.C. is regarded with mixed emotions. Many college administrators praise it wholeheartedly and work hand in hand with it toward its goal of "raising fraternities to a high standard of excellence." Other educators consider the N.I.C.'s activities as equivalent to those of a well-intentioned busybody, a sort of off-campus Mary Worth. From several notable institutions, the National Interfraternity Conference has received several notable snubs.

Fraternities themselves, in spite of the history and organization behind them, are the subject of widely differing opinions. They have received temperate criticism from men like Pres. Charles W. Cole of Amherst, who says that they exert, on the whole, "a mildly negative influence." They have been soundly denounced by men like Sloan Wilson, formerly Education Editor of the New York *Herald-Tribune,* who calls them "stupid, juvenile and purposeless." But Dr. Milton Eisenhower, of Johns Hopkins, feels that "fraternities and sororities are workshops in understanding and co-operation. They are anvils upon which the character of individuals may be fashioned for service beyond self."

The highest praise of all, understandably, comes from speakers at fraternity alumni gatherings. From one, I heard that the United States of America is nothing more than a huge fraternity. From another, I gathered that heaven is operated on the fraternity system. ("When we are all gathered to that Great Big Chapter Room Up There. . . ." he said, lifting his hand in the gesture, I suppose, of Saint Peter offering a pledge pin.) Considering the praise and condemnation of fraternities, I have decided that I must not have been a very impressionable youth: I can't see that belonging to a fraternity had any effect, either beneficial or adverse, upon me, although my mother once blamed fraternity life for the deterioration of my table manners. (To this day, I catch myself setting my dinner fork aside, saving it for my dessert.)

Even the stanchest supporters of fraternites admit that "fraternities can be good or bad, depending on the college." Just as there is no typical fraternity house, neither is there a typical fraternity system—whether in method, attitude, or the part it plays in student life.

At Harvard, for instance, there is only one fraternity, and joining it carries almost no prestige at all—none compared to the privilege of joining Harvard's august Porcellian Club. At the University of Illinois there are over fifty fraternities and to join one of them means everything to an undergraduate (though only one out of three gets a bid). At Amherst, there is "100 per cent rushing," which means that every man who wants to join a fraternity can, and that's that. Yale has a handful of fraternities called "junior societies," which carry nowhere near the weight on campus of Yale's "senior socities."

At a whole gaggle of state universities, fraternity and nonfraternity men create a two-party system in campus politics; the election of Campus Queen becomes an annual interfraternity scrap. There is, of course, a geographical pattern involved here. Being a fraternity man means more if you live in Dallas than if you live in Boston. It means more in Cleveland, Detroit, Milwaukee, Seattle or Fresno than it does in New York. But the East-West pattern is not entirely consistent. A prominent fraternity man told me, "If you want to see fraternities at their worst—from a national standpoint—go to Dartmouth. And if you want to see them at their best, go to Gettysburg College in Pennsylvania. Dartmouth is sloppy about fraternities. But Gettysburg has one of the most beautiful fraternity systems in the world."

There are certainly tremendous differences between these two colleges. Dartmouth is a vigorous, cheerful, all-male college whose men have the wind of the north in their veins, as a Dartmouth song boasts. A Dartmouth man is proud of his prowess on the ski slopes, his stamina with a beer stein and his way with a maid. Dartmouth is expensive as colleges go, is in the Ivy League, and, as a result, is socially "correct." Dartmouth is cocky, given to breeziness and raccoon coats, and, though it takes education seriously, it loves a good time. Dartmouth is famous for its parties. The girl who is invited to a Dartmouth Winter Carnival doesn't say no (to the invitation, that is), and the same thing goes for the parties that pop up explosively nearly every Saturday night of the college year.

Gettysburg, on the other hand, with its root in the Lutheran

Church, is quiet, purposeful and, by Dartmouth standards, stuffy. Liquor is prohibited on the Gettysburg campus. Gettysburg is co-educational, which means that the Gettysburg man uses less colorful language, shaves every day and dresses more carefully. Gettysburg is considerably less expensive, has no "social" pretensions and, since its students come from a lower socioeconomic scale, has few ties to the Edgartown Regatta, Rugby Week in Bermuda, Palm Beach and the New York Debutante Cotillion.

Second only in importance to getting a B.A. at Gettysburg is getting a fraternity pin. A Gettysburg freshman told me earnestly, "I've been praying every night that I'll make Phi Delta Theta." And the chances of a Gettysburg man making a fraternity are good, since 80 per cent of the students are in fraternities and the rest are mostly commuter students who would not want to join anyway.

Rush Week at Gettysburg is an intensely serious affair. Freshmen are invited to different houses and, in a series of long, carefully planned dates, are wooed with lunches, dinners, trips to plays, movies, stock-car races; they are taken on picnics, hikes, swimming trips and steak roasts, plied with soft drinks and cigarettes. "The freshman is king during Rush Week," a fraternity man told me. "The competition is keen, so if we really want the man we've got to show him how *much* we want him."

Besides being on their best behavior themselves, Gettysburg fraternities offer freshmen helpful hints on how they can make the best impression. A fraternity booklet called *The Greeks at Gettysburg* suggests, "Give a *firm* handshake, but not a *bone-crusher*. A *dead-fish* grip is *definitely* against you. Be friendly and take part in the conversation, but do not *monopolize* it. Be yourself at all times."

Dartmouth fraternities don't take members until the sophomore year, which means that many men, by the time they are eligible to join a fraternity, have lost interest. Only about half of Dartmouth's student body is in fraternities, so there is little stigma attached to the man who fails to make one. "It was like losing a girl," an "axed" Dartmouth man told me. "It hurt for a few days, but I got over it."

Opposite from Gettysburg, Dartmouth lower classmen "rush" the fraternities. This turns Rush Week into a nonchalant, informal affair with sophomores wandering from house to house paying calls. Walking down Dartmouth's fraternity row one night during rushing I overheard one sophomore yawn and say to another. "Aw, it's getting pretty late. Let's skip every other house." "Sure," his friend replied. "Who cares?" Inside the houses, rushing is a casual stand-up affair, a little like a diplomatic cocktail party. There is a certain amount of steady-eyed smiling and firm handshaking, but mostly there is cocktailish small talk about summer, friends, sports and classes. Bowls of potato chips are passed around. A particularly "hot" sophomore may be taken off to a member's room for a serious sales talk but, other than that, nothing much breaks the mood of a pleasant get-together. In the old days of "sudden-death" rushing, hot men were met at the Hanover station, escorted to fraternity houses and plied with beer until, resistance lowered, they groggily signed pledge agreements. Now beer is prohibited until the final night of rushing.

I attended "hash sessions" at both colleges—the long meetings that take place each night of Rush Week when the men seen that day are screened. At Gettysburg these sessions are serious, sometimes lasting until dawn. Each candidate is soberly analyzed as to clothes, handshake, appearance, high-school career, manners, voice, sincerity, his interest in the house. Next they begin a process which actually speculates on the rushee's future. "Joe wants to be a teacher" one members will say. "I think he'll make a good one. He has qualities of leadership and he may end up as a college president."

At Dartmouth hash sessions are conducted with all possible expediency. "Who met Joe?" the house president shouts, banging a gavel and, for a moment, there is noisy whispering and page-turning as the house members riffle through their classbooks for Joe's picture in order to see who actually did meet him. Then one man may say, "Yeah, I met him. Nice guy. Owns a convertible. Give him an A." Then Dartmouth's ditto system begins as the other members who met Joe, and feel the same way about him, chime in with, "Ditto—ditto—ditto." There is a quick show of hands, then on to the next man.

Pledge Night, or Sink Night as it is called in some colleges, is always akin in spirit and mood to a wedding reception. The exhausting business of Rush Week is over; the fraternity men have chosen their new mates; pledge pins have been bestowed, and ahead of everyone lie the long and happy years of fraternal association. To continue the metaphor, Pledge Night at Dartmouth is like a wedding reception at the Scarsdale Country Club. Beer flows like champagne, the party grows loud and raucous, someone puts a lampshade on his head and stands on the piano.

Pledge Night at Gettysburg is like a wedding reception in the church social room—cheerful but restrained and, of course, beerless. At Gettysburg, the pledge period, or honeymoon, that follows lasts from September until early spring. It is a period of sacrifice and learning during which the members-to-be, under the guidance of the Pledge Training Committee, embark upon a strictly supervised program learning fraternity ideals, history and lore. Each freshman is assigned a "big brother" who sees that studies, both fraternity and academic, are not neglected. Some fraternities enforce evening study hours. At Dartmouth, the honeymoon is shorter. Most fraternities initiate their pledges by Thanksgiving. Pledge training is either brushed over or completely ignored. "That business of learning fraternity lore is a lot of Mickey Mouse," one Dartmouth man told me.

When I was initiated into my fraternity I went through Hell Week. For five nerve-racking, if not exactly hellish, days, I had my bed short-sheeted three times, got dumped into a cold shower once and was sent on a fruitless search through a chilly night for a Bennington girl's garter. (Bennington girls, among other things, do not wear garters.)

But times change. Hell Week at Williams is no more. Since the tragic night in 1956 when an M.I.T. freshman, abandoned on a lonely road by his fraternity as part of Hell Week, was drowned in a reservoir trying to find his way home, fraternities everywhere have been understandably leery of pranks that might prove dangerous. Dartmouth still observes a mild form of Hell Week before its fraternity initiations, but, rather than hell, it is characterized by harmless, if zany, horseplay. (Sample assignment: Stand over an open manhole with a fishing pole baited with a dead flounder. When passers-by ask you what you are doing, explain that all intellectuals have gone underground and you are fishing for them.)

Hell Week at Gettysburg is called Help Week or Campus Cleanup Week. For the few days before initiations pledges busy themselves with useful chores around the college and community. One pledge assignment was to repaint local mailboxes to conform with new post-office standards. Another was to patch up and paint the local old folks' home.

The contrasts between the two colleges are many, but the most interesting is the difference between the functions that fraternities serve at these institutions. Fraternities at Gettysburg seem to exist, essentially, for the glory and betterment of fraternities at Gettysburg. At Dartmouth, fraternities exist for fun. "This house taps a keg every Saturday night," one Dartmouth man said. "That's what I like about it." "We don't bother trying to build ideals or instill values," another said. "The college does that." One house president said, "We've got the Scholarship Trophy this year, but we're trying to get rid of it. It makes us look like a bunch of bookworms. What this house really needs is a good trombone player."

With a central eating system and most students living in dormitories, Dartmouth fraternity houses are tomblike during the week. But on a weekend like Winter Carnival, fraternity houses are ablaze; lights glitter on the famous snow sculptures that grace their lawns, and all through each house not a creature is stirring, unless he is stirring a Martini. Music and laughter float from the windows. ("Girls aren't

allowed on our upper floors," one man said, "at least not legally.")
New Hampshire winters are long and vigorous, which may be one
reason for Dartmouth's penchant for party giving. As one student
said, "When you're snowed in up here a thousand miles from nowhere,
what else is there to do?"

With so little else to do, belonging to a Dartmouth fraternity can
be expensive. The college estimates that, in addition to an initiation
fee of fifty to a hundred dollars, three years of fraternity living cost
a student $525 extra. And this is conservative. The operating budget
of a Dartmouth fraternity house can easily run as high as $16,000 a
year. One house spends $3000 a year on parties alone; another, $4,200.
Breakage—glassware, china, windows, lamps and furniture—becomes
a sizable figure on fraternity bills. "How did you manage to perform
twenty-three dollars' worth of breakage last month?" a father testily
wrote his son, who explained that the actual breakage figure for the
month was $1150, "so we voted to divide it up between us."

A common matter of business at fraternity-house meetings is what to
do with leftover liquor from the previous weekend. ("We have three
alternatives: sell it, drink it, or save it for the next big weekend.")
Aware that the life they offer is costly, Dartmouth fraternities offer free
"rides" to certain students who can prove financial need. In return,
these members perform odd jobs around the house. But the commonest
argument against joining a fraternity at Dartmouth is simply that it
costs too much. "It makes no sense to me," a nonfraternity junior said
to me. "I don't drink. Why should I pay for some other guy's booze?"

There are also hidden costs to belonging to a fraternity. In the Eastern college circuit several artists have made a nice thing out of traveling from college to college sketching caricatures of fraternity men for
ten or fifteen dollars a head. These caricatures are framed and used to
decorate the walls of the fraternity bar or party room. (A good artist
can dash off deft caricatures of forty or fifty fraternity men in the
course of an evening.)

Beer mugs are another traditional item of purchase. The standard
crockery beer mug, bearing the fraternity seal and the member's name,
is fairly inexpensive. But at Stanford University members of one
fraternity have been know to buy mugs of sterling silver, handsomely
engraved, and, at graduation, present them to the chapter house.
Through the years this house has amassed a collection of silver mugs
informally appraised at somewhat more than the house itself. Jewelry
is another item. Although each fraternity has only one "official" pin,
there are also sweetheart pins, pins for mothers, sisters, grandmothers,
pins with pearl borders, special crown pearl borders, recognition buttons, tie clasps and rings.

However, fraternity membership does not *have* to be expensive, as proved, once again, by Gettysburg College. There, through thrift and careful planning—and with help from house mothers (which Dartmouth doesn't have) who market and plan menus with a feminine eye on the budget—it actually turns out to be somewhat cheaper to belong to a fraternity than to live in a dormitory.

Gettysburg fraternities, of course, do not go in for the amount of socializing that Dartmouth does. They keep busy along other lines. As Larry Gaenzle, a young alumnus and last year's president of Gettysburg's powerful Interfraternity Council, explained it to me, "Our fraternities have a four-fold program—educational, recreational, spiritual and service. By service, I mean that we try to serve the individual, the college and the local community."

Gaenzle told me that one of the most important and waited-for events in the school year is Gettyburg's "Greek Week." This, too, is divided into four sections.

The educational part of the week consists of dinner discussion groups held in the fraternity houses at which members, faculty and alumni debate questions of "vital interest." (Sample questions: Does etiquette change? What are the responsibilities of a chapter to its alumni? What should we do with chaperons at house parties? Will freshmen become better Christians by joining a fraternity?)

A typewritten report of these discussions and their conclusions runs to twenty-seven pages single spaced. (The answers to the vital questions above are "Yes, etiquette changes but the 'spirit' remains the same; the responsibilities of a chapter to its alumni are many; chaperons should be treated with respect and made to feel at home; freshmen will become better Christians by joining fraternities if they apply themselves.") The recreational part of Greek Week consists of an interfraternity get-together where the houses conduct singing contests and put on skits. For service, the fraternities join in some worth-while community project. And, to close the week on a spiritual note, the fraternities and sororities join at a special chapel service.

It would be unfair to say that Dartmouth fraternities are completely frivolous. A number of them support refugee students from Hungary and have adopted war orphans abroad. They give Christmas parties for needy children. But this, according to national fraternity officers, is not enough; they shake their heads gloomily over Dartmouth and wax rhapsodic over Gettysburg. One reason for this is that Gettysburg listens attentively to everything the national officers say, whereas Dartmouth ignores them. And this, of course, explains why true-blue fraternity men single out Dartmouth as a horrible example.

There is a strong trend at Dartmouth for fraternities to sever their national ties, and a number of houses already have, generally as the result of membership disputes. Dartmouth is proud of its integration policy; most of its fraternities accept Negroes and Jews without a second thought. "We want to make our own decisions," a Dartmouth man told me. "We do what *we* think is right—not what some guy in Chicago tells us is right." By becoming local, most Dartmouth men feel, a fraternity loses nothing. In fact it may gain, since the national dues it has been paying can then be kept for itself. "The only thing members of local houses lose is the free sack," a Dartmouth man explained, pointing out that the free-sack service that nationals offer can be important during the football season. "I'm glad I'm a Beta when there's a bed for me at the Beta house at Penn after the Penn-Dartmouth game," he said.

At the same time, a number of colleges—Amherst, for example—have been cracking down on free sacks. Amherst lies roughly in the geographic center of the Eastern-college road map, and also within shouting distance of two popular women's colleges—Smith and Mount Holyoke. For years, Amherst fraternities put up with flagrant sack-mooching and, doing so, nearly depleted their treasuries. Finally, it was discovered that Amherst's reputation for hospitality was spreading to the noncollege world—to itinerant encyclopedia salesmen, drummers and road-show impresarios. Today, Amherst fraternities give practically all non-Amherst men a chilly reception.

Dartmouth and Gettysburg are certainly isolated examples, and the two attitudes they represent are not typical of fraternities everywhere. They are only at opposite poles. At bigger colleges—Ohio State, University of California, University of Illinois, Indiana, Michigan—in fact, almost anywhere—you might find one fraternity that takes itself as seriously as Gettysburg fraternities do and, at the other end of the scale, a fraternity as nonchalant as any of Dartmouth's.

And you would probably find a whole range of attitudes in between. On any campus, fraternities tend to stratify themselves. One house will be considered "top" and another *infra dig*. One house will be known for its party boys, another for its bookworms. And, from year to year, these ratings keep changing. When I was in college, my fraternity was the bookworm house; we had three Phi Beta Kappas and no football players. (And, of course, in the curious pattern of undergraduate snobbery, bookishness was pretty odd-ball.) But when I visited it a few years after graduating, I found that the pendulum had swung the other way. It had become quite "jock"—long on athletes and short on Phi Betes. Now, the pendulum is back again; it is known as "the egghead house."

Still, it is true that fraternities on the vast campuses of the Midwest and West are generally more important—or, rather, that the gulf between fraternity and nonfraternity men is wider—than at most Eastern colleges. One reason for this is certainly size. That vague feeling of "belonging" is more easily achieved in a group of fifty men than it is in a student body of twenty-five thousand. Often, at these giant schools, a shortage of dormitory space means that the nonfraternity man must find his diggings in a local rooming house, or commute and, for social life, he must fend for himself.

Another reason for the strong position of fraternities on these co-educational campuses has to do, of course, with girls and the presence of sororities, or "women's fraternities" as they are officially called in the peculiar parlance of the fraternity world. Whether it is solid fact or artful sorority propaganda, I don't know, but sorority girls are always promoted as the most desirable girls on any coed campus, and this means that sororities and fraternities are continually bolstering each other's prestige.

No right-thinking Ohio Wesleyan girl would deign to date an Ohio Wesleyan boy who was not in a fraternity. The Ohio Wesleyan boy, in turn, loyally prefers to date sorority girls. If he finds a girl he especially likes he can eliminate competition by "hanging" his pin on her. Pin-hanging is often accompanied by elaborate ritual. One popular practice is for the boy's fraternity brothers to join together and serenade the "hung" girl from the front lawn of her sorority house. Charming though this sounds, it is not always so regarded by residents in the neighborhood of the university. At the University of Illinois, for example, so many quiet evenings were being shattered by male voices raised in song that the citizens of Urbana sang out in protest. Serenades can still take place at Illinois—provided the serenaders first register with the local police.

In trying to figure out why fraternities differ so widely from place to place—why two fraternity systems can be as dissimilar as Gettysburg's and Dartmouth's—I have concluded that almost always the responsibility for what a fraternity is, does and means rests with its alumni. Being constantly visited, supervised, counseled and supported by a loyal and devout group of older men seems to have given Gettysburg its austerity, its conservatism, its sobriety and its slight tendency to self-righteousness.

Dartmouth has a generous and loyal alumni body, too—but Dartmouth alumni never seem interested in fraternity affairs. At his class reunion, the Dartmouth alumnus rarely goes back to his fraternity house. Dartmouth fraternities are less dependent on alumni financial support. "When we need a little money we have a cocktail party for the parents," one Dartmouth man said. "Then we get the fathers aside and sort of pass the hat."

A Gettysburg alumnus took me through the handsome new chapter house that he and his fellows had raised the money to build. At the door of the chapter room, which was locked, our tour ended. I asked whether I might see inside and he looked at me with horror. "The chapter room is sacred!" he said. "The only thing I can tell you about it is that it's designed in an oval shape."

But at Dartmouth I was taken into several chapter rooms. And, to the dismay I am sure of all serious-thinking fraternity men, I was even told all about one house's secret ritual. "It's a riot," my guide at Dartmouth said. "We all put on black robes and hoods for initiation. Then we put each pledge into a coffin and carry him into the chapter room. Everybody stands in a circle and starts chanting. We knock thrice on the lid of the coffin and say, 'Out of the darkness, into the light!'—and lift the lid." From this description, and remembering my own initiation ceremony with its masks, chants and choreography, it seems safe to say that as far as ritual goes, most fraternities are pretty much alike.

Fraternities, whether taken seriously or not, seem to fill some sort of gap in college life. Colleges with fraternities recognize this, I think; most of the college administrators I talked to said they would honestly be sorry to see fraternities go. It is not simply that fraternities provide roofs over students' heads and, in the majority of cases, meals. It is a little more subtle. When college fraternities came into being, there were no cars, no telephones, no planes flying to Bermuda for Easter Week. Colleges were cloistered, life was monastic and home was far away. Fraternities then provided relief from the tedium of college classrooms and study.

They still do. You can conquer boredom—as Dartmouth does—by tapping a keg on Saturday night. Or you can conquer it—as Gettysburg does—by indulging in projects, committee work and ritual.

Meanwhile, fraternities show no signs of going. With their shortcomings and inequities—the most important of which is the matter of discrimination—they are growing by leaps and bounds. In the last fifty years the number of fraternity chapters in America has more than quadrupled. In 1900 there were 140,000 fraternity men in the United States. Right now there are over a million and a half. And, at each college in the country, each fraternity chapter continues to mean nothing more nor less than each chapter at college decides to make it mean.

When I was seventeen I suppose I did not analyze things too much. I joined a fraternity because it was the thing to do. I sometimes wonder whether, if I had it to do over again, I would or not. Alas, unless Saint Peter is waiting for me with a shiny pledge button, I shall never have the chance.

Suggested Topics

1. What fraternities do *for*—and *to*—a person
2. "The freshman is king during rush week"
3. Hell week
4. Scholarship and the "Greeks"
5. Discrimination and fraternities
6. Should fraternities be outlawed?
7. The honorary scholarship fraternities

THE CASE FOR CAMPUS LIFE

Grace and Fred Hechinger

A former president of the Education Writers Association, Fred Hechinger is education editor of *The New York Times.* His wife, Grace, has worked for the Ford Foundation, Brandeis University, and *Newsweek* magazine. Their comparison of metropolitan and campus colleges is based on personal experiences: Mr. Hechinger is a graduate of the City College of New York; Mrs. Hechinger, of Wellesley College.

Commuting, by train or car or bus or by some combination of these, is the new metropolitan American way of life. As the suburbs grow denser and spread farther from their centers, husbands commute to their daily work, wives to weekly afternoons in town, families to evenings at the theatre (with a mad rush for the last commuter train before the final curtain is down). It is no more than natural that the country's college youth should also be acquiring the commuting habit.

To be quite fair, it is more than a habit; it has become a necessity. Less than two decades ago, colleges were anxiously seeking students. In those incredible days, college catalogues spared no effort to advertise the advantages of campus life. The "view books" of the most respectable colleges often resembled slick resort literature, and rolling hills and tree-shaded lawns vied for attention with the academic prestige of the faculty.

Reprinted from *The New York Times Magazine,* March 29, 1959. By permission of *The New York Times* and the authors.

Going to college then was almost synonymous with going *away* to college. Few students commuted to institutions of higher learning, and those who did so made no secret of the fact that they would prefer to "go away" if they could afford to. "The College on the Subway," as the College of the City of New York was known, was the exception (somewhat underprivileged) to this rule.

Today, with three and a half million students already enrolled in colleges and universities, and with double that number forecast for 1970, the campus colleges not only don't have to lure students to their residential oases but don't know how to cope with those who want to come. As a result, colleges on the subway—or at a bus stop, for their numbers have been growing faster than urban transit systems—have become an increasingly important part of the higher educational scene. They seem likely, in fact, to become numerically the most important part.

An inevitable accompaniment to this change is that the public images of campus and commuting colleges are being reversed. Spokesmen for commuter institutions boast that anything the campus can do they can do better. And cheaper, they add, scoring a point that even the most loyal campus alumnus cannot contest. The commuting college, as Dr. John C. Adams, president of Hofstra College in Hempstead, L. I., recently pointed out, can even afford to pay higher faculty salaries because, aside from the maintenance of parking lots, its nonteaching expenses are so much lower.

Before we all become slaves of the slogan "Commuting is good for you," this seems to be the time to ask whether the virtues of the campus are just a myth. Are there any real and lasting advantages in "going away" to college?

A chance to go away to college is, for many high school seniors, the only possible break from adolescence and the shelter of the home. David Boroff, a lecturer at Brooklyn College and faculty adviser to one of its student magazines, recently quoted a 19-year-old coed: "As long as I'm home, I'll never grow up." While her complaint may smack of teen-age exaggeration and self-pity, it contains more than a kernel of truth.

"The most important fact about the student when he finally reaches the college campus is that he has been reared in what the professional educators call a 'child-centered' society," says Harold W. Stoke in his new book, "The American College President." He adds: "I suppose parents in all times and places have loved their children, but I doubt whether the anthropologists can find any other society in which, directly and indirectly, children are the object of so much privilege and special attention as they are in America."

The college freshman's plunge into a completely new situation on the campus is an important aid to growing up. Instead of being a child on whom the family's attention is focused, the student suddenly is part of a community of peers. He no longer has to "escape" from parental care to do things together with young people of his own age: they are all around him.

With this new freedom come new responsibilities. He must make his own decisions. Which hours to play or study? Which clubs to join or spurn? In addition, there are (at least on most modern campuses) such new duties as a certain measure of housecleaning and even waiting on tables, regardless of the student's economic and social background.

There is no easy substitute for the experience of the campus community itself. One serious limitation of the commuter college is that it draws most of its students from one region, and, frequently, from a relatively narrow economic group. It is perhaps ironic that the residential college, traditionally accused of snobbishness, has become more of a melting pot, through liberal scholarship aid and insistence on nation-wide representation.

A high-ranking administrator at Columbia, who said that he would not trade the excitement of the metropolis for a rural campus at any price, nevertheless admitted that even on Morningside Heights commuting students are at a serious disadvantage compared with their residential colleagues. "The mere fact of living together makes all the difference," he said. "On-campus men are housed with students from all over the country; in fact, from all over the world. The differences rub off—and that's a vital part of education."

Horace Hewlett, secretary of Amherst College, put it this way: "Students from different economic, social and geographic backgrounds find themselves involved in a community of interests from which a sense of both group and individual responsibility cannot help but emerge."

Whether it is the student-operated honor system of a Haverford College, with its strict rules and student courts independent of the "real life" authorities, or the community manager plan of an Antioch College, or the community government of a Bard College or a Bennington—to name only a few—each offers a rare opportunity (for most students the only one in a lifetime) to help shape the laws and enforce the rules instead of just conforming to them. An unreal situation? An ivory tower? Perhaps. But is not one of the important ingredients of education simply the challenge to find personal, if not always original, solutions to life's problems?

The search for independent judgment and opinions is another ingredient of education that the campus fosters. The family protects; it also establishes set ways of thinking and set social patterns. These may be fine patterns and sound philosophies. But, for the most part, teen-agers adopt rather than understand them. Even their brief outbursts of revolt are instinctive rather than reasoned.

Can independence, or even a groping for independent thought, be given a fair chance when each day's new discoveries are subjected to immediate review at the parental dinner table at night? Perhaps the problem is best described by an anecdote recorded two years ago during commencement at a New England women's college.

The main speaker, an executive of one of the educational foundations, had just finished presenting an urgent picture of a world in crisis. He had appealed for compassionate and liberal American action at home and abroad. The applause was beginning to subside. Suddenly the speaker's wife, seated in the audience, heard a mother whispering to her sputtering husband: "Now, don't you worry, dear. When Susie gets home, we'll wash all that nonsense out of her hair."

Perhaps they did. Perhaps they even should. But exposure to a great variety of ideas in a concentrated dose will put the student's mind and personal strength to a far greater test than will exposure in brief spurts during the "commuter run." Thus, the campus becomes a more realistic preparation for the many severe tests to which independent judgment will later be subjected in the "real" world.

What about the purely academic side of education in any comparison between the resident and the commuting student? Here, too, the campus has built-in advantages. Take, as an example, the now widely imitated new Amherst curriculum. Its most important course, taken by all sophomores, "Problems in American Democracy," involves faculty members of almost all departments and requires attendance of all second-year students at lengthy guest lectures and debates. Could such an academic community enterprise be compressed into a commuting framework?

Or could a commuting student fit his hectic schedule to the tea-and-symposium pattern of a Swarthmore honors seminar, conducted for four or more hours, interrupted only by a sandwich tray, in a professor's living room?

The commuter college may leave the doors of library and laboratory open after classroom hours, but it is much harder for the commuting student to find the road back to books or test tubes after dinner at home or downtown than it is for the residential student whose dormitory is only a short walk from the academic buildings. Nor does a handy cafeteria meal have as much extracurricular educational value as the daily round-table of a college dining room.

Advocates of the commuter college point to the great wealth of cultural offerings in the big city. But the very mass of riches has disadvantages. There may be far fewer books in the library of the residential college than in the vast collection at Forty-second Street. But the modest red-brick rotunda is likely to be much closer to the center of the student's mind.

Similarly, there are probably far better performances offered at Carnegie Hall every week than are likely to show up at "Ivy Auditorium" or "Memorial Chapel." But the occasional guest performance on campus not only reaches the interested student but has a chance of capturing the marginal one. "It's a revelation to see some of our freshmen get excited over a string quartet, even if some of them have never thought of spending an evening listening to chamber music before," said a Mount Holyoke College faculty member.

In a famous Phi Beta Kappa address at Harvard, Woodrow Wilson once said: "My plea then is this, that we now deliberately set ourselves to make a home for the spirit of learning; that we reorganize our colleges on the lines of this simple conception, that a college is not only a body of studies but a mode of association. * * * It must become a community of scholars and pupils * * *."

Granted that the best of the commuter colleges strive for that "mode of association," the cards are stacked against them. Commuting teachers are as busy and—often against their will—as unaccessible after classroom hours as their students are rushed and on the run.

Listen to the reminiscing of Judge Harold R. Medina about Princeton's Dean Christian Gauss: "The Dean's house on Sunday afternoons was usually filled with undergraduates, and if the Dean wasn't there, Mrs. Gauss was always on hand to make the students feel at home with tea, cookies and doughnuts. A side door of the house was kept unlocked for undergraduate use, and the Dean was on call day and night. * * *"

This is admittedly an ideal picture. Not every dean's home is as open—or as full of wisdom—as was that of Christian Gauss. Nor has the college campus escaped the impact of modern times. The automobile has surrounded even the ivory tower with parking lots. George F. Kennan of the Institute for Advanced Study at Princeton once said that the automobile may be the greatest menace to undergraduate intellectual life: mobility has curtailed leisurely conversation and reflection.

But even this is a matter of degree. If the campus student has become too mobile by choice, the commuter is condemned to daily rush hours by necessity.

This comparison is in no way intended to condemn the commuter college. The student who earnestly seeks an education will find it in the most crowded city college and on the most hectic commuter schedule. Such men as Dr. Jonas Salk and Bernard Baruch, both graduates of New York's City College, have shown this. Many students at commuter colleges approach their work with far greater determination and maturity than do their campus counterparts, and their intellectual purpose often makes them more exciting to teach.

Moreover, the college-Gothic facades of many residential colleges hide only a smug isolation. Mere "togetherness" promises little more than the stamp of the finishing school unless the minds of the community are fired by the spark of intellectual leadership. Nor should it be overlooked that on some campuses the wrong kind of stress on fraternities and sororities has shattered the very cohesion for which the academic community had been created.

Even if this were not so, the sheer weight of numbers of the incoming freshmen classes in the years ahead will make the commuting colleges an increasingly vital part of the fabric of American higher education. But this is exactly why we must not lose sight of the values of "going away" to college. The problem of the future will be to select even more carefully than in the past the boys and girls who can benefit most from campus life.

At the same time, the best efforts of all those interested in the future of higher education must be devoted to instilling the Wilsonian concept of "a community of scholars and pupils" even in the hectic milieu of the commuter colleges. It is more important than ever before to prevent the ivory tower from becoming obsolete.

Suggested Topics

1. Advantages of attending college in a large urban center
2. The campus college as a melting pot
3. Can you grow up more easily away from home?
4. College—"a community of scholars and pupils"
5. It all depends on the college—and the student.
6. "Country club" colleges
7. Evening colleges present a special problem.

COLLEGE ATHLETICS: EDUCATION OR SHOW BUSINESS?

Harold W. Stoke

Now President of Queens College, New York, Harold W. Stoke served in a number of colleges as a teacher and as an administrator. He has been President of the University of New Hampshire and of Louisiana State University and Dean of the Graduate School of Arts and Science of New York University.

I

On the morning of December 7, 1951, in the General Sessions Court in New York City, fourteen tall young men stood before Judge Saul S. Streit. The scene was the climax of the notorious basketball scandals in which players had been convicted of receiving bribes from professional gamblers for throwing basketball games in Madison Square Garden. The judge was stern, but for the culprits he tempered justice. Jail sentences and fines were few and light. Judge Streit then looked over the heads of the defendants and hurled angry words at the colleges and universities they represented. He charged that these institutions had so far forgotten their educational mission and had so overemphasized athletics that they themselves had made this scene in his courtroom all but inevitable.

Addressing himself to the colleges, Judge Streit demanded immediate and drastic reforms. Among these were the restoration of athletic responsibilities to faculties and to the academic administrative authorities; the revitalization of the National Collegiate Athletic Association; the establishment of an amateur code and of a capable, well-financed policing authority.

While there was some dismay (if little surprise) in university circles at the basketball scandals, there was genuine puzzlement about the judge's suggestions for reform. The point that had escaped him was that all his proposals had been tried for years—uniformly without success. If Judge Streit and the countless educators who have tackled this problem had asked themselves why Bradley University, Kentucky, New York University, North Carolina State, or any other university should ever play basketball in Madison Square Garden, they would have started on a line of inquiry which would have brought

From *The Atlantic Monthly,* March, 1954. By permission of *The Atlantic Monthly* and the author.

about a better understanding. Obviously it was no educational interest that brought the teams there, no huge concentration of alumni, no
essential training program. It wasn't wholly a matter of money. They
were there in response to a far more complex and subtle compulsion:
to assist their schools as a part of the system of American higher education to carry out that system's latest and growing responsibility—
namely, to provide public entertainment.

In our American society the need for entertainment is an inevitable
consequence of the changing conditions of our lives—the lengthening
life span, the shorter work week, speed and mobility, industrialization and prosperity. These changes create social vacuums, and for
filling social vacuums the American system of education—and particularly higher education—is one of the most efficient devices ever
invented. It is flexible, highly varied, and in touch with virtually the
entire population; furthermore, it is characterized by a genuine spirit
of service. It is manned by aggressive and accommodating people; it
is suffused with a thoroughly practical philosophy. Hence, to its already great and growing array of services—its teaching, research, adult
education, military training, and general public service—it has added
another, public entertainment. This responsibility has been accepted
in some instances eagerly, in some instances reluctantly, but nonetheless accepted. Drama, music, radio, and television widen the educational as well as the entertainment services of the universities;
wherever these touch the public they possess more of the characteristics of entertainment than of education. Yet of all the instrumentalities
which universities have for entertaining the public, the most effective
is athletics.

What educational institutions thus far have not seen is that the
responsibility for supplying public entertainment is a responsibility
different in kind from those they have previously performed. The
failure to understand this fact has led to endless strain in the management of athletics, to bewilderment among educators and the public,
and even to outright scandal. Conceived as education, athletics is in-
explicable, corrupting, and uncontrollable; as public entertainment,
and even as public entertainment to be provided by educational institutions, athletics becomes comprehensible and manageable.

The most essential distinction between athletics and education lies
in the institution's own interest in the athlete as distinguished from
its interest in its other students. Universities attract students in order
to teach them what they do not already know; they recruit athletes
only when they are already proficient. Students are educated for something which will be useful to them and to society after graduation;
athletes are required to spend their time on activities the usefulness
of which disappears upon graduation or soon thereafter. Universities

exist to do what they can for students; athletes are recruited for what they can do for the universities. This makes the operation of the athletic program in which recruited players are used basically different from any educational interest of colleges and universities.

The fundamental distinctions between athletics and education are somewhat obscured by several arguments frequently heard. The first is that athletics has "educational values." This is the familiar "character building," "team spirit," "sportsmanship" argument. Anyone who knows the actual operations of athletics will admit that such values could be realized far better if athletics were handled as recreation and physical education. The second argument is that many fine athletes make fine scholastic records—implying that there must not, after all, be any conflict between athletics and education. Again the answer can be short. Big-time athletics requires 20 to 28 hours per week of its devotees, aside from the time spent away from the campus; hence it is bound to detract from an athlete's education. But how can an impoverished athlete get a chance at a college education? I'll answer that question with another: Is he any more entitled to it than anyone else?

II

College athletics *is* public entertainment. Last year football audiences numbered 40 million, and now basketball is outstripping football in attendance. It is estimated that the public pays $100 million a year to the colleges for admission tickets, and television has added enormously to the number of spectators and to the revenue. Public interest as measured in publicity, newspaper coverage, and attention is far beyond that given to any educational activity. In no major school does the attention given to the appointment of a president compare with that given to the appointment of a coach, and the general public can name many more coaches than presidents.

The organization of this public entertainment is intricate. Most of the larger colleges and universities, private and public, are organized into athletic conferences managed by highly paid commissioners. Through them, complicated athletic schedules are worked out with all the finesse of the international bargaining table, and considerations of finance, publicity, the prospective careers of coaches and even of presidents, are balanced in equations which would baffle electronic computers. Stadiums, field houses, and playing fields are constructed with the entertainment-seeking public primarily in mind. At the time the Yale Bowl was built it would have seated the entire adult population of New Haven, while Michigan could have put twice the population of Ann Arbor into its stadium. The University of Southern California and the University of California at Los Angeles are big schools, but even they would scarcely need the Memorial Stadium for their students and faculty. Obviously the real underwriters of bonds which build athletic plants are not students, but the public. Many an athletic director caught in a squeeze of high costs and inadequate gate receipts wishes to heaven he had all of the student tickets to sell to the people willing to pay more for them.

The same force lies back of the other feature of athletics—the numerous and high-priced coaching specialists, the elaborate half-time shows, the colorful bands (supported almost as completely by scholarships as are the athletes and for the same purpose), the frolicsome majorettes, the carefully planned and executed spontaneous student rallies and demonstrations, the food, drink, and program concessions. None of these could possibly serve any educational purpose for which a college or university exists, but they are wonderful aids to public entertainment.

Perhaps most significant of all is the fact that the rules of the games themselves are now constructed and reconstructed with their entertainment value uppermost. Like dramatic coaches and directors bringing into being a Broadway production, the coaches and athletic directors gather each year to adjust the rules of football and basketball for the purpose of heightening the dramatic and entertainment value. The substitution rule, who may run with the ball, what may be allowed to happen within the ten-yard line or within the last four minutes, the nature of the penalties, and, currently, the one- or two-platoon system in football are matters which are governed by their effect upon the entertainment and upon the welfare of the enterprise. In basketball, the rules have been changed to encourage high scoring, constant running and action, alternate chances at scoring in order to provide the murderously exciting finishes which now characterize the game. Revisions are made each year only after the most elaborate study and consideration and with a wariness which would do credit to the fuse workers in a munitions factory.

Consider the Bowl games. They are important influences on athletic policies and at the same time irrefutable evidence that athletics, so far as the Bowls are concerned, have no educational significance whatsoever. So far as I know, no one seriously claims that they do.

All of the Bowls for obvious reasons are located in the South or in winter vacation areas. They are immensely successful business promotions; there is nothing about them remotely related to education. As one man put it: "Rose Bowl, Sugar Bowl, Orange Bowl—all are gravy bowls!" A half-million people saw the games in the eight major bowls last January 1, and it is estimated 70 million more heard them on radio or saw them on television. Receipts were almost $2.5 million.

The distribution of the money follows a kind of formula in each conference—a large percentage to each school participating in the Bowl, a smaller percentage to each school in the conference and to the conference treasury itself. A more subtle formula to ensure support for Bowl games could hardly be devised. Participation in one of the Big Four Bowls—Rose, Sugar, Cotton, and Orange—may bring each participating school as much as $125,000. Everyone profits—except the players, whose amateur status has thus far confined them to such grubby rewards as gifts of gold watches, blankets, free tickets which can be scalped, sometimes a little cash—the last usually secretly. Under pressure from the players and perhaps from a sense of institutional guilt at the indefensible exploitation, the rewards to players are improving, but they still are far below the A.S.C.A.P. and Equity pay scales for big-time entertainers.

III

How is all this to be made compatible with the nation's educational system? Most troubles arise from the failure of colleges to see that in supplying public entertainment they have embarked upon an operation which is different from their educational functions—and one that requires different management. Colleges have acted as if athletics were merely an extension of student recreation. Since athletes come from the same high schools as other students, are about the same age, and do get a kind of education, it has been assumed that the academic regulations applicable to the general run of students should also apply to athletes. We overlook completely the different reasons for which each is there. Hence schools have prescribed the same formal academic requirements for both the athlete and the nonathlete —a minimum number of hours must be taken, a certain number of courses must be passed, systematic progress, however slow, must be made toward a degree, and a host of other regulations must be followed.

Yet athletics, like a corrosive acid, has eaten through every academic regulation—to the great frustration, bewilderment, and cynicism of the educational community. It has defeated faculties, forced the resignations of presidents, wrecked coaches, and undercut the support of institutions where the efforts to apply academic regulations have been insistent. Where such regulations have been successfully applied they have all but killed the athletic programs, or put them in abeyance, as at New York University, Fordham, or Pittsburgh, until a more "understanding" attitude permits revival. There are, of course, many schools—Oberlin, Swathmore, Haverford, Bowdoin, to name a few—that attract little attention from the entertainment-seeking public because they make little attempt to supply public enterainment.

The truth is that the appetite of the public cannot be satisfied by the quality of entertainment which can be provided by athletics governed by academic regulations. Consequently, at institutions which are meeting the public's demands, academic regulations must be ignored, compromised, or eliminated. Admission requirements for athletes have become less formidable than they used to be, and usually an arrangement can be made for the boys to make up high school deficiencies. The requirements as to courses, progress toward degrees, and even grades can generally be met by either a flexible elective system or the "tailored curriculum" leading to a highly specialized "degree" in which many hours of handball, swimming, and coaching can be included. Where this does not suffice, every athletic department of any size provides at its own expense counseling and tutoring service for any of its men likely to get into trouble. Not all athletes need these negations of educational regulations, but the point is that when required the negations must be available. How compelling the necessity is can be estimated by the situations which come to light when these compromises are not sufficient—the wholesale cheating at West Point, the alteration of records at William and Mary, special examinations, and countless other devices involving various degrees of accommodation or even fraud and misdemeanor. No matter what the regulation, if it prevents athletics from supplying the public entertainment for which it exists, a way around must be found. This has been the fate which has uniformly attended the regulative efforts of faculties, administrators, code committees, accrediting associations, and even the N.C.A.A. itself.

Why should this conflict be so irreconcilable? There are many reasons, but perhaps the most compelling is that adequate entertainment can only be provided by winning teams. No amount of gushy sentiment about "playing the game" will conceal the fact that the public wants its teams to win. Victory is a part of the total titillation. If the public can't have it from one source it will transfer its loyalties and money to some other. Chick Meehan filled Yankee Stadium with football fans roaring for N.Y.U., but when de-emphasis came, N.Y.U. found that 6000 was a good crowd to watch it play Fordham, the arch-rival. "When Michigan loses, someone has to pay" may be a slogan at Ann Arbor, but it sums up the attitude of all schools with athletic entertainment programs. This means that to supply the entertainment, the schools must get the entertainers.

The recruitment of players is the key to most of the athletic anxieties of college presidents, the desperation of coaches, the pressure of alumni, and the activities of outside influences, business and otherwise. A chain reaction of undesirable consequences follows. The school must get the player, and the best one; the player knows this, and the bidding starts. Sometimes negotiations are carried on by a parent or other relative in order that the player may be technically free of all nonamateur bargains; otherwise he becomes a part of a corrupt bargain about which, if questions arise, he must lie or forever keep silent. Gradually the "board, room, and tuition" formula—plus a little extra, if necessary—has won acceptance. Sometimes the myth of employment persists as the justification for such payments, but it is now generally acknowledged to be a myth. The effort to limit the number of such scholarships is actually an effort to equalize competition between schools. The conferences often set a limit—but there are ways around it, the junior college "farm system" for one.

The bidding, of course, is highest for the best. In this field rumor is rife. There is the cartoon of the coach who angrily turns to one of his players and says: "Jones, you're through! Turn in your suit and your convertible." The deal may have a hundred variations, from a pledge to help the ambitious athlete on through medical school to assistance to various relatives. My own experience leads me to believe that the bizarre bargain is less frequent than educators and the public think, but is crucial nonetheless. One or two stars can transform a team into a winner and are worth what they cost. Schools bargain with all kinds of appeals—the prestige of the Ivy League may appeal to the boy from the Middle West; religious affiliation may take a boy to Notre Dame; the lavish dormitory facilities for athletes may tip the scales for Louisiana State or Texas. Most conferences have rules which prevent an athlete who has signed with one school from leaving it to join another, even though he later discovers the immense advantages of the second school. Conferences resent scouts from outside their territory, yet raiding is universal. By a dozen devices high school coaches are encouraged to become feeders for particular colleges and universities, sometimes by the flattering appointment to a coaching school staff, support for a bigger job, or even cash. Thus the web of recruitment is widespread, subtle, and effective.

The services of the American educational system in the field of public entertainment cannot be taken lightly—least of all by the educational institutions themselves. It may not be an ideal use of an educational institution to supply public entertainment, but the public interest exists; and for the institutions, either the necessity or the willingness to supply it also exists. The schools which would like to refuse will be compelled to supply it to keep up with their willing rivals. Their only choice is whether they will manage the entertainment in such a way as to prevent damage to themselves as educational institutions—damage which the present methods certainly entail. These methods frequently create financial obligations which imperil educational development because they have contractual priority over educational budgets. Those who recruit players and the players who are recruited are too often corrupted not because of the bargains they strike, but because the bargains are in violation of pledges all have agreed to uphold. Influences outside universities are encouraged to seek control of educational operations—influences which are seldom willing to confine their interests to ₐathletics. Athletics requires an atmosphere of academic accommodation to its necessities, to the great cynicism of faculties and students. It has bred a kind of humiliating schizophrenia in educational administrators who are compelled to defend with platitudes what they do not believe or to keep an uneasy silence. It has created a kind of amused tolerance toward institutions on the part of the very public which buys the entertainment—a tolerance which says that whatever the virtues and respectability of higher education on all other scores, it must be given the privilege of this secret sin.

IV

At the risk of scornful disagreement let me outline how, it seems to me, the great strain in our educational institutions can be reduced. The first and most crucial step is purely intellectual: to make the admission, both inside and outside the universities, that our programs of intercollegiate athletics are operated primarily as public entertainment and not as educational responsibilities. This will lay a foundation for entirely new solutions to the problem.

With the acceptance of this concept most of the undesirable stresses and strains will begin to disappear. Athletics—that is, *winning* athletics—now becomes a legitimate university operation. Recruiting becomes not only legal but justifiable. To get the best athletes becomes not only understandable but commendable in exactly the same way that one seeks for excellence in any department of the university. One gives the athlete what the resources will allow—just as Illinois offers the graduate assistant in history or chemistry what it can to attract the best. No one thinks the less of Illinois because it can outbid Montana for graduate students. In short, athletic practices which are not at all appropriate to "educational" activities become acceptable and legitimate as parts of a program of public entertainment.

The same principle clarifies the position and character of the coaching staff. Let it be the best that can be obtained, as large and specialized as the situation requires. Let it be freed to meet its obligations without the moral strain imposed by the necessity to circumvent impossible requirements. The financial situation likewise becomes manageable. Since athletics is to be managed as entertainment, it need not in logic or in fact be a charge on the educational budget; and just as no educational institution expects to support itself from athletics, so athletics should not expect to be a charge on education. Self-support for athletics as public entertainment is at once a financial liberation and a restraint.

And why should there be concern about the academic record of a young man who comes to a university primarily to play on a team and whom the university has brought for exactly that purpose? I submit that nothing is lost by relieving all athletes of the obligation to meet academic requirements, if they cannot or do not wish to do so. Let us be courageous enough to admit that the university's interest in them is that they be good athletes, not that they be good students. It is the insistence that they be students which creates the problem both for the faculty and for the athletic managers, and to the detriment of both. Of course, if a boy wishes to be a student as well as an athlete, by all means encourage him, but in that case the fact that he is an athlete need not enter into his status as a student any more than his grades as a student should be made to affect his effectiveness as an athlete. The athlete will then for the first time be on a par with every other student who works his way through school. His academic progress will be exactly proportional to the time and interest he has beyond the demands of his employment.

What if the athlete has no interest whatsoever in his further education? A team entirely made up of professionals is not the solution for the colleges. The best solution is a prescription of academic work suited to the tastes and talents of the athlete but with the clear understanding by professors and athletes alike that the record as a student will be neither a hindrance nor a help to athletic success.

What! someone says. Have unbridled bidding for athletes? No eligibility rules? No discipline? By no means—but let these things arise, as they will, from athletic and not from academic sources and necessities. Let eligibility rules be drawn and enforced by those who are most concerned about them—the athletic managements—not by faculties. Who can be counted on to expose infractions of eligibility rules? Opponents! Every roster of players is exchanged between coaches—why should a faculty committee bother? Who is hurt if the ineligible player plays? The opposition! Who is the best insurance that he won't? The opposition! No, faculties and administrators have gratuitously assumed a lot of unnecessary burdens—and to what purpose or to what effect it is hard to see.

The relinquishment of formal academic—not institutional—control over athletics will have very substantial advantages both for athletics and for education. The first is the restoration of institutional and personal integrity. Gone will be the necessity to keep up the pretense that at the present time suffuses the discussion of athletics as a part of an educational program. The establishment of single-mindedness will be the greatest advantage, for educational institutions are basically devoted to intellectual honesty. Such honesty will free athletics as well as education from the schizophrenia from which they both now suffer.

A very valuable outcome will also be the dissipation of the sentimentality which currently surrounds college athletics in the mind of the public. This myth is carefully preserved not for its truth but for its utility. Listen to any major coach talk about his team and you will see how little such sentimentality is justified. He refers to his "material," not to boys; he discusses weakness at end and tackle and backfield, completely oblivious of the feelings of his men. There is not a player whom he will not instantly displace if he can get a better one. One of the most unhappy tasks that athletic managements must perform is to get rid of players to whom scholarships have been given—commitments made—but who can't quite make the grade on the field. Perhaps the public which sees the universities as operating departments of public entertainment and sees athletes as assistants in the department will come to think of the whole matter a little differently —to the great relief of everyone concerned.

When doctors find that a given treatment results in no improvement, they re-examine their diagnosis; when scientists find that experiments produce no anticipated results, they revise their basic hypothesis. Educators now find that what was once the recreation of students in school has been transformed into a responsibility of the educational system to supply the public with entertainment. It is essential that educators carry through a fundamental revision of concepts of athletic management appropriate to this transformation.

Suggested Topics

1. Athletic scholarship—a contradiction in terms
2. Colleges and the public entertainment business
3. Athletics can have "educational values."
4. The "gravy bowls"
5. Intramural vs. Intercollegiate athletics
6. Big-time athletics and gambling

ARE WE MAKING A PLAYGROUND
OUT OF COLLEGE?

Jerome Ellison

A journalist, writer, and teacher, Jerome Ellison served at various times as an editor of *Life, Reader's Digest, Liberty,* and *Collier's.* He has taught at New York University and Indiana University.

During a sunny day one autumn a colleague of mine was counseling a freshman girl at the University of Georgia. He explained that a certain course could not be taken without prerequisites amounting to about two years' work. "But I won't be here that long," the lass protested. "At the end of this school year I'm getting married."

Just to be nice my friend asked who the lucky man was. "Oh, I've just got here," said the miss, "and haven't met him yet." Out of curiosity, the professor kept tabs. The wedding took place in a burst of orange blossoms just after the close of the next semester, as planned.

This sort of thing is so common in the large, tax-supported coeducational plants that turn out more than half of all our college graduates, that most people assume it's probably all right.

After four years on the inside, as a member of a university faculty, I, for one, am not at all sure it's all right. It's part of a growing national inclination to push education aside whenever it interferes with love or comfort, money or fun.

In today's world I question whether we can afford it. Communists and free men agree on at least one thing—the abler, better-informed side in this contest is more likely to prevail. Higher education will play an increasingly vital role in the struggle. We water it down, it seems to me, at our own great peril. And watering it down we certainly are.

The boys, I have noticed, go along in the business as readily as the girls. In one of my own courses at Indiana University there enrolled, not long ago, a male predentistry student. He was a sophomore, personable, fairly intelligent, had a car, and was going steady with a girl in his home town, a hundred miles away.

"Man, this is wearing—driving back and forth to Kokomo twice

Reprinted from *The Saturday Evening Post,* March 7, 1959. By permission of the author.

a week!" he said one time when on the carpet about a late assignment. Later, on a like occasion, "Man, this is killing—all these science courses!"

He shortly solved all his problems by marrying the girl, moving into a university-subsidized apartment on campus, and switching from dentistry to recreation—a curriculum which allows one to become a bachelor of science without ever having to study mathematics, language, chemistry, physics, history or science, but only things like volley ball, archery, lacrosse, deep breathing and refereeing.

My quarrel here is not with the change in career, but with the reasons. Our crowded, roaring slums testify to our need for trained recreation people. But this young oaf switched, not because he had discovered a national need, but because he thought recreation would be easier. One has a feeling that when the sun beats hot on the city pavements and the slum kids really need him, he'll be at home in front of the air conditioner.

Frequently, when counseling a bright student, I point out that we live in an age of science, that one of the bases of science is mathematics, and that the educated man of our day should have a little math. The point that math matters is never questioned. "But," I am almost always told, "it's hard!" The student paws through the catalogue again, seeking a course which is easier but probably irrelevant to his total plan.

Similarly, we often cite the need—in a nation that has a mere 6 per cent of earth's people, and must for its survival learn to get on with the other 94 per cent—for language training. Here again, the cry goes up, "Too hard!"

Some students go to extremes to avoid a language. I worked with one lad who planned from the first to be a journalist, and who has now, at last, become one. But the course in journalism required eighteen hours of a foreign tongue. He enrolled in a teacher-training course, which did not require a language for a degree, and took his journalism in electives—"on the side"!

The prevalence of this sort of thing, and the extent to which school authorities play along with it, is something, I here assert, really to be exercised about.

I have seen too much of the power of higher education to widen and ennoble human life to stand by without protest while this vital power is vitiated. It was through a land-grant university that my father worked his way from the rudest of back-country farms into the vastly expanded horizons of a respected profession. A similar school helped me to spend my own life in the kind of work I love. And if I have learned anything from that work—twenty-five years of editing, writing, teaching and publishing—it is that the fate of man depends now more than ever before upon an educated citizenry. Half-educated won't do. Man's survival hangs now upon his wisdom.

In the light of this conclusion, some things about our mass higher education seem basically immoral. I am not here referring to the sexual aspect of morality. An informal consensus of deans seems to be that the standard in this particular is possibly a shade higher than that of the parents of today's students. Of course, young people in and out of college, today as always, get into scrapes through mismanagement of their sex lives. But for sheer bawdy brazenness I have seen nothing to vie with the letter to the Wisconsin student paper which opened: "We who are not virgins smile at the notion that we have lost our self-respect," and went on to expound the "fuller" life. This was written in the 1930's by a girl who may now be a staid grandmother.

The thing that concerns me is an intellectual immorality—the encroachment upon the main business of college of an accumulation of irrelevancies which together make up a "Second Curriculum" that often takes precedence over the first.

The Second Curriculum is that odd mixture of status hunger, voodoo, tradition, lust, stereotyped dissipation, love, solid achievement, and plain good fun sometimes called "college life." It drives a high proportion of our students through college chronically short of sleep, behind in their work, and uncertain of the exact score in any department of life.

To gain some notion of the extent to which the Second Curriculum has taken over, we'll whisk through, in a moment, an ordinary year's calendar at a Big Ten school. First let us set the scene. You start with a broad expanse of tree-studded lawn, perhaps half a mile square, dotted with buildings rendered in several versions of collegiate architecture.

One of these structures is the student union, a rallying point for snacking, dalliance and amusement. From morning until night it resounds to the blare of the jukebox, the clink of coffee cups, the clatter of bowling pins, the click of billiard balls, the slap of playing cards, the gentle creak of lounge chairs and, in the plushier ones, the splash of languid bodies in tepid swimming pools. There's likely to be an informal dance here every Friday and Saturday night. They have a ball—banquet or name-band dance—about every weekend in the ballroom.

Fringing the main campus and sprawling for a mile in every direction are student living quarters—fraternities and rooming houses both stately and squat, trailer camps, huge residence units resembling, according to the architectural mood, medieval castles or modern luxury hotels.

The whole panorama—so well has Joe College sold his old man on the principle that a car is needed for study—is overrun with automobiles. Our big campuses are churning in a traffic turmoil that almost has to be seen to be believed. Some schools—Indiana is one—issue stickers, dubbed "hunting licenses," permit the student to park on campus if he can find a space. Others, following a method used at Wisconsin, provide parking at some distance from the university and charge a fee, which covers shuttle-bus service to school.

In some of the better-motorized universities, more than half the students have cars. Duke, Fairleigh Dickinson, Johns Hopkins, Houston, Louisiana, Maryland, Nebraska, Oregon State, Syracuse, Texas and Iowa all average—according to a study made at the University of Houston—over half a car, and up to one car, per student. Ohio State's 19,000 students operate 11,640 motor vehicles. The student-to-car ratio at Wisconsin, 15,000–5800; at Purdue, 13,000–5100; at Northwestern, 15,000–2500; at Illinois, 23,000–5000; at Indiana, 11,000–4500; at Michigan State 19,000–6400. These cars support enterprises—drive-in restaurants, drive-in theaters (known in college jargon as "passion pits"), miniature golf courses, roller-skating rinks, gin mills—many miles from the campus.

More than a fifth of the students are married. This statistic has profoundly affected university life at all levels. For one thing, the housing people have been caught short. The Indiana campus, which is typical, was several hundred units short in married-student housing last fall, while newly completed quarters for single students stood vacant. The big coed plants are building married housing pell-mell, trying to catch up with a growing trend. In eleven state universities with a total enrollment of 160,000, more than 21 per cent of last autumn's students were married. The expected figure for four years hence is one in four.

The large married minority strongly influences the single majority. Most of the girls are striving, sometimes with unladylike eagerness, to get married—the Georgia coed mentioned earlier has her counterparts in every state. The steps to success are going steady, "pinning"—exchange of fraternity badges or other club symbols—formal engagement and marriage. Monthly box scores of pinnings, published by some college papers, are read with sports-page avidity.

Since even the bottom rung of the coed success ladder cannot be mounted unless one is dated, the pressure to date is enormous. The emotional backlash of failure to date is profound, particularly among women students. A Wisconsin coed, writing in the student daily, reports that half the sorority pillows are "wet with tears" of a Saturday night—no dates. I know of one attempted suicide over the business.

The male reacts to the same pressures in a variety of ways. He may

affect a cynical Don Juanism or a guarded wariness. Or his own pillow may be wet with tears, or he may simply yield to community
pressure and start populating the nursery school the university main-
tains for married students' children. In any event, both male and
female live in daily tension, varying from mild to acute, over some
aspect of dating or mating.

It is in this over-all atmosphere that the Second Curriculum is
pursued. An important part of it is, of course, the standard, souped-up
program of professionalized athletics. Since this phenomenon has been
ably dealt with in a number of recent articles, it is enough to note
here that a normal season may include eight major basketball games
and four football games. Each has its influx of alumni and visitors, its
bands and cheering sections, its squads of bench warmers, its round of
dances and fights, its frenzy of warm-ups, post-mortems, hospitality
and decorations.

For the Homecoming Game, each housing unit prepares elaborate
lawn statuary, built of papier-mâché and crepe paper on the colossal
scale. These devices, illuminated and sometimes animated by intricate machinery, consume vast ingenuity and time. The control panel
for one of the displays at Indiana was hardly less complex than the
switchboard of a fair-sized telephone exchange. A recent prize winner
was an enormous red bull (Indiana) towing a corn cutter which mowed
down cornstalks (Iowa men) and delivered them in bags. There were
fifty-one entries in Wisconsin's Homecoming decoration contest. The
winner was a gigantic prostrate Indian whose eyes lighted up and
moved from side to side, whose head moved on a swivel and whose
chest heaved.

Each spring has its special big weekend. Indiana has a fifty-mile
bicycle relay race in May. Work on it begins the preceding November,
with the appointment of a student committee of 192 persons. The
bike teams practice all year. One rider makes weekend trips to Indi-
anapolis, fifty miles away, on his bike, just to keep in shape. The big
weekend itself offers a tricycle relay race featuring costumed sorority
girls, a golf tournament, social activities at each of the university's
fifty fraternities and sororities, two all-campus dances and a home-
talent vaudeville show, in addition to the main race.

Every weekend is special for something. Illinois has a Dad's Day
Revue, a stunt show, a Hawaiian-hoop contest, the John Street Pajama
Race, the burning of a twenty-five-foot statue called Winter's Gloom,
and Men's Economic Recovery Campaign Week, during which coeds
make dates and pay for them. Ohio State has a Circus Party with real
elephants, a Greek Week, a May Week Carnival, a Rose Formal and
a Pumpkin Prom.

All-campus dances at Indiana include the Freshman Frolic, the

First Fling, the Sophomore Cotillion, the Junior Prom, the Dames Ball, the Military Ball, the Mardi Gras Ball, the Blanket Hop, the Bicycle Bump, the Opening of Formal, the Street Dance, the Wellhouse Waltz and a jitterbug contest. Wisconsin fraternities specialize in costume dances inviting the nearest tolerable approach to nudity— a Mammoth Brawl, simulating caveman days, a Roman Party in togas, the Cherokee Chugalug in loincloths and the Pajama Party.

Each week has its list of home-talent entertainments and stunts. Our calendar brings us the Jordan River Tug of War, The Watermelon Mess, the Fall Carnival (coeds dressed as underworld characters, running wheels of chance and performing skits for charity), the all-university competitive sing, numerous pep rallies, including the burning in effigy of John Purdue; the Gridiron Banquet, the Football Banquet, the Athletic Banquet, the Turtle Derby, the Greek Week Chariot Race, the Fun Frolic (rides, concessions and a Ferris wheel), a fashion show, a Panhellenic Circus, a Barbecue, a Round-up and a Sports-Car Rally. Wisconsin has all this plus a Man-with-the-Most-Beautiful-Legs Contest, a Yell-like-Hell Contest and the Haresfoot musical show, in which the boys dress up as girls.

In the big coeducational schools an immense amount of time and energy goes into the election of "queens"—a reflection, perhaps, of the statistic that 35 per cent of all college students are females. At Indiana the queen season opens in September with the nomination of two queens from each women's dormitory or sorority to appear at a pep rally, where one of them is designated football queen. Later in the same month, after an all-campus sweepstakes, including preliminaries, semifinals and finals, somebody is crowned sweater queen.

In October and November various queens and sweethearts—a sweetheart of, say, Beta Theta Pi, Signa Chi or Dodds House, is about the same as a queen—are elevated. With sandwich men, posters, torchlight and sports-car parades, students elect a homecoming queen, a military-ball queen, a queen of the autumn formal, a yearbook queen, a queen of the athletic lettermen, a junior-prom queen, and some others. This year some publication students, seeking a device to promote the sale of the college annual, came up with the idea of electing a *queen* queen. Nobody was eligible who had not previously been a queen of something. Forty-three young women qualified.

Our queen program, my research has revealed, lags somewhat behind Big Ten standards. Ohio State has everything we have plus a pumpkin-prom queen, a rose queen, a Greek Week queen, a May queen, and a boat-race queen. Illinois has a men's-residence-hall queen, a sno-ball queen, a dolphin queen, a Miss Photoflash, a star-and-scroll queen, a Sheequon queen and a plowboy-prom queen.

As with the goose, so with the gander—bachelors and kings are selected from among the male students. The Indiana campus elects a bachelor of the year, Illinois elevates a most-eligible bachelor, Ohio State elects a Greek Week king, Wisconsin honors a campus clown, a dorm duke, a KD king and a Kat's Meow.

Once a year at Indiana there's a protest against the whole silly business in the form of a "most-useless-man" contest. Typical campaign ad: "He's so useless the state has paid his tuition for ten years to keep him out of industry."

One time a few years ago some pranksters, fed up with queens, ran a nanny goat for prom queen. Horrified campus politicians protested that she was not female and therefore not eligible. When her backers produced a veterinarian to attest her femininity, her foes finally got her disqualified on the ground that she had not been in residence on campus the preceding year. Nevertheless, she ran a strong third in the voting.

These diversions are, of course, over and above those amusements which are considered by school authorities to have cultural, educational or recreational value. Every university schedules a dazzling string of road shows for its auditorium. A typical year will bring two Broadway musical comedies, two celebrated violinists, two world-famous symphony orchestras, a renowned opera company, two first-rate ballet companies and an assortment of nationally advertised jazz musicians, pianists, sopranos, bands and lecturers. Besides this, university academic departments, particularly those of music, theater and dance, offer several entertainments and lectures weekly for the diversion of the student.

But come, does not all work and no play make Jack a dull boy? Lest ennui overtake Jack, the typical student union offers a bridge club, an arts-and-crafts club, a chess club, a photo club, a sailing club and a golf club besides bowling, billiards and record concerts. We shall have sound minds in sound bodies—as long as both can stand the strain. The year-round program of intramural sports is open to all students—touch football, softball, badminton, golf, table tennis.

In schools which offer what is considered an adequate Second Curriculum, each college generation is expected to produce its quota of pranks, "outbreaks" and illegal highjinks. Last year, five Ohio State freshmen got drunk in Kentucky, stole a corpse from an undertaking parlor, transported it a hundred miles and placed it in front of the union building on the Columbus campus.

The same year, Athens, Ohio, police had to use tear gas to break up a riot, over nothing in particular, of 3000 students who invaded the city's business district. The riot started with a few students pelting each other with oranges, and wound up with twenty-eight of them in jail on charges of disorderly conduct, assault and battery, throwing firecrackers, resisting arrest, blocking traffic, and unsafe operation of motor vehicles.

Illinois' contribution to this lore is the celebrated water fight of April, 1958, in which 6000 berserk students opened fire hydrants, routed the local fire department and drenched the dean of students. I am impressed by the fact that the year in which college students in Hungary started an immortal revolution to free their country from tyranny, the big thing on the Indiana campus was a panty raid. On the day in which a local school was bombed and the countdown began for one of our major satellite attempts, a Big Ten student paper carried the headline, LIZ HAMILTON ELECTED HOMECOMING QUEEN.

Fun, yes; love, certainly; marriage in good time, of course. But shall these things be gained out of season, at too dear a price? Some of us are beginning to ask what very little work and an awful lot of play makes Jack.

What should be done? Half a dozen useful suggestions are in circulation and receiving minority support among the faculties of our colleges and universities. All that is needed to place them on the action agenda is a little public outcry.

The first step would be to prohibit automobiles. There would be a pitiable bleating, but all, I am sure, would pronounce the action a benefit. Princeton men do not appear unhappier than most, and their scholarship ranks with the world's best. Yet they are not allowed to operate motor vehicles while attending college.

The next step would be to disband fraternities and sororities. Here, I must confess, my heart skips a beat as I turn in my old badge. I have even shed a quiet tear, for the associations of my college fraternity are deep and dear. But the plain fact is that the system has outlived its usefulness. This fact must be faced, even by sentimental fraternity men like myself. Glenn H. Goodman, of the Ohio State faculty, has let fly at fraternities for "picking top men and isolating them in an atmosphere of football, adolescent discussions, dating and drinking."

I could add other serious charges. Besides providing the prime breeding grounds of the "minimum effort" attitude, fraternities too often breed a tawdry Don Juanism, a callow and provincial snobbishness, the habit of getting drunk and a world view no broader than a dollar bill. Worst of all, they consume quantities of time, effort, money and emotional stress—with their chronic financial troubles, panicked rushing season, and social-alcoholic-political monkeyshines—out of all proportion to the good they offer in terms of fellowship.

My apologies are tendered to chapters which do not deserve such harsh words. But enough of them do, and have deserved them for so long a time that they doom the whole system.

The same apology goes to those students—and I have known quite a number—with the integrity and plain nerve to resist the pressures of the conforming mob, place the Second Curriculum firmly in second place and do a job in college. The fact that a few unusual individuals can win through to an education does not, however, weaken my case—which is that universities have no right to make it almost impossible for students to study.

Several other things might be done to cut down ill-formed attitudes toward scholarship, toward marriage, and toward the relationship between them. Plush university housing should not be offered until the head of the house is at least a senior, usually achieved at the age of twenty-one. This would remove cheap, pleasant, subsidized living—an abnormal condition which the young couple cannot expect to find later on—as a temptation to impulsive teen-age marriage. At the same time it would not obstruct love so deep and true, though young, that it is determined to find a way.

Standards of scholarship are responsive to public expectation. Our state universities face a rising—and, in my thinking, justified—public opinion that education beyond high school is every child's right. Let us, then, offer a two-year university curriculum, crowned with an associate-in-arts degree for those who pass it successfully. Our many junior colleges have set the precedent. Let it be tough, and let it be the same for everybody. Those who wish to go on for the full four years would return to college in a frame of mind to get down to business. A re-entrance examination at the beginning of the junior year should be tough enough to weed out those who are in college mainly for the Second Curriculum.

These are some of the suggestions currently in the air, and there are others—the problem is nationwide. Citing popular pressure for easy, fun-packed college degrees, Richard B. Hovey of Western Maryland College, addressing the College English Association, has come down smartly on the head of the nail.

Hovey has pointed out that a shocking number of college graduates can't even write grammatically or spell correctly, and has asked the reasons. He finds that standards are shot, and that there's not much a teacher can do about it. "An individual teacher cannot suddenly decide to have standards; let him fail half or more of a class, and he will soon be in trouble with his administrators." He finds, moreover, that students understand this and take advantage of it: "Our student knows that unless he is . . . unforgivably negligent, he will get by."

The burden of the Second Curriculum is wryly acknowledged everywhere. To him who may question its baleful effect, I extend the invitation to take my place some morning. Let him face an early class he's knocked his brains out to prepare for. Let him address the blank stares and vacant faces of a roomful of students who knocked their brains out the night before at the Sophomore Twitch, the Winter Willies, the Monumental Maul, the Greek Tweak or, in short, at goofing off.

Now that we're over on the teaching side, what about the teachers? The faculty, as certain current novels suggest, is far from perfect. Entering the academic life from the "outside world," one is disappointed by the banality of conversation at social gatherings, and by attitudes of old-fashioned trade-unionism centering on "tenure," a word which means that after they've kept you on for seven years it's almost impossible for them to fire you. This concern for tenure bends many teachers toward cautious utterance, often blunting the kind of searching, outspoken discourse that might explode into exciting teaching and learning.

Here, though, I'd like to say a word in defense of the kind of repetitious teaching called "time serving." There are certain foundation subjects, often humdrum, that the student simply has to "get." These are the barren places in the terrain of learning which must be crossed to reach the thrilling peaks beyond. The work is a rut, and here the patient Mr. Chips serves well.

For inspiration one looks to the faculty "stars," and every faculty has some bright ones. When my own resolve flags, I can look to men like H. J. Muller, our Nobel Prize winner in genetics; Bob Byrnes in history; Bill Wilson in English; Schuyler Otteson in economics and Bill Moore in physiology, and I become refreshed. These men have broken the confines of their own specialties to look at the universe and have found courage to state their views regardless of what special interest may be offended.

In intellectual daring of this order we may hope to find, through education, the glory of the future. And what a future beckons! The purely mechanical side already has been pretty well publicized—the two-day work week, the trips through space, world tours as a standard part of grade-school education, the time when the deserts will bloom and the jungles will be made into gardens.

The new day of the human soul has, however, scarcely been mentioned. Some think the long-sought substitute for war is close to being found—that peaceful means actually exist for converting an enemy into a co-operative and willing friend. In the resulting leisure and plenty, man might begin to develop his potential in art and philosophy. The artist and poet in each of us would find expression. We would stand before the goal of goals for all men—the penetration into the deepest meaning of life itself.

These wonders will not drop into our laps without our effort. Indeed, to avoid a quick catastrophe, we'll have to work as never before. And the kind of work most urgently demanded is work of the mind.

We'll have to *think* our way out of this one. We need tough, seasoned, disciplined thinkers, incorruptible, enormously well informed, skilled in their chosen specialties, but with an appreciation of all specialties—thinkers who cannot be diverted to limited or shoddy goals—and we need a lot of them.

For these reasons, the Second Curriculum must be trimmed. This must be done, not in spite or through outraged morality, but to make room for something wonderfully better.

We who are concerned about Jack and Jacqueline would like to see more, not less, love on the campus. Besides the inevitable and proper love of comfort and fun, of boy for girl, of status and position, of exercise and sport, of family and children, we'd like to see some love of truth and intellectual achievement, of discovery and high adventure, of beauty, harmony design and great precision, of mankind and its farthest destiny. We would like, in short, to see the First Curriculum come first.

Suggested Topics

1. The "Second Curriculum"
2. All play and no work . . .
3. Should automobiles at college be prohibited?
4. Early marriage and education
5. The intellectual level of the American campus
6. Unnecessary frills on our campus

ARE WOMEN'S COLLEGES OBSOLETE?   *Harold Taylor*

Appointed president of Sarah Lawrence College, Bronxville, New York, in 1945, when he was only thirty years old, Harold Taylor left the presidency of that well known women's college in 1959 to return to his first love—teaching and writing. A graduate of the University of Toronto and of the University of London, he has published widely on aesthetics, social philosophy, educational theory, academic freedom, and contemporary issues.

Are women's colleges obsolete? There are many educators who believe that they are. The women's colleges, they say, after 100 years of existence have accomplished their mission. Women can now go to college, to almost any college in the country. Women are recognized in most quarters as the intellectual equals of men. More than a third of the present 3,000,000 students in college are women.

The trend has firmly set toward coeducation and coordinate education, with coordinate colleges now joining together men's and women's institutions, each retaining its own identity, with joint classes, joint student organizations and shared projects of all kinds, from theatre groups to language clubs. The most familiar example is the coordination of Harvard with Radcliffe, a human condition which, according to reports, has produced an enrichment of educational quality for both institutions.

Dartmouth and Wesleyan have both been speculating on the possibility of adding women's institutions to their present establishments. Smith and Mount Holyoke are cooperating with Amherst and the University of Massachusetts, with joint classes in special fields. Swarthmore, Bryn Mawr, and Haverford have done the same for some time.

At Yale, where two years ago the mere suggestion that women undergraduates be added to the university sent alumni and administration to the barricades with prepared statements, a small group of undergraduates from Smith and Vassar has now been accepted for a special program.

Two Midwestern colleges for women, Rockford and MacMurray in Illinois, after 100 years have now added coordinate men's colleges to

Reprinted from *The New York Times Magazine*, September 7, 1958. By permission of *The New York Times* and the author.

their existing campuses. A poll of 3,100 Midwestern high school students taken by Rockford College four years ago showed a 3 per cent preference for a separate women's college, 3 per cent for a men's college, and 94 per cent for some form of coordinate or coeducation.

What lies behind the strength of this movement away from separate education?

The main reason given by the educators is that to segregate women in separate colleges to be taught mainly by other women is, in the present age, unhealthy and unsound. It isolates women from the normal life of society; it inhibits their personal growth; it confines them to a narrow, cloistered and unreal world when they should be part of the main stream of the society for which they are being educated.

Similarly, to segregate men and women from each other's company during the college week is to make an exaggerated and artificial social institution of the college week-end and thus to distort the normal personal relations between young men and women.

There is also a very practical reason—the growing numbers of married students. At present, 14 per cent of all college students are married. On some campuses the number is 25 per cent. At Stanford University, 20 per cent of the student body or 1,532 students are married and are raising, while in college, a total of 1,579 children. In the women's colleges, the number of young women who drop out in order to marry college men—thus ending promising college careers before they are well begun—is often as high as 45 to 50 per cent over the four undergraduate years.

All these factors have strengthened the trend toward coeducation. Today, only 14 per cent of the 1,019,000 women in college are in separate colleges for women, most of them along the Eastern seaboard, some in Roman Catholic institutions throughout the country. As the total college population increases to 6,000,000 by 1970, the percentage of women in separate colleges will be even smaller, for the possibility of expansion of the present women's colleges is limited, and most of the increased numbers will be absorbed in coeducational institutions. In the Midwest and on the West Coast it is simply assumed that women will go to coeducational colleges. Only in special cases will a girl travel East to a college for women.

Does this mean that the day of the women's college is over?

For a number of reasons it does not.

It means that the women's college as we have known it in the past has already changed and will change still further. The students in the women's colleges are not young women who intend to educate themselves for spinsterhood. Approximately 85 per cent of them marry—usually college men—within five years of graduation, most of them hold jobs before marriage, they raise families and maintain independent interests or careers outside the home.

Nor do they feel isolated from the real world while in college. They are not. They are interesting young women who have chosen a women's college in order to obtain the education they want, and in many cases are more directly connected with the "real" world by their interest in politics, literature, the arts, and the study of society than are the students on coeducational campuses. Their colleges are organized not to segregate women from men but to provide a particular time and place for the full development of the student's power.

It is true that the women's colleges are, and will remain, a minority movement in American education. This is one of the most important things about them. They can remain free to be themselves and to attract to their campuses the students who genuinely want to be there, those who wish to break away from the patterns of their age group and of their society, those who wish to be themselves.

Over the years the women's colleges have developed a body of educated women who possess intellectual independence, initiative and resourcefulness, women who form at this moment one of the most potent forces we have for sustaining a liberal and enlightened American society. They have set the pace for the education of women.

The tradition of the women's colleges from the beginning has been one of continuing concern for intellectual, moral and cultural values. Partly because they have been free from some of the vocational pressures which exist in men's colleges and the coeducational institutions, partly because in their origin they were inspired by a sense of mission on behalf of women's education, they have always been intensely concerned with the quality of education itself.

It is no accident that many of the most interesting experiments in liberal education have developed within the women's college movement. These colleges have been free to experiment—to invent the Junior Year Abroad, to include the creative arts in the curriculum, to break with academic tradition, to put to use advanced educational ideas which, unless tested and judged in action, would never find their way into the country's educational system.

The combined education of men and women does have positive values which separate education lacks. In comparison with women, men are likely to be less respectful of authority, more practical-minded, they are likely to press harder in argument, they have usually had a wider range of experience and a greater mobility in their society. In comparison with men, women college students are often more mature emotionally and intellectually than men of the same age, more interested in ideas, more conscientious in carrying out assignments, more sensitive to nuance, more understanding in personal relationships. Men and women have a great deal to contribute to each other's education, both in personal and in social terms.

However, it does not follow that therefore the best education for women is to be found in coeducational institutions. Often the social distractions and social competition of the coeducational community are so overwhelming that they destroy the possibility of a rich intellectual life for the student. The college woman may certainly live in the world of male companionship on a coeducational campus, but, as in the case of her life in the world after college, she is often forced into a secondary role in the society of which she is a part.

In many instances the overriding purpose in the minds of men students on a coeducational campus is to gain a practical education leading directly to a business or professional career. This cannot fail to affect the total intellectual environment and the attitude toward women. Women are then regarded not as intellectual companions or even as fellow-students, but primarily as "dates," among whom can be found those most suitable for becoming wives of business and professional men. In this situation women either conform to a dominant anti-intellectual pattern, or, at some cost to their personal lives, struggle to maintain a sense of independence and intellectual purpose in an environment frequently hostile to such values.

Women may find their personal development thus inhibited and their own interests deflected at the source. This is particularly the case for the college woman who marries during college, bringing a premature responsibility both to herself and to her husband. Fewer risks are then taken in choosing careers and life-patterns, since family responsibilities and a concern for security lead young husbands to the path of the higher paying careers at the expense of those which might be both more interesting and more spiritually rewarding.

It is for reasons of this kind that there can be no blanket endorsement of coeducation as the ideal educational plan for the modern woman. It depends on the woman, it depends on the institution. For a great many women, the women's college is better able to provide an environment in which the student can achieve her identity as a person through an education in the liberal arts. "What we need," says David Riesman, "is some form of adult protection for our young people who, at the moment, do not want to pursue each other."

The women's colleges do give this kind of protection to the girl who wishes to concentrate on her education without the distractions of pursuit.

Over a year ago, as part of a study of the future of the college, Sarah Lawrence students were asked to comment on the possibility that a coordinate college for men might be added to the existing campus. I was surprised to find that the majority of the students was against the idea. The students pointed to the personal values in their present education—the freedom from social pressure, the absence of competitive social attitudes, the acceptance by students of each other in their own terms, the opportunity for comparatively undistracted work during the college week, the ultimate privacy of being allowed to develop as an individual.

What they were asking for was a time to grow strong as persons, to form a character of their own at a level they wished to reach before facing the challenge and influences of a male-dominated society. The opportunity for a continuing relation with men on a campus adjoining their own was less important to them than the opportunity for personal independence.

When these students looked around them to see the men's colleges and the coeducational universities where values of conformity and social status express themselves in "shoe" types, or in fraternity and sorority patterns of the "successful," they did not like what they saw, nor did they want it for themselves. They preferred to work out their own destinies. They preferred to see the men they knew or to make new friends at various times during the week and over the week-ends, rather than to adapt themselves to the demands of a social life dominated by campus dating practices.

Their testimony is, of course, that of women who deliberately chose to come to a women's college. It cannot be taken to mean that only in the women's colleges can such individual freedom be found. This is a matter of how colleges are organized.

The real question to be asked about a college, whether for men, for women, or for both, has to do with the quality and character of the individual institution and the human values it expresses. What difference does the college make in the lives of its students? Aside from what it can teach the student to know and to do, what does it teach him to want, to cherish and to love?

At present, according to one research study and the evidence from a number of others, most college students are learning, in educator Philip Jacob's words, "to be unabashedly self-centered"; they aspire to "material gratification, for themselves and their families. They intend to look out for themselves first and expects other to do likewise."

It is here, in the matter of human values, at the deepest level of educational thinking, that the women's colleges have their greatest opportunity and largest responsibility. They must use to the full the characteristic sense of mission with which their history has endowed them. Having achieved the intellectual emancipation of women, a new mission presents itself.

It is twofold: to find ways in which the liberal arts college can raise the level of idealism and enlightenment in a society dominated by a concern for material values; and to find ways in which the modern woman, in this society, can fulfill her talents in the new role in which she finds herself.

That role no longer separates itself into a choice between marriage and a career. As Agnes E. Meyer puts it, "Devotion to one family is no longer a lifetime job." The role of the educated woman is one which fuses together elements of family life, personal interests and community life with the possibility of an independent career.

In every phase of her new role, in relation to her husband, her children, and to her society, the modern educated woman has an extraordinary range in the use of her knowledge and her education to affect the lives of those around her. The pattern of her life now releases the modern woman to resume her interests outside the family from the age of 35 onward. What is she to do with these years of maturity?

This question calls for fresh insight on the part of educators as to the needs of the contemporary woman and the nature of a changing American society. One of these changes is the relation of men to women. Such changes must be reflected in the college curriculum and in the approach to education. In the past, the women's colleges were part of a protest movement against the claims of men for domination of their society and their family life. The women's colleges are now part of a society which accepts them warmly for their special contribution to cultural and social affairs.

They no longer need to protest. Instead, they can now extend the range of their educational invention to include collaboration with men's colleges and coeducational institutions. Their educational planning should be done not as women's colleges whose deans, faculty members, presidents and students meet with each other to discuss women's college problems, but as colleges which are part of a system of education serving an integrated society.

The women's colleges should take the initiative in educational experiment, in projects ranging from the fusion of the liberal and the technical elements of science, to the development of a new content and methods for teaching the humanities. Such experiment can include, among other things, the exchange of faculty members with men's and coeducational institutions, joint classes with men students, week-end institutes, joint summer sessions, field trips, and social events planned around the common intellectual and personal interests of young men and women—in theatre, literature, politics, painting or science.

In those instances when geography makes it feasible, women's colleges in the future will no doubt move toward more formal cooperation with men's institutions. The Radcliffe experience makes further experiment in various forms of coordinate education feasible and desirable. In other instances men's colleges will no doubt move toward greater coordination in academic and social programs with women's institutions, and in some cases may establish women's colleges coordinate with their own. There need be no loss of identity or invasion of privacy in such coordination.

In the meantime, the Eastern women's colleges are flourishing, there are many more thousands of able students who wish to attend them than they can presently accommodate. They are strong and vigorous. In the future, we can conceive of the ideal situation as one in which the colleges for women work within their own tradition, join forces with men's institutions when appropriate, find new ways of meeting the educational needs of women in a new age, and throughout the whole of their endeavor teach the members of both sexes a respect for each other, for the ideals of a democratic society, and for the life of the mind.

Suggested Topics

1. Coeducation—bane or boon?
2. The problems of married college students
3. Coeducation—a slice of life
4. Education vs. "the distractions of pursuit"
5. The denominational college—its strengths and weaknesses
6. The future of the one-sex college
7. The career woman and the women's college
8. Cooperative enterprise among nearby colleges

THE WORLD OF BOOKS

BUILD YOUR OWN LIBRARY
Gilbert Highet

> The author or editor of a considerable number of scholarly
> works, a gifted translator from the classics, and a lecturer of
> extraordinary ability, Gilbert Highet is Professor of Greek and
> Latin at Columbia University. He came to the United States in
> 1937, after being educated at Glasgow University and at Oxford,
> where he later taught.

You should build your own library, as though you were building
something which would last all your life, and perhaps longer. Not
the bookshelves and such external things; the books themselves,
chosen, and read, and placed, with understanding and affection. Everyone except illiterates and quasi-illiterates has a little library of his
or her own, even if it is only a few novels picked up haphazardly or
a shabby collection of paperbacks. Everyone starts with *some* books:
a Bible, a do-it-yourself manual, a mystery story. The standard of
education throughout the United States is more or less paced by the
sales of books in various regions: the stupider any area is, the fewer
good schools it has, the fewer books its inhabitants buy and borrow
from libraries. Books are not all of civilization, but they are one of
the essential carriers of civilization.

Since we are nearly all building our own libraries, here are a few
hints which might be useful, hints from an old lover of books who
acquired his first volume forty-eighty years ago, bought his first volume
forty-five years ago, and bound his first volume with his own hands

"Build Your Own Library" by Gilbert Highet. Transcript of a radio broadcast,
printed by the Book-of-the-Month Club. Copyright 1958 by Oxford University Press,
Inc. Reprinted by permission.

forty years ago. (I still have it too, though the glue is beginning to dry up and the sewing to come apart.)

Naturally, we start with the few indispensable books for consultation, not for reading—the books of reference without which we can scarcely have an intelligent discussion or read an intelligent book: the dictionary, the encyclopedia, and all the other settlers of arguments. Every week, sometimes every day, people take the trouble to telephone me or write me at Columbia University in order to ask me some perfectly simple question which they themselves could have solved within five minutes if they had had two or three simple, cheap, and widely distributed reference books at their hand. Ridiculous.

Beyond those, we all have our individual look-it-up shelves, depending on our personal interests and hobbies. Everyone ought to have a first-aid book; most people need cookery books; anyone who spends any time in the country needs a garden book and a bird book and a tree book; there are books on the maintenance of automobiles, on income tax, on child care. (Just make sure that you buy reasonable books, and not the works of crackpots: I still remember a period of great unhappiness when my wife and I were misdirected by a book about raising small babies, and when we all three suffered a great deal. It is a grave responsibility to write a book.)

Now for real reading. We begin with the central books, which are part of almost every educated person's mind, which are thought about and referred to (consciously or unconsciously) every day: the Bible and Shakespeare. From these we go on to the more or less permanent works of fiction which have been created during the last century or so: Tolstoy's *War and Peace* and *Anna Karenina*; Dostoevsky's *Crime and Punishment* and (probably) *The Brothers Karamazov*; Melville's *Moby Dick*; a few of the best of Mark Twain and Charles Dickens; the perverted pageant of Proust; some of Thomas Mann; Faulkner's central works; add to these the novels which have most powerfully impressed you and seem unforgettable.

Now you have part of the core of a library. You need poetry also, and good nonfiction. In buying poetry to keep, follow your own taste. If your taste is still developing, then buy several good anthologies of poetry, ancient and modern, original and translated; keep them; read them off and on for a year or two, and then your taste will form itself. You will know whether you prefer Robinson Jeffers or Robert Frost, Browning or cummings. Personally, I buy every anthology of poetry which looks intelligent and varied and rich; even if I find only a dozen good poems in it which I did not possess, they are my reward. As for permanent nonfiction, that depends entirely on your habit of mind. If you are inclined to philosophy or to religion, to science or to economics or to history, there are many good books which promise to last.

But then you should have a couple of shelves devoted purely to fun: ease, relaxation, pleasure—something to pick up in odd moments when you cannot face the logic of life or the effort of thought; something to read while in bed with a mild virus infection; something for a peaceful evening when you cannot stand any more guffawing audiences and shouted commercials. (YES! SHOUTED COMMERCIALS!) Something easy. Similar books should be put in every guest room. Not *Whither Are We Drifting?* books, nor books about *Our Role in Tristan da Cunha,* but books which produce the same effect as a chicken sandwich and a glass of champagne: the works of James Thurber; some fantasy fiction; some intelligent whodunits; light books of travel; some well-written ghost stories (like those of M. R. James, *Ghost Stories of an Antiquary*)—books which you need not read, but go on reading for pure diversion.

Now this is becoming a personal library. As you read books and buy them, you will find that your own tastes come out more and more strongly. There are special hobbies which interest you. There are problems still unsolved on which good books are written. Neglected aspects of human activity deserve more attention. You have been to some strange and charming place, and wish to explore its past and its present. For all these reasons you will buy books. A man who was captivated by a lecture on astronomy which he heard at school may well recall it twenty years later, and begin to read more about modern astronomy; or else he may pass on to the new topic of space travel, or to the important and still misunderstood subject of weather and climate. The young fellow who deciphered one of the ancient Greek scripts called Minoan was not a professional scholar at all: he was an architect by profession, but he recalled that he had heard, when he was still a schoolboy, a lecture on the problem of these scripts by Sir Arthur Evans, who had dug up many of the clay tablets on which they are written; the problem fermented in his mind for years; he devoted his mind to it as soon as he had some leisure; he collected books and articles about it; and, with the brilliance of an amateur (which sometimes brings tears to the eyes of the professionals), he solved it. Another man, who recognizes reluctantly that his temperament will never allow him to be a good chess player, will still collect books on the history of the game, biographies of its masters, analyses of its problems. Another, again, may buy books on mathematics, its puzzles and its personalities; on extra-sensory perception; on business cycles; on psychoanalysis; on the ballet; on local and family history; even (I am glad to say) on nonsense.

Your library will now go on growing, almost by itself. But it needs a little care. It is not an external thing, like a doormat; it is more personal than a car. Like your furniture and pictures and ornaments, it is a reflection of your feelings and your mind. No more than you would have a cracked piece of linoleum under your dining-room table, should you have a collection of dirty, dog-eared, crippled books on your shelves. No more than you would have your phonograph blaring out a random selection mixing Tebaldi with Spike Jones and old Carusos with new Presleys, should you have shelves in which Mickey Spillane leans against Edith Sitwell. Books need a little arranging, and a little maintenance.

To make sure that they will remain with you it is a good idea to have your own bookplate inside the front cover. There are many pleasant bookplates which can be adapted for individual use on sale in stationers' shops. Or you can persuade an artist friend to design one specially for you; or if you are a photographer you can make your own. Back in 1929, when I had just a few books which I treasured, a friend of mine who was an artist and a calligrapher designed a bookplate for me. Those were the days of sharp, angular, modernist designs, and this bookplate was highly unfashionable, being calm and balanced and reposeful and harmonious—a head and a landscape out of the pictorial tradition of the early Italian Renaissance. But I liked it; I save up some money and had a plate made of it; I have used it ever since. James Wardrop, who drew it for me, is dead now, but his friendship and his sensitive taste remain alive for me whenever I open one of my books.

As well as putting your own bookplate into your books (by the way, you know that you should never lend a book? Never, unless you have at least two copies. You always lend books that you like; the other fellow likes them too; and you never see them again), you might also jot down the date you bought them: just a few figures, the month and the year, will be enough later to remind you of a stage in your life which had been half forgotten.

There is also an almost indispensable addition to your library, which is not a book, but a collection of book material. This is a box file, or a large decorative envelope, or anything more or less permanent and not too disagreeable to look at, into which you can put newspaper clippings, and magazine articles, and interviews, programs of concerts and catalogues of art exhibitions, and so forth. It is surprising how many things like this turn out to be worth keeping. There is no need to make a system of it; but if some particular piece seems interesting when you read it, drop it into the file. In five years or so you will be surprised to find how much that is curious and stimulating has survived, which might otherwise have perished. Of course there will be a lot of rubbish too, and you can throw that into the wastebasket; but there will be some interviews with authors which have never been reprinted in book form, and which supplement what you yourself have been thinking about them; there will be some reviews of new plays or first novels which confirm, or perhaps contradict, later impressions; there will be some impressive or amusing public utterances, when some prominent writer breaks into speech. You will often reread an article from your own file, when you would not think of handling the back numbers of the magazine in which it first appeared.

One further hint, which is sometimes forgotten. Public libraries are fine things, and we all ought to use them; but they do not replace a personal library. When you see a book which really attracts you, *buy* it. Take it out of the library first if you like, and read it to see whether you are sure. But if you are sure, then buy it. In part, this is a kindness to the author, who has to live and pay his taxes and his mortgage; one of the surest ways to wound any writer however insignificant, is to write telling him that you *loved* his book even though you had to wait *six months* before your name came up on the waiting list at the lending library. In part, it is insurance. Books are apt to go out of print, when their authors die; they disappear even before that, and cannot be discovered except with inordinate effort. There is a story about a Southern farmer who was sitting on his porch whittling, when his wife screamed at him. "Joe," she cried, "Joe, an alligator just et one of our chillun!" He thought for a while, and then he said, "You know, Polly, I thought something been getting our chillun." Even if an author births a good book, and nourishes it, and teaches it to stand by itself, some alligator is apt to get it; and you and I ought to make sure that it has some chance of survival, by buying it and putting it on our shelves.

Remember also that there are many guides to help you in building a good personal library. To begin with, there are some very competent level-headed, and candid book critics in the United States. If you pick two or three of them and read their reviews regularly, you will recognize their strengths and their weaknesses, and learn within limits to trust their taste. Again, at the end of every calendar year, the best magazines and newspapers usually list the hundred books produced during that year which have most chance of surviving with distinction; from these lists you could easily assemble two or three highly interesting shelves. Then there are a number of exceedingly useful books about books, which classify and describe hundreds, even thousands, of important works in all fields. The best is probably Hester Hoffman's *Bookman's Manual* (Bowker, New York, 8th edition, 1958); there is a fine paperback called simply *Good Reading* (New American Library), which would keep most people going for a lifetime; and I often recommend a book list made up for Trinity College, Hartford, Connecticut, by Professor Harry Todd Costello, called *Books for a College Student's Reading* (Trinity College, Hartford, 1951). When in doubt, always ask a librarian. Trained librarians always have lists ready at hand; some even distribute their own; they are always willing to help, for they love books.

I have been talking about forming a personal library as though it were a pleasure and a way to pleasure; and indeed so it is. But it is also something of a duty. It is the mind that makes us truly human. If the mind is never fed on anything more than television stunt programs and old movies and short reports in the newspapers and casual conversations, it will never operate at more than half its capacity; it will start to atrophy like an arm with a withered muscle. A house without books usually means a mind without either knowledge, or thought, or enjoyment of its own powers.

Suggested Topics

1. My core library
2. The fate of the lent-out book
3. Are the best-sellers the best books?
4. If I were limited to ten books . . .
5. Browsing in the book stalls
6. Why I respect a particular book critic

DICTIONARIES: OUR LANGUAGE RIGHT OR WRONG   *Felicia Lamport*

Felicia Lamport is the author of an amusing family biography, *Mink on Weekdays (Ermine on Sundays)* and of a number of light poems.

Some people are born to dictionaries, some achieve them as Confirmation presents, and others have them thrust upon them by schools. Nevertheless, at some time in the lives of most people it becomes necessary actually to choose a dictionary. Often the bright lexicon of one's youth tends to exert an umbilical pull through life. Many a man who has lost his dictionary or worn it to tatters will set out to buy the same one all over again, in the identical edition, if possible; a new type face in his dictionary would be as unsettling to him as a new type of face on his father or mother—probably because, in these uncertain times, so many people look confidently to the dictionary as the last stronghold of immutable authority.

Actually it is nothing of the sort. The modern lexicographer prides himself on being as mutable as mercury and quite as responsive to climatic change. In the jargon of the trade, the approach has changed from "prescriptive" (telling people what language they ought to use) to "descriptive" (recording what language they *do* use). The old rigid corset of correctness has given way to a flexible girdle of usage.

This policy is enunciated in most dictionary introductions, but with approximately the effect of a gnat's scream, possibly because of the small type, but more probably because dictionary jackets, with their claims of supreme authority, persist in implying the opposite. Lexicography may be a philological science to editors, but to publishers it is big business: the most recent edition of the Merriam-Webster unabridged dictionary cost well over a million dollars to bring to market. Usage is a demanding master, and a costly one to serve. Corps of experts are needed to read millions of pages a year, winnowing new words and meanings, noting change or obsolescence in old ones. These readers cover a vast range of newspapers, magazines, and books, marking up a page with symbols until it looks like the bottom of a canary's cage, and then extracting "citation slips" for each context in which each word appears. Other experts monitor the spoken word on radio and television to keep up with current pronunciation. Editors are rigorously guided by these citation slips.

The smallest and newest publishers work mainly with free-lance lexicographers. They begin with an out-of-copyright dictionary as a base, or with a word-list assembled, according to one candid editor, "by gosh, by golly, and by plagiarism"—this last euphemistically described in the trade as "knowing one's competition." From this point on, editors of large dictionaries and small alike see themselves as devoted and scholarly spaniels, following the path of usage. However, they seem to balk at a number of well-worn turnings. Their image of "correctness" as a concept broad enough to include the consensus of literate error pales before several glaring examples.

Consider the word *jejune,* familiar to many people and defined by 99 per cent of them as "youthfully foolish, naïve," doubtless because of its resemblance to *jeune.* The editors of dictionaries give it only its classic meaning: "meager, scanty, barren, unsatisfying to the mind."

Fey, construed to mean "elfin" by most literate people, is defined as "fated to die"; its popular meaning has only recently crept into a single dictionary. Confronted with this lag, editors say that the citation slips have not yet shown sufficient evidence to justify the new sense.

There is no mathematical formula for the dictionaries' seal of approval. Editors exercise a judgment based not only on frequency but on range. A word may accumulate a foot-high pile of citation slips, but if it appears only in a single publication it will not make the grade; otherwise *Time* and *Variety* alone could make a shambles ("a slaughterhouse; abattoir") of existing dictionaries. Editors must also be prophets of longevity: slang words often crop out in epidemic proportions only to vanish, leaving no more trace than a measles rash (*e.g., making whoopee, ruptured duck,* and, it is to be hoped, *square* and *cool* used as antonyms).

Dictionary makers must also deal with word coiners who press for the inclusion of their inventions. Their neologisms are often ingenious, but are admitted to the word sanctuaries only through the gate of popular acceptance. The word *humiture,* more succinct and less alarming to Chambers of Commerce than *discomfort index,* was recently submitted to the Merriam Company's scholarly editor, Dr. Philip Gove (Merriam prides itself on its Ph.Diesel-powered staff). Dr. Gove views the word with interest and will watch the citation slips to see if it catches on.

From out in left field (an expression not yet and possibly never to be included in the word-books) has come perennially another pressure on the man behind the thumb-indexing of the brain. Ever since Warren Gamaliel Harding—an unlikely neologist if there ever was one—accidentally added *normalcy* to the language, there has been a rumor that a kind of royal prerogative adheres to any Presidential slip, making it a must for all future dictionaries. "There's nothing to that rumor," one lexicographer says. "If there were, we'd have had to reset half the book for several Presidents I could mention."

Editors are often confronted with pressure to keep words *out* of dictionaries. While they may sympathize with those who campaign against terms with invidious racial or ethnic implications, they maintain that it is their job to report usage, not to change it. Occasionally, however, they slip in a hint of disapproval by defining such terms as "used by prejudiced people." Further pressure for omission comes from the proprietors of trade-marks, who, having spent fortunes making their catchwords familiar, then spend further fortunes trying to prevent them from becoming so generic that they are no longer the sole property of the original holders. *Aspirin, cellophane,* and dozens of other trade names have been popularized right into the public domain. Here again the editors politely disclaim all right to control.

They observe, record; perhaps permit themselves a secret smile or grimace.

The idea that the lexicographer is the man who lays down the *lex* is one with strong classic antecedents. In the late sixteenth century, the *Accademia della Crusca* was formed to refine the Italian language and preserve its purity for all time in an official dictionary. The *Académie française* was organized a few years later in France to assure the permanent inviolability of that country's excitable tongue. The effectiveness of these undertakings has been something less than complete: Not long ago, the *New York Times* reported that the 3,500 members of *L'Office du Vocabulaire français* had met to consider the alarming pace at which the corruption of the language has been proceeding. English has been creeping in—and not good English, either. The French alarm themselves.

In England the purifying, refining, and smelting movement developed rather more slowly. Most of the early English glossographers devoted themselves to defining the unfamiliar or "hard" words, largely for the benefit of women, children, and foreigners. But the eighteenth century began with a trumpeting of the "prescriptive" note when Swift, writing to the Lord Treasurer "in the name of all the learned and polite persons of the nation," complained of the corruptions, absurdities, and gross improprieties of the language. Remedial action was undertaken by Samuel Johnson, who made no bones about being as prescriptive as R. It was his candid intention not only to stem the current of linguistic change but actually to turn back the stream. The syntax of the fathers was to be visited on the children.

Johnson felt that the language had "spread, under the direction of chance, into wild exuberance" since the days of the Elizabethan writers, whom he considered "the wells of English undefiled." He proposed to cleanse English of its impurities and secure it against future decay by producing a dictionary that would record all "good" words and set a permanent standard for proper diction. Undaunted by the reminder that forty French academicians had labored forty years to produce such a work, Johnson undertook to do the job alone in three ("As three is to sixteen hundred, so is the proportion of an Englishman to a Frenchman"), for fame, the honor of his country, and the unprecedented advance of £1,575 from a syndicate of booksellers.

By the time he had finished his great *Dictionary of the English Language,* the three years had stretched to eight, the advance had long since been used up, and he was no longer sanguine about the likelihood of "embalming his language." Yet for the next hundred years Johnson's dictionary was the standard for most Englishmen and many Americans. One Massachusetts judge still uses it exclusively, on the ground that "the language has gone plumb to hell since Johnson."

Most Americans, however, turned from Johnson to Noah Webster, who gave us our first truly American dictionary in 1828. Despite Webster's genius for the clear, concise definition, his dictionary was not notably well received during his life. His price was too steep for the public, his etymologies were too unscientific for the scholars, and his attempts to reform spelling met with such frenetic resistance that he was forced to drop many of them. He succeeded in knocking the "u" out of such words as *honor* and *glamor,* in substituting *jail* for *gaol,* and in making many Americans so unsure of whether they were going to the *theater* or the *theatre* that many of them eventually took to the movies; but he failed to popularize *wimen* or to reduce our tongue to a reasonable *tung.* Benjamin Franklin, Theodore Roosevelt, and G. B. Shaw all tried in vain to simplify our spelling. It seems unlikely that our letters will ever achieve happy togetherness with our phonemes: fonetik speling stil haz implikashunz uv unejukatid absurditi.

In 1857, a revolution in dictionary making was launched in England by Dean Richard Chenevix Trench of Westminster. Dr. Trench felt that a dictionary should not be a standard of the language but an inventory, that the lexicographer should be a literary historian, not a critic, and collect not merely the "good" words but all words. His suggestions started the wheels turning on the vast project that resulted, more than seventy years later, in the publication of the Oxford *New English Dictionary.*

The compilers of this lexicon proposed to include every word recorded in the English language since the middle of the thirteenth century, the obsolete as well as the current, giving the full biography of each, illustrating every change in form or meaning by a quotation, proving etymology by the word's history—not by ingenious conjecture, as Webster had done.

This new approach required not just a highly determined man with a quill but a highly financed organization with a staff. The Philological Society sent out a call for collaborators to help with Dr. Trench's proposed "drawing as with a sweep-net over the whole extent of English literature." Before the dictionary was published, over 2,000 volunteers were helping in the monumental task. Every parson worth his psalter was busily seining the language and making extractions; literary-minded ladies and gentlemen in England, the United States, and all other English-speaking countries were sending in quotations by the thousands, one man reaching a total of 165,000. When finally completed in 1933, the great thirteen-volume work became the dictionary maker's dictionary and the scholar's delight. One can wander through its acres of quotations with endless pleasure—given the $300 to buy it, the shelf space to store it, and a back sufficiently free from slipping discs to handle it comfortably.

A dictionary without quotations was described by Voltaire as only a skeleton, but the average or non-scholarly American favors the skeletal in dictionaries. With several hundred of them now on the market, he faces a difficult choice. He is confronted by yards of dictionaries: multilingual, bilingual, encyclopedic, general, and specialized. In the specialized field alone a single publisher, with the resplendent name of Dagobert D. Runes, claims to have published 250 volumes, including dictionaries of Americanism, folklore, mysticism, psychology, and even tobacco. Narrowing the field to the general English dictionary, there are still some eighty-odd titles, ranging in price from 25 cents to $300, in size from a few ounces to 90 pounds, and in quality from hastily patched-up offsets to fine scholarly works. Yet all of them claim to be the most supremely authoritative, complete, and up-to-date in a given category and to have the most entries with the fullest definitions in the most compact form and the most readable type.

These claims are somewhat puzzling to the prospective buyer. To begin with, he is unlikely to know what an "entry" is (it's any word that appears in boldface type). Nor has he any conception of where a category begins or ends: Is a "desk" dictionary more advanced or less advanced than a "college," bigger or smaller than a "concise"? (The terms are used loosely: the "college" claims roughly 125,000 to 175,000 entries; the "desk" and "concise" are more or less interchangeable, running from 70,000 to 100,000; the "shorter" Oxford is longer than any in this last group. However, as one lexicographer says: "Most dictionary publishers either lie or equivocate in their entry claims: no one is likely to sit down and count." Exaggerations of up to 20 per cent are considered sporting in the trade, but the claim of 100,000 by a dictionary with 50,000 is *infra dig.*)

For some, the name "Webster" might be reassuring if it were not for the tangled web of Websters now in print. The original claim is held by the G. & C. Merriam Company, which bought the unsold copies of Webster's dictionary at his death and popularized it by astute merchandising and scholarly revision. Webster's name was a fertile source of litigation for decades, producing, in some years, more suits than Brooks Brothers. His dictionary is now out of copyright, can be used by any publisher, and is currently in brisk circulation. Merriam and World, the two leading Webster publishers, each cautions the public against confusing "the" authoritative Webster (*i.e.,* its own) with any others. Merriam, somewhat obsessed by the idea of confusion, goes so far in its biographical dictionary as to include under the sketches of Noah and Daniel a warning against confusing them with each other.

The Merriam Company tends, on the whole, to exude an air of superiority, perhaps because of its lofty position on the heights of Springfield, Massachusetts, and dictionary sales charts, but more probably because of its well-merited reputation for consistently fine scholarship. The faint antiseptic aura that occasionally emanates from this company may spring from its ties to Noah Webster, who undertook at one time to bowdlerize the Bible.

The first article of lexicographic faith is that the dictionary should provide the user with the information he wants. Dr. Johnson carried this premise to the extent of listing several words under two headings (*soap, sope; fuel, fewel*), "that those who search for them under either form may not search in vain." The modern lexicographer is too space-bound for such a courtesy, even though it would have spared Clarence Barnhart, the editor of the Thorndike-Barnhart dictionaries, the wrath of a lady who recently wrote in: "There is no excuse for a dictionary the size of yours leaving out a word like 'phsychology'!"

There are necessary limits to the province of the dictionary, but the public, reluctant to recognize them, writes in such questions as: "Does the fire engine, the ambulance, or the mail truck have the right of way?" The editor, if not too busy, will try to oblige (the mail truck has the technical right but never enforces it), but his patience gives out during the mammoth word-puzzle contests. Librarians are equally annoyed by such competitions: during one recent contest the New York Public Library had to call in the police to prevent contestants from frustrating their rivals by tearing relevant pages out of dictionaries.

Editors are also irritated by the practice of selling dictionaries by creating anxiety neuroses ("Are *you* guilty of these common errors?"), or imparting snob appeal to sesquipedalian words. They are articulate and learned men themselves, but they speak with notable simplicity, appearing as anxious as morticians to keep the flavor of their work from creeping into their conversation. They are, however, tolerant of such word-play as the search for the longest word in the language. According to *The American College Dictionary*'s amiable managing editor, Jess Stein, the old standby *antidisestablishmentarianism* (28 letters) has been topped by *floccinaucinihilipilification* (29 letters adding up to "estimation as worthless"), and again by an obscure lung disease, *pneumonoultramicroscopicsilikovolcanikoniosis* (45), and finally by the one-word description of the spa waters at Bristol, *aqueosalinocalcinocetaceoaluminosocupreovitriolic* (51), pronounced salutary by an eighteenth-century physician.

Editors prefer to confine such frivolities to publicity releases or supplements; space is too limited in the book itself. Since the public demands encyclopedic material in dictionaries, even the abridged ones include a sprinkling of biographical, geographical and historical nuggets in the main alphabet. The supplements, which are as broadly stocked as drugstores, are likely to include such essentials as: Lists of

Proper Names (segregated by sex), Flags of All Nations, Sign and Symbols (from Astronomy to Zodiac), Lists of Colleges (Junior, Senior, and Canadian), Pronouncing Gazetteers, Letter Writing Guides, Tables of Weights and Measures, Population Statistics, Forms of Address (Written and Spoken, from Ambassador to Vice-President), Usage Guides, Glossaries of Foreign Words, Rules of Simplified Spelling, Vocabularies of Rhymes, Alphabets for Semaphoring and Telegraphing, Foreign Alphabets, and the chewing gum left by a visiting child.

To the regret of the dictionary makers, the average American demands very little in the way of etymology, and so misses the delights of peeling back layers of meaning.

The *gossip* (*god* + *sib,* as in *sibling*) becomes a full-bodied character when seen first as "a baptismal sponsor," then as "a close friend or chum," only lately reaching the present status of "a tattler." The *cad* is far more interesting historically than face to face, originating as "an unbooked passenger on a coach," becoming "an assistant, as a bricklayer's laborer," shifting to "an omnibus conductor," and finally generalizing into "a fellow of low and vulgar manners." A bland word like *pretty* picks up piquancy when one discovers that it meant "sly" in its infancy, moved on to "clever," and only developed its "beautiful" implications quite late in its history.

Occasional words, too lively to sink into obsolescence, spring back into action every so often. Dean Trench argued eloquently but in vain for such beauties as *cankerfret* and *witwanton;* his list of synonyms for *miser* (*nudge, curmudgeon, cuff, gripe, pinchpenny, clutchfist, penifather, nipfarthing*) should certainly be hoarded by any word-lover.

The word-lover is generally a mild man, but, like the animal-lover, he can be stung to action by any abuse of his pets. The use of *like* as a conjunction has driven some members of this species to give up cigarettes entirely. Others have committed assault on hearing *literally* used as a kind of double-strength *figuratively* (as in the great blooper, "The pastor was literally the father of his flock"). At such times the emotional word-buff is likely to descend on the dictionary editors, demanding that they abandon their eulogy of usage and return to the good old prescriptive ways. But the sensible logophile simply retires to the nearest dictionary, where he roots about with all the joy of a pig in a truffle field.

This man will probably have the Oxford at his elbow, but he has a deeper interest in words than most Americans. The man who wants a dictionary principally as a prop against malapropisms would be illadvised to use the Oxford. American unabridged dictionaries are far less cumbersome. In this field, scholars and sales charts agree on the superiority of the Merriam-Webster *New International, Second Edi-*

tion. This dictionary is a splendid one to have in a man's library, but if his space is limited to a desk top, he may find that it nestles there rather like a St. Bernard in a window box, and decide on something smaller.

In the "college" class there are a number of fine dictionaries. Although publishers tend to guard their figures as zealously as fashion models, bookstores reports indicate that here again Merriam, the Abou Ben Adhem of the field, leads all the rest with *Webster's New Collegiate Dictionary*, but the Random House *American College Dictionary* and *Webster's New World Dictionary of the American Language, College Edition* (published by World) offer lively competition. All three are good. Winston and Funk & Wagnalls also publish good ones.

Choosing among all these is largely a matter of personal taste, of calculating, weighing, and evaluating their many minor differences. To consider a few: Merriam has the largest reputation but the smallest type; World has the most pages, Random House the most illustrations; World and Merriam put derivations before definitions, Random House after; Random House and World include all entries under a single alphabet, Merriam lists biographical and geographical material under separate alphabets; Random House lists meanings in order of frequency of use, World and Merriam emphasize historical order; World and Random House repeat their pronunciation key on the bottom of every page, Merriam gives it only at the start.

If harmony with the color scheme of a room is a decisive factor, it may be useful to note that Random House is jacketed in black and bound in russet. World has a gray jacket and a red binding, Merriam has a crimson jacket and is bound in blue.

School dictionaries are issued by the five publishers mentioned above; in addition there is the Thorndike-Barnhart series, which ranks with the best and is the most comprehensive.

In the event of total confusion, it may be useful to remember Samuel Johnson's dictum: "Dictionaries are like watches: the worst is better than none, and the best cannot be expected to go quite true."

Suggested Topics

1. "Usage is a demanding master"
2. Prescriptive vs. descriptive usage.
3. How words get into our language
4. Let's reform English spelling.
5. How to choose a good dictionary

BOOKS ARE AN ESCAPE INTO EXPERIENCE

Harry Golden

The author of *Only in America* and *For 2¢ Plain,* works of appealing humor, satire, nostalgia, and compassion, Harry Golden has a national following through *The Carolina Israelite,* of which he is editor and publisher.

The winter of 1917 was one of the coldest ever to descend upon the Eastern Seaboard. Because of the war there was a severe shortage of coal. The kitchen stoves, which rarely warmed the tenements anyway, smoked for only an hour a day, enough time to cook the evening meal. In the schools, the ink froze solid in the little glass inkwells in each desk. It was even impossible for a while to heat the water for the public baths at the University Settlement House. At the height of the cold, the schools closed for a week. The one place in New York that remained heated and warm—and accessible—was the New York Public Library on Fifth Avenue and Forty-second Street. I was one among many who walked past the couchant lions up those marble steps and into the spacious entryway.

It was my first distinct impression of how important a public library was. I went there every day to get warm. There were thousands like me—school children, adults, even mothers with their babies in a go-cart, which I remember they wheeled to and fro in the main entrance hall.

Long before this I had learned to make use of a library. How long does it take you to become an American? The library of the University Settlement House had a big placard:

> *I love the name of Washington*
> *I love my country, too*
> *I love the flag, the dear old flag, the Red, the White and Blue.*

A lesson in English as well as in history. A simple verse which helped open the door and it was all before you on the shelves—and free.

Later on, I began to use the Rivington Street Branch (long since torn down) of the New York Public Library system in downtown New

Reprinted from *The New York Times Book Review,* April 12, 1959. By permission of *The New York Times* and the author.

York, and here, too, there were no restrictions and only one law. You had to show your hands, both sides, to the lady at the desk. If they weren't clean, you had to wash them before they let you touch the books. The adult factory workers who came in at night lined up for inspection, too.

I remember the methods of censorship the Rivington Street librarian used. If there was a book in the stacks that she thought unsuitable for children, it was placed on a high shelf you couldn't reach. The reasoning was that if you were tall enough to get your hands on it, you were old enough to read it. I am a product of the Rivington Street Library, and I did my "graduate" work at the main branch, and it has been my good fortune in recent years to have had communication with many of the men who sat at some of the other library tables; the boys who teach now at Harvard and Princeton, M. I. T. and Antioch, as well as the fellow who produced New York's last hit play, and a man who writes that I always said "hello" to him in the reading room and that he now does social work in Los Angeles.

If the winter of 1917 had never happened, I would have remembered the Public Library system in only a general way—as a place where thousands of immigrant boys and girls, then as well as now, were caught up in the process of becoming American citizens.

Yet it is no mockery to say that my first responsible impression of the library was that it was warm on a cold day. It offered an escape, an escape from the cold. It is a responsible impression because that is exactly what the library offers, an escape—an escape into experience.

What kind of experience this is, I shall have to leave to the philosopher, the psychologist, the neurologist and the esthetician. And there will be many who will argue that this sort of escape is not an important experience. It doesn't lead to anything. It is purposeless. To suggest that books and libraries are simply an escape, they will say, is to apply an unfair analogy to writers and their audience. Books and libraries, they insist, have a utilitarian purpose.

Well, I admit that this is true, that books and libraries have their uses, but those uses are not simply to help students prepare for the chemistry examination or to help market researchers determine how many gross tons of soybeans were imported last year.

I cannot offer the logical definition for what I mean perhaps, but let me point to the racks of paper-bound books in airline terminals, bus depots and railroad stations. These publishers have built a tidy empire by offering these books at a cheap price to people on the go. Travel, we say, is broadening. Why a book? Because no matter how much people praise travel, the actual process of getting from one place to another is a stationary process. You have one seat in a plane, or one berth in a sleeper, and to sit in that one place for hours on end is ultimate boredom. People escape from this boredom by reading, for boredom is simply the absence of experience. By reading you escape, and I am the first to admit it. And I will go even further and say that the great argument against the car as a mode of travel is that it is impossible to read in it.

Libraries and books offer an escape, but it is an escape *into* something larger, not *from* something larger; it is an escape into hazard, not from hazard. A dictator escapes not by fleeing into a library, but by a midnight flight to the Dominican Republic. The ruined broker does not ease his anxiety with the latest fiction but by jumping from his office window on the sixteenth floor.

Despite the plethora of visual-aid devices the colleges are using these days, it is worth repeating that there are no short cuts to reading. In economics you start with land, and in knowledge you start with books. A book tolerates no arguments and any modification makes it less than it is.

A book, in short, has a total, global effect, and the public library has, by and large, kept this faith. To use a library you do not have to subject yourself to a battery of personality and value tests as you do to get a job as a typist. The library, I believe, is the last of our public institutions to which you can go without credentials. You don't need a college degree as you do at the Graduate Association. Nor do you need a Statement of Business Venture as you need for the Chamber of Commerce. You don't even need the sticker on your windshield that you need to get onto the public beach. All you need is the willingness to read.

In the reading room of the Cooper Union Institute, which is downtown in New York City, where Third and Fourth Avenues split off, there used to be free nighttime lectures. The auditorium, in which Lincoln first became a national figure, often held a few Bowery tramps as well as the many interested members of the community. After a while you'd stop being surprised in the discussion periods about how much the tramps knew about Keats or the Single-Tax because you reasoned the tramp, after all had·more leisure. Whatever the books had to offer, they gave to the tramp as much as to you.

Thus the library is a picture of America in miniature. America is always absorbing the immigrant, only to reproduce the pioneer. I would like to recommend how best to preserve this principle. It is a simple injunction. See that the local library contains those books you don't like or don't want to read.

The best argument ever forwarded for this principle was enunciated almost a century ago by an English woman named Anne Gilchrist, who wrote "An English Woman's Estimate of Walt Whitman." "Leaves of Grass" had a long unfortunate history before it became required reading in college freshman courses, and one of its first defenders was Mrs. Gilchrist who wrote: "A quarrel with words is more or less a quarrel with meanings. If the thing a word stands for exists (and what does not so exist?) the word need never be ashamed of itself; the shorter and more direct, the better. It is a gain to make friends with it, and see it in good company."

The free and uncensored library where young children begin to read and where old men know a morning of warmth and peace is the truly great joy of liberty.

Suggested Topics

1. A book that changed my mind
2. Reading—an "escape into experience"
3. The library: "a picture of America in miniature"
4. The value of knowing how to use a library
5. Good librarians are good teachers.

BOOKS: GUNPOWDER OF THE MIND   David Riesman

A perceptive student of American culture, David Riesman has had a distinguished career as a social scientist at the University of Chicago and Harvard, following earlier training in biochemistry, the law, and industry. His writings include *The Lonely Crowd, Faces in the Crowd,* and *Individualism Reconsidered.*

Inventions are as much the mother of necessity as the reverse, and the Western world as we know it now is inconceivable without print— just as World War II could hardly have been fought without the telephone and the IBM machine. This is one reason why it is hard for the print-raised generations to contemplate the decline of reading relative to the rise of other media, for each medium of communication not only brings in its wake an elite attuned to its potentialities but alters the forms of perception, the bonds of sympathy, and the channels of conflict that hold a society together.

I should like to present here certain suggestions, highly tentative

Reprinted from *The Atlantic Monthly,* December, 1957. By permission of the author.

and exploratory, concerning three questions: first, what are the differences between cultures which depend entirely on the spoken word and those which depend on print; second, what will be the significance of the written word now that newer mass media, less demanding psychologically and yet perhaps more potent politically, have developed; third, what is likely to happen in those countries where the tradition of books is not fully established and where the new media are already having a decisive impact.

In Ruth Underhill's transcript of the autobiography of a Papago Indian woman are some passages which convey a sense of the impact of the spoken word in a culture where no other modes of communication compete with it. One passage goes as follows:

> The men from all the villages met at Basket Cap Mountain, and there my father made them speeches, sitting with his arms folded and talking low as all great men do. Then they sang war songs. . . . Many, many songs they sang but I, a woman, cannot tell you all. I know that they made the enemy blind and dizzy with their singing and that they told the gopher to gnaw their arrows. And I know that they called on our dead warriors who have turned into owls and live in the Apache country to come and tell them where the enemy were.

In the many passages of this sort that one can find in ethnographic accounts, we become aware of the immense emotional force that can be harnessed by the spoken word in such a group—so powerful here that at least in fancy it can shatter the morale of a distant enemy. Implicit here is the fact that a society dependent on oral traditions and oral communications is, by our standard, a slow-paced one: there is time enough, for grownups as well as children, to roll back the carpet of memories: nobody has to miss the ceremonies in order to catch the 8:05 the next morning from Scarsdale—or to run the train itself. To be sure, the teen-age girls today who learn by heart the lyrics of popular songs do seem to have time enough on their hands to memorize verses, but even they must learn a new repertory every year and will surely not, as parents, sing these songs of their dating years to their own children.

What I have said needs to be qualified in several respects familiar to those of you who have done group singing informally. I do have the impression, strengthened by assiduous reading of juke-box labels, that there is a kind of sediment of tunes and ballads—"Stormy Weather," for example—which binds at least the jazz generations into an occasional songfest, more or less barber-shop-quartet style. Then there are the folk songs and madrigals sung by the college-educated, such as the highbrow variants of "Boola Boola" and "10,000 Men of Harvard." But for none of these songs is it terribly important to know the right words—the lyrics are not altogether meaningless even, I suppose, in the so-called "nonsense" songs, but neither do they encapsulate the history of the tribe or the patterns of heroic behavior.

What I am getting at is that the spoken or sung word is particularly impressive when it monopolizes the symbolic environment; but once books have entered that environment the social organization can never be the same again. Books bring with them detachment and a critical attitude that is not possible in a society dependent on the spoken word. We can occasionally have second thoughts about a speech, but we cannot hear it, as we can read a book, backwards as well as forwards—that is, the writer can be checked up on in a way that the speaker cannot be.

People tend to remember best the things they have felt most deeply. The memorable words in a culture wholly dependent on the spoken word will often be those most charged with group feeling; and we would expect communication to keep alive in an individual the childhood sense of dependence, childhood's terrors and elations, and something of its awe for the old.

The shift to a literate culture, historically decisive as it is, does not of course occur all at once; only a tiny minority could read prior to the age of print, and the reading of manuscripts altered styles of communication rather less than one might today think. For one thing, manuscripts, having to be slowly deciphered, promoted memorization, which in turn promoted arguments by quotation and commentary. Manuscripts were often read aloud and, with their beautiful illuminations, were regarded not simply as rationalistic vehicles of knowledge but also as shared artifacts. By exteriorizing, by making palpable, the processes of thinking and discussion, they promoted individuation only partially, while also promoting adherence to tradition.

The book, like an invisible monitor, helps liberate the reader from his group and its emotions and allows the contemplation of alternative responses and the trying on of new emotions. Max Weber has stressed the importance of the merchant's account book in rationalizing the merchant and his commerce; and other historians have made familiar the role of the printed Bible in encouraging dissident sects to challenge the authority of the Roman Church—indeed, to challenge the given forms of social life itself. At the same time, while the printed book helped people to break away from their family circle and parish, it helped link them into noncontiguous associations of true believers.

Arthur E. Morgan, speaking in *Search for Purpose* of his childhood among small-town folk of limited horizons, remarks, "This library [in the town] was like foster parents to me." Thomas and Znaniecki describe an analogous process in their book on *The Polish Peasant in Europe and America;* the Polish peasant who learned to read and write became identified with the urban world of progress and enlightenment, of ideology and utopia, even while physically still in the peasant world. This identification had many of the elements of a conversion, print itself and the world it opened up being a kind of gospel. Today, in this country of near-universal literacy, we have forgotten the enthusiasm for print which can burst on people newly literate: the "each one teach one" movements of Mexico, the Philippines, and elsewhere; the voracity for books in the Soviet Union and other recently industrialized lands.

Among the highly educated, and in the countries of long-established literacy, there is little comparable enthusiasm. We have become less excited about books as such, or even about "good books," and instead are more discriminating in terms of fields, of tastes, of literary fashions. Our world, as we know all too well, is full of many other things which compete with books, so that some of that minority who were avid readers as children, shutting out parents and peers with faces (as the latter would charge) buried in a book, are now buried as adults in activities that exclude books or push them to the periphery of attention.

In any case, our experience in recent years with mass literacy and mass communications has generally been disillusioning—much as with universal suffrage. Thus, we no longer believe, as numerous thoughtful people did in the 1920's, that radio offers a second chance for stimulating adult education and civic literacy. Likewise, despite a few shining hours, few observers today regard educational TV as anything like an adequate counterweight to the endlessly smiling, relaxed informalities and (for many in the audience) lack of challenge of low-pressure uneducational TV. Paradoxically, however, the coming of TV has given new possibilities back to the radio in the bedroom, for the TV audience is now the mass audience, and the radio can appeal to the wish for privacy, and to specialized tastes and minority audiences. With rare exceptions, it is now the massness of the mass media, rather than their mediating and individuating power, which frightens and depresses many educated people—so much so that we frequently lose faith in enlightenment itself as a goal, let alone in the three easy lessons with which our predecessors sought to reach it. Sometimes, in fact, despair goes to such lengths that the writers of bombast on behalf of books, as if in answer to the spreaders of bombast on behalf of TV, are apt to urge that if only people would read books once more, long and serious books that require close attention, the evils of the modern world would be undone and we would be saved.

The fact is, however, that books, whatever their liberating power in society as a whole, can be used, of course, in nonliberating ways. For instance, a child can be forced into slavery to print through the fanaticism of parents or pedagogues. Indeed, we tend to consider the education of John Stuart Mill by his high-pressure father, in which he learned to read at three and studied the classics before he was ten, as monstrous as it is amazing. We think the French and the Orthodox Jews are cruel to make small children mind their lessons with no time out for sports, let alone for cultivating the "whole child."

But few are the American homes today, or the schools and colleges (even those run by Catholic orders), where these patterns still prevail; on the contrary, both home and school seek to come to terms with life at its most unbookish (just as many books for children—and TV shows, too—are not in search of fantasy but in search of documentary detail).

While the classics are having a small revival at a few colleges and schools, the more general situation is that Americans, with increasing world power, will insist that everyone learn to speak American while not compelling our children to learn any other language—and in many schools not even our own in any full measure. Yet languages, like systems of musical notation, must be carried in the bones and bodies of the living if the accomplishments and experiences of the dead are not to be lost to us. It may be that some residual feeling of this sort— some fear that children may be growing up as barbarians and away from us of the older generations—may be one element behind the ominous success of Rudolf Flesch's demagogic best seller, *Why Johnny Can't Read,* a book that would lose the exaggerated edge of its power if *its* readers could read, or were not too frightened to keep their wits about them. Flesch and his followers never ask the crucial question I am asking here: namely, what distribution of not only reading skills but reading enthusiasms, for what systems of notation (including music, languages, and mathematics), is desirable if we are not only to pass on the heritage—the world's library of art and imagination—but also to contribute to it? They take it for granted that Johnny should read just because John Alden or John Adams did read; in the case of most of the reactionary critics of our public schools who are riding so high today, such terms as "heritage" are merely snob tags, status labels, which they can use to pull rank on schoolteachers, educationists, psychological counselors, and other relatively defenseless people. I suspect that many such critics would like to restore drill and to make reading more of a chore than it needs to be as a sublimated form of hazing the young though some chore and bore elements will certainly be part of any educational program which aims to reach all who can possibly be reached by books or by any other media which connected people with a non-contiguous world, the world of yesterday and tomorrow as well as of the here and now.

Certainly, in an era of abundance we can afford to read books for pleasure, and it may on the whole be a good thing that a boy in school or a soldier in camp can unself-consciously pull out a pocketbook without feeling that there is anything esoteric or status-labeled in the act. Even so, casual pleasures in our society, hard as they often are to come by, will not suffice to absorb young people's energies and aspirations. On the contrary, young people need at some time in their lives to extend themselves, to work at the height of their as yet untapped powers (indeed, lacking better ways, some seek to do this in forms the society defines as delinquency). Since the world's work no longer offers this opportunity for exertion for most nonfarm Americans, we may think it fortunate—though in some respects arbitrary—that the world's storehouse of culture unfailingly does. While we can perhaps imagine a post-literature culture in which people are challenged primarily by other media than print and musical scores, and no doubt we have already a culture in which even in the most bookish strata many media cooperate, yet at the moment I think it is not just prejudice and snobbery which lead us to rely heavily on books as our traditional badge of enlightenment and on libraries as the great storehouse of our culture.

These problems I have been discussing—and I cannot emphasize too strongly the tentativeness of what I have said—would be less important and less apparently insoluble if the book, and other printed matter, stood at the end of the road of social development, as was true from the fifteenth century to the end of the nineteenth. The rule of black print on white paper may be said to mark the epoch of the rise and increasing influence of the middle class, the class of clerks and bookkeepers, merchants and engineers, instruction-givers and instruction-readers, the class of the time-attentive, the future-oriented, the mobile. Reading and education were the highroads this class made use of to rise in the world and to move about in it during the great periods of colonization.

Even the novel, denounced as frivolous and sensuous by the Puritans, had an important function in the changing society. I think not so much of its use as a device for reform and civic adult education, like *Oliver Twist* or *Uncle Tom's Cabin,* as of its less obvious use as a device by which people might prepare themselves for novel contacts and novel life-situations, a form of what psychologists term "anticipatory socialization"—that is, a preparation in imagination for playing roles that might emerge in one's later career. In fact, the very conception of life implicit in the notion of a career is facilitated by the dramatic structure of the novel, especially the *Bildungsroman,* with its protagonist, its interest in motive, its demand on the reader that he project himself into the experiences portrayed.

The rise of the newer media of communication has coincided with a certain loss of power by the older, print-oriented middle class. Yellow journalism, coming on top of universal suffrage, did begin to shake that hegemony. Indeed, the very term "yellow journalism" is significant as marking a change from the monotone of black on white (just as the fact that only 10 per cent of the cars turned out this year are black and all the rest are technicolor says a good deal about our loss of Puritan inhibitions). The comic book, also, is part of this same revolution. And of course the movies and broadcasting, while not displacing the book, shake its monopoly and with it the monopoly of the middle class.

But the consequences of these shifts in the focus of attention and in the emotional impact of the media differ very much depending on whether one speaks of a country where print has long been institutionalized or of a country which had previously been largely illiterate. In the former, the shifts of power tend to be subtle and unclimactic. Thus, it is not a major revolution in America that TV has made preadolescent children even more hep than they were before, more apt to be one up on their parents even about politics, more ready psychologically to empathize with other conditions of man than their own. But in the less industrially advanced countries the shift can be explosive. A study (done by Daniel Lerner at Columbia University) of foreign radio listeners in seven Middle East countries is illuminating. In many villages such people as the grocer who has a radio, or the young bus driver who has seen movies in the capital and can bring news of the great world, are displacing the village elders in positions of leadership. To rise in such a way, these upstarts do not need to acquire the stern discipline typical for the print-oriented person; rather, they need the same equipment American children have who go about in Davy Crockett suits—a willingness, often quite passive and unstrenuous, to let fancy roam at the dictates of the mass media. The political parties of the Middle East are now beginning to make use of this willingness, and as we all know, programs can be fanatically pursued which promise to supply Cadillacs and cinemas to peasants who are told they can have these things without working, just as Americans do, if only they will vote and believe. Thus, in the illiterate masses there tends to be created a new kind of literacy, an often terrifying emotional and political fluency, with all the emancipations of print and hardly any of its restrictions and disciplines.

The movies, of course, are a boundary-annihilating form, easily transmissible past linguistic and cultural barriers (as well as barriers of literacy). They may also be, as Arnold Hauser suggests in *The Social History of Art,* a democratizing form because of their mobility, the absence of traditional stage conventions and properties. Art historians have recently noted that when Renaissance painters shifted the Virgin Mary from frontface to profile it marked a decline of Catholic religiosity and a less devout approach to the Trinity. The camera can be even more impudent, and can put aesthetic laws to use in all kinds of ways, leading the audience, as Hauser says, to the events, rather than

leading and presenting the events to them, with the voyeuristic intimacy which we can see in such a film as Hitchcock's *Rear Window*.
A movie can tell its story as though we are telling it to ourselves, or as
though we are actually dreaming it; it can force us to identify with
its chosen moods and people. The camera, by moving around, subtly
invites us to embrace one character and exclude another; to look up
and feel awe of a hero or fear of a villain; to look down and feel contempt or pity. A sidelong glance of the camera alerts us for trouble; a
right-to-left pan, reversing the righthandedness Hermann Weill discusses in his book on symmetry, invests people and places with a
spooky feeling. I need not labor the catalogue of the director's powers,
aided as they are by the near-hypnotic effect of the concentrated bright-
ness of the screen while other sights and sounds are at a low ebb. The
movie is the novel in motion; it is potentially the least rationalistic,
the most subjectivized medium. And like the broadcast, the rally, or
the fireside council of the tribal chief, it demands attention now, this
minute, in this time and at that place; unlike a book, it cannot wait
for your mood.

Where the movies and the book are both in circulation, the written
word and the screen image compete in making our sensibility mobile
and empathic, though for many of us even now the movies have pretty
well replaced the novel as the powerful medium for anticipatory socialization. Conceivably, when every man has his own movie camera
and home projector, and his own movie library as we now have our
record collections, he will become more critical and less vulnerable—
this being the usual effect of do-it-yourself. Likewise, study of the
movies, as it is encouraged by some of the documentary film societies,
can help put movie-goers in the director's place, permitting them to
be more critical of him.

But all this betokens a society like ours in which radio and film
are cumulative media for the better-educated strata—a society in which
a certain uneasy balance of powers exists among the media, a society
in which the librarians have been vigilant of freedom, while the movie
magnates have generally failed to fight down their fears of the Legion
of Decency and the other censoring groups who to some degree have
tempted the films in the direction of sadism in exchange for the often
circumvented pieties surrounding sex. In the Middle East, where the
movies and radio arrived ahead of the book, there is no such balance—
though I suppose Turkey comes paradoxically closest, where Kemal
Ataturk detached the young from even the literate old by imposing
the Roman script; here the print-oriented are not simply the students
of the Koran but are up-to-date and Westernized.

Oral communication keeps people together, binds people to each
other, while print in our day loosens these bonds, creates space around

people, even isolates them in some ways. People who would simply have been deviants in a preliterate tribe, misunderstanding and mis-understood, can through books establish a wider identity—can under-stand and even undermine the enemies of home and hearth and herd. While the geographic migrations of preliterate peoples have something in common with the incomprehending movement of flocks of deer, the readers of the Age of Discovery were prepared mentally for some of the experiences of their geographic mobility—they had at any rate left home in imagination even if they had not roamed as far or among as strange people as they were actually to meet. The bookish education of these inner-directed men helped harden them for voyages; they wanted to convert the heathen, civilize them, trade with them. If any-one changed in the encounter, it would be the heathen, while they, as they moved about the globe or up the social ladder, remained very much the same men. The epitome of this was the Englishman in the tropics who, all alone, dressed for dinner with home-guard ceremonial, toasted the Queen, and, six months later, read with a proper sense of outrage the leader in the London *Times*. His ties with the world of print helped steady him in his course far from home.

Today, the successors of these men are men molded as much by the mass media outside their formal education as by their schooling; men who are more public-relations-minded than ambitious; men softened for encounters rather than hardened for voyages. If they move about the globe it is often to win the love of the natives or to try to understand their mores, rather than to exploit them for gain or the glory of God. Meanwhile, as we have seen, the natives (as they used to be called) are themselves in many cases on the move, and the sharp differences between societies dependent on the oral tradition and those dependent on print are tending to be less important with the coming of radio and film. Often the decisive difference is among the peasants themselves within a country now moving out of the stage of oral tra-dition—the difference between those who listen to the radio and go to movies and those who shut these things out as the voice of the Devil or as simply irrelevant for them. In the Middle East studies it was found that those peasants who listened to Radio Moscow or the BBC or the VOA already had, or perhaps acquired, a different sensibility from those who did not.

It is too soon, however, to say whether the epoch of print will be utterly elided in the underdeveloped countries, just as, with the com-ing of electrical and atomic energy, they may skip the stage of coal and water power. Conceivably, the movies and broadcasting will eventually help to awaken a hunger for print, when their own novelty is worn off and when they come to be used as tie-ins with print—as in Lyman Bryson's *Invitation to Learning*. Just as the barbarians of Europe in the Middle Ages pulled themselves up by Greek bootstraps, so the non-industrial countries can for a long time draw on the storehouse of Western science and technology, including the science of social organization; and there are still enough inner-directed men in our society who are willing to go out and help build the armies of Iran and the factories of Istanbul.

In this connection, it is striking that the Soviet Union, paying at least nominal heed to the scriptures of Marx and Lenin, has created what is in some ways a replica of the Victorian industrial world rather than the modern consumer world. As a result, treatises on Marxism and Hollywood movies may be seen as alternative lures to the pre-industrial nations, with national pride voting for steel plants and Karl Marx, and personal taste for cars, Coca-Cola, and the stereotype of America. To be sure, Communism may seem the quickest way to the consumers' utopia, with its apparent power to mow down all vested interests, including one's own. I should parenthetically add that the appeal to the consumer mentality in the East, the glamour of America's image, is almost never the result of our official propaganda concerning the alleged "American Way of Life," but is rather a by-product of the characteristic American virtuosity in the newer media and the products of American enterprise they bespeak.

It is apparent that the mass media, like other forms of technological innovation, bring about new polarizations in society and between societies. The readers and the nonreaders, the listeners and the non-listeners, may belong to the same castes, the same economic and social groupings, and yet may slowly diverge as they form different values and tastes and turns of mind. In this way, feudal and other hierarchical forms are upset, with the spread of literacy beyond a small group of clerks; and it is perhaps no accident that self-taught and self-made men like Ben Franklin and Andrew Carnegie should have put such emphasis on libraries: in their day, books were the gunpowder of the mind, the way of nonmilitary glory and social and intellectual mobility.

Today, in contrast, there are many thoughtful Americans who despair of the role of the book as a vehicle either of social enlightenment or of personal mobility. They point to the low percentage of Americans (compared with Danes or Japanese, Britishers or Germans) who ever read a book when through with school; they point to the rarity of book stores (even when we include those that sell mainly greeting cards) and to the financial crisis of the libraries (not to speak of the frequent pressure on them to censor their shelves). The newer media seem in tune with the times in a number of ways; they often require less close attention than a book, and they are "social" in two senses: they are usually viewed in company, and they present celebrities or "just folks" in a kind of pseudo intimacy with the viewer—so much so that for TV performers "sincerity" has become the symbol both of what they admire and of what they are cynical about. Discussion, as in this article, of historical developments sometimes engenders a feeling of inevitability, and a cause, such as that of books, is declared lost because not everyone votes for it and because research brings us the latest returns from the worldwide competitive election campaigns of the several media.

Yet one's own pleasure in books does not rest, beyond a certain break-even point, on the numbers who share such pleasures, but rather on the whole quality of life in a culture. What books can do for that quality, in broadening horizons, in encouraging fantasy, in promoting individuation, can in some measure be done by other media—witness the Third Programme in England, the great post-war Italian films, and some television drama in this country. The newer media can be used to promote empathy and vicariousness in terms of emotional depth, and not simply in terms of political nationalism and consumer-goods sophistication. Even so, what the newer media can seldom do is to promote privacy. As I have just remarked, the people on the TV screen are "company" for the viewer, even if they don't seek to make him a pseudo participant along with the rubberneck studio audience. The people in a book are "company" for the reader in a different sense: to "see" them the reader must make an effort, and he must do so—whatever guidance he gets from critics, teachers, and friends—in relative isolation (in a recent cartoon, one person at a cocktail party asks another if he's read a certain book, and the latter answers "not personally"). In a world which threatens us with a surfeit of people, this role of the book becomes again as important as in the preliterate tribes where, also, there was no escape from others; and, as America becomes one vast continental pueblo, the book—whatever its residual trajectory as a revolutionary social force—comes into its own as a guarantor of that occasional apartness which makes togetherness viable.

Suggested Topics

1. The decline of reading
2. The need for reading skills *and* reading enthusiasms
3. The impact of the newer communication media on our society
4. Are books still the "gunpowder of the mind"?
5. What books mean to me

WRITING AND THE
POWER OF LANGUAGE

COMPOSITION AT THE BARRICADES   *Louis Zahner*

> Head of the English Department at Groton for close to forty
> years, Louis Zahner is in a position to observe the serious
> changes which, as he says, "have worked against the teaching
> and learning of effective English" in the secondary schools in
> the past twenty years.

The present state of English composition is apparently more than
a temporary, local decline that can be arrested and restored by a little
tinkering with teaching and testing here and there in American schools
and colleges. When, in early June,* the congregation of Oxford University rescinded a month-old decision and restored Latin as a compulsory subject on entrance examinations, the case was put by one of
its members: "The decline of Latin in the schools here, and its virtual
disappearance in America, is one cause of a growing incompetence in
the writing of our English. I am thinking of politicians, journalists,
preachers, essayists—and, I fear I must add, learned persons."

The fact that written English is slipping in England as well as in
America suggests that the reasons for the decline may be more deep-
seated than we realize, that the condition may be a symptom of pro-

* [This was in June, 1959. The next year, Oxford again reversed its stand and
dropped Latin requirements—the editors.]

Reprinted from *The Atlantic Monthly*, November, 1959. By permission of the
author.

found changes common to English and American culture. It would be interesting to know whether there are non-English-speaking countries in which the writing of the mother tongue is likewise degenerating.

If the remedy lies in education, it is in education in the broadest sense: in whatever goes on, for better or worse, in the entire life of the pupil, of which the classroom is an almost infinitesimal part. At best, the English teacher must be prepared to take some of the responsibility, most of the initiative, and, when anything goes wrong with language anywhere, all of the blame.

That changes have worked against the teaching and learning of effective English can hardly be doubted. Many of them may still lie hidden. Others are far from established. A few may be reasonably held as certain. In any event, some thought about such changes in the schools and in the society of which they are a part may be a step toward seeing just what the problem is.

The rapid growth in the numbers attending school and college, with the consequent overloading of the teacher, is well known. The question uppermost in the minds of four out of every five high school teachers is this: "How can I teach a class of thirty-five pupils whose I. Q.'s range all the way from eighty to a hundred and forty?"

And the second question is similar to it: "With five classes a day of thirty-five pupils each, how can I assign enough compositions, even short ones, to get anywhere with the teaching of writing?" The teacher might go on: "If my pupils write only one paper a week, I can't honestly read them all. I can only mark the mechanical mistakes, like spelling. That isn't teaching. You must stop to think about what a student writes if you hope to teach him anything about either thinking or writing. You must get into his mind. Teaching composition isn't dealing with words; it's dealing with people. I've given up. I have had to go to workbooks—the self-correcting kind with a teacher's answer booklet."

Smaller classes, with students grouped according to ability and ambition, and fewer of them per teacher are, of course, the only remedy. But the realization of that goal is still far in the future. Meanwhile, what we need is some hardheaded thinking and experimentation on how to do a better job of teaching under conditions as they are and as they are likely to remain for some time.

In his struggle to save the written language, today's teacher of English stands almost alone. There was a time when the study of other subjects called naturally for written reports and essays and, at the least, for written answers of some length on examinations.

The essay test—that is, the examination which demands original thinking and writing—is dead. It had a decent funeral, with orations, and its many mourners have now left the churchyard. But the fall of the essay examination as a college entrance test is perhaps the greatest single cause of the decline of the teaching of composition in the schools. The use of objective tests in schools and for college entrance has not only decreased practice in writing. It has given the schools the idea that the colleges do not put much value any more on a sound training in writing. If a student can enter college without ever having written a composition in his school, is composition worth teaching? Under these conditions, who can blame the teachers for wondering whether writing is any longer one of the essential three R's?

The colleges and their examining agencies are in no way culpable. To save the essay test they have tried every known means and experimented with countless new ones. They have met today's more and more complex and exacting demands of testing for college entrance brilliantly and fairly. In their determination not to direct the schools, however, they have underestimated an inevitable power that they never wished to have. The colleges once exerted considerable influence upon written composition through their entrance examinations; they could, if they would, bring to bear such influence quietly but effectively through other means. If, in doing so, they would unobtrusively consider their obligation to be the improvement of the teaching of composition not only to the college-bound but to every student everywhere who has it in him to think and write straightforward prose, an abandoned salient will have been re-established and widened.

In addition to removing the necessity and the incentive for writing, the objective test has had a less obvious but even more corrosive effect upon writing. Calling for facts and information rather than original thinking, it does not require the student to reach and support generalizations and conclusions of his own. Under its influence, teachers are putting more and more emphasis on memorization of facts and storage of information rather than on understanding. Expressed another way, students do not have much to write about. They can put facts together like glass beads on a string, and if they can do it without making any mistakes, they get the impression that they are writing. Teaching the mechanics and techniques of writing to empty students is an immoral business, a waste of everybody's time.

The only remedy is an increase in the number of enlightened teachers in all subjects, teachers who are bent on educating their pupils, tests or no tests. They will soon discover that the best preparation they can give their students for taking an objective test is to forget the test and to get to work on reading, thinking, and writing. Mere facts and information take care of themselves in the process.

The schools are beset by another difficulty that cripples the teaching of language. It is a commonplace that year by year, subject by subject, more and more ground has to be covered. Not enough of the old can be jettisoned to make room for the new. Hence, to save time, subject matter must be presented condensed and processed. More and more, teaching is by abstractions and prefabricated generalizations and conclusions, not by cases, particulars, or illustrations. There is no time for inductive teaching.

The result is a learning through mere words almost wholly removed from any firsthand experience, even from any suspicion that words have anything to do with experience. They are just words that, at a pinch, can be defined by other words, generalizations that can be supported by other generalizations, or even by a rewording of the same ones. Here are the seeds of what later flowers into pure jargon and rich gobbledygook.

Holding fast the connections between words and the realities of experience is the essence of all use and understanding of language, its use in thinking and in writing and speaking, its understanding in reading and listening. Fortunately, making these connections is a natural process. It is the way a child learns his native language. His first question is, "What is that?" He sees and touches the object before he asks for and is given the word that names it. Later, the question becomes, "What does that word mean?" That is the critical point in his whole education in language. If the answer is given by specific examples within his own experience, he is learning language. If it is given as a rewording in equally abstract and remote words, he is learning incantation.

When this natural process asserts itself in the English classroom it can fare badly. Asked to define "terror," a child naturally says something like "Terror is when you are almost hit by an automobile." The teacher corrects him: "It is wrong to say 'Terror is *when*.'" The learner keeps trying until he gets "Terror is a state of fear approaching panic." He wins an A and the damage is done. Similarly, much isolated vocabulary drill hopefully undertaken by the schools in preparation for aptitude tests is excellent training in the use of language as incantation and as an ornate cloak for vacuity.

The remedy for this lies in the lower grades. Teaching in the eleventh and twelfth grades must continue to be carried on in relatively high abstractions. But in the lower grades, little by little, a habit of mind can be established that will not let any generalization slip by without a quick mental checkup by illustration and example, or any abstraction without a down-to-earth operational definition. Taught and practiced in the grades, the process of relating language to actual experience can become the established way the mind works. There have been and are mature men incapable of thinking in any other way. Mr. Justice Holmes and Judge Learned Hand come readily to mind.

This matter of dealing with abstract words and generalizations is only one detail of a large issue—the teaching of language in the schools. It is an open question whether what is taught in the schools really is the English language.

The idea that English grammar and structure are identical with those of Latin is implicit in much of the teaching, and methods once used for teaching Latin live on under a disguise of very fancy modern dress. Contemporary studies of the language are beginning to take hold, but much remains to be done for, and to, the classroom teacher before he can use them effectively.

The study of the intricate ways of language in the interchange of ideas and feelings—what it can state, what it can suggest; how it can clarify, how mislead; the almost limitless variety of meanings and shades of meaning it can convey—this also is beginning to gain a foothold.

But the linguists and the operationalists (to coin a stand-in for "semanticists," which seems to have taken on an emotional tinge) still work apart and even at cross-purposes. What must come if the English language is to be effectively taught in the schools is a revival of the trivium, the union of grammar, logic, and rhetoric, done into modern English, and with the full enlistment of modern knowledge.

Teachers should also take a new look at usage. The old formalist view that nothing is right unless it conforms to classical grammar and the best literary standards mercifully has gone. In its place, however, is established an equally undiscriminating pronouncement, "Anything goes. If enough people use it, it is right." The obvious exception is made of illiterate expressions which, though clear in meaning, damage the user: "I seen him when he wasn't hardly trying."

In addition to making heroic and mildly manic efforts to banish such expressions, teachers and others keep alive the venerable argument about locutions that depart from traditional grammar but are not as yet fully accepted. It is more generally understood that such usage will in time be accepted and called idiom. The slang dictionary of fifty years ago reads today like a list of literary, even diplomatic phrases. But there is always a line where the advancing front encounters rear-guard action. "It's me" is no sooner in occupied territory than the battle rages at the *like—as* salient.

All this ado is harmless except that, in treating current usage as a matter of manners, not of meanings, it diverts attention from the important issue.

The distinction between inventive and preventive usage is never considered. New usage can be inventive, bringing into the language useful and vitalizing expressions—"egghead," for example. Or it can be preventive, destroying the power of the language to make useful distinctions, or even to express what its users want to say. If, within the space of half an hour, someone hears, as (or, if you prefer, *like*) I recently did, that it is a "terrific" day (the sun was shining, the air balmy), that these new birthday cards are really "terrific," obviously "made up by some artist with a terrific sense of humor," and that a new policy is "a terrific deal insurancewise," what can he call a hurricane that scared him to death and blew his garage roof away? And will he be fully understood and considered to be moderately literate if he says "It doesn't cost me much to run my car" instead of "My car is terrific expensewise"? Or does an admissions officer reading on a candidate's report that "he does not take too much interest in athletics" know for sure whether the writer means that the candidate takes scarcely any interest at all or that he takes a great deal but does not let athletics interfere with his studies? One principal might mean the first, another the second. The admissions officer can only wait and see.

A detailed study of usage that does more than record and count and describe is overdue. The key question is not whether a new expression is considered by so many people to be at this or that level of usage but whether it is inventive or preventive.

The teacher of language, especially of writing, is working under another handicap. The gap between speech and proficent writing is widening. The student does not hear much good, let alone distinguished, English. Reading aloud in the home is an archaic pastime. Conversation is a lost art. Radio and television, their language aimed at catching and entertaining the customer, talk to him in his own easy jargon and patois. There are a few programs on which guests, commentators, and even announcers speak literate English. There are still some great preachers. But all these put together are far outnumbered. The language our pupils hear is not the language from which clear, coherent writing is easily developed.

Nor does the student's reading help his writing much. Radio cut into his reading, though not dangerously; he learned to read against a background of music and voices. Television cuts deeper; it does not mix with reading.

More detrimental to the student's reading than the possible falling off in the amount he reads, however, is the emphasis now put by schools and colleges upon the speed of reading. If he is to get through the amount of reading required by his school and college, he must be trained to read faster. He is drilled to read by eye alone. Hearing in the mind the sound of the language being silently read is a fault that must be overcome.

The result is that writing too becomes the business of the eye alone. The mind's ear grows deaf. Unless the pupil's pen is the tongue of a ready speaker, we cannot hope for even moderately effective writing.

The teacher and poet in Robert Frost spoke together when he wrote: "A dramatic necessity goes deep into the nature of the sentence. Sentences are not different enough to hold the attention unless they are dramatic. No ingenuity of varying structure will do. All that can save them is the speaking tone of voice somehow entangled in the words and fastened to the page for the ear of the imagination. That is all that can save poetry from sing-song, all that can save prose from itself."

Methods for the use of the voice in teaching composition could quite easily be developed. They would include the use of the pupil's own voice in the writing and revision of his work. Supplemented by sound films and recordings made especially for the purpose and by facilities for pupils to read aloud to themselves, they might well help to solve the problem of teaching compositon to large classes and reduce the teacher's overwhelming load of students' papers to correct.

Whatever is done to improve the writing of English must be done in the elementary and secondary schools. The freshman year at college is too late. By that time bad habits have become ingrained and prejudices against writing have been established in the mind of the student who writes badly or has never written at all. But there is a more urgent reason: freshman English does not help the boys and girls who do not go on to college. Even without benefit of the college instructor, they should still somehow be taught the power of articulate speech and articulated writing.

All in all, the high school teacher of composition has his work cut out for him. He is half inventor and explorer, pushing into new territory with whatever tools he can devise. He is half repairman, doing what he can to mend the damage done both in the school itself and in the world of which it is a part. At the moment, he does not appear to be holding his own. He may even be resigned to a retreat so gradual that nobody will recognize it as ultimately a defeat, especially if he calls it "Keeping abreast of the times" or "Adjustment to the modern world."

Paul Diederich, of the Research Division of the Educational Testing Service, writes: "Since I am skeptical of the possibility of widespread improvement in writing except at a rate that is truly glacial, I find myself in sympathy with our committees of outstanding school and college teachers who devise our College Board examinations in writing. They expect very little, they get less, and our scores are based on what college-entering students do, not on what we wish they could do."

It may be that we shall have to accept with grace and a show of gratitude downward-spiraling standards dictated by high school students. It may be that we shall have to rest content with examinations that test a smaller remnant of writing with greater accuracy.

It may be getting late. But it is still far too early to give it all up with a shrug. English teachers are a resourceful, resilient, determined breed. Parents want the best for their children and are willing to find out what that best is.

More and more people are hearing the alert and beginning to realize how much is at stake. It is no less than our survival as a civilized people—perhaps even as a people at all.

For, menacing and obdurate, Caliban still crouches in his cave, the eternal archetype of the savage state of man:

"You taught me language, and my profit on't
Is, I know how to curse."

Suggested Topics

1. Why we don't write as well as we should
2. Essay vs. objective tests
3. The widening gap between spoken and written English
4. Is a knowledge of grammar important?
5. Various levels of English usage
6. Let's go back to the old trivium—grammar, logic and rhetoric.

ENGLISH AS SHE'S NOT TAUGHT   Jacques Barzun

A student of cultural history, Jacques Barzun has written extensively on education, musicology, and criticism, and is now Provost of Columbia University. His books include *Teacher in America* (1945), *God's Country and Mine* (1954), and *The House of Intellect* (1959).

I

At an educational conference held in Vancouver last summer, leaders of the Canadian school system generally agreed that from half to three quarters of their students in the first year of college were

Reprinted from *The Atlantic Monthly*, December, 1953. By permission of the author.

incompetent in grammar, syntax, and analysis of thought. What was notable in the discussion was that nearly every participant used the English language with uncommon force and precision. Any looseness or jargon heard there came from the three American guests, of whom I was one. Most of our hosts—Canadian teachers, principals, supervisors, and university instructors—had obviously gone through the mill of a classical education; the chairman made a mild pun involving Latin and was rewarded with an immediate laugh. Yet they declared themselves unable to pass on their linguistic accomplishment to the present school generation, and they wanted to know why.

In the United States the same complaint and inquiry has been endemic, commonplace, for quite a while. You come across it in the papers. You hear parents, school people, editors and publishers, lawyers and ministers, men of science and of business, lamenting the fact that their charges or their offspring or their employees can neither spell nor write "decent English." The deplorers blame the modern progressive school or the comics or TV; they feel that in school and outside, something which they call discipline is lacking, and they vaguely connect this lack with a supposed decline in morality, an up-surge of "crisis." Like everything else, bad English is attributed to our bad times, and the past (which came to an end with the speaker's graduation from college) is credited with one more virtue, that of literary elegance.

The facts seem to me quite different, the causes much more tangled, and the explanation of our linguistic state at once more complex and less vague. For many years now I have been concerned with the art of writing and kept busy at the invidious task of improving other people's utterance, and I cannot see that performance has deteriorated. The level is low but it has not fallen. As a reader of history I am steadily reminded that the writing of any language has always been a hit-and-miss affair. Here is Amos Barrett, our chief source on the battles of Concord and Lexington: "It wont long before their was other minit Compneys . . . We marched Down about a mild or a mild half and we see them acomming . . ." and so on. An illiterate New England farmer? Not so, since he could write; he had been taught and in some way represents "the past." The question he poses is, how do people write who are not professionals or accomplished amateurs? The answer is: badly, at all times.

Writing is at the very least a knack, like drawing or being facile on the piano. Because everybody can speak and form letters, we mistakenly suppose that good, plain, simple writing is within everybody's power. Would we say this of good, straightforward, accurate drawing? Would we say it of melodic sense and correct, fluent harmonizing at the keyboard? Surely not. We say these are "gifts." Well, so is writing, even the writing of a bread-and-butter note or a simple public notice; and this last suggests that something has happened within the last hundred years to change the relation of the written word to daily life.

Whether it is the records we have to keep in every business and profession or the ceaseless communicating at a distance which modern transport and industry require, the world's work is now unmanageable, unthinkable, without *literature.* Just see how many steps you can take without being confronted with something written or with the necessity of writing something yourself. Having been away for a couple of weeks during the summer, I find a bill from the window washer, who luckily came on a day when the cleaning woman was in the apartment. He has therefore scribbled below the date: "The windows have been cleaned Wed. 12:30 P.M. Your maid was their to veryfey the statement"—perfectly clear and adequate. One can even appreciate the change of tenses as his mind went from the job just finished to the future when I would be reading this message from the past.

Call this bad writing if you like, it remains perfectly harmless. The danger to the language, if any, does not come from such trifles. It comes rather from the college-bred millions who regularly write and who in the course of their daily work circulate the prevailing mixture of jargon, cant, vogue words, and loose syntax that passes for prose. And the greater part of this verbiage is published, circulated, presumably read. A committee won't sit if its drivelings are not destined for print. Even an interoffice memo goes out in sixteen copies and the schoolchildren's compositions appear verbatim in a mimeographed magazine. Multiply these cultural facts by the huge number of activities which (it would seem) exist only to bombard us with paper, and you have found the source of the belief in a "decline" in writing ability—no decline at all, simply the infinite duplication of dufferism. This it is which leads us into false comparisons and gloomy thoughts.

II

The apparent deterioration of language is a general phenomenon which is denounced throughout Western Europe. One had only to read the Catalogue of the British Exhibition of 1951 to see the common symptoms in England. Sir Ernest Gowers's excellent little book of a few years earlier, *Plain Words,* was an attempt to cure the universal disease in one congested spot, the Civil Service, which is presumably the most highly educated professional group in Britain.

In France, the newspapers, the reports of Parliamentary debates, and the literary reviews show to what extent ignorance of forms and insensitivity to usage can successfully compete against a training obsessively aimed at verbal competence. And by way of confirmation, M. Jean Delorme, a native observer of the language in French Canada, recently declared the classic speech "infected" on this side of the Atlantic too. As for Germany, a foreign colleague and correspondent of mine, a person of catholic tastes and broad judgment, volunteers the opinion that "people who cultivate good pure German are nowadays generally unpopular, especially among the devotees of newspaper fiction and articles. The universal barbarism of language has already gone well into the grotesque."

So much for the democratic reality. But great as has been the effect of enlarged "literacy," it does not alone account for what is now seen as linguistic decadence. The educated, in fact the leaders of modern thought, have done as much if not more to confuse the judgment. For what is meant by the misnomer "pure speech" is simply a habit of respect toward usage, which insures a certain fixity in vocabulary, forms, and syntax. Language cannot stand still, but it can change more or less rapidly and violently. During the last hundred years, nearly every intellectual force has worked, in all innocence, against language. The strongest, science and technology, did two damaging things: they poured quantities of awkward new words into the language and this in turn persuaded everybody that each new thing must have a name, preferably "scientific." These new words, technical or commercial, were fashioned to impress, an air of profundity being imparted by the particularly scientific letters $k, x,$ and $o = $ Kodak, Kleenex, Sapolio. The new technological words that came in were sinful hybrids like "electrocute" and "triphibian," or misunderstood phrases like "personal equation," "nth degree," or "psychological moment"—brain addlers of the greatest potency.

The passion for jargon was soon at its height, from which it shows no sign of descending. Every real or pseudo science poured new verbiage into the street, every separate school or -ism did likewise, without shame or restraint. We can gauge the result from the disappearance of the Dictionary properly so called. Consult the most recent and in many ways the best of them, *Webster's New World Dictionary,* and what you find is a miniature encyclopedia filled with the explanation of initials, proper names, and entries like "macrosporangium" or "abhenry," which are not and never will be words of the English language.

Under the spate of awe-inspiring vocables, the layman naturally felt that he too must dignify his doings and not be left behind in the race for prestige. Common acts must suggest a technical process. Thus we get "contact" and "funnel" as workaday verbs—and "process" itself: "we'll process your application"—as if it were necessary to name the steps or choices of daily life with scientific generality. I know a young businessman who makes jottings of his business thoughts; when he has enough on one topic he *folderizes* them.

What is wrong with all this is not merely that it is new, heedless, vulgar, and unnecessary (all signs of harmful vice in a language) but that jargon swamps thought. The habit of talking through cant words destroys the power of seeing things plain. "I'll contact you to finalize the agreement." What does it mean? The drift is plain enough, but compare: "I'll call at your office to sign the contract." The former raises no clear image or expectation, the latter does. Moreover, the former smells of inflated ego, it fills the mouth in a silly bumptious way.

But who cares? Why fuss?—good questions both. Nobody cares much because—we all think—it's the deed (or the thing) that counts, not the words. This conviction, too, is a product of modern technology, and its effect is great though unremarked. The power of words over nature, which has played such a role in human history, is now an exploded belief, a dead emotion. Far from words controlling things, it is now things that dictate words. As soon as science was able to chop up the physical world and recombine it in new forms, language followed suit; and this not only among scientists making up new vocables, but among the supposed guardians of the language, the poets and men of letters. It is highly significant that around 1860 writers deliberately began to defy usage and turn syntax upside down. Lewis Carroll and Edward Lear made good fun with it; "obscure" poets such as Rimbaud sought new depths of meaning. There was in this a strong impulse to destroy all convention, for Victorian moralism had made the idea of conventionality at once suspect and hateful. The revolt succeeded and its spirit is still alive; novelty-hunting is now a linguistic virtue, or to express it differently, a common influence is at work in Jabberwocky and James Joyce, in the scientist's lingo and in the advertiser's "Dynaflow," "Hydramatic," or "Frigidaire"—which end by becoming household words. In short, modern man is feeling his oats as the manipulator of objects and he shows it in his manhandling of words.

This helps to explain why the predominant fault of the bad English encountered today is not the crude vulgarism of the untaught but the blithe irresponsibility of the taught. The language is no longer regarded as a common treasure to be hoarded and protected as far as possible. Rather, it is loot from the enemy to be played with, squandered, plastered on for one's adornment. Literary words imperfectly grasped, meanings assumed from bare inspection, monsters spawned for a trivial cause—these are but a few of the signs of squandering. To give examples: the hotel clerk giving me a good room feels bound to mention the well-known person whom "we last hospitalized in that room." Not to lag behind Joyce, the advertiser bids you "slip your feet into these easy-going *leisuals* and breathe a sigh of real comfort."

Undoubtedly these strange desires are often born of the need to ram an idea down unwilling throats. We all fear our neighbor's wandering attention and try to keep him awake by little shocks of singularity, or again by an overdose of meaning. Unfortunately, novelty-hunting proceeds from the known to the unknown by a leap of faith. "It was pleasant," writes the author of very workmanlike detective stories, "to watch her face and find his resentment *vitiate* as he made excuses for her."

III

The notable fact is that all this occurs in printed books, written by writers, published (usually) by first-rate firms that employ editors. In speech, the same blunders and distortions come from educated people. It is all very well to say, as one expert has confidently done, that "what certain words really mean is moving toward what they seem to mean," the implication being that after a while everything will be in place. Actually, this leaves meaning nowhere, if only because we're not all moving in step. The *New Yorker* spotted a movie theater sign on which "adultery" was used to mean "adulthood." From an English periodical I learn that some new houses "*affront* the opposite side of the street." If Mrs. Malaprop is going to become the patron saint of English, what is going to prevent "contention" from meaning the same thing as "contentment" or the maker of woodcuts from being called a woodcutter?

There is no getting around it: meaning implies convention, and the discovery that meanings change does not alter the fact that when convention is broken misunderstanding and chaos are close at hand. Mr. Churchill has told how Allied leaders nearly came to blows because of the single word "table," a verb which to the Americans meant dismiss from the discussion, whereas to the English, on the contrary, it meant put on the agenda. This is an extraordinary instance, and the vagaries of those who pervert good words to careless misuse may be thought more often ludicrous than harmful. This would be true if language, like a great maw, could digest anything and dispose of it in time. But language is not a kind of ostrich. Language is alive only by a metaphor drawn from the life of its users. Hence every defect in the language is a defect in somebody.

For language is either the incarnation of our thoughts and feelings or a cloak for their absence. When the ordinary man who has prepared a report on sales up to June 30 rumbles on about "the frame of reference in which the co-ordination campaign was conceived," he is filling the air with noises, not thoughts.

For self-protection, no doubt, the contemporary mind is opposed to all this quibbling. It speaks with the backing of popular approval when it says: "Stop it! You understand perfectly well what all these people mean. Don't be a dirty purist looking under the surface and meddling with democratic self-expression." To haggle over language *is* quibbling of course. All precision is quibbling, whether about decimals in mathematics or grains of drugs in prescriptions—fairly important quibbles. The question is whether in language the results justify the quibble. Well, the public is here the best judge, and it is evident that as a consumer of the written word, the public is always complaining that it cannot understand what it is asked to read: the government blanks, the instructions on the bottle or gadget, the gobbledygook of every trade, the highbrow jargon of the educators, psychiatrists, and social workers, and—one must also add—the prose of literary critics. The great cry today is for improved communication, mass communication, the arts of communication, and yet under the pretext of being free and easy and above quibbling, those who do the most talking and writing indulge themselves in the very obscurities and ambiguities that cause the outcry.

They are abetted, moreover, by another offspring of the scientific spirit, the professional student of language. In his modern embodiment, the linguist takes the view that whatever occurs in anybody's speech is a fact of language and must not be tampered with, but only caught in flight and pinned on a card. This is "scientific detachment," and it has gone so far that under its influence in many schools all the categories of grammar, syntax, and rhetoric have been discarded. The modern way to learn English or a foreign language is to absorb a phrase-by-phrase enumeration of all that might conceivably be said in ordinary talk—a directory instead of a grammar.

This brings us back to our first difficulty, how to teach the millions the use of their mother tongue *in composition*. We have made nearly everybody literate in the sense of able to read and write words. But that is not writing. Even those who profess disdain for the literary art and the literary quibbles respond automatically to good writing, which they find unexpectedly easy to read and retain, mysteriously "pleasant" as compared with their neighbors' matted prose. The linguists themselves pay lip service to "effective" speech, approving the end while forbidding discrimination among the means.

Now many thousands of people in the United States today exercise this discrimination; there is amid the garbage a steady supply of good writing, modestly done and published—in every newspaper and magazine, over TV and radio, in millions of ads and public notices, in railroad timetables, travel booklets, and printed instructions on objects of daily use. Good writing is good writing wherever it occurs, and some of the impugned comics which are supposed to defile the native well of English in our young are far better than acceptable.

It is therefore idle and erroneous to condemn "the newspapers" or "the radio" en masse. Here too one must discriminate, and the failure to do so is one cause of the trouble—the strange cultural trait whose origin I have sketched and which makes us at once indifferent to our language, full of complaints about it, and irresponsible about mangling it still more. In these conditions people who write well learn to do so by virtue of a strong desire, developed usually under necessity: their job requires lucidity, precision, brevity. If they write advertising copy they must not only make it fit the space but make the words yield the tone.

Tone—that is the starting point of any teaching in composition. What effect are you producing and at what cost of words? The fewer the words, and the more transparent they are, the easier they will be to understand. The closer the ideas they stand for and the more natural their linkage, the more easily will the meaning be retained. Simple in appearance, this formula is yet extremely difficult to apply, and even more arduous to teach. You cannot work on more than one pupil at a time and you must be willing to observe and enter into his mind. On his part, the discipline calls for a thorough immersion in the medium. He must form the habit of attending to words, constructions, accents, and etymologies in everything he read or hears—just as the painter unceasingly notes line and color and the musician tones. The would-be writer has the harder task because words are entangled with the business of life and he must stand off from it to look at them, hearing at the same time their harmonies and discords. It is an endless duty, which finally becomes automatic. The ideal writer would mentally recast his own death sentence as he was reading it—if it was a bad sentence.

IV

Now such a discipline cannot be imposed from without, and not everybody needs it in full. But its principle, which suffices for ordinary purposes, should be made clear to every beginner, child or adult. Unfortunately, the school system, even when progressive, makes writing an irrational chore approached in the mood of rebellion. The school does this in two ways: by requiring length and by concentrating on correctness. I know very well that correctness was supposedly given up long ago. The modern teacher does not mention it. But if the teacher marks spelling and grammatical errors and speaks of little else, what is a child to think? He gets a mark with the comment "imaginative" or "not imaginative enough" and most often: "too short," and he is left with no more idea of composition than a cow in a field has of landscape painting. How *does* one judge the right length and get it out of a reluctant brain? Nobody answers, except perhaps with the word "creative," which has brought unmerited gloom to many a cheerful child. Who can be creative on demand, by next Tuesday, and in the requisite amount? In all but a few chatterboxes, mental frostbite is the only result.

Meanwhile the things that are teachable, the ways of translating the flashes of thought into consecutive sentences, are neglected. They have been, most often, neglected in the teachers themselves. How do *they* write or speak, what do *they* read? If they read and write educational literature, as they often must for advancement, are they fit to teach composition? And what of the teachers of other subjects, whose professional jargon also infects their speech, what is their countervailing effect on a child to whom a good English teacher has just imparted a notion of the writer's craft? Suppose the teacher of a course on family life has just been reading *Social Casework* and his mind is irradiated with this: "Familial societality is already a settled question biologically, structured in our inherited bodies and physiology, but the answer to those other questions are not yet safely and irrevocably anatomized." Unless this is immediately thrown up like the nux vomica it is, it will contaminate everybody it touches from pupil to public—in fact the whole blooming familial societality.

The cure is harsh and likely to be unpopular, for it must start with self-denial. It can be initiated by the school but it must not stop there. As many of us as possible must work out of our system, first, all the vogue words that almost always mean nothing but temporary vacancy of mind—such words as "basic," "major," "over-all," "personal," "values," "exciting" (everything from a new handbag to a new baby); then all the wormy expressions indicative of bad conscience, false modesty, and genteelism, as in: "Frankly, I don't know too much about it"—a typical formula which tries through candor and whining to minimize ignorance while claiming a kind of merit for it; finally, all the tribal adornments which being cast off may disclose the plain man we would like to be: no frames of reference, field theories, or apperception protocols; no texture, prior to, or in terms of; and the least amount of co-ordination, dynamics, and concepts.

After the vocabulary has been cleansed, the patient is ready for what our Canadian friends at the Vancouver conference deplored the lack of in the modern undergraduate: analysis of thought. To show what is meant and let criticism begin at home, I choose an example from a New York City report of 1952 entitled "The English Language Arts." It begins: "Because language arts or English is so—" Stop right there! What are language arts?—A perfectly unnecessary phrase of the pseudo-scientific kind which tries to "cover." Besides, "language arts or English" is nonsense: ever hear of another language? Moreover, "language arts . . . is" doesn't sound like a happy opening for a report by and to English teachers. Let us go on: English is so what? Well, "language arts or English is so intimately connected with all knowledge and all living, it is the subject which most often bursts the dikes separating it from others." What do you mean, language is *connected* with living? And how does English connect with *all* knowledge and *all* living? Is the practical knowledge of the Russian engineer intimately connected with English? Do the amoebas speak English? And if this intimacy does exist, then what are these dikes that separate English from other subjects? Are these subjects not part of "all knowledge" with which English is connected—or rather, of which it too is a part?

Cruel work, but necessary if anything akin to thought is to arise from the written word. The Neanderthal glimmer from which the quoted sentence sprang is irrecoverable but its developed form should run something like this: "English, being a medium of communication, cannot be confined within set limits like other subjects; to the peoples whose speech it is, all theoretical knowledge, and indeed most of life, is inseparable from its use."

And this is so true that it justifies the operation just performed on the specimen of non-thought. For although it is possible to think without words and to communicate by signs, our civilization depends, as I said before, on the written word. Writing is embodied thought, and the thought is clear or muddy, graspable or fugitive, according to the purity of the medium. Communication means one thought held in common. What could be more practical than to try making that thought unmistakable?

As for the receiver, the reader, his pleasure or grief is in direct proportion to the pains taken by the writer; to which one can add that the taking of pains brings its special pleasure. I do not mean the satisfaction of vanity, for after a bout of careful writing one is too tired to care; I mean the new perceptions—sensuous or intellectual or comic—to be had all day long in one's encounters with language. Imagine the fun people miss who find nothing remarkable in the sentence (from Sax Rohmer): "The woman's emotions were too tropical for analysis"; or who, trusting too far my disallowance of "contact" as a verb, miss the chance of using it at the hottest, stickiest time of year: "On a day like this, I wouldn't contact anybody for the world."

Suggested Topics

1. Are good writers born—or made?
2. Is a knowledge of grammar important?
3. The "blithe irresponsibility of the taught"
4. Gobbledygook in government (or academic) prose
5. English as it's taught in high school
6. Informal vs. formal English

FELL SWOOP ON A FINE CLICHÉ KETTLE   *Bergen Evans*

Since 1942 a Professor of English at Northwestern University, Bergen Evans has attained a national reputation through his appearances on television and radio as an authority on English usage and popular fallacies. He has written on eighteenth-century English literature and is co-author of *A Dictionary of Contemporary American Usage.*

Clichés flourish in our speech like crab grass in our lawns. Perhaps the sober times we live in have something to do with it. Without being entirely conscious of the fact, we lean toward the sententious, the emptily formal. Often it looks as if we did not want to use words at all, but only the husks of words to serve as recognition signals, pass-words into the group, indications of not-too-committal amiability.

We are not wholly to blame. The torrent of printed and broadcast wordage that is dumped over us every day exceeds all possibility of fresh supply. The happiest day in the history of the language never produced one-thousandth of what the press and radio and television pour out every hour. And since most of this stuff is prepared in furious haste, it is bound to be repetitious, woven of the worn phrases that come to jaded minds writing under compulsion about things that don't really interest them. Ninety per cent of what the public reads and hears is expressed in fossilized fragments of once-living phrases.

There are times, of course, when triteness is not merely excusable, but a means to an end. One becomes forcibly aware of that fact during an election year such as this. Politicians, civic leaders and other such declaimers find clichés useful to avoid meaning and to win audiences. Before the third cliché has been delivered—usually around the end of the first sentence—the auditors relax, perceiving that they are listening to a sound man who is full of recognizable wisdom.

Reprinted from *The New York Times Magazine,* July 27, 1958. By permission of *The New York Times* and the author.

They know they are in the presence of a man who gets down to brass tacks, hits the nail on the head and doesn't beat about the bush; a man who means business, who is fully aware that although we have entered the atomic age we have not relinquished the faith of our fathers, and who believes that although we cannot rest upon our laurels we must not rush in where angels fear to tread. Such a speaker is a man after their own hearts. He has his feet on the ground. He knows the score.

The mark of a cliché is this intrinsic meaninglessness. Once it may have been clever or brilliantly precise or movingly passionate; chances are it was, or it wouldn't have been repeated so often. But after the ten-billionth repetition it no longer startles or shocks or amuses or excites. It simply doesn't register; it has become a conglomerate of syllables which the mouth pronounces while the mind rests.

Originally, most clichés had meaning beyond that of plain words. But all this has been battered out of them, and their use characterizes the user as a mere parroter of musty turns of phrase—and as a dull person at the very moment he wants to be thought witty.

Thus, when John Bogart told a young reporter on The New York Sun sixty years ago, "When a dog bites a man, that is not news, because it happens so often. But if a man bites a dog that is news," he hit on a felicitous illustration that tickled the national fancy. Bogart was to be congratulated. And the first hundred million or so who repeated his words were to be envied for getting a good thing cheap. But when one hears them now, usually accompanied by the speaker's self-gratulatory chuckle, they can only be received with stoicism.

Many clichés are alliterative. Our minds seem to file our vocabularies in alphabetical order and if we scoop up a word carelessly it often brings with it another word beginning with the same consonant. It is not the thoughtful but the thoughtless who say *cool as a cucumber, slow but sure, rack and ruin, bag and baggage.*

And there are clichés that once were proverbs. But proverbs and clichés differ in the most fundamental way that forms of speech can differ: proverbs concentrate a people's wisdom, clichés concentrate their *lack* of thought.

Some have tried to defend clichés on the ground that, if usage establishes anything, they are surely established. If usage, they say, can change the meaning of words, alter grammar and gain acceptance for idioms that defy logic and grammar, surely it also makes clichés acceptable. But the difference is that usage has given the words and idioms their meaning; whereas overuse has drained clichés of theirs. So that those who insist that clichés must be accepted on this ground are arguing that there is no difference between meaning and nonmeaning.

How worn many phrases that we hear daily actually are can scarcely be believed. It was said of ancient Athens that it was a wonderful place to visit but one wouldn't want to live there!

Jonathan Swift—our first cliché expert—published in 1738 a frightening book entitled "Complete Collection of Genteel Conversation * * * Now Used in the Best Companies of England," in which he gathered a huge heap of moldy platitudes, stale witticisms and meaningless tag ends of phrases to show what passed for sprightly talk among the members of the smart set of his time. And what makes the book frightening is that one could swear that most of it had been tape-recorded yesterday. Such tag ends as "talk of the devil," "It's all in the day's work" and "a sight for sore eyes." Such profundities as "Marriages are made in heaven," "You can't have your cake and eat it" and "Oh, the wonderful works of nature, that a black hen should lay a white egg" (William Jennings Bryan wowed the Chautauqua circuits with that one for forty years). Such gastronomic witticisms as "I love it [some food], but it doesn't love me" and "He was a bold man that first ate an oyster."

Swift assured the reader that "there is not one single witty phrase in the whole collection which hath not received the stamp and approbation of at least one hundred years."

But then, as now, there was one use of clichés so satisfying that it almost justified their existence: as the basis of a great deal of wit. The familiarity of a cliché can be relied on to lead the listener's or hearer's mind into a definite groove where the wit can lie in wait for him. The opening words suggest an inevitable conclusion and in the expectation of this inevitability is the wit's chance.

So Oscar Wilde's "Punctuality is the thief of time," Samuel Butler's "It's better to have loved and lost than never to have lost at all," and Addison Mizener's "None but the brave desert the fair."

Exquisite wits will sometimes use a cliché unaltered, but in a context where its common meaning becomes ludicrous. And sometimes, most delicious of all, where its literal and original meaning is thrust upon us with unexpected freshness and force. Thus Clifton Fadiman, speaking of the cool reception accorded the first number of "Pickwick," says that it was successful "only in a Pickwickian sense."

But these, of course, are anti-clichés, golden transmutations of some of the world's dullest lead. Intent is all. If a phrase has meaning for speaker and hearer, then no matter how often it may have been uttered, it is not a cliché. No one who heard Edward VIII's abdication broadcast can forget the pathos of the opening "At long last." All triteness was purged and the hackneyed phrase was vibrant with meaning.

When the writer or speaker has his metaphor vividly in mind, he isn't using a cliché. Haystacks do not come naturally to our urban minds, and it has been centuries since jack was a generic term for men.

But if one actually thinks of a needle in a haystack as an effective trope for something difficult to find, or of a jack-of-all-trades as a concise and vivid way of describing a man of many abilities but few talents, then he should speak these words.

If the phrase is sincerely meant, spoken deliberately with a full awareness of its exact meaning and its shopworn state, or gaily borrowed in ridicule, it is not a cliché, no matter how often it has been spoken. It is a cliché only when it comes without meaning, though often with a most pompous pretense of meaning, from an unmeaning mind.

Watch That Cliché

Clichés crop up frequently in table talk and have a blighting effect on the conversation. Here are some questions that may be used to get the talk moving naturally again. They are guaranteed to infuriate the cliché user and to annoy the hostess.

—B.E.

1. What is the difference between *kith* and *kin?*

2. When things are *touch and go,* what touches and what goes?

3. Is a *moot* meet, or could a meet be moot?

4. Does a *Cheshire cat* have exceptional risibilities?

5. Is the *fell* of *one fell swoop* akin to *felony,* a *woolfell* (i.e., a hide) or the past of the verb *to fall?*

6. Use *minion* of the phrase *minion of the law* in any other context.

7. What shade of color lies *beyond the pale?*

8. Are *palmy days* connected with palm trees or the inner surface of the hand?

9. What is the distinction between *bag* and *baggage?*

10. The halcyon is a kingfisher. What are *halcyon days?*

11. What causes a *flash in the pan*—gold teeth?

12. Was *Job's turkey* impoverished or feeble?

13. When you *steal someone's thunder* what do you do with his lightning?

14. To what *manner* was who born?

15. When you give someone *the cold shoulder,* do you turn your back with chilly disdain or offer him an unheated hunk of mutton?

Answers

1. *Kith* are those known to you, *kin* those related to you.

2. The keel of a ship touches a reef or sandbar and the ship still moves.

3. The *moot* was an Anglo-Saxon assembly for argument and discussion.

4. Nobody knows. Some think that a whimsical (or incompetent) painter of inn signs in Cheshire depicted his lions rampant with too amiable countenances.

5. *Felony.*

6. *Minion*=darling. It is akin (just to confuse matters further) with the *mignon* of *filet mignon.*

7. *Pale* here=paling.

8. Palm trees.

9. *Baggage*=the property of an army collectively; *bag*=the property of the individual soldier.

10. The seven days preceding and the seven days following the winter solstice.

11. The firing of the priming powder only, in a flintlock musket.

12. Feeble.

13. Nothing. The thunder here was caused by shaking a sheet of tin or rolling wooden balls in a trough, in the theatre.

14. Hamlet, to the custom of drinking too much and firing off cannon to celebrate drunken orgies.

15. The mutton.

Suggested Topics

1. "But what has he said?"
2. The art of saying nothing at length
3. Clichés as a propaganda device
4. When a cliché is not a cliché
5. An analysis of a political speech

GREAT CLICHÉ DEBATE (CONT.)   *Joseph Wood Krutch*

Until his retirement as Brander Matthews Professor of the
Drama at Columbia University, Dr. Joseph Wood Krutch has
had a distinguished career as a scholar, critic, and teacher. He
has written extensively on contemporary culture and ethics,
and for many years was drama critic of *The Nation*.

For some years now I have been letting Bergen Evans correct my
errors and set me right on all sorts of matters involving fact and
opinion. But worms will turn and I reached my turning point when I
read his warning against clichés in the July 27 issue of this magazine.
Mr. Evans went out on a limb (if I may coin a phrase) and then let
someone cut it off near the trunk.

Challenged to find something better than the phrase "Jack-of-all-
trades," which he reprehended, he was unable to come up with anything better than "One who can turn his hand to any (or to many
kinds of) work." And I don't believe even he thinks that preferable.
"Jack-of-all-trades" may, as he says, have long ceased to be vivid or
original; but his substitute never was. And it is fourteen words instead
of four. That is going a long way about to avoid a phrase which is
clear, exact and universally understood. The same may be said of
"brass tacks," "have your cake and eat it, too" and his other examples
of phrases to be avoided.

In the two paragraphs I have just written there are at least five
other clichés, but I submit that every one of them is economical and
perspicuous. To those who still prefer one of Mr. Evans' clumsy
periphrases I can only reply that "one man's meat is another man's
poison." Or, as Mr. Evans would perhaps put it, "That which, to one

Reprinted from *The New York Times Magazine*, August 31, 1958. By permission
of *The New York Times* and the author.

individual, has a pleasant flavor and is at the same time nourishing may be both distasteful and positively noxious to another."

Actually, neither "Jack-of-all-trades" nor "brass tacks" is a cliché in the most precise meaning of the term. Both started out as fresh metaphor. Then, possibly, there was a time when both had become real clichés—that is to say, phrases still used with a certain air of being novel when they were already very familiar. But by now they have passed beyond that stage. When you hear "brass tacks" you no longer think of a tack at all. It is not now a stale metaphor but simply an accepted term and no more objectionable than any familiar word used over and over again because it is both *pre*cise and *con*cise— the last two words being, by the way, a couple of clichés since the one means literally "cut off" and the other "cut short."

A very important part of the standard vocabulary is composed of words that were originally metaphors, though many of them are now unrecognized as such except by philologists. Is "dependent" a cliché to be avoided because it means "hanging from"? Should we refuse to say "palliate" because it means "cover with a cloak," "astonish" because it means "struck by thunder" or "lunatic" because it means "struck by the moon"? Their origins may be hidden by the fact that they are borrowed from a foreign language, but "brass tacks" is almost as much a word and almost as little a mere, tired metaphor as any of the examples from the Latin. And it is no more reprehensible. How about, to give a few more random examples, "easel," "sincere," "martinet," "assassin," "etiquette," "glamour," "sabotage" or "ostracize"? If we refused all such words, we should be hard put to it to express any abstract or general idea. Anyone who is determined to avoid everything that is, by Mr. Evans' definition, a cliché, had better know no Latin and stay away from dictionaries or he will find it difficult to say anything at all.

When a cliché really is objectionable, it is rarely only because it is familiar expression. Usually, it is inept; it does not accurately convey what the user means to say. Or else it is open to some other objection— as when, for instance, the speaker brings it out with a flourish or a chuckle (e. g. "*Cherchez la femme,* as the French say") as though unaware that it is no longer surprising or witty and has become merely useful instead. "Allergic to" may some day be inoffensive—but not now, if the speaker thinks he is being up-to-date and "smart." Almost equally objectionable are phrases used as meaningless substitutes for either shorter phrases or single words, as when we say "besetting sin" and "common or garden" when we do not mean anything more than "sin" and "common."

Metaphors that recently were striking but are now in the twilight zone between genuine metaphor and mere familiar term are especially likely to be used inappropriately or to trick the users into a mixed metaphor just because the metaphorical sense is almost, but not quite, lost. "Bottlenecks must be ironed out" and "The economy of the Ruhr is bound to move within a vicious circle of bottlenecks" (both quoted in Sir Ernest Gower's "Plain Words") are howlingly absurd, not because "bottleneck" should nearly always be avoided or because even "vicious circle" is sometimes not an accurate term; they are grotesque because bottlenecks are not ironed out and they don't move in circles, vicious or not. It is hardly necessary to add that a familiar phrase should not be used unless one can get it straight and knows what it really means. To have said "like Caesar's wife, all things to all men" was a unique achievement in ineptitude; but "psychological moment," for instance, and "to the manner born" seem to be more often used wrongly than rightly.

Anyone who undertakes to write about how one should write is sticking his neck out—if Mr. Evans will pardon the expression. And, like pretty nearly everyone who has attempted it, Mr. Evans gives us some unintentional examples of what to avoid almost as striking as his precepts. As Jacques Barzun pointed out in a recent review of Bergen and Cornelia Evans' "Dictionary of Contemporary American Usage," an enemy of the trite phrase should not refer to someone as being "cheerfully unaware" or characterize a locution as "the darling of the pompously ignorant."

To lump together, as is done in the same dictionary, "wear and tear," "tilting at windmills" and "more in sorrow than in anger" as equally objectionable is to overlook important differences. In many contexts, "wear and tear" would be hardly more objectionable than "brass tacks." Whether "tilting at windmills" is or is not acceptable will often depend upon just how specifically it is appropriate. "More in sorrow than in anger" is usually a mere parroting of literacy at fifth hand.

Mr. Evans' besetting sin is (tut, tut, please strike out "besetting") his frequent failure to make distinctions—either those already mentioned or various others. When, for instance, he writes, "The mark of the cliché is [its] intrinsic meaninglessness * * * It simply doesn't register," he is forgetting that while "brass tacks" or, say, "pig in a poke" may not register as the metaphors they once were, they are far from being meaningless. They do, in fact, convey meaning and are preferable to the kind of roundabout substitutes he offers us.

And when he cites from an imaginary political speech the declamation that "although we cannot rest on our laurels we must not rush in where angels fear to tread," he does not sufficiently stress that while the clichés may be objectionable for other reasons, what is most offensive is the fact that the speaker is not saying anything at all. Clichés may be made to conceal the absence of thought as well as to express thought; but that is equally true of all words. We would not think the speech of Mr. Evans' politician any better if, having determined to avoid clichés, he substituted for "rush in where angels fear to tread" something like "hastily embark upon a course of action men wiser than ourselves would hesitate to enter upon without mature consideration."

Determine to avoid clichés at all costs and you are almost certain to be led into gobbledygook. To say that the race is not always to the swift nor the battle to the strong may be to adopt a cliché. But it is still preferable to George Orwell's translation into gobbledygook: "Success or failure in competitive activities exhibits no tendency to be commensurate with innate capacity." Fowler gives five rules for good writing, of which the first three are to prefer the familiar word to the far-fetched, the concrete word to the abstract, and the single word to the circumlocution. Orwell's burlesque translation violates all three.

The greatest of all faults in writing is obscurity. The greatest single cause of all the other faults is self-consciousness. That is why even good rules often do as much harm as they do good until following them has become a habit rather than the result of conscious effort. Winston Churchill's secretary must have put a great deal of thought into how to avoid ending a certain sentence with a preposition before he achieved the result that led his employer to pencil in the margin. "This is the kind of English up with which I will not put." And I shudder to think (another good cliché) of the prolixities into which some may be led in their effort to avoid every thing Mr. Evans stigmatizes as a cliché. Clichés, of course, are often painful. But I am not here going to be shamed out of saying that "the remedy is often worse than the disease."

A cliché is, in the realm of speech, what a platitude is in the realm of belief, and each has become what it is for a similar reason: the one because it is so true and the other because it is so useful. A wise man will not scorn the one nor a good writer the other. That honesty is the best policy is a platitude to which it is sometimes necessary to call attention, and when it is there is no better way of stating the platitude than by means of the cliché.

G. K. Chesterton once wrote that there are two ways of being a slave to public opinion. One way is to be afraid to disagree with it and the other is to be afraid to agree. Superior people, as he did not find it necessary to add, are particularly prone to the second fear. And that is equally true of the cliché and the platitude. Paradox and wit are delightful, but they do not always wear well. Oscar Wilde's "Nothing succeeds like excess" was brilliant as phraseology and as a half-truth. It was far better than "Nothing succeeds like success" the first time it was

said. But not the fiftieth. And to use it once more with the idea that
one is being clever is to use a cliché far more objectionable than the
one it parodied.

Neither Mr. Evans' rules nor mine are going to eliminate all dispute. It is always said that the cultivated writer and the cultivated
reader are the final judges, but there will still be cases when men with
equally good claims to one designation or the other will disagree.
One of them may have heard a certain phrase more often, or may
differ with the other as to whether it has ceased to be a tired metaphor
and become, like "palliate" or "astonish," merely the best way of
conveying a meaning.

Bernard Shaw, certainly not a careless writer, used "throw out the
baby with the bath," though this happens to be one of Fowler's examples of really overworked phrases. I do not know how we could decide
who, in this case, should be followed. But I do think it is very much
worth while to attempt discrimination rather than to denounce every
familiar phrase under a "blanket indictment"—which is one more good
cliché to end with.

Suggested Topics

1. Precisely what is a cliché?
2. The tongue in Professor Krutch's cheek
3. If we had to avoid every cliché . . .
4. "The remedy may be worse than the disease."
5. Some clichés I'd like to avoid
6. "Gobbledygook" may be the alternative.

"NO-ENGLISH": Why College Students Can't Write Their Native Tongue   Willard Thorp

A Professor of English at Princeton University, Dr. Willard
Thorp has written extensively on Restoration literature and on
American literature of the eighteenth and nineteenth centuries.
His edition of Melville's *Moby Dick* is highly regarded.

I have been red-pencilling student papers for a good many years
and I ought by now to have become resigned or cynical. But I am
not, and the reason for my present concern is a sinister change in the
kind of writing we have lately been getting from our students.

Reprinted from *The Wall Street Journal*, November 11, 1958; condensed from
the *Princeton Alumni Weekly*. By permission of *The Wall Street Journal* and the
author.

We are now too often presented with a kind of prose—if that is the name for it—which is inviolable. A red-pencil used against it becomes as impotent as a sword in a folk-tale which has had a spell put on it. Sometimes this prose resembles remotely a bad translation from a foreign language. Sometimes it suggests that the writer has squeezed together under pressure the jagged ends of several assorted ideas. The only name I have for this monstrosity is No-English.

The writer of No-English is unconscious of the fact that his pages resemble nothing else under the sun. If you say to him, "This is not English. You must tear this up and try again," he will answer plaintively: "But you know what I mean, don't you?" He will be indignant if you reply, "I can guess, but only because I know what you are supposed to mean."

Let me read you a few choice samples of No-English. These come, alas, from examination papers in my sophomore course in American literature. I shall save the honor of the writers, though not of Princeton, by withholding the names of the perpetrators.

A change from the optimastic view of the individual man as put forth in transcendentic philosophy to the pessimistic view of mankind frought with invalide morals living a superficial life with no direction such as T. S. Eliot flitting bug-eyed from Antwerp to Brussels to London.

He was a man who had dispared to the nature of man and although he had these tendencies of subjection he soon gained aspirations and broke away from the school of disparants and strove on his own beliefs.

When Twain was writing Huckleberry Finn he decided to implement the voyage as a cohesive catalyst. Twain used a general local. Faulkner has a restrictive local, and Thoreau wrote for everybody in the universal.

To one who cares about the well-forged instrument by which those who use English communicate with one another there are, I submit, some very alarming symptoms of decay and defilement in these passages of No-English. Listened to with half an ear they sound impressive, authoritative, and even powerful. Though their authors were composing complete nonsense, they put down these jumbled words with the self-assurance of an advertising copy-writer.

Why is the tide of No-English flooding in with such power that we cannot stand against it? I think I know some of the reasons.

First in importance is the influence of officialese. This is the age of the official statement from government, of communiques, of press releases from public relations officers. All writing of this sort must sound impressive and authoritative, for it is composed to be believed in without dissent.

My long-suffering ear tells me that my students are more often than not trying to write officialese. And why not? This is the way very important people in our society "reveal" or "announce" what are supposed to be matters of life-or-death. This is the interminable voice of the age—or one of its voices.

The evident desire of the writers of No-English to pack power into their prose I think I can trace to another defiler of the well of English. Almost every magazine an undergraduate picks up is likely to be written in a hot-rod style which bursts with energy in every sentence. Authors who wish to sell their wares to Time, Look, and Life, must write in a 500-horse-power style. And their editors, as well, seem to live in constant fear that if they take the foot off the accelerator the reader will drop off to sleep between sentences or, bored and indifferent, turn on the television set.

Much more to be feared than the poison-vials of officialese is the expensively distilled poison of advertising-style. Students cannot escape it—nor can we.

One of the most insidious things about advertising-style is that it burns up the language at a furious rate because there is so much oxygen in it. The new Plymouth, the ad-man says, is "newest," "most modern" of the low-price three. Also, "biggest." Its Power-Flow 117 motor is "brilliant." Its Power-Flite no-clutch transmission is the "finest made." The next ad-writer for Plymouth is going to find ashes all over his cubicle. What can he dig out of the dictionary which is newer than "newest," bigger than "biggest," higher than "highest horsepower in the field"?

I come finally to the chief defiler of undergraduate writing. And I regret to say we professors are certainly the culprits. And what we are doing we do in all innocence and with the most laudable of motives. This is a serious accusation, and I must justify it or shut up.

There is one predicament in our present kind of collegiate education which, I am convinced, confuses the student who desires to write good English, which may, indeed, lead him to believe that there is no necessity for trying to write in the great tradition of English prose. What I am referring to is the tremendous specialization which the subjects in our curriculum have undergone in this century.

Because the fields of learning now share very little common ground, they (and we) no longer possess a common language. The historian cannot understand the equations of the physicist and the physicist cannot understand the new vocabulary developed by the sociologist. The professor of literature who lectures about "levels of meaning," the "texture and tension of poetry," the wonderful "ambiguities" in Melville's prose, and the "personal symbolism" in the poetry of Robert Frost, opens the eyes but not the ears of his colleague in chemistry who had no idea literature was "that" difficult.

I have begun to notice lately that our better students take an unholy pride in the specialized vocabularies they encounter as they move through their academic day.

Who, among the student's faculty friends will tell him that although it is important to know all he has learned during the day, and that the beginning of wisdom is the certitude of fact, nevertheless there is something beyond fact which is of the utmost importance for him. If, in his pride of knowledge, he refuses to learn how to communicate his knowledge, his ideas and his aspirations, in language that is simple, sensuous, passionate, direct, honest, precise, varied, strong though quiet, and eloquent, he will never bring men to his way of thinking. He will have condemned himself to the prison of the public relations officer or the life of the Madison Avenue ad-man or to the drudgery, without the final reward, of the narrow specialist-scholar.

He deserves to win a better fate. He might become a member of the company of those who have moved men to laudable action. He might, through his skill with words, join, in time, John Milton whose "Areopagitica" still defines the rules of free enquiry, and Jonathan Swift who spoke for the oppressed in Ireland and so for enslaved men everywhere, and Thomas Jefferson, and John Stuart Mill, and Tom Paine, whose words were more useful to Washington than ten thousand fighting men.

Who among us is ready to speak sternly to that student, our pride and our hope, though he still writes No-English?

Suggested Topics

1. The "No-English" of advertising
2. Isn't it enough if you know what we mean?
3. Specialized jargons and our common language
4. Why Johnny can't write
5. The importance of an ability to communicate
6. What makes differences in style?

GETTING AT THE TRUTH   *Marchette Chute*

> A writer of poetry and books for children and adults, Marchette
> Chute is best known for her biographies, popular yet scholarly,
> of English historical and literary figures such as Chaucer, Shake-
> speare, and Ben Jonson.

This is a rather presumptuous title for a biographer to use, since
truth is a very large word. In the sense that it means the reality about
a human being it is probably impossible for a biographer to achieve.
In the sense that it means a reasonable presentation of all the available facts it is more nearly possible, but even this limited goal is
harder to reach than it appears to be. A biographer needs to be both
humble and cautious when he remembers the nature of the material
he is working with, for a historical fact is rather like the flamingo
that Alice in Wonderland tried to use as a croquet mallet. As soon
as she got its neck nicely straightened out and was ready to hit the
ball, it would turn and look at her with a puzzled expression, and any
biographer knows that what is called a "fact" has a way of doing the
same.

Here is a small example. When I was writing my forthcoming biography, "Ben Jonson of Westminster," I wanted to give a paragraph or
two to Sir Philip Sidney, who had a great influence on Jonson. No
one thinks of Sidney without thinking of chivalry, and to underline
the point I intended to use a story that Sir Fulke Greville told of him.
Sidney died of gangrene, from a musket shot that shattered his thigh,
and Greville says that Sidney failed to put on his leg armor while
preparing for battle because the marshal of the camp was not wearing
leg armor and Sidney was unwilling to do anything that would give
him a special advantage. The story is so characteristic both of Sidney
himself and of the misplaced high-mindedness of late Renaissance
chivalry that I wanted to use it, and since Sir Fulke Greville was one
of Sidney's closest friends the information seemed to be reliable
enough. But it is always well to check each piece of information as
thoroughly as possible and so I consulted another account of Sidney
written by a contemporary, this time a doctor who knew the family

Reprinted from *The Saturday Review*, September 19, 1953. By permission of the
author.

well. The doctor, Thomas Moffet, mentioned the episode but he said that Sidney left off his leg armor because he was in a hurry.

The information was beginning to twist in my mind and could no longer be trusted. So I consulted still another contemporary who had mentioned the episode, to see which of the two he agreed with. This was Sir John Smythe, a military expert who brought out his book a few years after Sidney's death. Sir John was an old-fashioned conservative who advocated the use of heavy armor even on horseback, and he deplored the current craze for leaving off leg protection, "the imitating of which . . . cost that noble and worthy gentleman Sir Philip Sidney his life."

So here I was with three entirely different reasons why Sydney left off his leg armor, all advanced by careful writers who were contemporaries of his. The flamingo had a legitimate reason for looking around with a puzzled expression.

The only thing to do in a case like this is to examine the point of view of the three men who are supplying the conflicting evidence. Sir Fulke Greville was trying to prove a thesis: that his beloved friend had an extremely chivalric nature. Sir John Smythe also was trying to prove a thesis: that the advocates of light arming followed a theory that could lead to disaster. Only the doctor, Thomas Moffet, was not trying to prove a thesis. He was not using his own explanation to reinforce some point he wanted to make. He did not want anything except to set down on paper what he believed to be the facts; and since we do not have Sidney's own explanation of why he did not put on leg armor, the chances are that Dr. Moffet is the safest man to trust.

For Moffet was without desire. Nothing can so quickly blur and distort the facts as desire—the wish to use the facts for some purpose of your own—and nothing can so surely destroy the truth. As soon as the witness wants to prove something he is no longer impartial and his evidence is no longer to be trusted.

The only safe way to study contemporary testimony is to bear constantly in mind this possibility of prejudice and to put almost as much attention on the writer himself as on what he has written. For instance, Sir Anthony Weldon's description of the Court of King James is lively enough and often used as source material; but a note from the publisher admits that the pamphlet was issued as a warning to anyone who wished to "side with this bloody house" of Stuart. The publisher, at any rate, did not consider Weldon an impartial witness. At about the same time Arthur Wilson published his history of Great Britain, which contained an irresistibly vivid account of the agonized death of the Countess of Somerset. Wilson sounds reasonably impartial; but his patron was the Earl of Essex, who had good reason to hate that particular countess, and there is evidence that he invented the whole scene to gratify his patron.

Sometimes a writer will contradict what he has already written, and in that case the only thing to do is to investigate what has changed his point of view. For instance, in 1608 Captain John Smith issued a description of his capture by Powhatan, and he made it clear that the Indian chief had treated him with unwavering courtesy and hospitality. In 1624 the story was repeated in Smith's *General History of Virginia,* but the writer's circumstances had changed. Smith needed money, "having a prince's mind imprisoned in a poor man's purse," and he wanted the book to be profitable. Powhatan's daughter, the Princess Pocahontas, had recently been in the news, for her visit to England had aroused a great deal of interest among the sort of people that Smith hoped would buy his book. So Smith supplied a new version of the story, in which the once-hospitable Powhatan would have permitted the hero's brains to be dashed out if Pocahontas had not saved his life. It was the second story that achieved fame, and of course it may have been true. But it is impossible to trust it because the desire of the writer is so obviously involved; as Smith said in his prospectus, he needed money and hoped that the book would give "satisfaction."

It might seem that there was an easy way for a biographer to avoid the use of this kind of prejudiced testimony. All he has to do is to construct his biography from evidence that cannot be tampered with —from parish records, legal documents, bills, accounts, court records, and so on. Out of these solid gray blocks of impersonal evidence it should surely be possible to construct a road that will lead straight to the truth and that will never bend itself to the misleading curve of personal desire.

This might be so if the only problem involved were the reliability of the material. But there is another kind of desire that is much more subtle, much more pervasive, and much more dangerous than the occasional distortions of fact that contemporary writers may have permitted themselves to make; and this kind of desire can destroy the truth of a biography even if every individual fact in it is as solid and as uncompromising as rock. Even if the road is built of the best and most reliable materials it can still curve away from the truth because of this other desire that threatens it: the desire of the biographer himself.

A biographer is not a court record or a legal document. He is a human being, writing about another human being, and his own temperament, his own point of view, and his own frame of reference are unconsciously imposed upon the man he is writing about. Even if the biographer is free from Captain Smith's temptation—the need for making money—and wants to write nothing but the literal truth, he is still handicapped by the fact that there is no such thing as a completely objective human being.

An illustration of what can happen if the point of view is sufficiently strong is the curious conclusion that the nineteenth-century biographers reached about William Shakespeare. Shakespeare joined a company of London actors in 1594, was listed as an actor in 1598 and 1603, and was still listed as one of the "men actors" in the company in 1609. Shortly before he joined this company Shakespeare dedicated two narrative poems to the Earl of Southampton, and several years after Shakespeare died his collected plays were dedicated to the Earl of Pembroke. This was his only relationship with either of the two noblemen, and there is nothing to connect him with them during the fifteen years in which he belonged to the same acting company and during which he wrote nearly all his plays.

But here the desire of the biographers entered in. They had been reared in the strict code of nineteenth-century gentility and they accepted two ideas without question. One was that there are few things more important than an English lord; the other was that there are few things less important than a mere actor. They already knew the undeniable fact that Shakespeare was one of the greatest men who ever lived; and while they could not go quite so far as to claim him as an actual member of the nobility, it was clear to them that he must have been the treasured friend of both the Earl of Southampton and the Earl of Pembroke and that he must have written his plays either while basking in their exalted company or while he was roaming the green countryside by the waters of the river Avon. (It is another basic conviction of the English gentleman that there is nothing so inspiring as nature.) The notion that Shakespeare had spent all these years as the working member of a company of London actors was so abhorrent that it was never seriously considered. It could not be so; therefore it was not.

These biographers did their work well. When New South Wales built its beautiful memorial library to Shakespeare, it was the coat of arms of the Earl of Southampton that alternated with that of royalty in dignified splendor over the bookshelves. Shakespeare had been re-created in the image of desire, and desire will always ignore whatever is not relevant to its purpose. Because the English gentlemen did not like Shakespeare's background it was explained away as though it had never existed, and Shakespeare ceased to be an actor because so lowly a trade was not suited to so great a man.

All this is not to say that a biography should be lacking in a point of view. If it does not have a point of view it will be nothing more than a kind of expanded article for an encyclopedia—a string of facts arranged in chronological order with no claim to being a real biography at all. A biography must have a point of view and it must have a frame of reference. But it should be a point of view and a frame of reference implicit in the material itself and not imposed upon it.

It might seem that the ideal biographical system, if it could be achieved, would be to go through the years of research without feeling any kind of emotion. The biographer would be a kind of fact-finding machine and then suddenly, after his years of research, a kind of total vision would fall upon him and he would transcribe it in his best and most persuasive English for a waiting public. But research is fortunately not done by machinery, nor are visions likely to descend in that helpful manner. They are the product not only of many facts but also of much thinking, and it is only when the biographer begins to get emotional in his thinking that he ought to beware.

It is easy enough to make good resolutions in advance, but a biographer cannot altogether control his sense of excitement when the climax of his years of research draws near and he begins to see the pieces fall into place. Almost without his volition, A, B, and D fit together and start to form a pattern, and it is almost impossible for the biographer not to start searching for C. Something turns up that looks remarkably like C, and with a little trimming of the edges and the ignoring of one very slight discrepancy it will fill the place allotted for C magnificently.

It is at this point that the biographer ought to take a deep breath and sit on his hands until he has had time to calm down. He has no real, fundamental reason to believe that his discovery is C, except for the fact that he wants it to be. He is like a man looking for a missing piece in a difficult jigsaw puzzle, who has found one so nearly the right shape that he cannot resist the desire to jam it into place.

If the biographer had refused to be tempted by his supposed discovery of C and had gone on with his research, he might have found not only the connecting, illuminating fact he needed but much more besides. He is not going to look for it now. Desire has blocked the way. And by so much his biography will fall short of what might have been the truth.

It would not be accurate to say that a biographer should be wholly lacking in desire. Curiosity is a form of desire. So is the final wish to get the material down on paper in a form that will be fair to the reader's interest and worthy of the subject. But a subconscious desire to push the facts around is one of the most dangerous things a biographer can encounter, and all the more dangerous because it is so difficult to know when he is encountering it.

The reason Alice had so much trouble with her flamingo is that the average flamingo does not wish to be used as a croquet mallet. It has other purposes in view. The same thing is true of a fact, which can be just as self-willed as a flamingo and has its own kind of stubborn integrity. To try to force a series of facts into a previously desired arrangement is a form of misuse to which no self-respecting fact will willingly submit itself. The best and only way to treat it is to leave it alone and be willing to follow where it leads, rather than to press your own wishes upon it.

To put the whole thing into a single sentence: you will never succeed in getting at the truth if you think you know, ahead of time, what the truth ought to be.

Suggested Topics

1. Fact and prejudice
2. Political biographies in presidential campaign years
3. "No man is a hero to his valet."
4. Is it true that George Washington never told a lie?
5. "Nothing can so quickly blur and distort facts as desire."

THE RECONSTRUCTION OF HIDDEN VALUE JUDGMENTS
Felix Cohen

Prominent as an attorney, author, teacher, and legal philosopher, Felix Cohen (1907-1953) was a close student of American Indian affairs and the author of *A Handbook of Federal Indian Law, Combating Totalitarian Propaganda,* and *Readings in Jurisprudence and Legal Philosophy.*

1. Locating prejudices

What I can do in society depends pretty much on what my neighbors will tolerate. Or, to put the matter more abstractly, the limits of my liberty are the limits of my neighbors' tolerance. Prejudice is the chief enemy of tolerance and therefore the chief enemy of freedom.

Reprinted from *Symbols and Values: An Initial Study,* edited by Lyman Bryson, Louis Finkelstein and Robert M. Mac Iver. Copyright by the Conference on Science, Philosophy and Religion in Their Relation to the Democratic Way of Life, Inc. By permission of Harper & Brothers.

In order to eliminate prejudice we must identify it. But here we are met by the threshold difficulty that none of us can easily recognize his own prejudices.

For some years I have been asking my students whether any of them had any prejudices, and I have not by this method of inquiry found anybody who had any prejudices and admitted to having them. I can think of only three possible explanations of this fact: (1) that my students have prejudices and know they have them, but are attempting to conceal this fact from me; (2) that my students are actually without prejudices; and (3) that it is normal for people not to see their own prejudices.

As my students are, generally speaking, of the highest moral character, I must reject this first alternative theory of conscious deception. And as my students are a fair cross-section of humanity, I must reject the second alternative, the possibility that my students are in fact unprejudiced. This leaves me with the third alternative theory, at least as a working hypothesis, the theory, namely, that prejudice is something that we are more apt to recognize in others than in ourselves.

In this respect prejudice is not unique. Take the relation, for instance, of *fact* to *theory*, of *reverence* to *idolatry*, of *orthodoxy* to *heterodoxy*, of *common sense* to *metaphysics*. Generally, the theories we believe we call *facts*, and the facts we disbelieve we call *theories*; the attitude of respect for objects we respect we call *reverence*, the attitude of respect for objects which we hold in contempt we call *idolatry*; we are all familiar, of course, with the observation that *orthodoxy* is my doxy and *heterodoxy* is the other fellow's doxy.

Less familiar, perhaps, is the reflection that ways of looking at the universe to which we are habituated we generally call *common sense*, while ways of looking at the universe that are unfamiliar to us we are apt to call *metaphysics*. Even the recognition that the world is not divided between Americans and foreigners, but that Americans are themselves foreigners in most of the world, requires a degree of sophistication which few members of Congress ever consistently attain. For example, in June of 1952, it was not possible to find one-third of either house of Congress willing to support the President's veto of the McCarran-Walter Omnibus Immigration Act, which sets up a new and drastic regime for the stranger in our land. And the sponsors of this law were nearly all professed believers in the infallibility of the Bible, which again and again insists that we should not vex the stranger, but should have one law alike for the home-born and the stranger in our midst, ". . . for remember that ye were strangers in the land of Egypt."

In order to avoid confusing ourselves with the center of the universe, it is necessary to recognize that statements about *strangers* or *strange ways,* or *prejudice,* or *idolatry,* or things *foreign,* involve certain points of reference and lines of direction, and that different minds may operate with different points of reference and different lines of direction. Thus what is the core of life's wisdom and experience and the basis of all reason to me may be seen as the extreme of prejudice by somebody else, and *vice versa.*

Skipping, for the time being, the question of how we can determine which of two divergent moral standpoints is right, and concentrating on the more elementary question of how we can determine whether two moral views are divergent, we face the difficulty that people of the most diverse moral outlooks will often express exactly the same abstract value judgments, that is to say, they will prefer courage to cowardice, justice to injustice, and good to evil. Such preferences may be considered, in effect, verbal conventions. Moral divergencies are generally reflected not by challenges to these conventions, but by disagreements as to the content or denotation of such value concepts as courage, justice, and goodness. Such disagreements as to the content of value concepts are commonly reflected in our application of honorific or pejorative terms to a given set of circumstances or persons.

It is hoped that this hypothesis may serve to illumine the divergencies of value attitude that are the sources of prejudice and may suggest a technique for locating such sources capable of wider and more scientific application.

As the field of racial and national feeling is generally conceded to be a field in which prejudice plays a major role, it may be helpful to examine some of the semantic data in this field to see what light such data may throw upon the problem of prejudice identification.

2. The semantics of prejudice

Perhaps the simplest way to recognize racial or national prejudice (in others) is to notice the ways in which people refer to other people. A person who uses the common contemptuous or patronizing terms, *nigger, coon, darkie, redskin, paleface, Chink, Jap, Wop, Spick, Dago, Hunkie, Kraut, Siwash, half-breed, Gook, Frog,* etc., may be quite unaware of the value overtones of these terms, but the sensitive listener, especially if he has been sensitized in a particular direction by repeated impact of these barbed words against his own skin, immediately spots the attitude of contempt that these terms convey. Of course, the user of such terms, when challenged, may reply that these are the terms in common usage in his group, and that he means no offense by them. "He didn't know it was loaded." Almost all of us repeatedly offend others by a word, a tone, or a gesture, without being aware of the fact. It is reasonable to suppose, however, that one who takes up, however innocently, from his environment various word usages that offend others also commonly takes up, perhaps just as innocently, the implicit racial and national attitudes of separateness, distance, and direction that prevail in that environment.

Why, one may ask, should the use of these terms indicate an attitude of contempt? In some cases, this question is easily answered. The name itself may indicate association with something mean or revolting or contemptible in the experience of the name caller, perhaps with something that typifies the basic avoidance reaction which human and other animals exhibit toward various forms of filth and danger.

Such is the case, for instance, with words associating the eating habits of a racial group with some cheap or, to the word user, bad-smelling or repelling food, as, for example, *Frog, Kraut, Spick,* or *Greaser.* In other cases the name itself has a downward-pointing direction, e.g., *coon* (likening a person to a subhuman animal), or *half-breed* (animals breed; humans marry and bear children), or *Siwash* (a corruption of *sauvage*).

In still other cases, the name identifies a human being with what he justly regards as a trivial aspect of himself such as his skin color, as in the terms, *Negro, darkie, redskin,* or *paleface.* The moral overtone of the designation is: the person so designated is peculiar; his outstanding characteristic is the abnormality of his skin. Such overtones may be created by repeated usage. The practice of most American newspapers of referring to arrested or suspected criminals as "Negro" or "alien," if they are either, but not as "White" or "seventh generation American," or "Protestant," or "freckled," is a technique that builds popular impressions as to the criminality of Negroes or aliens which are often very far removed from the facts. What may be called "the technique of the irrelevant adjective" is a smear technique that is difficult to answer. When a New York Congressman objected to Congressman Rankin's referring to him as a "Jewish Congressman from New York," Congressman Rankin's answer was, in effect: "Well, you are Jewish, aren't you? Why be ashamed of it?"

The real issue here is not whether a racial or religious adjective is accurately descriptive of an individual but whether the adjective is properly relevant to the context in which it is used. The adjective, *Negro,* may be entirely relevant to a discussion of the medical effects of sunburn, and the adjective, *Jewish,* may be entirely relevant to a discussion of religious ritual. The relevance of these adjectives to a report of a crime wave, however, may depend upon the inarticulate premise that Negroes or Jews are especially disposed to criminal activity. Such inarticulate premises make the difference between sympathetic and unsympathetic accounts of the same event.

In some other instances it is more difficult to understand why the racial designation should be felt as a term of disparagement. (To say that this is so because the term has been used historically in a disparaging way only pushes our question one stage back.) *Dago,* for example, began apparently as a shortening of the honored Italian name, *Diego,* and *wop* as an abbreviation of *guapo* (meaning handsome), yet both terms now carry definitely disparaging overtones as do such originally harmless abbreviations as *Jap, Chink,* and *Hunkie.*

Is there something about the sound of certain words that makes them carry overtones of contempt? (Is it merely a coincidence that the English language uses one-syllable words ending in *unk* to designate so many unhonored objects—*e.g., bunk, chunk, dunk, drunk, flunk, hunk, junk, punk, sunk, skunk, slunk, stunk?*) Does a one-syllable word that can be uttered in less time than it takes to think, perhaps, carry an overtone of contempt more easily than a polysyllabic word or a precise phrase *(e.g., American of Chinese descent,* instead of *Chink)?*

Or is there a more subtle difference between racial terms that are nouns and those that are adjectives? Would this explain why *Chinaman* is so offensive a term to most Chinese, why *Scotchman* is so offensive to most Scots, and why a boy who is Jewish normally resents being called "Jew boy?" Is it that the adjective by its form reminds us that there is always more to be said on the subject, perhaps something more important to say than has yet been said, while the noun, by its form, seems to equate an individual with a single distinguishing characteristic, so that if the chosen characteristic is trivial the individual is thereby labeled as a trivial individual?

I ask these questions not rhetorically, but in hopes that some answers may emerge. Such answers might help us to extend the bits of empirical knowledge that we have all acquired, from time to time, in this field of discourse, and make it possible to develop a more comprehensive and scientific understanding of the semantics of prejudice.

3. Semantic egocentricism

What my revered teacher, Ralph Barton Perry, has called the ego-centric predicament shows itself with particular clarity in the language of comparative religion. Almost every religious group has a special term, generally carrying a down-grading connotation, by which it refers to outsiders. Thus to the Mohammedan, the outsider is an infidel; to the Mormon a Gentile; to the Jew a Gentile or pig-eater; and to the Christian an unbeliever or heathen. Thus, if somebody calls me a Gentile, I can be pretty sure that he is a Mormon. A man who calls me an infidel I can generally classify as a Mohammedan. And if

I am referred to as an unbeliever I can generally assume that the person who so refers to me is of a Christian faith. These terms when applied to me do not give me information about myself; they do give me information about the speaker. The use of "outsider" terms thus helps to reveal the religious perspective of the user, in so far as it reflects the true believer's estimate of the relation of his own to other faiths.

If we follow Bentham's division of words into the eulogistic, dyslogistic, and neutral, we may note whether a religious reference to a particular group is sympathetic, neutral, or disparaging, by noting the word choice used in such reference. If we take four of the Western world's leading faiths and list for each faith the "insider's" eulogistic or upgrading term for his own faith as "U," list the neutral or middle term as "M," and list the "outsider" dyslogistic or downgrading term as "D," we get the following scheme:

	1		2
U	Believer		True Believer
M	Jewish		Moslem, Mohammedan
D	Kike		Heathen, etc.
	Christ-killer		

	3		4
U	Christian		True Christian
M	Catholic		Protestant
D	Romanist,		Atheist
	Papist, etc.		

4. The tongue's second dimension

What is important to note is that the choice between columns 1, 2, 3, and 4 on the same horizontal line, referring to four different objects, purports to tell us something about the object of discourse, while the choice of terms in any given vertical line between columns U (up, eulogistic), M (middle, neutral), and D (down, dyslogistic), all relating to the same object, tells us something about the person who is discoursing, perhaps something he did not intend to tell us, in the same way that a fossil skeleton tells us something about the animal of which it was a part. Ordinarily people are trained to observe the horizontal or denotative distinctions in discourse. The anthropologists, however, have developed a special listening technique in order to note the vertical or connotative distinctions which mark out the value perspectives of the speaker. Thus, when an anthropologist listens to a native discourse on ghosts or witches, he may be learning a great deal, not about ghosts or witches, but about the value judgments of his informant.

This is a technique of observation that may be equally useful in analyzing the inarticulate moral premises of judges or legislators, who often strenuously and sincerely insist that they have no moral theories but are merely carrying out the "spirit of the Constitution," the "common law," the "dictates of precedent," or the "will of the people." Indeed, whenever a court announces, "This is a court of law and not of morals," the careful reader of judicial opinions must be prepared for a vigorous application of some moral theory as to what judges ought to do. And the more vigorously a court insists that it cannot accept social theories, no matter how plausible, the more certain we can be that the court is embarking upon a social theory that must be kept secret even from its most devoted supporters because if it were recognized as a theory, and exposed therefore to criticism, it would fade in the sunlight of open discussion.

A judge's denial of the relevance of morality or social policy may thus serve as a good indicator of his own views of morality or social policy if we read his opinion with special attention to the choices he makes between upgrading and downgrading terms.

5. The conjugation of irregular adjectives

Bertrand Russell has called attention to the possibility of conjugating value-weighted adjectives in such form as:

1. I am firm.
2. You are obstinate.
3. He is a pig-headed fool.

More generally, we can say that almost any human characteristic may be described either in honorific or in pejorative terms. Consider, for example, how the choice between upgrading, downgrading, and neutral words to describe a given human trait or inclination may reflect a speaker's value judgment in any of the following cases:

Eulogistic	In-Between	Dyslogistic
Discreet	Cautious	Cowardly
Loyal	Obedient	Slavish
Careful	Meticulous	Fussy
Devoted	Self-subordinating	Fanatical
Kind	Soft	Mawkish
Warmhearted	Sentimental	Mushy
Tolerant	Non-discriminating	Nigger-lover, Indian-lover, etc.

Generous	Liberal	Spendthrift
Courageous	Bold	Reckless, Foolhardy
Mature	Old	Decayed
Youthful	Young	Immature
Sound	Conservative	Reactionary
Openminded	Liberal	Unsound
Practical	Aware of material factors	Mercenary
Realistic	Suspicious	Cynical
Humanitarian	Idealist	Do-gooder

6. Verb and noun choices as value indicators

More subtle than the choice of adjectives (and therefore more useful in tracking down concealed value perspectives) is the value orientation that is involved in the choice of a noun or a verb to describe a given activity, operation, or institution, or to identify the position of an individual in society. Consider, for example, the varying connotations of respect or disrespect involved in the choice among the following ways of describing the position of a given individual:

Eulogistic	*In-Between*	*Dyslogistic*
Official	Office-holder	Bureaucrat
Statesman	Policy-maker	Politician
Officer	Policeman	Cop
Investigator	Detective	Flatfoot
Governess	Nursemaid	Servant
Business Executive	Employer	Boss
Financial Leader	Banker	Moneylender, Moneychanger
Doctor	Druggist	Shopkeeper
Pilgrim	Migrant, Refugee, Immigrant	Alien
Orator	Influential Speaker	Rabblerouser

While deferential forms of speech have not attained the same high-development in Western society as in the Orient, a considerable part of our vocabulary of polite intercourse consists in using to a person's face words we do not use behind his back (*e.g.,* your Honor, your Excellency, Dear Sir, "you all"). In Vienna, for example, where politeness is carried to a high degree, it used to be (perhaps still is) customary to address a policeman by a title two grades above his actual rank.

Peculiar individual tastes have relatively little permanent impact upon a social institution like language. But where many individuals in a society share a common value standard, it is natural for them to develop a common code. Such a professional or political code will ordinarily embody, and by constant reiteration will reinforce, the standards that are implicitly held by the group in question.

These codes become particularly important in a political campaign. Our candidates may *inspire;* they never *inflame,* as do the other fellow's candidates. Our candidates may *demonstrate;* only the opposing candidates *allege.* Our candidates may *clarify;* only their opponents will *admit error.* Our candidates may *discern, enlighten, assist, serve, catalyze, counsel,* or *cooperate.* On no account will they *theorize, propagandize, abet, interfere, instigate, incite,* or *conspire.*

California's Governor Warren is reported to have made the sage observation: "When government does something for us, that's social progress; when it does something for the other fellow, that's Socialism." Political oratory may thus offer a wealth of enlightenment to the careful listener, not about the events discussed but about the value-system of the orator. Perhaps this is what was in the mind of the Talmudist who, when asked to define "a wise man," replied; "A wise man is a man who can learn from anybody."

Thurman Arnold has pointed out that the professional jargon of judges and lawyers has influenced the American mind to a point where a whole shift of vocabulary takes place when a judicial function is transferred to an administrative agency: *Procedure* becomes *red tape;* the *rule of law* yields to *bureaucratic discretion;* precedent disappears and *force of habit* takes its place, and so on down the line.

The language of colonial administrators offers a particularly impressive exhibition of double bookkeeping in the political field, for here professional and political value standards are largely reinforced by racial or national prides and prejudices. Even in the United States today, where at least lip service must be paid to the traditional American dislike for colonialism, a highly developed system of administrator's double-talk has made it possible for our colonial officials to profess a firm resolve to liquidate their jobs, and allow their so-called wards (for example, American Indians) full rights of citizenship, while in practice they press steadily for increased powers and increased appropriations. Under this system of double-talk, colonial officials "assist," "counsel," "serve," and "enlighten" natives, while other persons never *assist,* but only *abet,* never *advise* but only *incite,* never *serve* but only *interfere,* never *enlighten* but only *propagandize.* When native chiefs or councils make decisions for themselves, this is called *politics;* when decisions are made by colonial officials, that is called *policy-making.* When decisions are put into practice by natives, this is called *manipulation;* when colonial officials handle such matters the preferred term is *administration.* When native property is handled so as to increase its productive yield, this is called *development* if colonial officials or their licensees are doing the handling, and *exploitation* if some one else is doing the handling. When natives take advice from the colonial officials this is called *cooperation;* when they take advice from others this is called *conspiring.* By carefully keeping the two vocabularies distinct it is generally possible for a professionally trained group of administrators to persuade the public that pays its salaries that its "wards" are not yet fit to run their own businesses, manage their own lands, hold their own free elections, make their own contracts, or even decide when to go to bed and when to get up in the morning, and that increasing appropriations and powers should be granted to white officials to enable them to make such decisions for their non-white subjects.

Any white man who speaks up in defense of native freedom and thus impedes the power-drive of the colonial office is officially classified as either a "crank" or a "grafter" or a "paid agitator"—a "grafter" if the natives pay him for his help, a "paid agitator" if white sympathizers pay him, and a "crank" if nobody pays him.

When the white officialdom uncovers acts of dishonesty among its employees, this is called "raising the level of government service"; when an outsider uncovers such acts, this is called "undermining confidence in the Government."

The same semantic techniques are used on a much larger scale in the Communist world, where the "withering away of the state" is the justifying slogan for a vast increase in state power.

The following table of social action words could be expanded indefinitely if time and space permitted. It covers only a few of the key word-choices that, when applied to any given subject matter of a controversial character, may help us to identify the moral or political standpoint of the word-user:

Eulogistic	In-Between	Dyslogistic
Discern	Think	Theorize
Demonstrate	Assert	Allege
Cooperate	Act in concert	Conspire
Assist	Aid	Abet
Clarify	Retract	Admit Error
Serve	Control	Interfere
Administer	Manage	Manipulate
Service, Administration	Office	Bureau
Ownership, Property	Power to exclude	Monopoly
Develop	Create value increment	Exploit
Enlighten	Report	Propagandize
Inspire	Motivate	Inflame
Catalyze	Stir to action	Instigate
Counsel	Recommend	Incite
Social Progress	Expansion of Public Service	Socialism
Orderly Procedure	Procedure	Red-tape

7. "We" words and "they" words

Generally speaking, words of the first column in the foregoing three tables may be classed as "we" words. They are words which we customarily apply to our own actions and to the actions of those for whom we have a strong fellow feeling. Words of the third column, on the other hand, are "they" words, used to describe the actions of those from whom we are inclined to separate ourselves. Sometimes the relation between "we" words and "they" words involves no more than the addition of the three-letter pejorative suffix, "ism." Thus one who disapproves of peace, or psychology, or social progress, or isolation, is likely to sound much more persuasive if he denounces *pacifism, psychologism, Socialism, progressivism,* or *isolationism.* In other cases the relation of upgrading "we" words to downgrading "they" words is subtler and more difficult to delineate. But generally it is conducive to clarity to ask of any word: Is this a term I would apply to myself?

Just as the choice between "we have sinned" and "you have sinned" so often may mark the difference between effective shared effort at reform and the kind of preaching that moves only the preacher, so the subtler choice between "we" words and "they" words can often reveal moral premises of which the speaker himself may be quite unaware.

When, for example, a court begins an opinion in an Indian property case by referring to Indians moving from one place to another as *roaming, wandering,* or *roving,* we can be pretty sure that it will end up by denying the claimed property rights of the Indians. For these words are words that are commonly applied to buffalo, wolves, or other subhuman animals. They suggest that the relation of an Indian to land was a purely physical relation and not a social relation. There are plainly "out-grouping" or "they" words to describe movements which most of us, thinking of ourselves, would describe by means of such words as *traveling, vacationing,* or *commuting,* words that we would not apply to animals, words that are distinctively human. These latter words connote purpose in movement. Only when we regard a person as strange or perhaps subhuman do we customarily impute aimless motion to him. Thus, if I or a friend should move from one place to another, this physical motion will ordinarily either be described in "we" terms or be assimilated into a more highly descriptive term. We might speak of ourselves as transporting merchandise, or surveying, or berry-picking, or selling life insurance, or settling the West, depending on the occasion and purpose of the physical motion. An unfriendly Indian might disregard all these nuances and describe our action in "they" terms as *trespassing* or *invading the Indian country*. And, conversely, white judges, or white settlers who do not consider Indians quite human will be apt to disregard the purposes and occasions of Indian travel and refer to any moving Indian as a *nomad*, thereby implicitly justifying the taking of Indian lands and homes by more civilized "settlers" or corporations.

More generally, we may say that we are, each of us, likely to place ourselves and those to whom we are especially attached closer to the top than to the bottom of our value worlds. This means that "we" words will generally have a higher value direction than "they" words. For example, when a white judge refers to a defendant as a Negro, Indian, or savage, he is using an "out-grouping" line of demarcation that separates himself from the defendant. On the other hand, a judge who refer to the same defendant as a citizen, a taxpayer, a father, a husband, or a veteran, is using an "in-grouping" delineation that includes himself or honored friends. Perhaps the most significant effort of the attorneys on opposite sides of a case is the effort to persuade the judge or the jury or both to think of the defendant in "we" terms or "they" terms. This, however, is not yet part of what is generally taught in law schools. Certainly a large part of what is involved in this analysis is not yet understood by the present writer. That is why this paper is submitted, in this tentative form, in the hope that it may provoke all possible destructive criticism. . . .

10. Conclusion

The technique of semantic analysis will not eliminate human prejudice. It will not even provide a touchstone for distinguishing between truth and prejudice. It will not prove or disprove the hypothesis that there is an absolute relativism of values (*i.e.,* that any value system is absolutely as good as any other system). But the technique of semantic analysis, if it can be developed beyond the bare rudiments here sketched, may help us to uncover the inarticulate value premises of others and even of ourselves and thus to understand the similarities and dissimilarities that exist between any two value perspectives. Such understanding may itself lead to greater tolerance of cultural diversities. At the same time, it may help us to see more clearly the moral implications of our human egocentric limitations. Having achieved such understanding of our own limitations and distortions, we may be in a better position to help others to see theirs. To that extent, semantic analysis may help us to identify and eliminate prejudice, and thus aid us, in the long run, to achieve a greater degree of tolerance and freedom in our society.

Suggested Topics

1. Prejudice—the chief enemy of tolerance
2. "We" words and "they" words
3. "The technique of the irrelevant adjective"
4. The semantics of prejudice
5. A look at my own prejudices

THE POPULAR ARTS

JAZZ MAKES IT UP THE RIVER — *Gilbert Millstein*

A member of the Sunday staff of *The New York Times,* Gilbert
Millstein is at home in a variety of fields, ranging from reviews
of books to sprightly and penetrating feature articles on such
subjects as the theatre, the Jet Age, colorful personalities, tip-
ping, etc. etc.

Although the art of jazz has only lately been certified by, among
others, the State Department and ministers of several faiths, and has
arrived no closer than a scrabbling handhold to a comfortable definition, the fact is that more of it is being played and written by more
musicians and listened to by more people with more catholic tastes
than at any time since the sainted Charles (Buddy) Bolden is reputed
to have shouted, "Let's call the children home," stuck his cornet out
of the window of a New Orleans dance hall and blown loud enough
to be heard ten miles away.

"You can't hold it in your hand or encompass it," the pianist
Thelonious Monk remarked on a recent night, immediately subsequent
to his choice in an international critics' poll as the outstanding performer of the year on his instrument. "It's something to enjoy. I never
tried to think of a definition. I never had time to think of it. *Listen,*
that's all, *listen, listen, listen!* You supposed to know jazz when you
hear it. You can't talk it. What do you do when someone gives you
something? You feel glad about it; you take it." Monk's adjuration,
like Bolden's before him, has been obeyed; it is there, but no one has
said, beyond cavil, what it is.

Reprinted from *The New York Times Magazine,* August 24, 1958. By permission
of *The New York Times* and the author.

Among the anti-romantic proofs that jazz has finally stopped coming up the river from New Orleans, obscured in the mists of nostalgia, are these: the sales of jazz records of all kinds are at an all-time high. The number of night clubs devoted exclusively to jazz has grown markedly in the past three years, while those committed to standard entertainment have declined. The music has become a regular fixture on radio and a reasonably regular, if not always expertly produced, fixture on several television programs.

The jazz concert, an occasional promotion in the past, has become an enormously profitable and institutionalized business. Not until the early Fifties was the interdict placed on jazz by major concert halls lifted. (Exceptions were made for such men as Benny Goodman and Duke Ellington.) This was largely the work of a persistent promoter named Norman Granz, who began touring his "Jazz at the Philharmonic" troupe in 1945. In the colleges, jazz, once the coteric possession of a few fraternity brothers, is now the province of entire student bodies as a result of the campus tours pioneered by Dave Brubeck in 1950 and taken up later by the revered Louis Armstrong and the astringent Modern Jazz Quartet.

An accompanying manifestation has been the growth of the jazz festival. The first of these, according to the critic and historian, Leonard Feather, was held in Wilkes-Barre, Pa., in February, 1951. Since then they have proliferated: Newport, Randalls Island, Stratford, Ont., Great South Bay, French Lick, Ind., and Monterey, Calif. As pointed out recently by Nat Hentoff, another expert, the number of books on jazz published in the past five years is greater than the total output of the preceding quarter century, and Down Beat, the Good Book of the jazz fan, has doubled in circulation in the past year. A stunningly final evidence of the recognition the music has achieved may be seen in the decision of S. Hurok, an impresario of the classical all his life, to take on his first jazz client, Errol Garner, the pianist.

There are a good many reasons—some cultural, some economic and sociological, some seemingly contradictory, a few bordering on the mystic—why jazz has reached its present eminence, an elevation not quite so likely to be abandoned in a hurry as it has been several times in the sixty or so years of its recognizable existence. For one thing, it has achieved respectability—in a manner having little or nothing to do with the music. From its beginnings jazz was associated—correctly, often as not—with sporting houses, sporting women, whisky, disorder and, more latterly, narcotics. Its practitioners were seen—hazily—as artists *manqués,* a picturesque lot with great talents, souls, lusts, hangovers and neuroses, and they were ticketed for the sort of destruction Zola unfortunately was born too early to write about. They were also

barefooted, unable to read music, or both, and gave their finest performances only after hours in illegal saloons. Sometimes this was true.

The portrait was fine for coterie types, sentimentalists, historians
and the writers of bad naturalistic novels, but repellent to the general
public. Today, while the level of morality among jazz musicians is no
higher than it is in the lay population, it is possible to find a heavy
percentage of instrumentalists married for long periods to one woman
(and having children), who read music (and may even, like Dave
Brubeck, have studied with Milhaud), wearing shoes (and Brooks
Brothers suits), playing openly in bosky dells and giving many indications of staving off physical and psychic rot for decades.

As Gunther Schuller, a composer and instrumentalist of both jazz
and "serious" music remarked not long ago, "These people are much
more organized as people, and they gave others the assurance that
they could behave like normal, everyday, decent citizens—they showed
up on time for a job; they knew what they were doing, and they weren't
drunk." Having read of jazz's glamorously disheveled past, audiences
were thus in the highly titillating position of being able to approve
jazz's sanitary modern morals and, at the same time, savor its steamy
antecedents. The imaginative could equate Mahogany Hall with
Carnegie Hall, and, if the musician's soul were not rent, it at least
burst its seams in the corridors of the Juilliard School of Music.

The standard intellectuals—not the jazz cabalists, talkers of hip
language and wearers of beards, berets and dark glasses—whose gauges
of respectability are more apt to be bookish, were, at long last, drawn
to jazz as its academic qualifications rose to suit their tastes. Once they
had decked jazz in ivy and scholarship (the Brubeck album, "Jazz
Goes to College," is, incidentally, one of many bearing roughly similar
titles), the intellectuals then discovered it offered them something
classical music did not.

Classical music is fixed in form; one symphony orchestra's or one
performer's interpretation differs from another's, but the notes are forever the same and the market has lately been glutted with different,
if not too much differing, renditions of the serious warhorses. But
jazz, being an improvisational music, must renew itself constantly and
its freshness appealed to the academics.

Another factor is what the saxophonist, Paul Desmond, calls the
"indescribable worsening" of popular music in the last decade, coupled
with the spread of rock 'n' roll (which, it is true, has its origins in
jazz, but which bears it as much resemblance as a city dump does a
vinaigrette), and the growth of a glutinous kind of mood music made
portentous by the use of such devices as the echo chamber. The relatively mature listener—not particularly a classicist—was, respectively,
alienated, irritated or bored. There were others to whom the swing

bands of the late Thirties represented, whether they were aware of it or not, a smooth, satisfying wedding of popular music to jazz, but these bands were no longer in existence. For them, as for a generation of college students, the void appears to have been filled with the sound of jazz.

The element of fashion is present in the usual disingenuous way, in this instance with a small sprinkling of irony. The Europeans have, by and large, been serious students of American jazz for well over twenty-five years and, with the exception of a few *avant-gardists* in this country, were well ahead of America in recognizing it as an art form. This became known here shortly after the end of the Second World War and hot music was taken up with the same avidity reserved for Italian shoes and British sports cars.

In his "The Story of Jazz" Marshall Stearns has taken note of the "protest-music" appeal theory of jazz as laid down by several psychiatrists. Summarized, the proposition runs this way: the music has such flagrantly disreputable associations that "it takes real courage and * * * rebellious spirit to identify oneself with it." On the one hand, the rebel can defy society with complete safety—he has only to listen —and, on the other, make cause with a small band of like-minded rebels. One hot musician, unaware of the ground broken by the psychiatrists, remarked, half in earnest, one night to a friend, "People wonder why we get paid relatively well. Man, we take people's chances for them." Nat Hentoff has put it still another way: "In an era of compulsive conformity we want something that connotes freedom; we can always shut it off when the boss comes to dinner."

Not the least important aspect of the music's current popularity is linked to changes in attitude toward the Negro. In its earliest days jazz was widely regarded as an exclusively Negro music. Even when this was found not to be the case, the Negro musician was permitted to play only with Negroes and the Negro audience was rigidly segregated, excepting only in the freemasonry of dives. Negros and mixed orchestras were barred from hotels. Until only a relatively few years ago some intellectuals compounded the crime by condescending to jazz as something "inherent" in the Negro personality (like shiftlessness, good humor, the ability to dance and to take a punch in the head, although not in the belly), and they also made a foolish distinction between what they termed "white jazz" and "Negro jazz." The reversal of these conditions and states of mind, while it has yet to constitute an idyll, is gradually increasing, with "all deliberate speed."

The most obvious reasons are economic and technological. Where audiences are concerned, the nearly uninterrupted rise in the standard of living since the beginning of the last war has been reflected in an increase in leisure and of money to spend it on. Some of it has been spent on jazz. In terms of the musicians, the process is a little more complicated. Artistic reasons apart, they were, in a sense, forced into playing the jazz for which they had yearned unrequited previously. A great many talented jazz musicians played in the big bands of the late Thirties. The draft broke up most of these bands; the 20 per cent Federal entertainment tax drove almost all the rest out of the hotels, motion-picture presentation houses and some night clubs.

For the most part, jazz is played by small groups. Small bands cost less to hire than large ones and these were hired by night club owners whose interest in art may be termed, at its highest, peripheral. Few musicians will concede it, but the iron of economics has also, admittedly to a small extent, even helped to change jazz from a dancing music into a listening music. There is no 20 per cent tax in clubs where there is no dancing. There are also more tables if the owner has a dance floor he can cover with them.

Technologically, the long-playing record had two effects. In the first place, it enables the jazz musician to free himself of the straitjacket imposed by those which revolved at seventy-eight revolutions per minute and limited a performance to three minutes or less. An uninhibited jazz performance is apt to last anywhere from five to twenty minutes or more, depending on the number of choruses the players are moved to take. Thus, the conditions under which jazz is at its best were met on long-playing records. Furthermore, it became possible to reissue on one record large numbers of much older and still cherished short selections. The over-all cost was smaller and the general gained easy access to the collector's caviar.

The reasons jazz has gained the acceptance it has are easily come by, by comparison with attempts to define what it is. Very likely, the classic utterance on the subject (as beautifully succinct as Carlyle's injunction to Margaret Fuller, upon hearing that she had accepted the universe: "By God, she had better!") was made by the late Fats Waller who was called upon for a definition. "Ma'am," he replied, "if you don't know by now, don't mess with it."

In a chapter of his The Encyclopedia of Jazz, Leonard Feather reminded his readers: "It must be borne in mind that no two musicians at any time in jazz history have ever agreed completely on a definition, and that even when they find an area of agreement their opinions are bound to change as time goes by." And he added, "Where jazz begins and popular music ends is another question that I would hesitate to answer . . ."

Nevertheless, Feather and other students have suppressed their misgivings and managed to work out formulas which may not be all-embracing but have the virtue of being readily understandable. To take just two examples, jazz is the following to (a) Feather and (b) Stearns:

(a) The music we recognize today as jazz is a synthesis drawn originally from six principal sources: rhythms from West Africa; harmonic structure from European classical music; melodic and harmonic qualities from nineteenth-century American folk music; religious music; work songs and minstrel shows.

(b) Jazz: a semi-improvisational American music distinguished by an immediacy of communication, an expressiveness characteristic of the free use of the human voice, and a complex flowing rhythm; it is the result of a three hundred years' blending in the United States of the European and West African musical traditions, and its predominant components are European harmony, Euro-African melody and African rhythm.

It is possible to identify the *kinds* of jazz that are played and the periods in which they began—the experts speak of Traditional or New Orleans, Dixieland or Chicago, Kansas City, Swing, Bop, Progressive and Modern; Ragtime, Blues and Boogie-woogie—but from there on the definitions show an annoying tendency to grow highly technical and disputatious where they are not hedged about with splinters of qualification and fragments of interpretation. Opinion is no longer unanimous, for example, that the music even originated in New Orleans, some scholars contending that it simply had its greatest impact there. One critic stated positively that ragtime is not jazz, nor is jazz ragtime, and was set up by the others. Most of the attempts to make clear to the layman what a musician means when he says his music "swings" have ended in frustration, and, today, there is a fine, noisy controversy raging over where jazz is going and whether it is proper to call a lot of what is being played jazz.

Up to this time, improvisation on a theme by a soloist has been considered an absolute essential in jazz. However, a school of thought has come into being among some musicians, composers and commentators, the essence of which is that it is possible to have written music that can honorably be called jazz. The other day, at the conclusion of a heated argument along these lines among three modernists and a "moldy fig"—traditionalists are known as moldy figs—the fig cried out in pain, "This is the end of jazz as we know it."

The substance of the argument was relayed to Gunther Schuller and to Orrin Keepnews, the latter a former jazz critic and a founder of Riverside Records. Schuller's comment was that "jazz is a folk music in the process of becoming an art music. It may be absorbed into the stream of classical music as has happened before with folk music. But jazz is so strong a folk music, it may withstand absorption and form a third stream. The musicians aren't concerned with labeling it, just with playing it. Someone will label it later." Keepnews was a little more jazzy. "This music," he said, "is no innocent little maiden to be seduced by the big, bad stranger from Symphony Hall."

Suggested Topics

1. A jazz festival
2. "The glamorously disheveled past" of jazz
3. Why jazz has reached its present eminence
4. "Jazz in ivy and scholarship"
5. Rock 'n' roll
6. The "indescribable worsening" of popular music

HOW NO-TALENT SINGERS GET "TALENT"
John S. Wilson

John S. Wilson is on the staffs of *The New York Times*, for which he serves as a critic of jazz music, and of its radio station, WQXR, for which he supervises a highly esteemed jazz program. He is the author of *The Collector's Jazz: Traditional and Swing* (1958) and *The Collector's Jazz: Modern* (1959)

Last fall a recording company executive was sitting in front of his television set watching a private eye series called "77 Sunset Strip" when he was struck with a sudden loathing for one of the characters—a young, jive-talking parking lot attendant named Kookie who looked like a teen-ager's idea of a rock 'n' roll singer.

"I was offended that there should be someone who looked like that and talked like that," George Avakian, who produces pop disks for Warner Brothers records, recalled recently. "But in the same instant I was struck by an obvious inspiration—he should make rock 'n' roll records. I was sure that kids would like his talk and his looks, especially a way he had of looking out of the corner of his eye. And—the real clincher for his popularity with kids—parents would loathe him."

The fact that there was no evidence that Edward Byrnes, who played Kookie, could sing a single note did not dampen Avakian's

Reprinted from *The New York Times Magazine,* June 21, 1959. By permission of *The New York Times* and the author.

enthusiasm in the slightest. He was quite aware that singing ability is one of the least essential qualifications for success as a pop singer today. Recording techniques have become so ingenious that almost anyone can seem to be a singer. A small, flat voice can be souped up by emphasizing the low frequencies and piping the result through an echo chamber. A slight speeding up of the recording tape can bring a brighter, happier sound to a naturally drab singer or clean the weariness out of a tired voice. Wrong notes can be snipped out of the tape and replaced by notes taken from other parts of the tape.

This last process—splicing—once enabled comedian Jerry Lewis to sing a completely breathless record called "Busybody." Lewis made several takes of the song, breathing in a different place on each take. In the final editing, all the breathing spaces were cut out, leaving an exhausting listening experience.

The move toward the synthetic singer has been progressing slowly ever since Whispering Jack Smith found that the microphone eliminated the need for real vocal projection early in the Nineteen Twenties. But not until the past few years has the gadgetry of electronics and tape taken a dominant role in the creation of pop recordings. The gadgetry dam really burst after Elvis Presley's recorded voice was so doctored up with echoes that he sounded as though he were going to shake apart. Since then "sounds" have often taken precedence over music.

In today's highly competitive bedlam of pop recordings, the bulk of the disks are propped up by some form of gimmick or engineering acrobatics, although it is still possible for "singing" singers—Perry Como, Frank Sinatra, Patti Page, Nat "King" Cole or such more recent arrivals as Pat Boone and Johnny Mathis—to produce consistently successful disks without resorting to non-musical crutches. In fact, it is to the advantage of these singers to avoid trickery because the individual sound of their singing is a potent element in selling their records.

Yet a successful popular singer today may actually be nothing more than the product of a recording engineer's creative ingenuity. Last Christmas' inescapable popular hit recording, "The Chipmunk Song," was ostensibly sung in shrill, piping voices by three English-speaking chipmunks named Simon, Theodore and Alvin. Their voices were all produced by one man, Ross Bagdasarian, who wrote the song. He recorded each voice on separate tapes which were later played at double speed and blended by a process called overdubbing.

If three nonexistent chipmunks could make a hit record, there was no reason for Avakian to hesitate about using a live TV actor who seemed to have teen-age appeal. But even Avakian was not prepared for Byrnes' monumental lack of talent as a singer. When the actor reluctantly submitted to an audition, it was found that he not only could not carry a tune (a failing so common among potential pop singers that it is almost taken for granted) but he had no sense of pitch, practically no range and his grasp of rhythm was so uncertain that his accompanist was unable to stay in line with him.

This seemed to be more than even the most skillful recording techniques could rectify. But meanwhile Byrnes' popularity with teen-agers was building week by week and his potential value as a record star was increasing. Some means had to be found to get him on a record.

The solution hit upon was to have a girl do the singing while Byrnes interjected an occasional spoken line. The girl, Connie Stevens, was written into the TV script so there would be an excuse to have her on the record. Tying in even more closely with Byrnes' booming popularity on TV, a song was created for him which stressed the name of the character he played and his compulsive habit of combing his hair—"Kookie, Kookie (Lend Me Your Comb)." By the time the recording was made, Byrnes had been taking singing lessons for several weeks and it was daringly decided to let him sing six bars so that the record would not be dominated by Miss Stevens.

Six months after Avakian had first flinched at the sight and sound of Kookie, Edward Byrnes' record was released. Three weeks later it had leaped to first place in Variety's weekly compilation of the nation's most popular recordings.

Byrnes' success in a medium for which he would appear to have no talent stems from one of the odder aspects of a very odd business. Although a singer's popularity is measured today by his record sales, the crucial elements in his appeal are visual and non-recordable—his appearance and personality. When non-singing television and movie stars with teen-age appeal, such as Byrnes, Tab Hunter and Tony Perkins, attempt to transfer their appeal to disks, their limitations as singers have been no handicap.

Television or movie reputations can simplify the process of creating a recording star but they are not essential. During the past year an unknown teen-ager with no noticeable talent has climbed a remarkable route to popularity.

Two years ago 14-year-old Fabian Forte was observed sitting on the front steps of his South Philadelphia home by Bob Marcucci, head of a small record company. To Marcucci, he looked a bit like Elvis Presley or Ricky Nelson but with the down-to-earth quality of the boy next door. With nothing more than this visual impression to go on and despite young Forte's insistence that he could not sing, Marcucci began calling regularly at his home to urge him to try. ("Ma, that crazy guy's here again," Fabian called out to the kitchen one night. "He still wants to teach me how to sing.")

Fabian eventually tried out his vocal wings by singing along with a Ricky Nelson record. The demonstration proved that the boy was right—he was no singer. Marcucci sent him to a voice teacher. The teacher sent him back, advising, "Don't waste your money." A second teacher made the same suggestion. When Marcucci took the boy to a third teacher, he beat the teacher to the punch.

"Don't tell me not to waste my money," he said. "Just work on the kid for a few months and try to teach him to sing a little."

The teacher managed to open up Fabian's voice slightly, although he was not able to inculcate any sense of pitch. Nevertheless Marcucci decided that his find was ready to be recorded. His first disk, on which he was billed simply as "Fabian," was an excellent example of what the music trade knows as a "bomb"—a complete failure. But when Fabian made personal appearances to promote his record, teen-agers responded to him excitedly. Appearances on Dick Clark's TV show made him known, visually, to a wider audience.

Since February, 1958, Fabian has spent every school holiday (he is still in high school) and every week-end appearing before teen-age audiences. His second record, with his picture emblazoned on the sleeve, sold a respectable quarter of a million copies. His most recent effort, "Turn Me Loose," reached the top ten in the popularity charts. He was seen on the Perry Como show in April, with Ed Sullivan in May, returns to the Sullivan show tonight, and starts his first film for Twentieth Century-Fox in July.

Fabian's singing has improved since he made his first record but it is his physical attraction rather than his voice which has carried him upward so fast. Part of this attraction may lie in the fact that he is the opposite of the stereotyped conception of the rock 'n' roll singer. He does not wiggle. He simply stands up and tries to sing and, in the view of one of his fans, "projects a kind of joy of living." He dresses neatly but informally and he is well-mannered.

"Gee!" exclaimed a startled camera man on the Como show. "He called me 'sir!' "

A carefully created performer such as Fabian is still a rarity in pop music. More typical are singers or groups, as obviously untalented as Fabian was when Marcucci found him, who flash across the pop music charts with a single meteoric success and then disappear.

"Usually they are a group of kids who hang around a street corner together," a recording supervisor has explained. "They can't really sing but they work up one song and bring it to a record company. If we like it, we try to think which of the people we have under contract could use it. Usually it's not suitable for any of them. The only ones who can do it are these kids, so we record them. But then it's good-by because they can't come up with a follow-up."

Performances by these amateurs give recording engineers an opportunity to call up all the ingenuity and trickery at their command, although almost every pop recording made today, even by well established talent, carries some evidence of the use of echo chambers, tape
reverberation, equalizing, speeding, over-dubbing or splicing.

A singer's voice is now piped through an echo chamber—a room
with solid walls, a solid ceiling and a high reflecting surface—almost
as a matter of course to give it a big, resonant sound. Ten years ago,
when echo was a new toy, makeshift echo chambers were used. Two
early echo advocates, engineer Bob Fine and recording director Mitch
Miller, sent Frankie Laine's "Mule Train" cascading up and down
a circular stairwell to give it echo, and they piped Vic Damone's "Ave
Maria" through a bathroom.

A variant of the echo chamber, tape reverberation (or "tape reverb")
gave Elvis Presley's early records their distinctive, frantic, jangling
sound. Unlike an echo chamber, which sustains a sound, "tape reverb"
repeats it like a very rapid echo. This is a common device on rock 'n'
roll recordings because it is a simple method of covering up a paucity
of instruments or poor voices.

It is even possible for engineers and recording directors completely
to rearrange a recording after the performers have left the studio. The
sequence of choruses can be shifted, certain instruments or voices can
be given more prominent roles, others can be deleted entirely.

Two hit recordings by the Coasters, a vocal group—"Charlie Brown"
and "Yakety Yak"—were created in this fashion. Tom Dowd, chief
engineer for Atlantic Records, recorded the original performances on
eight channels, producing eight different tapes. Then he mixed these
tapes in whatever proportions or sequence he desired, first putting
down the lead voice and harmony, then adding the bass voice, next
running in a guitar, implementing that with a second guitar, then a
saxophone—slowly building and shaping the final record as though
he were working with colors or clay instead of sounds.

Because so many pop disks are a product of the recording engineer's
skill, it is often impossible for a singer to reproduce his hit recordings
in personal appearances. This is one reason why lip synchronization,
or "lip synch," is so prevalent on television, particularly on shows
which feature pop recording stars. In lip synching, a vocalist mouths
the words of a song while his recording is being played. This guarantees that the TV performances will sound exactly like the record.

But lip synching has its dangers. A young singer named Johnny
Sardo recently prepared for his appearance on the Alan Freed show by
painstakingly rehearsing his lip synchronization with his new record.
As he stepped confidently before the cameras, prepared to synch, he

froze in horror when he heard the first bars of music: They were playing the other side of his record.

Although the use of non-singers and engineering tricks in an effort to create hit records does not seem to disturb those who produce the records ("Pop music is in such a low state now that it can't be injured by non-musical performers," George Avakian has declared), others are less complacent. Alan Drake, a comedian, recently withdrew from a scheduled appearance on a bill which included Fabian because he felt that he would have nothing to offer the kind of audience that would be attracted by the recording star.

"A gifted singer takes literally years of painstaking work to become a polished entertainer," said Drake, "while someone like Fabian comes along with a gimmick in place of true talent and is immediately foisted on the public for purely monetary gain, offering nothing in the way of constructive entertainment in return. I feel it is an insult to the public to pass these wonderless wonders off as artists and I refuse to have any part of Fabian or his ilk."

However, these "wonders" are not "wonderless" to the teen-agers and sub-teen-agers who provide the bulk of the support for pop recordings. As long as teen-age taste is catered to, singers who reflect an immature concept of excitement and glamour are likely to remain in favor. Talent will not be a drawback. But, thanks to echo, tape reverb, over-dubbing and splicing, neither will lack of talent.

Suggested Topics

1. The decline of the popular singer
2. "Payola" and the popular record
3. How a recording is faked
4. The "highly competitive bedlam of pop recordings"
5. The repulsive idols of repellent teen-agers
6. The gadgetry of electronics and tape

THE AMERICAN THEATER   *Arthur Miller*

> An internationally known playwright with a strong and liberal
> social dedication and sense of responsibility, Arthur Miller is the
> author of such noted works as *Focus*, a novel (1944), and the
> plays *All My Sons* (1947), *Death of a Salesman* (1949), and *The
> Crucible* (1953).

The American theater occupies five side streets, Forty-fourth to
Forty-ninth, between Eighth Avenue and Broadway, with a few additional theaters to the north and south and across Broadway. In these
thirty-two buildings every new play in the United States starts its life
and ends it. There will undoubtedly be many objections to this statement—you cannot say anything about our theater without fear of
contradiction—and demurrers will come from professors of drama,
stock-company directors, and little-theater people in New York, Texas,
California and elsewhere who will claim that Broadway is not the
United States and that much theatrical production is going on in other
places. I agree, and repeat only that with practically no exceptions, the
new American plays originate on Broadway. I would add that I wish
they didn't, but they do. The American theater is five blocks long,
by about one and a half blocks wide.

It would seem a simple matter to characterize so limited an area,
but I write this with the certainty that whatever I say will appear not
only new and strange to many theater people but utterly untrue. And
this is because the man or woman whose tapping shoes you hear from
the second-story dance studio over the delicatessen on Forty-Sixth
Street is in the theater, the ballet girl hurrying to rehearsal in her
polo coat with a copy of Rimbaud in her pocket is in the theater, the
peasant-faced Irish stagehand sunning himself on the sidewalk with a
Racing Form in his hand is in the theater, the slow-staring, bald-headed
ticket broker blinking out through his agency window is in the theater,
the wealthy, Park Avenue-born producer is in the theater and his
cigar-smoking colleague from the West Bronx is in the theater.

In the audience itself, though the bulk of it is of the middle class,
there is no uniformity either. There will be the businessman in town
from Duluth sitting beside Marlene Dietrich whom he will probably

Reprinted from *Holiday*, January, 1955. Copyright © by Arthur Miller, July, 1955.

not recognize and behind them two esthetes from Harvard. The word theater means different things to different groups. To some its very pinnacle is *South Pacific,* which is despised by the esthetes, who in turn cherish a wispy fantasy whose meaning escapes the Duluth man. There is a vast group of people for whom the theater means nothing but amusement, and amusement means a musical or light comedy; and there are others who reserve their greatest enthusiasm for heavy dramas that they can chew on.

The actors, directors and writers themselves are just as varied. There are playwrights who are as illiterate as high-school boys, and there are playwrights like Maxwell Anderson, who have spent a good deal of their lives studying the Elizabethan drama and attempting to re-create its mood and luxuriance on Broadway. There are fine actors who are universally admired but who have absolutely no theory of acting and there are other actors, equally good or equally bad, who have spent years studying the history of acting, taking voice lessons and learning how to dance in order to walk more gracefully.

The theater, obviously, is an entirely different animal to each of these groups. As for myself, I cannot pretend to any Olympian viewpoint about it either. I believe there is a confusion in many minds between Show Business and the Theater. I belong to the Theater, which happens at the moment to be in a bad way, but since this word, when capitalized, usually implies something uplifting and boring, I must add that the rarely seen but very real Theater is the most engrossing theater of all; and when it isn't it is nothing. I make the distinction so that the reader will be warned where my prejudice lies and discount accordingly.

The "glamour of the theater," which is and always will be its most powerful attraction, is a subject of daily reporting by almost every newspaper, gossip columnist, and radio station. Every year, around the first cool days of fall, the illustrated sections of the press and the picture magazines and newsreels run the familiar photographs of the limousines gliding up to the lighted marquees, the taxis and cars pressing into Forty-Fourth Street for the opening of some musical or drama, the inevitable montage of Sardi's restaurant at dinnertime and so on. For anyone who has made the slightest mark in this occupation there is a line of type waiting when he so much as pays his rent on time. Soon after *Death of a Salesman* opened, it was reported that I was a millionaire, which was pleasant news, if not true, and that despite my new affluence I still rode the subways. I keep wondering who was watching me going through the turnstiles. And the importance of this news still escapes me.

In fact, while everybody in the business is worried about its future —and if there is a heart of uncertainty in the country its loudest beat may be heard on these five blocks—to read the columns and the usual sources of theatrical information you would think it was all a continuous carnival of divorce, practical jokes, hilarious wit, elopements and sudden acquisition of enormous wealth.

But there is evidently no way of glamorizing the often inspiring and heart-lifting experiences of the work itself, a kind of labor that began in the Western world about three thousand years ago, and which has provided some of the most powerful insights we possess into the way men think and feel.

The net result of this image of our theater, the carnival image, is that the out-of-towner strolling these streets may quickly sense that he has been bilked. He will discover, especially if he arrives in midday, that the theater buildings themselves are tawdry-looking, and may well be disillusioned when he sees that some of the marquees do not have even the electrically lit signs of his home movie house—only temporary cardboards painted with the title of the show within. When he ventures into the outer lobby he will perhaps be shocked to discover that a seat costs six—or even eight—dollars and, if the show is a hit, that he won't get a ticket for six months or a year unless he pays a scalper twenty-five to a hundred dollars. If it is not a hit, and he buys a ticket legitimately, he may learn that he could have bought two for the price of one; and by the time he gets inside for the performance, some of the glamour of it all may have worn a bit thin.

Once inside, however, our visitor may find certain compensations. He may recognize very important people, from statesmen to movie stars, sitting nearby, whom he would not see in the home-town movie house. He will notice a certain dressed-up air about people, a few even wearing evening clothes. There are ushers to show him to his seat, and there is a program, and possibly a little more surprising is the coat-check man waiting as he passes through the outer door. There is still a vestigial ceremony about playgoing from which one may derive a sense of self-importance if not careful, and it all may lead our visitor to feel that he is, indeed, among ladies and gentlemen.

Then, as the lights go down and the curtain rises, our visitor may feel a certain strange tension, an expectancy, and an intense curiosity that he never knew in a theater before. Instead of the enormity of the movie image before which he could sit back and relax, he is confronted by human beings in life-size, and since their voices do not roar out at him from a single point to which his ear may tune in once and then relax, he must pay more attention, his eyes must rove over a thirty-foot expanse; he must, in other words, *discover*. And if there happens to be something real up there, something human, something true, our visitor may come away with a new feeling in his heart, a sense of having been a part of something quite extraordinary and even beautiful. Unlike the movies, unlike television, he may feel he has been present at an *occasion*. For outside this theater, no one in the world heard what he heard or saw what he saw this night. I know that, for myself, there is nothing so immediate, so actual, as an excellent performance of an excellent play. I have never known the smell of sweat in a movie house. I have known it in the theater—and they are also air-conditioned. Nor have I known in a movie house the kind of audience unity that occasionally is created in the theater, an air of oneness among strangers that is possible in only one other gathering place—a church.

Nevertheless, by every account our theater is a vanishing institution. We have some thirty-two houses going today in New York as against forty or more ten years ago, and between seventy and eighty in the twenties. I could weave you such a tapestry of evil omens as to make it a closed case that we will have no theater in America in two decades. What I should like to do instead, however, is to wonder aloud, as it were, why it is that each year thousands of aspiring actors, directors and playwrights continue to press into these five blocks from every corner of the country when they know, or learn very quickly, that ninety per cent of the professional actors are normally unemployed, that most of the producers are dead broke or within three cigars of being broke, and that to become a director of a Broadway show one must be prepared to gamble five to ten to fifteen years of one's life. And yet, on all the trains they keep coming, aspiring actors and eager audiences both.

As for the aspiring actors, I will not pretend to hunt for an answer, because I know it. It is simply that there are always certain persons who are born without all their marbles. Even so, the fullblown actors are merely the completed types of the secret actors who are called producers, backers, directors, yes, and playwrights. The rest of us would have been actors had we had the talent, or a left and right foot instead of two left ones, or straight teeth, or self-assurance. The actor himself is the lunacy in full profusion—the lunacy which in the others is partially concealed.

All over the country there are nine-year-old girls, for instance, who are walking around the house like my daughter is at this very moment, in high-heeled shoes with the lace tablecloth trailing from their shoulders. If mine doesn't recover before she is sixteen she will wake up one morning and something will click inside her head and she will go and hang around some producer's office, and if he talks to her, or just asks her what time it is, she may well be doomed for life.

The five blocks, therefore, are unlike any other five blocks in the United States, if only because here so many grown people are walking around trailing the old lace tablecloth from their shoulders.

If you know how to look you will find them waiting on you in Schrafft's, or behind the orange-drink counter at Nedick's. As a matter of fact, I have got so attuned to a certain look in their eyes that I can sometimes spot them on Sixth Avenue, which is not in the theater district. I was passing a truck being loaded there one day when I noticed a boy, unshaven, his hair uncombed, wearing paratroop boots; he was pitching boxes into the truck. And he looked at me, just a glance, and I thought to myself that he must be an actor. And about three days later I was sitting in my producer's office interviewing actors for *The Crucible,* when in he walked. Characteristically, he did not remember seeing me before—actors rarely do, since they are not looking at anyone but rather are being looked *at*. When asked the usual questions about his experience he just shrugged, and when asked if he wanted to read for us he shrugged again, quite as though the questions were impertinent when addressed to a great artist, and I knew then why I had tabbed him for an actor. It was the time when all the young actors were being Marlon Brando. He was being Marlon Brando even when loading the truck, for a real truck driver would never show up for work looking so unkempt.

The blessed blindness of actors to everything around them, their intense preoccupation with themselves, is the basic characteristic of all Broadway, and underlies most of its troubles, which, in another industry, would have been solved long ago. But since it is glamour which brings the young to Broadway, as well as the audience, it cannot be so quickly dismissed. The fact is, it exists. But it is not the glamour you are probably thinking of.

The time is gone when the Great Producer kept four or five Great Stars in ten-room apartments on Park Avenue, and they waited in their gilded cages for days and weeks for the Impresario to call for them—for without him they were forbidden to be seen in public lest they lose their "distance," their altitude above the common things of life. The time is gone when the leading lady dared not arrive at the theater in anything but a limousine with chauffeur and lap robe, while a line of stovepipe-hatted men waited in the stage-door alley with flowers in their manicured hands. There are a few hangovers, of course, and I remember a show in Boston a few years ago whose leading lady, an hour before curtain time, phoned the producer to say she was ill and could not play. The poor man was desperate, but there was an old-time doorman in that theater who happened to be near the phone and he said, "Get a limousine and a chauffeur." The producer, a contemporary type who was as familiar with gallantry as any other businessman, mastered his uncertainty and hired a car and chauffeur and sent a mass of roses to the lady's hotel room. Her fever vanished in roughly four minutes and she played better than she ever had, and I must confess I couldn't blame her for wanting the glamour even if she had had to make it herself.

But leading ladies, nowadays, arrive in a taxi, and a lot of them come in by bus or subway.

I have been around only ten years or so and I never knew the kind of glamour that evidently existed. But a few years ago I had occasion to visit John Golden in his office, and I saw then that there was, in fact, a kind of bravado about being in the theater, a declaration of war against all ordinariness that I can find no more.

The average theatrical producer's office today consists mainly of a telephone, a girl to answer it, an outer room for actors to wait in, and an inner room with a window for the producer to stare out of when he has nothing to produce.

John Golden's office is different. It rests on top of the St. James Theater; you rise in a private elevator, and come out in a dark, paper-clutter reception room where an elderly and very wise lady bars you— with the help of a little gate—from entry. You know at once that behind her is not merely a man, but a Presence.

In his office the walls are painted with smoke. They are very dark and covered with hundreds of photographs, plaques, statuettes, hanging things and jutting things of gold, silver and shiny brass. There is an Oriental rug on the floor, an ornate desk at the distant end of the room, and there sits John Golden, who is now eighty years old.[1] Behind him stands an imposing ascent of bookshelves filled with leather-bound plays he has produced. In a smaller adjoining room is a barber chair where his hair is cut, his beard shaved, and, I presume, his shoes shined. The windows are covered with drapes and obstructing statuary, because when this office was created, the man who worked in it had no time to look out into the street.

It was a time when the railroads were freighting out one after another of his productions, winter and summer, to all sections of the country. It was a time when, unlike now, important performers and even playwrights were kept on long-term contracts, when a producer owned his own theater and used his own money and was therefore not an accountant, nor even a businessman, but an impresario. In short, it was the time before the masses had left the theater for the new movies, and the theater was the main source of American popular entertainment. This office is now a kind of museum. There were once many like it, and many men like John Golden.

Their counterparts, the reflected images of Ziegfeld, Frohman, Belasco and the others, appeared only later in Hollywood, for the masses are needed to create impresarios, or more precisely, a lucrative

[1] John Golden died on June 17, 1955.

mass market. In Golden's office I saw the genesis of so much we have come to associate with Hollwood: the stars under long-term contract, the planning of one production after another instead of the present one-shot Broadway practice, the sense of permanence and even security. None of these are part of Broadway now, and they appear in their after-glow above the St. James; for it is not the masses we serve any more, not the "American People," but a fraction of one class—the more or less better-educated people, or the people aspiring to culture.

Golden's eyes blazed with pleasure as he talked of plays long since gone, like *Turn to the Right* and *Lightnin'* and others I remember my father raving about when I was a boy, and finally he sat back and mused about playwriting.

"You fellows have a much harder time," he said, "much harder than in the old days; nowadays every show has to seem new and original. But in the old days, you know, we had what you might call favorite scenes. There was the scene where the mother puts a candle on the window sill while she waits for her long-lost boy to come home. They loved that scene. We put that scene in one play after another. You can't do things like that any more. The audience is too smart now. They're more educated, I suppose, and sophisticated. Of course it was all sentimental, I guess, but they were good shows."

He was right, of course, except you *can* do that now; the movies have been doing it for thirty or forty years and now television is doing it all over again. I remember a friend who had worked in Hollywood writing a picture. The producer called him in with a bright new idea for a scene to be inserted in the script. My friend listened and was amazed. "But just last month you released a picture with that same scene in it," he reminded the producer.

"Sure," said the producer, "and didn't it go great?"

The Golden species of glamour is gone with the masses; it went with the big money to Hollywood, and now it is creating itself all over again in television. The present-day actors and directors would probably seem tame and dull to their counterparts of thirty and forty years ago. David Belasco, for instance, had even convinced himself that his was a glamorous profession, and took to dressing in black like a priest —the high priest of the theater—and turned his collar around to prove it. He carried on as no contemporary director would dare to do. Toward the last days of rehearsal, when he wanted some wooden but very beautiful leading lady to break down and weep, he would take out a watch, the watch he had been displaying for weeks as the one his mother gave him on her deathbed, and smash it on the stage floor in a high dudgeon, thus frightening the actress to tears and making her putty in his hands. It need hardly be added that he kept a large supply of these watches, each worth one dollar.

The traditional idea of the actor with his haughty stance, his peaked eyebrow, elegant speech, artistic temperament, and a necessary disdain for all that was common and plain, has long since disappeared. Now they are all trying to appear as ordinary as your Uncle Max. A group of actors sitting at a bar these days could easily be mistaken for delegates to a convention of white-collar people. They are more likely, upon landing in a hit show, to hurry over to the offices of a tax consultant than to rush out and buy a new Jaguar. For a few years after the war a certain amount of effort was put into aging their dungarees and wearing turtle-neck sweaters and some of them stopped combing their hair, like the boy I noticed loading the truck. But you don't get Marlon Brando's talent by avoiding a bath, and gradually this fad has vanished. There are more "colorful" personalities up here in the tiny Connecticut village where I spend summers than you will find on all Broadway. The only real showman I know of is Joshua Logan, who can throw a party for a hundred people in his Park Avenue apartment and make it appear a normal evening. Logan is the only director I can name who would dare to knock a stage apart and build into it a real swimming pool, as he did for the musical *Wish You Were Here,* and can still talk about the theater with the open, full-blown excitement of one who has no reservations about it. The other directors, at least the half dozen I know—and there are not many more—are more likely to be as deadly serious as any atomic physicist, and equally worried.

There is a special aura about the theater, nevertheless, a glamour, too, but it has little connection with the publicity that seeks to create it. There is undoubtedly as much sexual fooling around as there is in the refrigerator business, but I doubt if there is much more. The notion of theatrical immorality began when actors were socially inferior by common consent; but now a Winnifred Cushing (of the Boston Cushings), the loose woman in *Death of a Salesman,* hurries home to her mother after each show.

Not that it is an ordinary life. There is still nothing quite like it, if only because of the fanaticism with which so many respond to its lure. One cannot sit in a producer's office day after day interviewing actors for a play without being struck by their insistence that they belong in the theater and intend to make their lives in it. In the outer reception rooms of any producer's office at casting time is a cross section of a hundred small towns and big cities, the sons and daughters of the rich families and of the middle-class families and of families from the wrong side of the tracks. One feels, on meeting a youngster from a way-station town or a New Mexico ranch, that the spores of this poor theater must still possess vitality to have flown so far and rooted so deep. It is pathetic, it is saddening, but a thing is only dead when nobody wants it, and they do want it desperately. It is nothing un-

usual to tell a girl who has come to a casting office that she looks
too respectable for the part, and to be greeted by her an hour later
dressed in a slinky black dress, spike heels, outlandishly overdone
make-up and blond dye in her hair that has hardly had time to dry.
One of our best-known actresses had her bowlegs broken in order to
appear as she thought she must on the stage, and there is an actor who
did the same to his knees in order to play Hamlet in tights.

There is, it must be admitted, an egotism in this that can neither be
measured nor sometimes even stomached, but at casting time, when
one spends hour after hour in the presence of human beings with so
powerful a conviction and so great a desire to be heard and seen and
judged as artists, the thing begins to surpass mere egotism and assumes
the proportion of a cause, a belief, a mission. And when such sacrifices
are made in its name one must begin to wonder at the circumstances
that have reduced it to its present chaos. It might be helpful to take
a look at how the whole thing is organized—or disorganized.

Everything begins with a script. I must add right off that in the
old mass theater that came to an end somewhere in the late twenties,
when the movies took over, the script was as often as not a botch of
stolen scenes, off-the-cuff inventions of the producer or director, or
simply pasted-together situations designed for some leading player.
The audience today, however, demands more, and so the script has
become the Holy Grail for which a producer dreams, prays, and lives
every day of his life. It being so valuable, and so difficult to write, it is
leased by the author on a royalty basis and never sold outright. He
receives, I am happy to report, roughly ten per cent of the gross
receipts, or between two and three thousand dollars a week if he has
a hit. (I would add that he resolves not to change his standard of living
but he has a wife, and that is that.)

Three or four times a year the playwrights have a meeting of the
Dramatists Guild, their union, in a private dining room of the St.
Regis Hotel. Moss Hart, the author of *Climate of Eden* and, with
George Kaufman, of a string of successes like *The Man Who Came to
Dinner* and *You Can't Take It With You,* is the current president of
the Guild. There is probably more money represented here than at most
union luncheons, the only trouble being that with a few exceptions
none of the playwrights has any assets; that is, you can't write a hit
every time so the three thousand a week begins to look smaller and
smaller when it is averaged out over a period of unfruitful years.
Oscar Hammerstein, another Guild member, put an ad in *Variety*
after his *South Pacific* opened, listing a dozen or so of his failures
that everyone had forgotten, and at the bottom of the page repeated
the legend of show business, "I did it before and I can do it again."

Between the turtle soup and the veal scallopine, various issues are discussed, all of which are usually impossible to solve, and the luncheons roll by and we know that our profession is on the edge of an abyss because the theater is contracting; and we all go home to write our plays. Occasionally we meet with a group of producers, and Max Gordon can usually be relied on to demand the floor; and red in the face, full of his wonderful fight, he will cut to the heart of the problem by shouting at the playwrights, "The producers are starving, you hear me? Starving!" Leland Hayward, who has scraped by on *South Pacific, Mister Roberts,* and other such titbits, will accuse me of making too much money, and Herman Shumlin, the producer of *Little Foxes, Children's Hour, Watch on the Rhine,* will solemnly avow that he is leaving the business forever unless we writers cut our royalties; and then we all go home. Once the late Lee Shubert came with the others to discuss the problems of the theater, and when he was asked if he would reduce the rentals of his many theaters, since the playwrights were willing to reduce their royalties, he looked as though the butter was, indeed, melting in his mouth, so he didn't open it. And we all went home again.

There are seemingly hundreds of producers, but actually only fifteen or twenty go on year after year. Few are wealthy, and money is usually promoted or lured out of any crack where it can be found. It is a common, although not universal, practice to hold a gathering of potential backers before whom either the playwright or the director reads the script. Established producers regard this as beneath their dignity, but some don't, or can't afford to. These readings usually take place either on Park Avenue or on swank Beekman Place, for some reason, and while I never attended one, I have known many playwrights who have, but never heard of one dollar being raised in that way.

Script in hand, then, and money either raised or on its way—usually in amounts under five hundred dollars per backer—the producer hires a director, also on a percentage with a fee in advance, and a scene designer; the set is sketched, approved, and ordered built. Casting begins. While the author sits home revising his script—for some reason no script can be produced as the author wrote it—agents are apprised of the kinds of parts to be filled, and in the producer's reception room next morning all hell breaks loose.

The basis upon which actors are hired or not hired is sometimes quite sound; for example, they may have been seen recently in a part which leads the director to believe they are right for the new role; but quit as often a horde of applicants is waiting beyond the door of the producer's private office and neither he nor the director nor the author has the slightest knowledge of any of them. It is at this point that things become painful, for the strange actor sits before them, so nervous and frightened that he either starts talking and can't stop, and sometimes *says* he can't stop, or is unable to say anything at all and says *that*. During the casting of one of my plays there entered a middle-aged woman who was so frightened she suddenly started to sing. The play being no musical, this was slightly beside the point, but the producer, the director and myself, feeling so guilty ourselves, sat there and heard her through.

To further complicate matters there is each year the actor or actress who suddenly becomes what they call "hot." A hot performer is one not yet well-known, but who, for some mysterious reason, is generally conceded to be a coming star. It is possible, naturally, that a hot performer really has talent, but it is equally possible, and much more likely, that she or he is not a whit more attractive, or more talented than a hundred others. Nevertheless, there comes a morning when every producer in these five blocks—some of them with parts the performer could never play—simply has to have him or her. Next season, of course, nobody hears about the new star and it starts all over again with somebody else.

All that is chancy in life, all that is fortuitous, is magnified to the bursting point at casting time; and that, I suspect is one of the attractions of this whole affair, for it makes the ultimate winning of a part so much more zesty. It is also, to many actors, a most degrading process and more and more of them refuse to submit to these interviews until after the most delicate advances of friendship and hospitality are made to them. And their use of agents as intermediaries is often an attempt to soften the awkwardness of their applying for work.

The theatrical agents, in keeping with the unpredictable lunacy of the business, may be great corporations like the Music Corporation of America, which has an entire building on Madison Avenue, and will sell you anything from a tap dancer to a movie star, a symphony orchestra, saxophonists, crooners, scene designers, actors and playwrights, to a movie script complete with cast; or they may be like Jane Broder, who works alone and can spread out her arms and touch both walls of her office. They may even be like Carl Cowl who lives around the corner from me in Brooklyn. Carl is an ex-seaman who still ships out when he has no likely scripts on hand to sell, and when things get too nerve-racking he stays up all night playing Mozart on his flute. MCA has antique desks, English 18th Century prints, old broken antique clocks and inoperative antique barometers hanging on its paneled walls, but Carl Cowl had a hole in his floor that the cat got into and when he finally got the landlord to repair it he was happy and sat down to play his flute again; but he heard meowing, and they had to rip the floor open again to let out the cat. Still, Carl is not incapable of landing a hit play and neither more nor less likely than MCA to get it produced, and that is another handicraft aspect of this

much publicized small business, a quality of opportunity which keeps
people coming into it. The fact is that theatrical agents do not sell
anyone or anything in the way one sells merchandise. Their existence
is mainly due to the need theater people have for a home, some sem-
blance of order in their lives, some sense of being wanted during the
long periods when they have nothing to do. To have an agent is to
have a kind of reassurance that you exist. The actor is hired, however,
mainly because he is wanted for the role.

By intuition, then, by rumor, on the recommendation of an agent—
usually heartfelt; out of sheer exhaustion, and upsurge of sudden hope
or what not, several candidates for each role are selected in the office
of the producer, and are called for readings on the stage of a theater.

It is here that the still unsolved mystery begins, the mystery of what
makes a stage performer. There are persons who, in an office, seem
exciting candidates for a role, but as soon as they step onto a stage the
observers out front—if they are experienced—know that the blessing
was not given them. For myself, I know it when, regardless of how well
the actor is reading, my eyes begin to wander up to the brick wall back
of the stage. Conversely, there are many who make little impression in
an office, but once on the stage it is impossible to take one's attention
from them. It is neither a question of technique nor ability, I think,
but some quality of surprise inherent in the person.

For instance, when we were searching for a woman to play Linda,
the mother in *Death of a Salesman,* a lady came in whom we all knew
but could never imagine in the part. We needed a woman who looked
as though she had lived in a house dress all her life, even somewhat
coarse and certainly less than brilliant. Mildred Dunnock insisted she
was that woman, but she was frail, delicate, not long ago a teacher
in a girl's college, and a cultivated citizen who probably would not
be out of place in a cabinet post. We told her this, in effect, and she
understood, and left.

And the next day the line of women formed again in the wings and
suddenly there was Milly again. Now she had padded herself from
neck to hemline to look a bit bigger, and for a moment none of us
recognized her, and she read again. As soon as she spoke we started to
laugh at her ruse; but we saw, too, that she *was* a little more worn
now, and seemed less well-maintained, and while she was not quite
ordinary she reminded you of women who were. But we all agreed,
when she was finished reading, that she was not right, and she left.

Next day she was there again in another getup and the next and
the next, and each day she agreed with us that she was wrong; and
to make a long story short when it came time to make the final selection it had to be Milly and she turned out to be magnificent. But in
this case we had known her work; there was no doubt that she was

an excellent actress. The number of talented applicants who are turned down because they are unknowns is very large. Such is the crap-shooting chanciness of the business, its chaos, and part of its charm. In a world where one's fare so often seems machined and standardized, and unlikely to suddenly change, these five blocks are like a stockade inside which are people who insist that the unexpected, the sudden chance, must survive. And to experience it they keep coming on all the trains.

But to understand its apparently deathless lure for so many it is necessary, finally, to have participated in the first production of a new play. When a director takes his place at the beaten-up wooden table placed at the edge of the stage, and the cast for the first time sit before him in a semicircle, and he gives the nod to the actor who has the opening lines, the world seems to be filling with a kind of hope, a kind of regeneration that, at the time, anyway, makes all the sacrifices worth while.

The production of a new play, I have often thought, is like another chance in life, a chance to emerge cleansed of one's imperfections. Here, as when one was very young, it seems possible again to attain even greatness, or happiness, or some otherwise unattainable joy. And when production never loses that air of hope through all its three-and-a-half-week rehearsal period, one feels alive as at no other imaginable occasion. At such a time, it seems to all concerned that the very heart of life's mystery is what must be penetrated. They watch the director and each other and they listen with the avid attention of deaf mutes who have suddenly learned to speak and hear. Above their heads there begins to form a tantalizing sort of cloud, a question, a challenge to penetrate the mystery of why men move and speak and act.

It is a kind of glamour that can never be reported in a newspaper column, and yet it is the center of all the lure theater has. It is a kind of soul-testing that ordinary people rarely experience except in the greatest emergencies. The actor who has always regarded himself as a strong spirit discovers now that his vaunted power somehow sounds querulous, and he must look within himself to find his strength. The actress who has made her way on her charm discovers that she appears not charming so much as shallow now, and must evaluate herself all over again, and create anew what she always took for granted. And the great performers are merely those who have been able to face themselves without remorse.

In the production of a good play with a good cast and a knowing director a kind of banding-together occurs; there is formed a fraternity whose members share a mutual sense of destiny. In these five blocks, where the rapping of the tap-dancer's feet and the bawling of the phonographs in the recordshop doorways mix with the roar of the Broadway traffic; where the lonely, the perverted, and the lost wander like the souls in Dante's hell and the life of the spirit seems impossible, there are still little circles of actors in the dead silence of empty theaters, with a director in their center, and a new creation of life taking place.

There are always certain moments in such rehearsals, moments of such wonder that the memory of them serves to further entrap all who witness them into this most insecure of all professions. Remembering such moments the resolution to leave and get a "real" job vanishes and they are hooked again.

I think of Lee Cobb, the greatest dramatic actor I ever saw, when he was creating the role of Willy Loman in *Death of a Salesman*. When I hear people scoffing at actors as mere exhibitionists, when I hear them ask why there must be a theater if it cannot support itself as any business must, when I myself grow sick and weary of the endless waste and the many travesties of this most abused of all arts, I think then of Lee Cobb making that role and I know that the theater can yet be one of the chief glories of mankind.

He sat for days on the stage like a great lump, a sick seal, a mourning walrus. When it came his time to speak lines, he whispered meaninglessly. Kazan, the director, pretended certainty, but from where I sat he looked like an ant trying to prod an elephant off his haunches. Ten days went by. The other actors were by now much further advanced: Milly Dunnock, playing Linda, was already creating a role; Arthur Kennedy as Biff had long since begun to reach for his high notes; Cameron Mitchell had many scenes already perfected; but Cobb stared at them, heavy-eyed, morose, even persecuted, it seemed.

And then, one afternoon, there on the stage of the New Amsterdam way up on top of a movie theater on 42nd Street (this roof theater had once been Ziegfeld's private playhouse in the gilded times, and now was barely heated and misty with dust), Lee rose from his chair and looked at Milly Dunnock and there was silence. And then he said, "I was driving along, you understand, and then all of a sudden I'm going off the road. . . ."

And the theater vanished. The stage vanished. The chill of an age-old recognition shuddered my spine; a voice was sounding in the dimly lit air up front, a created spirit, an incarnation, a Godlike creation was taking place; a new human being was being formed before all our eyes, born for the first time on this earth, made real by an act of will, by an artist's summoning up of all his memories and his intelligence; a birth was taking place above the meaningless traffic below; a man was here transcending the limits of his body and his own history. Through the complete concentration of his mind he had even altered the stance of his body, which now was strangely not the body

of Lee Cobb (he was 37 then) but of a sixty-year-old salesman; a mere
glance of his eye created a window beside him, with the gentle touch
of his hand on this empty stage a bed appeared, and when he glanced
up at the emptiness above him a ceiling was there, and there was even
a crack in it where his stare rested.

I knew then that something astounding was being made here. It
would have been almost enough for me without even opening the play.
The actors, like myself and Kazan and the producer, were happy, of
course, that we might have a hit; but there was a good deal more.
There was a new fact of life, there was an alteration of history for all
of us that afternoon.

There is a certain immortality involved in theater, not created by
monuments and books, but through the knowledge the actor keeps to
his dying day that on a certain afternoon, in an empty and dusty
theater, he cast a shadow of a being that was not himself but the
distillation of all he had ever observed; all the unsingable heartsong
the ordinary man may feel but never utter, he gave voice to. And by
that he somehow joins the ages.

And that is the glamour that remains, but it will not be found in
the gossip columns. And it is enough, once discovered, to make people
stay with the theater, and others to come seeking it.

I think also that people keep coming into these five blocks because
the theater is still so simple, so old-fashioned. And that is why, however often its obsequies are intoned, it somehow never really dies.
Because underneath our shiny fronts of stone, our fascination with
gadgets and our new toys that can blow the earth into a million stars,
we are still outside the doorway through which the great answers wait.
Not all the cameras in Christendom nor all the tricky lights will move
us one step closer to a better understanding of ourselves, but only, as
it always was, the truly written word, the profoundly felt gesture, the
naked and direct contemplation of man which is the enduring glamour
of the stage.

Suggested Topics

1. The theater as human revelation
2. Off-Broadway theater
3. The stage vs. the screen
4. The greatest actor I have ever seen
5. Is the theater a vanishing institution?
6. The special aura about the theater

THE WESTERNER   *Robert Warshow*

A frequent contributor of film criticism for *Partisan Review*
and other publications, Robert Warshow was managing editor
of *Commentary* till his untimely death in March, 1955.

The two most successful creations of American movies are the
gangster and the Westerner: men with guns. Guns as physical objects,
and the postures associated with their use, form the visual and emotional center of both types of films. I suppose this reflects the importance of guns in the fantasy life of Americans; but that is a less
illuminating point that it appears to be.

The gangster movie, which no longer exists in its "classical" form,
is a story of enterprise and success ending in precipitate failure. Success is conceived as an increasing power to work injury, it belongs to
the city, and it is of course a form of evil (though the gangster's death,
presented usually as "punishment," is perceived simply as defeat). The
peculiarity of the gangster is his unceasing, nervous activity. The exact
nature of his enterprises may remain vague, but his commitment to
enterprise is always clear, and all the more clear because he operates
outside the field of utility. He is without culture, without manners,
without leisure, or at any rate his leisure is likely to be spent in
debauchery so compulsively aggressive as to seem only another aspect
of his "work." But he is graceful, moving like a dancer among the
crowded dangers of the city.

Like other tycoons, the gangster is crude in conceiving his ends
but by no means inarticulate; on the contrary, he is usually expansive
and noisy (the introspective gangster is a fairly recent development),
and can state definitely what he wants: to take over the North Side,
to own a hundred suits, to be Number One. But new "frontiers" will
present themselves infinitely, and by a rigid convention it is understood that as soon as he wishes to rest on his gains, he is on the way
to destruction.

The gangster is lonely and melancholy, and can give the impression of a profound worldly wisdom. He appeals most to adolescents
with their impatience and their feeling of being outsiders, but more

Reprinted from *Partisan Review*, March-April, 1954. By permission of *Partisan
Review* and the Estate of Robert Warshow.

generally he appeals to that side of all of us which refuses to believe in the "normal" possibilities of happiness and achievement; the gangster is the "no" to that great American "yes" which is stamped so big over our official culture and yet has so little to do with the way we really feel about our lives. But the gangster's loneliness and melancholy are not "authentic"; like everything else that belongs to him, they are not honestly come by: he is lonely and melancholy not because life ultimately demands such feelings but because he has put himself in a position where everybody wants to kill him and eventually somebody will. He is wide open and defenseless, incomplete because unable to accept any limits or come to terms with his own nature, fearful, loveless. And the story of his career is a nightmare inversion of the values of ambition and opportunity. From the window of Scarface's bullet-proof apartment can be seen an electric sign proclaiming: "The World Is Yours," and, if I remember, this sign is the last thing we see after Scarface lies dead in the street. In the end it is the gangster's weakness as much as his power and freedom that appeals to us; the world is not ours, but it is not his either, and in his death he "pays" for our fantasies, releasing us momentarily both from the concept of success, which he denies by caricaturing it, and from the need to succeed, which he shows to be dangerous.

The Western hero, by contrast, is a figure of repose. He resembles the gangster in being lonely and to some degree melancholy. But his melancholy comes from the "simple" recognition that life is unavoidably serious, not from the disproportions of his own temperament. And his loneliness is organic, not imposed on him by his situation but belonging to him intimately and testifying to his completeness. The gangster must reject others violently or draw them violently to him. The Westerner is not thus compelled to seek love; he is prepared to accept it, perhaps, but he never asks of it more than it can give, and we see him constantly in situations where love is at best an irrelevance. If there is a woman he loves, she is usually unable to understand his motives; she is against killing and being killed, and he finds it impossible to explain to her that there is no point in being "against" these things: they belong to his world.

Very often this woman is from the East and her failure to understand represents a clash of cultures. In the American mind, refinement, virtue, civilization, Christianity itself, are seen as feminine, and therefore women are often portrayed as possessing some kind of deeper wisdom, while the men, for all their apparent self-assurance, are fundamentally childish. But the West, lacking the graces of civilization, is the place "where men are men;" in Western movies, men have the deeper wisdom and the women are children. Those women in the Western movies who share the hero's understanding of life are prosti-

tutes (or, as they are usually presented, bar-room entertainers)—
women, that is, who have come to understand in the most practical
way how love can be an irrelevance, and therefore "fallen" women.
The gangster, too, associates with prostitutes, but for him the important things about a prostitute are her passive availability and her
costliness: she is part of his winnings. In Western movies, the important thing about a prostitute is her quasi-masculine independence:
nobody owns her, nothing has to be explained to her, and she is not,
like a virtuous woman, a "value" that demands to be protected. When
the Westerner leaves the prostitute for a virtuous woman—for love—
he is in fact forsaking a way of life, though the point of the choice
is often obscured by having the prostitute killed by getting into the
line of fire.

The Westerner is *par excellence* a man of leisure. Even when he
wears the badge of a marshal or, more rarely, owns a ranch, he appears
to be unemployed. We see him standing at a bar, or playing poker—
a game which expresses perfectly his talent for remaining relaxed in
the midst of tension—or perhaps camping out on the plains on some
extraordinary errand. If he does own a ranch, it is in the background;
we are not actually aware that he owns anything except his horse, his
guns, and the one worn suit of clothing which is likely to remain un-
changed all through the movie. It comes as a surprise to see him take
money from his pocket or an extra shirt from his saddle-bags. As a
rule we do not even know where he sleeps at night and don't think
of asking. Yet it never occurs to us that he is a poor man; there is no
poverty in Western movies, and really no wealth either: those great
cattle domains and shipments of gold which figure so largely in the
plots are moral and not material quantities, not the objects of contention but only its occasion. Possessions too are irrelevant.

Employment of some kind—usually unproductive—is always open
to the Westerner, but when he accepts it, it is not because he needs
to make a living, much less from any idea of "getting ahead." Where
could he want to "get ahead" to? By the time we see him, he is already
"there": he can ride a horse faultlessly, keep his countenance in the
face of death, and draw his gun a little faster and shoot it a little
straighter than anyone he is likely to meet. These are sharply defined
acquirements, giving to the figure of the Westerner an apparent moral
clarity which corresponds to the clarity of his physical image against
his bare landscape; initially, at any rate, the Western movie presents
itself as being without mystery, its whole universe comprehended in
what we see on the screen.

Much of this apparent simplicity arises directly from those "cinematic" elements which have long been understood to give the Western
theme its special appropriateness for the movies: the wide expanses

of land, the free movement of men on horses. As guns constitute the
visible moral center of the Western movie, suggesting continually the
possibility of violence, so land and horses represent the movie's material basis, its sphere of action. But the land and the horses have also
a moral significance: the physical freedom they represent belongs to
the moral "openness" of the West—corresponding to the fact that
guns are carried where they can be seen. (And, as we shall see, the
character of land and horses changes as the Western film becomes
more complex.)

The gangster's world is less open, and his arts not so easily identi-
fiable as the Westerner's. Perhaps he too can keep his countenance,
but the mask he wears is really no mask: its purpose is precisely to
make evident the fact that he desperately wants to "get ahead" and
will stop at nothing. Where the Westerner imposes himself by the
appearance of unshakable control, the gangster's pre-eminence lies in
the suggestion that he may at any moment lose control; his strength
is not in being able to shoot faster or straighter than others, but in
being more willing to shoot. "Do it first," says Scarface expounding
his mode of operation, "and keep on doing it!" With the Westerner,
it is a crucial point of honor not to "do it first"; his gun remains in its
holster until the moment of combat.

There is no suggestion, however, that he draws the gun reluctantly.
The Westerner could not fulfill himself if the moment did not finally
come when he can shoot his enemy down. But because that moment
is so thoroughly the expression of his being, it must be kept pure. He
will not violate the accepted forms of combat though by doing so he
could save a city. And he can wait. "When you call me that—smile!"—
the villain smiles weakly, soon he is laughing with horrible joviality,
and the crisis is past. But it is allowed to pass because it must come
again: sooner or later Trampas will "make his play," and the Virginian will be ready for him.

What does the Westerner fight for? We know he is on the side of
justice and order, and of course it can be said he fights for these things.
But such broad aims never correspond exactly to his real motives; they
only offer him his opportunity. The Westerner himself, when an
explanation is asked of him (usually by a woman), is likely to say that
he does what he "has to do." If justice and order did not continually
demand his protection, he would be without a calling. Indeed, we
come upon him often in just that situation, as the reign of law settles
over the West and he is forced to see that his day is over; those are
the pictures which end with his death or with his departure for some
more remote frontier. What he defends, at bottom, is the purity of
his own image—in fact his honor. This is what makes him invulnerable. When the gangster is killed, his whole life is shown to have been

a mistake, but the image the Westerner seeks to maintain can be presented as clearly in defeat as in victory: he fights not for advantage and not for the right, but to state what he is, and he must live in a world which permits that statement. The Westerner is the last gentleman, and the movies which over and over again tell his story are probably the last art form in which the concept of honor retains its strength.

Of course I do not mean to say that ideas of virtue and justice and courage have gone out of culture. Honor is more than these things: it is a style, concerned with harmonious appearances as much as with desirable consequences, and tending therefore toward the denial of life in favor of art. "Who hath it? he that died o' Wednesday." On the whole, a world that leans to Falstaff's view is a more civilized and even, finally, a more graceful world. It is just the march of civilization that forces the Westerner to move on; and if we actually had to confront the question it might turn out that the woman who refuses to understand him is right as often as she is wrong. But we do not confront the question. Where the Westerner lives it is always about 1870 —not the real 1870, either, or the real West—and he is killed or goes away when his position becomes problematical. The fact that he continues to hold our attention is evidence enough that, in his proper frame, he presents an image of personal nobility that is still real for us.

Clearly, this image easily becomes ridiculous: we need only look at William S. Hart or Tom Mix, who in the wooden absoluteness of their virtue represented little that an adult could take seriously; and doubtless such figures as Gene Autry or Roy Rogers are no better, though I confess I have seen none of their movies. Some film enthusiasts claim to find in the early, unsophisticated Westerns a "cinematic purity" that has since been lost; this idea is as valid, and finally as misleading, as T. S. Eliot's statement that *Everyman* is the only play in English that stays within the limitations of art. The truth is that the Westerner comes into the field of serious art only when his moral code, without ceasing to be compelling, is seen also to be imperfect. The Westerner at his best exhibits a moral ambiguity which darkens his image and saves him from absurdity; this ambiguity arises from the fact that, whatever his justifications, he is a killer of men.

In *The Virginian,* which is an archetypal Western movie as *Scarface* or *Little Caesar* are archetypal gangster movies, there is a lynching in which the hero (Gary Cooper), as leader of a posse, must supervise the hanging of his best friend for stealing cattle. With the growth of American "social consciousness," it is no longer possible to present a lynching in the movies unless the point is the illegality and injustice of the lynching itself; *The Ox-Bow Incident,* made in 1943, explicitly puts forward the newer point of view and can be regarded as a kind of "anti-Western." But in 1929, when *The Virginian* was made, the present inhibition about lynching was not yet in force; the justice, and therefore the necessity, of the hanging is never questioned—except by the schoolteacher from the East, whose refusal to understand serves as usual to set forth more sharply the deeper seriousness of the West. The Virginian is thus in a tragic dilemma where one moral absolute conflicts with another and the choice of either must leave a moral stain. If he had chosen to save his friend, he would have violated the image of himself that he had made essential to his existence, and the movie would have had to end with his death, for only by his death could the image have been restored. Having chosen instead to sacrifice his friend to the higher demands of the "code"—the only choice worthy of him, as even the friend understands—he is none the less stained by the killing, but what is needed now to set accounts straight is not his death but the death of the villain Trampas, the leader of the cattle thieves, who had escaped the posse and abandoned the Virginian's friend to his fate. Again the woman intervenes: Why must there be *more* killing? If the hero really loved her, he would leave town, refusing Trampas's challenge. What good will it be if Trampas should kill him? But the Virginian does once more what he "has to do," and in avenging his friend's death wipes out the stain on his own honor. Yet his victory cannot be complete: no death can be paid for and no stain truly wiped out; the movie is still a tragedy, for though the hero escapes with his life, he has been forced to confront the ultimate limits of his moral ideas.

This mature sense of limitation and unavoidable guilt is what gives the Westerner a "right" to his melancholy. It is true that the gangster's story is also a tragedy—in certain formal ways more clearly a tragedy than the Westerner's—but it is a romantic tragedy, based on a hero whose defeat springs with almost mechanical inevitability from the outrageous presumption of his demands: the gangster is *bound* to go on until he is killed. The Westerner is a more classical figure, self-contained and limited to begin with, seeking not to extend his dominion but only to assert his personal value, and his tragedy lies in the fact that even this circumscribed demand cannot be fully realized. Since the Westerner is not a murderer but (most of the time) a man of virtue, and since he is always prepared for defeat, he retains his inner invulnerability and his story need not end with his death (and usually does not); but what we finally respond to is not his victory but his defeat.

Up to a point, it is plain that the deeper seriousness of the good Western films comes from the introduction of a realism, both physical and psychological, that was missing with Tom Mix and William S.

Hart. As lines of age have come into Gary Cooper's face since *The Virginian,* so the outlines of the Western movie in general have become less smooth, its background more drab. The sun still beats upon the town, but the camera is likely now to take advantage of this illumination to seek out more closely the shabbiness of buildings and furniture, the loose, worn hang of clothing, the wrinkles and dirt of the faces. Once it has been discovered that the true theme of the Western movie is not the freedom and expansiveness of frontier life, but its limitations, its material bareness, the pressures of obligation, then even the landscape itself ceases to be quite the arena of free movement it once was, but becomes instead a great empty waste, cutting down more often than it exaggerates the stature of the horseman who rides across it. We are more likely now to see the Westerner struggling against the obstacles of the physical world (as in the wonderful scenes on the desert and among the rocks in *The Last Posse*) than carelessly surmounting them. Even the horses, no longer the "friends" of man or the inspired chargers of knight-errantry, have lost much of the moral significance that once seemed to belong to them in their careening across the screen. It seems to me the horses grow tired and stumble more often than they did, and that we see them less frequently at the gallop.

In *The Gunfighter,* a remarkable film of a couple of years ago, the landscape has virtually disappeared. Most of the action takes place indoors, in a cheerless saloon where a tired "bad man" (Gregory Peck) contemplates the waste of his life, to be senselessly killed at the end by a vicious youngster setting off on the same futile path. The movie is done in cold, quiet tones of gray, and every object in it—faces, clothing, a table, the hero's heavy mustache—is given an air of uncompromising authenticity, suggesting those dim photographs of the nineteenth-century West in which Wyatt Earp, say, turns out to be a blank untidy figure posing awkwardly before some uninteresting building. This "authenticity," to be sure, is only aesthetic; the chief fact about nineteenth-century photographs, to my eyes at any rate, is how stonily they refuse to yield up the truth. But that limitation is just what is needed: by preserving some hint of the rigidity of archaic photography (only in tone and décor, never in composition), *The Gunfighter* can permit us to feel that we are looking at a more "real" West than the one the movies have accustomed us to—harder, duller, less "romantic"—and yet without forcing us outside the boundaries which give the Western movie its validity.

We come upon the hero of *The Gunfighter* at the end of a career in which he has never upheld justice and order, and has been at times, apparently, an actual criminal; in this case, it is clear that the hero has been wrong and the woman who has rejected his way of life has been right. He is thus without any of the larger justifications, and knows himself a ruined man. There can be no question of his "redeeming" himself in any socially constructive way. He is too much the victim of his own reputation to turn marshal as one of his old friends has done, and he is not offered the sentimental solution of a chance to give up his life for some good end; the whole point is that he exists outside the field of social value. Indeed, if we were once allowed to see him in the days of his "success," he might become a figure like the gangster, for his career has been aggressively "anti-social" and the practical problem he faces is the gangster's problem: there will always be somebody trying to kill him. Yet it is obviously absurd to speak of him as "anti-social," not only because we do not see him acting as a criminal, but more fundamentally because we do not see his milieu as a society. Of course it has its "social problems" and a kind of static history: civilization is always just at the point of driving out the old freedom; there are women and children to represent the possibility of a settled life; and there is the marshal, a bad man turned good, determined to keep at least his area of jurisdiction at peace. But these elements are not, in fact, a part of the film's "realism," even though they come out of the real history of the West; they belong to the conventions of the form, to that accepted framework which makes the film possible in the first place, and they exist not to provide a standard by which the gunfighter can be judged, but only to set him off. The true "civilization" of the Western movie is always embodied in an individual, good or bad is more a matter of personal bearing than of social consequences, and the conflict of good and bad is a duel between two men. Deeply troubled and obviously doomed, the gunfighter is the Western hero still, perhaps all the more because his value must express itself entirely in his own being—in his presence, the way he holds our eyes—and in contradiction to the facts. No matter what he has done, he *looks* right, and he remains invulnerable because, without acknowledging anyone else's right to judge him, he has judged his own failure and has already assimilated it, understanding—as no one else understands except the marshal and the bar-room girl—that he can do nothing but play out the drama of the gun fight again and again until the time comes when it will be he who gets killed. What "redeems" him is that he no longer believes in this drama and nevertheless will continue to play his role perfectly: the pattern is all.

The proper function of realism in the Western movie can only be to deepen the lines of that pattern. It is an art form for connoisseurs, where the spectator derives his pleasure from the appreciation of minor variations within the working out of a pre-established order. One does not want too much novelty: it comes as a shock, for instance, when the hero is made to operate without a gun, as has been done in several pictures (e.g., *Destry Rides Again*), and our uneasiness is allayed only when he is finally compelled to put his "pacifism" aside. If the hero can be shown to be troubled, complex, fallible, even eccentric, or the villain given some psychological taint or, better, some evocative physical mannerism, to shade the colors of his villainy, that is all to the good. Indeed, that kind of variation is absolutely necessary to keep the type from becoming sterile; we do not want to see the same movie over and over again, only the same form. But when the impulse toward realism is extended into a "reinterpretation" of the West as a developed society, drawing our eyes away from the hero if only to the extent of showing him as the one dominant figure in a complex social order, then the pattern is broken and the West itself begins to be uninteresting. If the "social problems" of the frontier are to be the movie's chief concern, there is no longer any point in re-examining these problems twenty times a year; they have been solved, and the people for whom they once were real are dead. Moreover, the hero himself, still the film's central figure, now tends to become its one unassimilable element, since he is the most "unreal."

The Ox-Bow Incident, by denying the convention of the lynching, presents us with a modern "social drama" and evokes a corresponding response, but in doing so it almost makes the Western setting irrelevant, a mere backdrop of beautiful scenery. (It is significant that *The Ox-Bow Incident* has no hero; a hero would have to stop the lynching or be killed in trying to stop it, and then the "problem" of lynching would no longer be central.) Even in *The Gunfighter* the women and children are a little too much in evidence, threatening constantly to become a real focus of concern instead of simply part of the given framework; and the young tough who kills the hero has too much the air of juvenile criminality: the hero himself could never have been like that, and the idea of a cycle being repeated therefore loses its sharpness. But the most striking example of the confusion created by a too conscientious "social" realism is in the celebrated *High Noon.*

In *High Noon* we find Gary Cooper still the upholder of order that he was in *The Virginian,* but twenty-four years older, stooped, slower moving, awkward, his face lined, the flesh sagging, a less beautiful and weaker figure, but with the suggestion of greater depth that belongs almost automatically to age. Like the hero of *The Gunfighter,* he no longer has to assert his character and is no longer interested in the drama of combat; it is hard to imagine that he might once have been so youthful as to say, "When you call me that—smile!" In fact, when we come upon him he is hanging up his guns and his marshal's badge in order to begin a new, peaceful life with his bride, who is a Quaker. But then the news comes that a man he had sent to prison has been pardoned and will get to town on the noon train; three friends of this man have come to wait for him at the station, and when the freed convict arrives the four of them will come to kill the marshal. He is thus trapped; the bride will object, the hero himself will waver much more than he would have done twenty-four years ago, but in the end he will play out the drama because it is what he "has to do." All this belongs to the established form (there is even the "fallen woman" who understands the marshal's position as his wife does not). Leaving aside the crudity of building up suspense by means of the clock, the actual Western drama of *High Noon* is well handled and forms a good companion piece to *The Virginian,* showing in both conception and technique the ways in which the Western movie has naturally developed.

But there is a second drama along with the first. As the marshal sets out to find deputies to help him deal with the four gunmen, we are taken through the various social strata of the town, each group in turn refusing its assistance out of cowardice, malice, irresponsibility, or venality. With this we are in the field of "social drama"—of a very low order, incidentally, altogether unconvincing and displaying a vulgar anti-populism that has marred some other movies of Stanley Kramer's. But the falsity of the "social drama" is less important than the fact that it does not belong in the movie to begin with. The technical problem was to make it necessary for the marshal to face his enemies alone; to explain *why* the other townspeople are not at his side is to raise a question which does not exist in the proper frame of the Western movie, where the hero is "naturally" alone and it is only necessary to contrive the physical absence of those who might be his allies, if any contrivance is needed at all. In addition, though the hero of *High Noon* proves himself a better man than all around him, the actual effect of this contrast is to lessen his stature: he becomes only a rejected man of virtue. In our final glimpse of him, as he rides away through the town where he has spent most of his life without really imposing himself on it, he is a pathetic rather than a tragic figure. And his departure has another meaning as well; the "social drama" has no place for him.

But there is also a different way of violating the Western form. This is to yield entirely to its static quality as legend and to the "cinematic" temptations of its landscape, the horses, the quiet men. John Ford's famous *Stagecoach* (1938) had much of this unhappy preoccupation with style, and the same director's *My Darling Clementine* (1946), a soft and beautiful movie about Wyatt Earp, goes further along the same path, offering indeed a superficial accuracy of historical reconstruction, but so loving in execution as to destroy the outlines of the Western legend, assimilating it to the more sentimental legend of rural America and making the hero a more dangerous Mr. Deeds. (*Powder River,* a recent "routine" Western shamelessly copied from *My Darling Clementine,* is in most ways a better film; lacking the benefit of a serious director, it is necessarily more concerned with drama than with style.)

The highest expression of this aestheticizing tendency is in George Stevens' *Shane,* where the legend of the West is virtually reduced to its essentials and then fixed in the dreamy clarity of a fairy tale. There never was so broad and bare and lovely a landscape as Stevens puts before us, or so unimaginably comfortless a "town" as the little group of buildings on the prairie to which the settlers must come for their supplies and to buy a drink. The mere physical progress of the film, following the style of *A Place in the Sun,* is so deliberately graceful that everything seems to be happening at the bottom of a clear lake. The hero (Alan Ladd) is hardly a man at all, but something like the Spirit of the West, beautiful in fringed buckskins. He emerges mysteriously from the plains, breathing sweetness and a melancholy which is no longer simply the Westerner's natural response to experience but has taken on spirituality; and when he has accomplished his mission, meeting and destroying in the black figure of Jack Palance a Spirit of Evil just as metaphysical as his own embodiment of virtue, he fades away again into the more distant West, a man whose "day is over," leaving behind the wondering little boy who might have imagined the whole story. The choice of Alan Ladd to play the leading role is alone an indication of this film's tendency. Actors like Gary Cooper or Gregory Peck are in themselves, as material objects, "realistic," seeming to bear in their bodies and their faces mortality, limitation, the knowledge of good and evil. Ladd is a more "aesthetic" object, with some of the "universality" of a piece of sculpture; his special quality is in his physical smoothness and serenity, unworldly and yet not innocent, but suggesting that no experience can really touch him. Stevens has tried to freeze the Western myth once and for all in the immobility of Alan Ladd's countenance. If *Shane* were "right," and fully successful, it might be possible to say there was no point in making any more Western movies; once the hero is apotheosized, variation and development are closed off.

Shane is not "right," but it is still true that the possibilities of fruitful variation in the Western movie are limited. The form can keep its freshness through endless repetitions only because of the special character of the film medium, where the physical difference between one object and another—above all, between one actor and another—is of such enormous importance, serving the function that is served by the variety of language in the perpetuation of literary types. In this sense, the "vocabulary" of films is much larger than that of literature and falls more readily into pleasing and significant arrangements. (That may explain why the middle levels of excellence are more easily reached in the movies than in literary forms, and perhaps also why the status of the movies as art is constantly being called into question.) But the advantage of this almost automatic particularity belongs to all films alike. Why does the Western movie especially have such a hold on our imagination?

Chiefly, I think, because it offers a serious orientation to the problem of violence such as can be found almost nowhere else in our culture. One of the well-known peculiarities of modern civilized opinion is its refusal to acknowledge the value of violence. This refusal is a virtue, but like many virtues it involves a certain willful blindness and it encourages hypocrisy. We train ourselves to be shocked or bored by cultural images of violence, and our very concept of heroism tends to be a passive one: we are less drawn to the brave young men who kill large numbers of our enemies than to the heroic prisoners who endure torture without capitulating. In art, though we may still be able to understand and participate in the values of the Iliad, a modern writer like Ernest Hemingway we find somewhat embarrassing: there is no doubt that he stirs us, but we cannot help recognizing also that he is a little childish. And in the criticism of popular culture, where the educated observer is usually under the illusion that he has nothing at stake, the presence of images of violence is often assumed to be in itself a sufficient ground for condemnation.

These attitudes, however, have not reduced the element of violence in our culture but, if anything, have helped to free it from moral control by letting it take on the aura of "emancipation." The celebration of acts of violence is left more and more to the irresponsible: on the higher cultural levels to writers like Céline, and lower down to Mickey Spillane or Horace McCoy, or to the comic books, television, and the movies. The gangster movie, with its numerous variations, belongs to this cultural "underground" which sets forth the attractions of violence in the face of all our higher social attitudes. It is a more "modern" genre than the Western, perhaps even more profound, because it confronts industrial society on its own ground—the city— and because, like much of our advanced art, it gains its effects by a gross insistence on its own narrow logic. But it is anti-social, resting on fantasies of irresponsible freedom. If we are brought finally to acquiesce in the denial of these fantasies, it is only because they have been shown to be dangerous, not because they have given way to a better vision of behavior.[1]

[1] I am not concerned here with the actual social consequences of gangster movies, though I suspect they could not have been so pernicious as they were thought to be. Some of the compromises introduced to avoid the supposed bad effects of the old

In war movies, to be sure, it is possible to present the uses of violence within a framework of responsibility. But there is the disadvantage that modern war is a co-operative enterprise; its violence is largely impersonal, and heroism belongs to the group more than to the individual. The hero of a war movie is most often simply a leader, and his superiority is likely to be expressed in a denial of the heroic: you are not supposed to be brave, you are supposed to get the job done and stay alive (this too, of course, is a kind of heroic posture, but a new—and "practical"—one). At its best, the war movie may represent a more civilized point of view than the Western, and if it were not continually marred by ideological sentimentality we might hope to find it developing into a higher form of drama. But it cannot supply the values we seek in the Western.

Those values are in the image of a single man who wears a gun on his thigh. The gun tells us that he lives in a world of violence, and even that he "believes in violence." But the drama is one of self-restraint: the moment of violence must come in its own time and according to its special laws, or else it is valueless. There is little cruelty in Western movies, and little sentimentality; our eyes are not focused on the sufferings of the defeated but on the deportment of the hero. Really, it is not violence at all which is the "point" of the Western movie, but a certain image of man, a style, which expresses itself most clearly in violence. Watch a child with his toy guns and you will see: what most interests him is not (as we so much fear) the fantasy of hurting others, but to work out how a man might look when he shoots or is shot. A hero is one who looks like a hero.

Whatever the limitations of such an idea in experience, it has always been valid in art, and has a special validity in an art where appearances are everything. The Western hero is necessarily an archaic figure; we do not really believe in him and would not have him step out of his rigidly conventionalized background. But his archaicism does not take away from his power; on the contrary, it adds to it by keeping him just a little beyond the reach both of common sense and of absolutized emotion, the two usual impulses of our art. And he has, after all, his own kind of relevance. He is there to remind us of the possibility of style in an age which has put on itself the burden of pretending that style has no meaning, and, in the midst of our anxieties over the problem of violence, to suggest that even in killing or being killed we are not freed from the necessity of establishing satisfactory modes of behavior. Above all, the movies in which the

---

gangster movies may be, if anything, more dangerous, for the sadistic violence that once belonged only to the gangster is now commonly enlisted on the side of the law and thus goes undefeated, allowing us (if we wish) to find in the movies a sort of "confirmation" of our fantasies.

Westerner plays out his role preserve for us the pleasures of a complete and self-contained drama—and one which still effortlessly crosses the boundaries which divide our culture—in a time when other, more consciously serious art forms are increasingly complex, uncertain, and ill-defined.

Suggested Topics

1. Guns in the fantasy life of Americans
2. The film gangster: what is he doing to our children?
3. The "Western"—an escape from reality
4. The so-called adult "Western"
5. The conventions of the typical "Western"
6. "The element of violence in our culture"

THE ART OF AN UNKNOWN FUTURE	The Times Literary Supplement

THE ART OF AN UNKNOWN FUTURE

The Times Literary Supplement

It is difficult to take the comic strips seriously and yet it is impossible not to do so. In America they have become a social force of great importance and they have made serious inroads into Europe's intellectual defences. In addition, the claim has been made repeatedly—and sometimes by eminent persons—that the comics represent a new literary form. Some warn us that the comic strips are a social and moral menace of the utmost gravity; others declare that this new form of expression is capable of creating—indeed, has already created—works of lasting merit. Mr. Gilbert Seldes asserted in *The Seven Lively Arts* (1924) that Mr. Charles Chaplin and Mr. George Herriman, the creator of a strip called *Krazy Kat,* were the only two great artists in the United States, adding that *Krazy Kat* was America's "most satisfactory work of art." He went on to link Krazy Kat's name with Dr. Johnson's, "to whom he owes much of his vocabulary." Mr. Chaplin declared that for him Mr. Al Capp, the author of another strip, *Li'l Abner,* opened "new vistas of broad buffoonery with inspirational [*sic*] satire." Mr. John Steinbeck stated: "I think Capp may very possibly be the best writer in the world to-day." The European reader—

Reprinted from *The Times Literary Supplement,* May 29, 1953. By permission of *The Times* Publishing Company, Limited, London.

who probably cannot have helped seeing a comic strip or two here and there—remembers the clumsy and often primitive drawings with the hideous balloons bubbling out of the characters' mouths and is surprised, annoyed or pained by such claims. Is the European reader right? Or is he, in his snobbery, rejecting a new form of literary expression simply because of its unaesthetic and, admittedly, repulsive appearance, without examining its merits and shortcomings? Perhaps the new medium should now be allowed to present itself and take its modest bow; but it cannot count on a warm reception. Some will receive it with polite interest, others with tight-lipped silence and others again with open hostility and contempt.

In the United States 50 million comic magazines are sold every month, and it is estimated that the comics have 70 million readers. "Surveys point to the likelihood," writes Miss Frank, "that 98 per cent. of all children between the ages of eight and 12 read comics. These readers come from all types of homes and cultural backgrounds, rich and poor, city and country, well-educated and uneducated. Intelligence quotients seem to make no difference. . . ."

To this number many millions should be added who follow the strips in daily newspapers. Altogether their number cannot be estimated, but with a few exceptions, it is an accepted fact, among newsagents as well as editors, that "it's the strips that sell the paper." In spite of the overwhelming popularity of the strips among children, 60 per cent. of the readers are grown-up people. During the war the American P.X. stores sold 10 times as many comic magazines to soldiers as the four other most popular publications—*Reader's Digest, Saturday Evening Post, Life* and *Time*—put together. There must be millions of people who read little else in the United States and it would be wilful blindness to ignore their increasing popularity in Italy, Germany and—to a smaller extent—in this country.

The expressions "comic strips" or "funnies" are—or rather have gradually become—misnomers. These picture stories are not necessarily funny—indeed, suspense and adventure stories are now in the majority—and as soon as they appear in pamphlet form they cease to be "strips," too. Their spiritual ancestor seems to be Wilhelm Busch's hilarious but slightly sadistic picture book, *Max und Moritz*. In America itself the early beginnings go back to 1896, to Outcalt's *The Great Dog Show in M'Googan's Avenue,* published in the New York *World*. These drawings were coloured in yellow of a most revolting kind, and it was they that provoked the notorious phrase "yellow journalism." The phrase, even in its original meaning, referred not only to the vulgarity of the colour—not much improved in the strips through the following six decades—but also to the almost impressive vulgarity of the artist. Soon the *Yellow Kid* and the *Katzenjammer*

Kids were born among a number of similar attempts. The Katzenjammer Kids were *Max und Moritz* after emigration to the United
States. In time, like all emigrants, they lost much of their native character and adjusted themselves to their environment. To-day, the third
generation of readers are still enjoying the first generation of Katzenjammer Kids, who are as alive and youthful as ever.

By the first decade of this century, the comic strips had developed
all their essential, modern characteristics. They were neither illustrated jokes nor ordinary comic pictures with captions, but true picture stories. Narration and orthodox captions were replaced by balloons—a technical term for dialogue bubbling out of the figures'
mouths. The balloon usually has a "string" to it, pointing towards
the mouth of one character or another, to indicate who is speaking.
Narration was reduced to such sentences as: "The next day . . ." or:
"In the meantime," or: "Back at the farm." Historians of the comic
strips disagree whether the original strips were intended for children
or for grown-ups. Did the children read them over their parents'
shoulders or *vice versa?* This riddle may never be solved. It is certain,
however, that in the early days the strips were meant to be funny and
their only aim was to entertain. The main subjects of hilarity were
naughty and uncontrollable children and henpecked husbands. Consequently, these early strips instinctively painted a distorted and
satirical but essentially true picture of a society in which children
and women are often the rulers. A reaction and revolt against this
unpalatable truth was bound to set in sooner or later. It was in the
late 1920s that the new heroes began to appear. Tarzan was the first
among them, followed by a long and dreary succession, until, in 1938,
Superman arrived. His one great accomplishment is flying. He can
take to the air with great and natural ease and without any mechanical aid and, in pressing emergencies, he can fly through walls, too. It
is obvious that America got tired of being satirized; people needed to
identify themselves with supernatural protagonists and the comic
artists were ready and eager to supply the new heroes. The first supernatural hero, however, was Popeye, the sailorman, who was often
riddled with bullets but never killed. Research in comic-strip genealogy yields surprising results and reveals odd family connexions.
Popeye is the father of Superman and Superman is the father of
Supermouse, Supercat, and the rest, with a fair sprinkling of Super-
women. As science progressed the comic-strip heroes had to rise to
greater and greater heights. To-day a fair contingent of them works
on various planets—not infrequently in neighbouring solar systems—
bravely defying giant ants or atomic swindlers. They reach Mercury
with greater ease than we reach a London suburb during the rush hour.
All this has caused a revolution in humour, too. The little, helpless

and lonely man—as incarnated by Mr. Chaplin's tramp—is dead and gone; the new comic hero is the Popeye type, as a rule more vulgar and much less endearing than Popeye himself, the rough and ridiculous brute who always has his own way and who, however stupid he may be, in the end triumphs and prevails.

The birth of the Superman and Tarzan type of hero coincided with the birth of the suspense story. In the old days the gag was concluded in the last drawing; to-day the story rolls on at dramatic speed and the reader is left in anguish, wondering, what next? There is only one way to find out: buy next morning's paper. In the meantime the technique of drawing has also sunk even lower. It was always extremely difficult to draw well in the small squares, in which the balloons occupied a large part even of that limited space. The best the more able artists could do was to give evidence of the fact that they could draw much better in more fortunate circumstances. Soon, however, they had to simplify matters even further. Nowadays villains are invariably ugly and terrifying, heroes angel-like and as beautiful as the ability of the artist permits, so that one single glance informs the reader—or viewer?—what to expect from each character. As the popularity of the strips went on increasing and the demand became almost insatiable, artists and editors racked their brains; new material and new heroes were needed each week. Old *clichés* would no longer serve; new *clichés* were needed.

The briefest survey of to-day's strips and comic magazines—the latter began to swamp America in 1933—proves that the horror- and crime-loving public is better served than the fun-loving public. Mickey Mouse, Donald Duck, other "animated animals" and Popeye are still popular and have kept much of their charm. Naughty children and innocently quarrelling couples still try to, and do, amuse. But the majority of the strips are of a different character and may be divided into these groups: Western, crime, sea adventure, horror, science-fiction, sex and pirate strips. Certain statistics, quoted by Mr. Seldes, based on 100 comic books and 1,000 comic strips from newspapers, gave this result: major crimes depicted, 218; minor crimes, 313; physical assaults, 531; sadistic acts, 87; physical monstrosities, 165. One comic book examined by Mr. Albert Deutsch in 1948 "demonstrates to the child reader how to gouge eyes with the thumb, choke off the windpipe, kick an opponent in the stomach . . . flatten his arch with the heel, bite his ears, kick him in the liver area, punch him in the spine . . . all under the protective title of self-defense." On one occasion an actual recipe for poisoning was taken from a comic book, and on many occasions juvenile delinquents have declared that they derived the impulse to commit crimes from them. In spite of this condemnatory evidence, one must not jump to a verdict of guilty. Are comic strips not used as scapegoats by some young criminals and a society tormented by a guilt-complex? It is far from certain that the strips actually create fear and brutality; it seems more likely that they only stimulate anxieties that lie beneath the surface in a great number of children and which would be brought out by other means, too. Dr. Lauretta Bender, Professor of Clinical Psychiatry at New York University and a member of the Editorial Advisory Board of "Superman National Comics," states that comics constitute an experience of activity. Their heroes overcome time and space. This gives children a sense of release rather than a sense of fear. In the child's fantasy life, continues Dr. Bender, using such symbols as comics present, he may be able to adjust himself to the world's trials and difficulties. Children's fantasies are no escape from reality but a constructive approach to it.

It should be added that even the basest comic strip should not be regarded as a general argument against comic strips, just as the lowest type of penny dreadful is no argument against literature. Even old-fashioned and generally approved fairy tales—with their witches, wicked stepmothers and supernatural heroes—contained enough debatable material. Besides, comics are also being used with the best of intentions for good purposes. They—as far as sheer numbers of people are concerned—did more to unite and steel America for war than President's Roosevelt's speeches. Bible-stories were published as comic strips and sold in a million copies. Classics—*Wuthering Heights, Cyrano de Bergerac, The Three Musketeers,* among others—are also popularized in comic-strip form.

It may be difficult to condemn the comics on their obvious failings; but it is perhaps justifiable to condemn them on their merits. For one reader at least, *Wuthering Heights* in comic-book form, although it was done as well as it possibly can be done, was a grimmer sight than the sheet called "Horrific ! ! !" or the heroic tales of the indomitable Space Cadets on one of the neighbouring planets. Again, though it may be questionable whether comic strips do or do not create fear, anxiety and criminal tendencies, it seems to be beyond doubt that they create mental laziness and stupidity. Mental laziness thus engendered creates a further market for new strips; the new strips create more stupidity and this vicious circle does not retrace itself on the same plane but may lead into the abyss. If the comics are a new literary form, they may well be a kind of literature to end literature. It is a kind of literature not to be read, only looked at. The comics may flourish and conquer; but their ultimate victory—supported by their powerful and somewhat related ally, television—may mark the end of the reading habit. It may also help to create a society with two classes: the thinking and intelligent minority and the strip-ridden majority which is incapable of independent thinking and accepts ready-made views, if presented by badly drawn pictures. The growing success of the strips—as has been pointed out by others—may, in time, create an added menace to democracy.

Do a few really good strips on a certain literary and moral level—such as *Barnaby, Pogo* or *Li'l Abner*—redeem the whole art? *Li'l Abner,* the best of them, although wildly overestimated by many, is drawn and written by an able satirist. His sallies are often witty and he frequently scores a bullseye on his main target, Big Business. No one would deny Mr. Al Capp's abilities. But the form in which his ability gains expression remains, even in his hands, ugly, unaesthetic and repulsive—and it is the form which is now under discussion. Some critics say that the comic strips may give birth even to great poetry and that they should be given a chance. This claim is more than doubtful; and the new form has had its chance. It is a novelty more than half a century old.

. . . I run into people [writes Mr. John Steinbeck] who seem to feel that literature is all words and that those words should preferably be stuffy. The literature of the Cro Magnon is painted on the walls of the caves of Altamira.

Mr. Steinbeck may be right. Literature began with comic strips; if we are not careful, it may also end with them.

Suggested Topics

1. Are comics a new literary form?
2. The comic book as adult reading
3. Comic books and juvenile delinquency
4. The "funnies" aren't funny any more.
5. "A kind of literature to end literature"
6. The classics in comic book adaptation
7. "Literature began with comic strips."

THE WORLD OF BUSINESS

THE BUSINESSMAN'S MORAL FAILURE *Louis Finkelstein*

Chancellor and Solomon Schechter Professor of Theology at
the Jewish Theological Seminary of America in New York City,
Dr. Louis Finkelstein is a student of the civil and ritual law of
the Talmud, and the author of a number of scholarly works in
the field of Judaism. He is one of the leaders of the Institute on
Ethics, an interfaith body of religious and educational leaders.

If American businessmen are right in the way most of them now
live, then all the wise men of the ages, all the prophets and the saints
were fools. If the saints were not fools, the businessmen must be.

Too many businessmen never stop to ponder what they are doing;
they reject the need for self-discipline; they are satisfied to be clever,
when they need to be wise. They worry about their place on the
economic ladder, but are not concerned sufficiently with whether the
civilization in which they work is likely to collapse. They can defeat
a local competitor, but may well be defeated by the competitor of us
all, which is moral decay.

Now the American executive is very often a man of some vision,
motivated by a spirit that generates great energy. Underlying the
efficiency of our business community there is the principle of team-
work, cooperation, a reasonable degree of pleasure in the success of
co-workers, a comparatively broad welcome to talent, and freedom
in human relationships. Granted, these are virtues of no mean order.
But the American businessman is losing his insight into the moral
sources of American economic strength.

Reprinted from the September, 1958, issue of *Fortune* magazine by special permission; © 1958 Time, Inc.

Our country could not have reached its present heights without the blessing of natural resources; but the U.S. would have failed at the outset without a philosophy developed by men more concerned with the betterment of the human spirit than the comforts of the body. These men were inspired by the writings of immortal philosophers and religious thinkers. The modern business leader is more often than not bewildered at the suggestion that the future of the Republic is in some way related to the ideals and ideas of John Locke, not to mention Spinoza, the medieval Scholastics, the Rabbinic sages, and the ancient Greek philosophers.

Ask the U.S. businessman why he is successful today, and he may explain to you the advantages of capitalism, the profit motive, and the "American system." He may, with due modesty, point out the superiority of his own products and marketing. But he will largely ignore the philosophic foundations of the American system. He tends to ignore the great ethical laws as they apply immediately to his work. The truth is that he is preoccupied chiefly with gain, coasting on the spiritual momentum of the past, divorced from our sources of inspiration. He is the leading citizen of a largely hedonistic nation propelled by meaningless drives toward materialistic and frequently meaningless goals.

Clearly no institution will survive if it is dedicated *only* to self-preservation. A business has a goal beyond simple success. It is not a biological organism whose survival is a virtue in itself. Rather, it is a man-created institution, an integral part of our culture, and as such must make a contribution of service to society (as well as a profit for itself) if it hopes to survive. It cannot do this out of a focus on self-gain or pride.

Why do I single out the American businessman for indictment, when he is probably no more materialistic than any of the rest of us? I do so because of the responsibility he bears, because his role in American society is so great. Ours is an industrial society, and the customs and morals and attitudes of businessmen pervade our whole life. Virtually all of us in America have adopted in some degree the pragmatic ethical standards of our business society; and to that degree we have abandoned our ethical and religious traditions.

Our American tragedy is that we fail to see the signs of our decay. But the signs are apparent in the vulgar ostentation all around us, in the sexual laxity revealed by the Kinsey studies, in the demoralization of American captives in the Korean war, in the widespread defiance of law. The signs are apparent in our general toleration of wrongdoing, which is itself an evil and corrupting force.

Curiously, this breakdown of moral discipline has occurred when institutionalized religion is flourishing as never before. But even religion in America now tends to be superficial. For many laymen it consists of writing an occasional check and sporadic attendance at church or synagogue, rather than in personal commitment. There is a dearth of saints, and many ministers themselves are unduly concerned with security in this world. While the percentage of truly dedicated pastors may be no smaller than in previous generations, today they suffer a special disability—a failure to communicate with the members of their flocks.

Human history is studded with the ruins of empires that came to a similar pass. Nations have been wrecked because they lacked an overriding moral goal to which individuals could commit themselves. History shows us that when we become success-dominated, we lose sight of our real reasons for living.

In its youth, America *was* ideal-dominated. Both individual citizens and the country as a whole had an impelling motive in life that was not limited to industrial, political, or economic growth. The men who gathered in 1787 could muster all their intellectual energies to formulate the national charter, overcome differences of background and interest—all because these men were laboring for a larger goal.

An equally vital role awaiting the American businessman today will be suggested at the end of this article. Time and again in American history the businessman has transcended his industrial role and become the buttress not only of government but of the public welfare. Today's crisis demands of him leadership in still another dimension—one where he has thus far conspicuously failed.

A young executive rapidly moving up the financial ladder unequivocally stated in private conversation with me, "It is impossible to conduct business in the U.S. today without breaking the law."

If the statement is exaggerated, it nevertheless retains distressing validity for one like myself who was educated in New York City and has resided there over half a century. A considerable portion of my time has been spent with men engaged in a great variety of businesses, who keep an equal variety of balance sheets.

The most casual observer is aware of the transgressions that go on daily in the American business community. He hears of tax returns that are outright perjury; he hears of purchasing agents who are taking bribes from suppliers, of businessmen offering bribes for false testimony or for police protection of some dubious enterprise. He reads of industries attempting to suborn state legislators for favorable legislation. He reads of businessmen bestowing favors on government officials to win special privileges. Even in my ivory tower on Morningside Heights, I have been urged by businessmen to accept a gift for the Theological Seminary in return for admitting a student—

and have been threatened by withdrawal of contributions to the school if I failed to do so.

We hear of businessmen using wire taps to obtain information about their competitors, of management acting in collusion with racketeers, of men using prostitution to promote the sale of their goods. We hear of businessmen violating the most elementary requirements of city building codes and profiting from rat-infested tenements. We hear of financiers deliberately lying about their operations and the financial condition of their companies to mislead investors so that insiders can make killings in stock.

There are less overt practices in the business community that may appear to be only on the borderline of unethical behavior: for example, concealing the true price of goods behind time-payment schemes that are actually usurious; employing advertising that is actually a flagrant misrepresentation of a product's worth. These and other clever dodges are accepted by many as normal phases of competition.

I would not deny that competition is the basis of our free enterprise and of our industrial success. Competition surely induces better efforts and greater production. But to compete in ways that are designed to destroy someone else is very different from competing in terms of doing better than your rival. Years ago in Lithuania, Rabbi Israel Salanter found two boys quarreling over which was the taller. One forced the other to stand in a ditch to settle the argument. Seeing this, Rabbi Israel sadly commented, "Isn't this characteristic of the world where to prove his superiority man must prove others inferior? After all, the same purpose could have been achieved by standing on a chair!"

When two companies are each trying to produce superior values, one may well be more successful than the other, and deservedly earn greater profits. But to seek a crippling advantage over another company is hardly fair competition and is certainly miserable ethics.

It seems to me that a management which is worthy of success is very different from a management which just wants success. One management conducts its affairs in the spirit of contribution, the other in the spirit of selfishness. Contributions to the general good have of course been made by men seeking only their own advantage, but selfishness cannot be made a principle of life and in our time might easily be fatal. Management worthy of success remembers that the true justification for profit is an incentive to serve the community. Success is paid to business by the community for the services is renders. In this sense, profits must clearly be an earned increment.

This reasoning can certainly be understood if stated in terms of the individual. We understand the meaning and value to the individual of "a good reputation." Every businessman knows that his reputation for integrity is one of his major assets. Certainly, a man's progress in a corporation depends in large measure on the reputation he earns through his daily behavior. It is immensely difficult to falsify such a reputation over any extended period of time. We are soon known by those around us for who we *are* rather than what we would like others to think about us. This is a man's "character" in the profoundest sense of the word.

I was interested to hear a major executive point out that the criteria he uses for selecting employees run in this order: character, intelligence, experience. "A really bright, executive picks up experience very quickly," he told me. "But the man we need and want most, in important places, is a man with character sufficient to resist many kinds of pressures when the going gets rough. We find, then, that character is the most important ingredient of all, particularly if the man is to be responsible for policy making. An executive can buy brains and can buy experience, but character is something he must supply himself."

And what *is* a man's character but his personal moral dimension, the goals he sets for himself, his sense of honesty and of responsibility, his relations with others? This does not mean, however, that the value of character derives from its contribution to success.

Unquestionably, ethics have a practical value, inseparable from their ultimate one: the creation of better men and women. Rivalry for goodness should, in the long run, make for pragmatic gain. But it is not enough for the individual or the corporation merely to mean well. Men as individuals and as corporations must make an effort to understand what they are doing, and why they are doing it.

The first step in the ethical life is self-criticism. As the Talmud puts it, "Cleanse yourselves, and then cleanse others." Ethics is a branch of thought starting with self-discipline. Discipline, whether among children or adults, whether self-imposed or external, is not popular in America today. And a welter of codes—in companies, in industries, in combines of industries, in labor—do not meet the situation.

Before anyone can think creatively about the moral life, he must feel in his bones a few principles that are part of any civilized ethic, without which civilization would be meaningless. I wish I could say with hope of being understood that of these the most important is awareness of God and love for Him. But as those words tend to become clichés, I say instead that we have to feel the wonder and significance of life and its unique opportunity for achievement. Each of us has only one life on earth. When that life is used unwisely, the loss is irreparable for oneself and for one's fellows.

A businessman who understands these truths will develop an almost automatic pattern of behavior. Certain ancient rules apply with equal force to Jew and Christian, atheist and agnostic, to all men in all situations. These immutable laws are expressed in various ways. The Pentateuch reveals the Decalogue and the Golden Rule of Leviticus 19:18: "Thou shalt love thy neighbor as thyself," which the Gospels restate in Matthew 7:12: "All things whatsoever ye would that men should do to you, do ye even so to them." Similar commandments are promulgated in the literature of the other great traditions of East and West.

Yet these and other binding commandments are often violated in the American business community. A man fears he may be risking his business if he obeys them, forgetting, however, that if he violates them he risks the world.

Business leaders who generously advised me in the preparation of this article said, "The majority of the American business community are not evil men, and want to do right. Let us say we admit the indictment and accept our responsibility—what can we do?"

To begin with, a businessman can develop an awareness that *every* decision of his life involves moral considerations. He can help develop this sensitivity in employees and associates, through example, through discussing with them the moral implications of company actions, through constant reminders that he has values in life above profit or economic security.

There are some corporations which insist that their executives assume responsibility for civic and community improvement. But the businessman can go further. In his training school for management he can introduce students of ethics, as well as management experts and psychologists, to consider the responsibilities of the business executive. He can overcome his anti-intellectualism. He can try to gain knowledge that will clarify the problems of wise decision making.

The businessman must realize that the inculcation of moral sensitivity starts in early childhood and continues throughout life. American society has achieved this kind of indoctrination in other fields. To take two familiar examples: virtually every American child is brought up with a concern for personal hygiene; virtually every female child is indoctrinated with the need to be as physically attractive as possible. Our culture is probably unique in the emphasis it places on these two patterns of education.

The businessman can, without "moralizing" (which would be deadening and self-defeating), transform his home into a school for moral responsibility. Avoiding precept, the businessman can make even his conversation at table serve the vital end of character education for himself, his wife, his children, and his guests. The stories he tells, the gestures he makes, the conversation he chooses and avoids, can all show that he has at least some notion of what life, America, and freedom are about. Without being in the slightest degree priggish, and eventually without self-consciousness, he may help his family and friends obtain insight into the ethical life.

The American businessman, then, should literally *place ethics on the agenda*—for himself at home and in the office, for his company and trade association:

His calendar should include regular meetings of management to discuss the moral dimensions in his specific business. One firm that instituted such meetings finds it continually gains valuable insights into new relationships with the many other organizations with which it does business.

He should seek expert advice on ethics. Existing resources in the field will gladly be made available to him.

He should put moral health on the same level as mental and physical health, indeed above them. This means he should read literature dealing with ethics; devote time to the study of ethics, alone and with colleagues and scholars; work for the establishment of research in ethics, as he has worked magnificently for the development of research in science and technology.

Whatever else may or may not be involved in the application of such principles, it will demand direction of effort—not merely doing what one happens to like at a given moment and following the easy path of self-indulgence. Wisdom begins with sacrifice of immediate pleasures for long-range purposes. There is a widespread view that belief in God and personal immortality leads to this discipline. The fact, however, is that the discipline itself is also indispensable to real belief in God and human immortality. That is why the role of the businessman in American ethics is no less crucial than that of the religious leader or scholar.

Today's crisis demands the businessman's leadership in the area of human behavior. The kind of criticism with which enlightened businessmen could confront philosophers and theologians could be a challenge. Then superficiality in religion would cease to be fashionable, and laymen would soon detect its shallowness. Morally sensitive and informed businessmen can compel American philosophy and religion to focus on the basic problems troubling mankind.

We Americans will then no longer warrant William James's description of us as worshippers of "the bitch-goddess, Success." Our best young minds would strive for genuine, rather than apparent, achievement. If we can overcome the tendency to measure intellectual productivity by quantity rather than quality, America might produce works and insights into the ethical realm comparable to the eternal creations that have emerged from other civilizations. Without such creations, rallying the spiritual energies of all men, America and the Free World will not endure.

Civilization needs men and women whose every act and decision will bear the stamp of responsibility. The world cannot long survive, at least in freedom, if decisions are made irresponsibly—that is, without disciplined consideration of individual and general consequences. At the present moment, this may seem almost impossible to achieve. Yet without many dedicated men and women exercising disciplined consideration of each of their actions, none of the great philosophic or religious traditions could have survived.

Modest steps to focus different types of experience on the complex issues of our day have been taken in various ways, one of which is the work of a group of scholars who drew together in 1939 in New York. The group includes physical scientists, social scientists, philosophers, and theologians of different faiths, who were stirred by the apparition of Nazism but recognized it as a symptom of a chronic disease of our time rather than the disease itself. They hoped they could clarify today's moral problems. Once a year, sometimes once in two years, these scholars have met. Some participants are frankly agnostic, some atheistic, others devout. For a long time their discussions were at cross-purposes. There were frequent outbursts when varied types of mind and experience confronted one another. Gradually, they arrived at an astoundingly simple conclusion: the problem of their concern may be summed up in a single word—"responsibility."

This conference of scholars is hopeful of establishing nothing less than a World Academy of Ethics and an Institute for Practical Ethics for Everyday Living, drawing on the wisdom not only of Christianity and Judaism but of Islam, Buddhism, Confucianism, and other traditions. The scholars need the help and participation of businessmen.

Does all of this sound as though the American businessman had to take on new burdens, and rush even more prematurely to his grave? On the contrary, one of man's primary duties to himself, his family, the community, and to God is preservation of his life on earth, so that he can realize his potentialities for good. The businessman who will take time to contemplate and to ponder the ethical dimension of life will discover new realms in which he can develop his talents, freeing himself from the bondage to private gain that menaces the maturing business executive. Clearly understanding the principles of a meaningful life, he will share them with his family, especially with his wife. He will accept philosophically the occasional defeats and frustrations of his business career. He will carry his burdens serenely and thus preserve his own life, as well as that of the community.

Before he decides that the moral discipline required to build a better society is too arduous for him and that he is too busy to master a new dialect of thought, before he flees his responsibility, he might do well to ponder the story of Moses in the third chapter of Exodus.

The father of Prophecy was heavy of tongue. He, too, preferred the ease of Midian and the pleasures of shepherd life to the burdens imposed by the leadership of men. He could not believe that the task presented to him could not be done by another. For a moment he doubted that it could ever be accomplished. But sometimes, because of unique combinations of circumstances surrounding him, an individual is indispensable for a specific role in history. Whether or not he wished it, Moses was one of the great spiritual leaders of mankind. He could neglect his duty, but he could not assign it to anyone else.

To rise in his full stature, the American businessman—who at his best embodies many of the Prophetic virtues—must also shoulder a unique burden of responsibility. The fate of the world hangs on his decisions, for above all the world needs ethical leadership from those it respects as supremely practical.

The words spoken by Moses to his contemporaries more than three thousand years ago apply literally to us in this latter day: "See, I have set before thee this day life and good, and death and evil." If the American businessman can bring himself to choose life and good, he can save not only our own but future generations. Surely he will heed the ancient Prophet's plea: "Therefore, choose life, that thou mayest live, thou and thy seed."

Suggested Topics

1. "Payola"—an old story
2. The philosophic foundations of the American system
3. The golden rule as an actual code of behavior
4. The superficiality of religious observance
5. The T.V. quiz scandal
6. "Fair competition" vs. "miserable ethics"

LIBERAL ARTS AS TRAINING FOR BUSINESS

Frederic E. Pamp, Jr.

Frederic E. Pamp, Jr., is President of the International Management Association, Inc. A Ph.D. in English, he has taught humanities at the University of Chicago and at Smith College.

It is not hard to predict that the practice of management will be profoundly affected by the rapidly approaching forces of automation and statistical decision making.

Any company with a decent regard for its survival must be trying to forecast the terms of those forces, for it must recruit and promote today the executives who will be running the company tomorrow. Can we write the job description for a vice president of X Manufacturing Company for 1965, or 1975? What will he have to know? What new skills, what new sensitivities will he have to possess to deal successfully with the new elements in management and (what is perhaps more important) the new combinations of old elements?

There have been enough changes just since the end of World War II to make the job grow alarmingly. These changes have in fact been largely responsible for the feverish attention that has been paid to management development in recent years. As Frederick Lewis Allen describes the complicated nature of present executive requirements:

The corporation executive today must be the captain of a smooth-working team of people who can decide whether the time has come to build a new polymerization plant, what the answer is to the unsatisfactory employe relations in a given unit of the business, how to cope with a new government regulation, how to achieve a mutually respectful understanding with union representatives and what position to take on price increases in order to maintain the good will of the public. In short, he is confronted with so many questions which require knowledge, intellectual subtlety, political insight and human flexibility that he desperately needs a mental equipment of the sort that the old-time tycoon could do without.

Up to now most of the increased demands on management have been quantitative. An executive has had to know more about en-

From *Harvard Business Review,* May-June, 1955. By permission of the *Harvard Business Review* and the author.

gineering, about accounting, about his industry, about the position of his company in the industry, about society and the world around him—all to the end of better control of masses of data and information, and better decision making on the basis of such material.

Now we are faced with the fact that many of the quantitative aspects of the executive's job are going to recede into the innards of a computer. Thus, in one company, dozens of clerks used to work laborious days on their slide rules to provide data for what were no more than calculated guesses, on top of which management built a whole pyramid of deliberate decisions. A computer can now take readings of the whole spectrum of data at any time desired, give the relevant figures their proper weights, and come up with production schedules, orders for materials, and financial budgets to ensure maximum efficiency of operation.

Nevertheless, the executive is not likely to join the ranks of the technologically unemployed, just because he will have shucked off many of the problems on which he formerly exercised his executive judgment and "feel." It is inevitable that new problems will crowd in to take the place of the old ones. And, in other than quantitative judgments, a new standard of accuracy and precision will be called for to match the level of accuracy displayed by the computer. A small fable for executives was played out before millions on television at the last election, when the computer performed faultlessly on faulty data and came out blandly with answers that could have ruined a company if they had concerned a gamble on marketing or capital investment.

In any event, the competitive edge acquired by one company by acquisition of a computer will not last long in any industry. Sooner or later all companies will be returned to the equilibrium defined recently by Albert L. Nickerson, Vice President and Director of Foreign Trade, Socony-Vacuum Oil Company:

> If one competitor has a material advantage today it—or a workable counterpart—is likely soon to become common property. An enterprise must rely for survival and progress on the personal qualifications of those who make up its ranks and direct its destinies.

Management development has already shaken down from an early concentration on executive manning charts and development of logical succession to key jobs, through a period of sorties into specialized training groups, to a generally accepted set of principles for assessment and development of the candidate on the job under realistic standards of performance. All this prepares for the job as it has shaped up in the past decade and as it exists today (as military staffs are always alleged to prepare for the last war). It is time for the focus to shift again—to the building of the kind of executive quality which will be at a premium tomorrow.

Straight-line extension of the norm that has led the company this far will not necessarily suffice to lead it in the future. Top management cannot expect to pick its succession exactly in its own image and get away with it. Neither is it enough to take the pattern of executive personality that has succeeded in one company (or a thousand) under present conditions. The first question a company must now begin to ask of its candidates for executive responsibility is: "What can you do that a computer can't?"

In more and more companies, the decisive factor is going to be the breadth and depth of executive judgment. As vast areas of what used to be decision making become subject to mechanical computations which are all equally correct in all companies, the edge will be won by the company whose executives do a better job of handling the qualitative factors which remain after the measurable factors have been taken out, and then of putting all the pieces together into a single, dynamic whole—what Peter Drucker calls "seeing a business as a whole in conceptual synthesis."

On one point all authorities have agreed. Narrow specialization is not enough; this is already responsible for most of the inability of middle management executives to be considered for promotion. John L. McCaffrey, President of International Harvester Company, puts it this way:

. . . the world of the specialist is a narrow one and it tends to produce narrow human beings. The specialist usually does not see over-all effects on the business and so he tends to judge good and evil, right and wrong, by the sole standard of his own specialty.

This narrowness of view, this judgment of all events by the peculiar standards of his own specialty, is the curse of the specialist from the standpoint of top management consideration for advancement. Except in unusual cases, it tends to put a road-block ahead of him after he reaches a certain level.

Thus, there has been a growing call for "breadth" in educational preparation for management, and a surprising degree of agreement on the need for more *liberal arts* in colleges.

Educators, especially those in state-supported colleges, may be forgiven a certain bewilderment if, after bending every effort—and many curricula—to answer insistent demands from business for more and more specialty and vocational courses on all levels, they are now abused for turning out graduates unprepared for the full scope of executive action in management for today, much less for tomorrow. They have responded by pointing out that the company recruiters still

come to the colleges with many more demands for technicians than
for liberal arts graduates.

Action has been taken to bring educators in the liberal arts and
business executives together to discuss the desirable objectives of education for management. A new respect is developing on the part of
businessmen for the standards which the privately endowed, liberal
arts colleges have been defending for many years. Agreement on ends
and, to some extent, on curricular means to these ends has been
worked out in conferences such as those held by the College English
Association at the University of Massachusetts in 1952, at the Corning
Glass Center in 1953, at Michigan State College and the Kellogg
Center in East Lansing in 1954, and the most recent one sponsored by
General Electric at Schenectady this spring.

Viewed in these terms many subjects and disciplines can lay claim
to a role in education for management. It is obvious that wider subject matter, more courses about more things in the contemporary
world, will give the student more breadth.

But it is also apparent that in a day when the executive will be
able to dial the electronic reference library and get all the facts about
all the subjects he wants, mere accretion of facts will not warrant his
putting in the time to prepare merely to know more facts. The call
is for more than "breadth" alone; it is for the ability to move surely
and with confidence on unfamiliar ground, to perceive central elements in situations and see how their consequences fall into line in
many dimensions. Tomorrow's executive must be able to move surely
from policy to action in situations that will be different from anything
any generation has experienced before.

There have been developments in traditional educational disciplines within the liberal arts which, much to the surprise of those
closest to them, will very likely turn out to be far more important to
educational preparation for management than many of the flashy
subjects that have seemingly been set up to serve business needs exclusively. The study of the *humanities*—of literature, art, and philosophy,
and of the critical terms that these disciplines use to assess the world—
is startlingly more pertinent and practical than the "practical" vocational preparation.

Executives should know that recent graduates in the humanities
have had a much different experience from those who went through
our better colleges ten years ago. They have experienced a much
more closely disciplined course in the examination of literature and
creative works—of the objectives and the tissue of meanings and
symbols which make up the over-all theme of the writing or the
painting or the composition, or other form of creative work.

These disciplines have of course other axes to grind than preparing executives to fill job descriptions. They are elements in our civilization which give it life beyond any technologies or economic systems. The arts, education, and management all serve a higher purpose, and business will do society no good if it demands, as do some business leaders, that education serve business directly and solely. That would be the same as insisting that a corporation be restricted only to working capital and forbidden to raise long-term funds.

But the very fact that the humanities serve a larger need than management training is one of the main reasons why they are so valuable for that purpose.

At first glance, the importance of training in these fields hitherto considered peripheral, if not downright irrelevant, to management may be difficult to see. The contribution of the physical sciences is obvious. Also, at long last, we have come to appreciate the significance of the social sciences, which appear to relate directly to business both because of their content and because of their disciplines. It is obvious that an executive must be able to interpret the social and political environment in which his company operates. Further, he must be familiar with as much of the growing body of knowledge of human behavior as possible. But the liberal arts have always been considered remote from the practical hurly-burly of daily decision making.

To demonstrate that precisely the reverse is true, let us examine the disciplines within which the executive moves. In so doing, we may alter our ideas of his job as it has traditionally been regarded, and bring into focus the parallels between the disciplines of the liberal arts and the disciplines of management.

If we analyze the central activity of the executive, his *process of decision,* we can see three kinds of disciplines which prepare directly for the skills and qualities needed:

(1) The executive must distinguish and define the possible lines of action among which a choice can be made. This requires imagination, the ability to catch at ideas, shape them into concrete form, and present them in terms appropriate to the problem.

(2) He must analyze the consequences of taking each line of action. Here the computer and operations research techniques can do much, but the executive must set the framework for the problems from his experience and imagination, and work with his own sensitivity and knowledge in the area of human beings where statistics and scientific prediction are highly fallible guides.

(3) Then in the decision he must have the grasp to know its implications in all areas of an organism which is itself far from being absolutely predictable: the company, the market, the economy, and the society.

Most executives act on the basis of a definite hypothesis about the nature of business, much as a scientist acts on a hypothesis about the universe. However, many of the elements subconsciously admitted to such a hypothesis are likely to be wrongheaded prejudices based on insufficient data. Indeed, one of the biggest contributions of operations research has been in identifying all the various factors that are involved and in establishing their net weighted relationships. The fact remains that a good proportion of business decisions have been proved pragmatically valid, to judge by the success of American management to date; and this casts real doubt on whether business is quite as "scientific" as many businessmen would like to think.

There has been a good deal of questioning for some time among more thoughtful management authorities whether management is or can be (or even ought to be) considered a science. . . . This question is important because of the possibility that much of top management's dissatisfaction with the executives available for promotion today has resulted from the educational and training assumption that management is a science or, worse, a collection of techniques, and can be prepared for in those terms alone.

There is the correlative danger that attempts to make management a science and only a science will destroy its essential nature and vigor in the American system. . . . Even if management were not faced with the great changes that are upon us, it would be essential to educate executives for the future who know how to ask impolite questions of the categories of science, just so as to avoid the danger that management as a body of knowledge will freeze into dangerously rigid controls on the whole enterprise system.

It is perhaps the most striking fact about the new techniques of management that when they have developed fully, we shall know much better how far the writ of science runs in management; we shall know how far beyond science a man must go to practice management.

I do not mean to deny that management needs a strong measure of scientific ability. But in organizing and systematizing education for the practice of management it has perhaps been forgotten that more dimensions of hypothesis and experience are involved than are available to science. The practice of management can repeat Hamlet's words to science today: "There are more things in heaven and earth, Horatio, than are dreamed of in your philosophy." The exclusively technical or scientific man is on a tennis court as compared to the generalist who has the added dimensions more like those of a squash court available to him. The latter can get the ball of decision bouncing off more walls.

In view of all this, what can the humanities offer that is pertinent to the executive's job? For one thing, there is plenty of testimony that a common factor in executive success is the ability to express oneself in language. To illustrate:

There have been many examinations of the background of executives to discover the secrets of success, which have pointed to other than technical accomplishment. In the most recent of these, by Wald and Doty in this magazine, which is more an examination in depth than any that have gone before, it is clear that the literary aptitude of the 33 executives examined was high compared to the scientific. These executives also felt that English was one of the most useful subjects they could take in college to help them toward success.

It is certainly true that the student in the humanities goes deeper into language, and must get more from it and do more with it. But to assume from this that language is only a tool is to stop far short of the possibilities.

Language is not only a tool; it is the person himself. He makes his language, but his language also makes him. "Speak that I may know thee" is the old saw. Any study of language that stops with "techniques of communication," that sees the relationship as one-directional, is stunting the student's growth as an individual. Thus the study of literature as communication only, and not also as experience, is short-changing the student. Study of literature for its own sake is an activity which widens and deepens the personality.

Arthur A. Houghton, Chairman of the Board of Corning Glass, poses the problem bluntly with his statement opening the College English Association Conference at Corning last year:

> The executive does not deal with physical matter. He deals exclusively with ideas and with men. . . . He is a skilled and practical humanist.

Human situations are controlling in a large proportion of business decisions. The executive, it is agreed, must be able to deal with these situations before all else. The instincts for plucking out the fullest implications and keys to human situations are not developed in technical courses of study, nor even in courses in human relations where the techniques pragmatically set the key for action.

There are numerical keys to situations, from accounting; there are quantitative keys, provided by operations research and other techniques drawn from the physical sciences; there are theoretical keys, such as those of Freudian analysis; and there are the keys of the social sciences, which claim to have no preconceptions or assumptions but which are guided by doctrines nonetheless. But none of these keys provides the executive with the ability to see situations as a whole after and above all the data that are available, to seize on the central elements and know where the entry of action can be made.

The fullest kind of training for this ability can actually be given by the practice of reading and analyzing literature and art. In his function the executive must do pretty much what a critic of literature must do, i.e., seize upon the key, the theme of the situation and the symbolic structure that gives it life. The executive must, moreover, create his object for analysis by himself, combining the ingredients of people and data. He must develop insight of an analytic, subjective kind—something he will never get in terms of pure science, for people and things in management situations just will not behave themselves with the admirable regularity and predictability of gases in a test tube!

The fact is, of course, that science itself has had to reconsider its assumptions about the nature of creative activity in its own field. In place of the mechanical concept of the mind as a computer patiently turning over the whole range of possible solutions one by one until it lights on the right one, explanations of scientific discovery now sound more and more like artistic or literary creation—much like John Livingston Lowes's description of how Coleridge inspiredly fused his whole range of experience and impression into "The Ancient Mariner."

The creative element in management, as in the humanities, is developed by the disciplined imagination of a mind working in the widest range of dimensions possible. Some of those dimensions can be more precisely stated. As Clarence Randall has put it:

My job today is in the realm of ideas. If I must delegate, I must delegate the things that are physical; the things that are material. . . .

Many others have agreed that the most valuable commodity in management is ideas. Yet those disciplines which explore ideas for their own sake, which treat ideas as having life and interaction of their own, have been set off by many as "impractical." Now that the range is widening for management problems, we shall do well to demand that the traditional disciplines, which have dealt in ideas as they interact, in situations as wide as the artist's view of life, become a major part of education for managers. The greater this range of resource for the minds of management, the more and better will be the ideas that emerge.

Because literature is the disciplined control and development of ideas, it deserves a prominent place in this educational plan. Furthermore, to deal with literature and the arts is to deal with ideas not in the stripped and bloodless way of science, but in the inclusive, pell-mell way that experience comes to us in real life—ideas and practice all muddled up.

Lyndall F. Urwick, in a lecture given a few years ago at the University of California said:

What the student needs is a universe of discourse, a frame of reference, so that when he encounters the raw material of practical life his mind is a machine which can work fruitfully upon that material, refer his own practical experience, which must be extremely limited, to general principles, and so develop an attitude, a guiding philosophy, which will enable him to cope with the immense responsibilities of business leadership in the twentieth century.

The executive's job, like life, is just one thing after another. The executive must be continually and instinctively making order and relation out of unrelated ideas—sorting, categorizing—to the end of action. The order he is able to impose on this mass of experience and the actions he initiates determine his success as an executive. He must find meanings for his company and his function, not only in control reports, balance sheets, market data, and forecasts, but also in human personalities, unpredictable human actions and reactions; and he must refer all to a scale of values. He must be prepared to answer the demand of the people who work for him: that their work contribute to the meaning of their lives. Without some awareness of the possibilities for meaning in human life he is not equipped for this central job of managing people. That awareness is a direct function of the humanities.

The key to the executive's situation and problem, then, is the fact and type of the network of meanings he must use and deal with. They are his stock in trade. He must remain aware of significance and meaning in the obvious: production rates, standards, absenteeism, and the rest. But today he must be acquiring more awarenesses to keep up. These can no longer be limited to the political and international. They are wider. Here the experience and criticism of the arts—especially literature—are direct preparation; for reading of this kind is above all a search for meanings. The mind that leads this search in literature and art—the author, the artist, the composer—is the most sensitive and aware. The mind that follows—the reader, the listener, the viewer—is itself stretched in the process; it too is going to grow more alert and aware.

Meanings on the widest possible level feed perception on a narrower one. The executive whose experience of meanings is thus widened has a suppleness of perception on narrower problems which can key them to effectiveness and coordination with policies and objectives on up the scale of management.

It is only prudent, then, that the executive's preparation include a participation (actual or vicarious) in the highest development of this process. Every novel and play and poem is an imposition of order in terms of human beings and of meaning in terms of a scale of values on the elements of experience that are found formless and pointless in any human experience. The terms by which this order is achieved over the whole scale of management action uses technology and science as tools, but it must have a sense of the whole and of values to be fully effective.

One of the most perceptive comments on the nature of the executive's job was made by Crawford H. Greenewalt, President of du Pont:

> . . . The basic requirement of executive capacity is the ability to create a harmonious whole out of what the academic world calls dissimilar disciplines.

This ability to see the whole of things is again a central function of the humanities. The sciences have flourished by acute concentration upon those elements of the universe that can be measured, but science itself will today admit that it is not a means to the knowledge of the whole of man or of the universe.

The whole of a play or a poem or a novel is the object of the studies of literature because the meaning and structure of each part of it make sense only in terms of the whole. Thus one can say that this feeling for completeness which must govern management even more in the future than it has in the past is directly served by the humanities.

Another, and perhaps the most important, aspect of the executive's job is the fact that he must operate in terms of values. Peter F. Drucker puts this at the center of the management job:

> Defining the situation always requires a decision on objectives, that is, on values and their relationship. It always requires a decision on the risk the manager is willing to run. It always, in other words, requires judgment and a deliberate choice between values.

Only in the humanities are values inextricable from the materials that are studied. The significance of this is pointed up by a comment in the Yale Report on General Education:

> The arts are distinguished by the fact that their order already exists in the material studied. . . . The student who works with them learns to deal with intuitive symbolic ways of interpreting experience, ways which combine into one order the rational, the descriptive, and the evaluative.

If there is a better description of the basic elements of management decision than that last sentence, I have not seen it. Men who must deal with situations above all in terms of values must be prepared by being exposed to those disciplines which admit that they are the stuff of all human life. It is here too that the most obvious reason usually advanced for the advantage of the humanities to an executive gains a new significance. With this equipment he is more likely to have interests outside the business. Not only is he thus likely to be less feverishly possessive about his status in the company, but he has available a far more extensive range of values against which to set his relations with others in the company and the policies of the company itself as well (when he is in a position to set those policies).

The tendency on the part of some social scientists—and some professors of literature—to assert the relativity of values is now going out of academic style. Even the most coldly objective of them now agree that some assumption of at least a hierarchy of values is necessary for worthy social action. This concession is of course not enough. The humanities can themselves be explained as the attempt to work out values in the arts, in all the possible terms of human action. Just as every poem, novel, or play is a representation of a scale of values, and thus has a life independent of the society that produced it, so the most objective study of value systems must admit that there are values by which the value systems themselves can be judged. The difference can be simply stated: for the humanities the values are inextricably linked to the materials; the sciences and social sciences attempt to divorce the materials from the value patterns. . . .

Those disciplines in education which provide human and traditional perspective on the sciences and social sciences have always been of the highest importance in developing this ultimate management skill; they will become more important as time goes on, for, as President Nathan Pusey of Harvard has remarked, "The humanities draw things back together."

The essence of the humanities, then, is meanings and value judgments on all levels. When they are well taught, they force the student to deal with things as a whole, with the gradations and expressions of meaning, worked out in terms of experience coordinated by values and communicated by the disciplined imagination of the artist or writer. These meanings, in a framework of fact, intellect, emotion, and social values, are pulled together in an essentially spiritual complex.

The key to management, and to the executives who make it up, is found in its very nature as an activity. It is easy to define management as a combination of resources, but the fact that the human resources in that combination are in a very special way unique is something that links the humanistic disciplines and management far more firmly than engineering links production to science. . . .

Participation as a student in the poetic process of turning vision into rhetoric is parallel basically to the central problem of the executive, when he works to get policy and company goals into action, integrating plans and objectifying them. And executive action in its own way is no less an art.

There are levels of organization in intellectual disciplines as well as in people. On the level of composition, rhetoric, and communication the humanities offer useful tools for the technician in business. But there also are higher levels of organization and integration in work of literary art, which correspond to the integrated personality for which management is looking. Only by exposure to these can we hope to get the character which is essentially the organization of the personality on the highest level of values.

To neglect the humanities in education is to accept the doctrine of the educationalists as set by John Dewey: "The educational process has no end beyond itself." Management has already discovered that the corporation cannot long exist if it has no end beyond itself. It has now seen its error in giving education the impression that the end of education should be the service of the technical needs of business. There is a new synthesis now in the making through which the true ends of both can best be served. It remains only for management to put it into effect.

Businessmen can of course do the obvious, such as recruiting liberal arts graduates on an equal footing with engineers and technicians. But they can do more. They can ask impolite questions of those who teach the humanities. Do they as teachers produce clarifications of value judgments in their students? Are the students compelled to wrestle with values, as real things or *as if* they were real? Are they driven to see situations as a whole and to analyze them with all the elements in their experience, including their moral values? Businessmen can make it known that their standards for education are not merely technical or specialized. They can thus deeply affect educational policy to the benefit of management and American society.

A realization of these facts can also affect the atmosphere in which potential executives are trained on the job. The procedures which now devote the potential executive's most imaginative years to apprenticeship to figures and techniques can perhaps be changed to take advantage of the stimulated imagination, the taste for general ideas with which the graduate emerges from college, without losing the advantages of buckling down to work and getting a responsible job done. Multiple management no doubt owes a good deal of its success in the many companies using it to its ability thus to harness the most creative elements in the thinking of younger men. There are other ways of working out plans that will tap the liberating qualities of study of the humanities which will not interfere with the necessity for technical training. They should be investigated.

The humanities in the colleges are now struggling to put the pieces of the specialties back together again in order to make the integrated men that management can best use. If they get the sort of direct support already given by Corning Glass Works, General Motors, and General Electric as expressed in their sponsorship of the College English Association's conferences, and in the research projected by that organization, these disciplines can prove the most valuable single resource available for the management of the future.

Suggested Topics

1. The specialist and the generalist
2. The practicality of liberal arts
3. Can we automate executives?
4. "What can you do that a computer can't?"
5. Education for management
6. Is management a science?
7. Ideas—the "most valuable commodity in management"

PUBLIC RELATIONS: THE INVISIBLE SELL

Robert L. Heilbroner

> A popularizer in the field of economics, Robert L. Heilbroner has written numerous articles on his specialty for leading magazines. His books include *The Worldly Philosophers* (1953) and *The Quest for Wealth* (1956).

Mixed up in the affairs of the Atomic Energy Commission, the Institute of Boiler and Radiator Manufacturers, Elvis Presley, and United States Steel; welcomed into the inner sanctum of church, corporation, and cabaret alike; as indispensable to a modern hospital as a surgeon and to a big labor union as an organizer, you will find the representatives of one of the newest, fastest growing, and certainly most significant professions of our times. These are the members of the public relations fraternity—a brotherhood of some 100,000 whose common bond is its profession, and whose common woe is that no two of the practitioners can ever quite agree on what that profession is.

Whatever it is, public relations is the wonder child of our age. Turn back to the Manhattan classified telephone directory for 1935 and look up the listing for public relations: you will find ten names.

Go through the catalogues of the universities twenty years back, and you search for a course on public relations in vain. Investigate the public relations staff of General Motors for 1931, and you will discover one man, Paul Garrett, who had just been hired.

Today the listing in the telephone directory runs on for seven columns and over seven hundred names—in Manhattan alone. Last year 653 colleges taught something called "public relations"; eleven (including such pillars of respectability as Columbia and New York University) offered it as an undergraduate major; and one, Boston University, had a School of Public Relations which gave an M.S. degree. And last December when Paul Garrett retired from General Motors as a full vice president (to set up his own public relations firm), his staff numbered some two hundred people, exclusive of clerical help, and cost well over $1,000,000 a year.

That is, however, only evidence of public relations' meteoric rise. Even more impressive is its present extent. According to *Fortune* magazine, nearly five thousand corporations now support public relations departments or engage public relations counsel. An already outdated report by the Bureau of the Budget lists 5,211 full-time "information officers" for the federal government. Add in the labor unions, the private welfare organizations, the charities, causes, and not least, the celebrities who also buy what public relations men sell, and you arrive at the not unimpressive figure of at least half a billion dollars spent for PR hired help alone. How much is spent not for the hired hands, but on public relations itself, nobody even hazards a guess.

And what is this thing called "public relations" on which all this money is expended? It is not one thing, but many, for the practice in which the brotherhood engages is indeed a motley one. In the name of public relations you will find the boys "institutionalizing" a TV comic, "personalizing" an institution, or just plain peddling a product or an idea. Public relations includes such virtuous aims as making the public "aware" of muscular dystrophy and such dubious ones as putting pressure on a legislature through phony consumer fronts. It runs the gamut from philosophizing on social trends before a board of directors, to advising that same board on how best to pulverize the opposition in a proxy fight. It takes in the planted item in the gossip column and the artfully contrived mention of a client's product in a magazine article ostensibly about something else. It embraces the cozy corporate brochure "About Us Folks," and the hard-breathing advertisement of the "facts" concerning a strike. In a word, public relations covers a lot of acreage—blurring out into advertising, slopping over into selling, dipping down into publicity, and touching—or at least aspiring to—the "making" of public opinion itself.

And what, one may ask, after reading this ill-assorted catalogue, *is* public relations? Perhaps we can sum it up by calling it the business of the Invisible Sell. Public relations is Dale Carnegie writ large: it is the professional winning of friends and influencing of people—only not for oneself, but for one's clients, and not by glad-handing or overtly campaigning for their favor, but by creating "situations of reality" in which their acquiescence and approbation are spontaneously aroused. The public relations man is the stage manager of real-life dramas which contain not a hidden moral, but a hidden commercial. In the arresting, if chilling, phrase of Edward L. Bernays, a pioneer in the field, public relations is "the engineering of public consent."

And this makes the brotherhood somewhat more interesting than just another bunch of guys out to make a buck. For we are all of us to some extent hooked by the Invisible Sell—enthusiastic about people we have never met, persuaded of the virtues of products and institutions with which we have no direct contact, contented captives of ideas we are scarcely aware of having picked up. If the public relations men are capable of *manufacturing* these enthusiasms, persuasions, and ideas, it would not be too much to claim that they practice the most important occupation of our day. Or perhaps one should say the most portentous. Or perhaps merely the most pretentious. Whatever the final verdict, it would certainly seem worth while to meet the fraternity members themselves.

This will not involve us immediately in a series of high-level conferences in paneled board rooms. On the contrary, a Cook's Tour of public relations land begins far from the fluorescent eyries of Madison Avenue, in the hole-in-the-wall offices of another, even dreamier avenue four blocks west: Broadway. For whereas it makes a public relations counselor (and how the trade does love that orotund title) cringe to be told so, he did not spring, full-formed, from the brow of Jove. He crawled up from a lower form of life called the Press Agent. And there on Broadway the evolutionary process can yet be witnessed, as small wriggling things hitch themselves up on the terra firma of respectability, take their first tentative gulp of air, and—if they are still alive —declare themselves to be public relations men.

Back in the primordial ooze itself are the press agents whose "offices" are often only the stuffy phone booths around the corner from Lindy's. At his wilder extremes the press agent is the man who says to his client cuties, "Now when you get turned down for the part, you just walk over to the window and jump. I'll be waiting down below with a net," but in his more prosaic moments he lives off plainer fare called Client Mention. And client mention is still an indispensable part of public relations, even at its most stratospheric. Ben Sonnen-

berg, for example, who is one of the best-known public relations men
in the country, has a special literary knack for leaving his clients' im-
prints on the sands of *Time*. Even Edward Bernays, who is today
about as far from a press agent as one can get, rode to fame on some
particularly gorgeous client mentions. One of them involved the
fiftieth anniversary of the invention of the electric light, for which
Bernays staged a Golden Jubilee at Dearborn, Michigan. Quite by
chance, the President of the United States contributed his presence to
the shindig and the Postmaster General issued a special stamp in its
honor. In the stamp, the Jubilee, the posters, and the news releases,
the Mazda bulb quietly glowed, reciprocally lighting up and lit by
the luminaries provided by its master PR.

Today the public relations counselor disapprovingly frowns at the
mention of the press agent whose motto reads, "Anything goes, so long
as you spell the name right." Nonetheless he owes much of his imaginative vitality to his rude forebears. Indeed at the lower echelons of
public relations you will find the direct descendants of the press
agents, who have learned that a quick and agile mind and some good
publicity ideas can be quickly parlayed into cash.

Of the 700-odd public relations firms in New York and the 2,000-
odd in the nation, a very considerable number—perhaps as many as
two-thirds—represent the ventures of bright young men, who start
with a general background in publicity, a client or two, and a few
hundred dollars in cash. This is where enterprising youth goes these
days, instead of West. A career in point is that of an ex-publicity man
named Alan Brandt. Good-looking, voluble, and an absolute garden
sprinkler of ideas, Brandt took the plunge sixteen months ago from
a well-paid position as publicity director of station WNEW in New
York, for which he had gained nation-wide notice with shows such as
a disc-less disc-jockey program (calliopes, music boxes, player pianos),
a 2:00 A.M. feeding show for parents up bottling their infants, and
Esoterica, A Program of Frankly Limited Appeal (Ethiopian music
and Gertrude Stein).

"I just got tired of working for someone else," says Brandt, "so I
went out and got myself a room with one window, one desk, one
phone, one size of stationery, one girl—and one client. I was in business."

The client was the producer of Captain Kangaroo, a TV kiddies'
show, and Brandt publicized it as the children's show that *parents*
would like. It was a good pitch and made several magazine breaks,
and thereupon the phone began to ring. A hair-products firm wanted
to know if Brandt could think of some way of publicizing buns and
chignons: Brandt got a TV hair styles contest started. A Boston radio
station showed up looking for a publicity idea: Brandt printed records

which fitted the new Chrysler car-phonograph and which interrupted their music with, "Are you missing the news? Tune in on station WHDH." A TV morning show wanted to be talked about: Brandt put Salvador Dali on to explain that the cauliflower was the basis of all art, and had an art dealer choose between six masterpieces worth over $100,000 and six fake copies worth less than $100, by slashing the fakes—while Brandt quietly perspired behind the camera. A book publisher wondered if something could be done about a novel set in a small New England town. Brandt got an item in the Associated Press about a book that would blow up Gilmanton, New Hampshire, and *Peyton Place* was a best seller before it even reached the bookstores.

It is now sixteen months later, and despite the fact that Alan Brandt is successful enough to need a personal tax lawyer, he sometimes worries about where he goes from here. For if the publicity end of the public relations game is a rich one (at least for those who make the grade), it is also rugged.

"Here I am," said another energetic hustler, "working like a beaver to get my client, call him Bill Blick, into the columns. He's a dog of a client, but finally I get something worth printing. Then I hear it's going to run in a big name column. I call my client's secretary and we all rush out to buy the early edition. And what does the item say?— 'What ever happened to Bill Blick?' "

Equally baneful to the publicity man is the fact that his client, a modest soul who just happens to have a few good pictures of himself in case they're needed, is usually blissfully unaware of the writing, the phoning, the glamorizing that have been done to make his pedestrian life fit to print. On the morning when months of patient work finally pays off, he cheerfully calls his PR and says, "Say, did you see what the *Times* wrote about me?" And worst of all is the call that comes on the day when a national break of great important has finally been landed. The client phones and enthuses.

"Great job! Just what we needed! Thanks a lot! Of course you understand that we won't be needing you any more now."

Hence those PRs who cultivate the flowers of publicity raise a lush but quick-wilting crop. It is not surprising therefore that the next step up the evolutionary ladder is to the less spectacular but hardier perennials of Product Promotion. Here is where you will meet nine out of ten PRs who have graduated from the publicity game, tirelessly plugging away for products the majority of which are hardly such as to inspire soaring flights of the imagination. Typewriters, for example. Or wool. Or dog food.

Now since there are very few magazines or newspapers which would be interested in running a story about typewriters, wool, or dog food, and still fewer which would give free advertising to Underwood, the

Wool Institute, or the Gaines Dog Food Company, the public relations man must disguise his hook with fancy feathers. The Underwood people therefore prepare "5 Sprightly Stories" on such themes as *How To Keep Your Boss Happy*, or *The Girl With the Halo* (your secretary); the Wool Institute offers *How's Your AQ?* (Appearance Quotient) and *Wool in History and Legend*—"the fascinating story of the thousands-of-years-old romance of the use of wool"; and the dog food people establish the Gaines Dog Research Center—"a research and educational institution created as a public service." These are offered free to editors.

Needless to say, the mortality rate of such PR productions reaches epidemic proportions, but since the birth rate is high, a certain number of brain-children survive. A considerable number as a matter of fact. No PR firm of any stature cannot boast of having "placed" stories in *Life, Look, Saturday Evening Post,* or *Reader's Digest,* not to mention the *New York Times*—although many is the chagrined PR who, having finally inspired a story on his client's industry or interest, reads it with fading smile to realize, at the end, that the goddam magazine never mentioned *his* client once.

One of the most successful product promoters is the firm of Ruder and Finn, which began like Brandt Public Relations, on a shoestring. Not quite ten years ago Bill Ruder, a young publicity man for Sam Goldwyn, and David Finn, a hopeful painter, decided to put their curiously diverse talents together in public relations. They took a room in the Hotel Lombardy—the size of which can be judged by the fact that it is now the hotel linen closet—and landed that essential First Account. It was a promotion job for Perry Como's records, and they performed it so artfully that Como thanked them publicly in an ad in *Billboard*. Then *their* phone began to ring. And they began to think.

"We didn't want to be just publicity boys all our lives," says Finn. "And while we were beating our brains to think of a way not to be, Bill remembered the nation-wide publicity network that Goldwyn used. We decided to try the same deal for product promotion." By writing to independent PRs around the country, Ruder and Finn established a gossamer-thin tie-up with small out-of-town public relations firms, and this they then hawked as the Ruder & Finn Field Network. Into its flimsy meshes promptly swam a whale. A major soap company was about to launch a new soap and it wanted just such point-of-sale promotion. The soap brass descended from its glassy heights to the brownstone basement into which Ruder and Finn had moved their operation (and where they had spent the previous twenty-four hours frantically adding twenty-seven men to their "network"), and—perhaps with suds in its eyes—approved of what it saw.

After that it was easy. Today, with seventy employees, a Field Network of over 190, and a gross take in excess of $1,200,000, Bill Ruder and Dave Finn run one of the six biggest PR firms in the country.

Walking through the pastel-tinted Ruder and Finn offices is not unlike walking through an advertising agency—a resemblance which makes both PRs and advertising men edgy. There is a writing department, a TV and radio department, a magazine department, an art department, and a long string of offices for account executives, supervisors of executives, supervisors of supervisors, and so on. For R & F does a great deal more than publicity for its clients. In fact it does public relations for them.

What is public relations at the R & F level? Of course it includes product promotion via the Invisible Sell, as witness a technique used to push Skotch Koolers, a picnic carrier. R & F sent samples of the Kooler to professional photographers and TV studios, merely suggesting that they might be used as studio props. They were. You may have noticed the Kooler along side the man with the beard in a Schweppes ad, or next to a bathing beauty extolling skin cream. Without spending a nickel on advertising, R & F dangled its product before the eyes of several million people, a pleasing number of whom swallowed the bait.

But the public relations bait does not consist of products only. Indeed, the publics to which R & F professionally relates its clients tend to include fewer and fewer customers, and more and more groups such as stockholders, employees, or even bankers. For these publics Ruder and Finn will design a client's annual report and compose dignified but warm letters to his shareholders, will edit his employee newspaper, or make his name known among the Wall Street community. Or, in the jargon of the trade, they will create and sell his "image."

It is not by coincidence that our Cook's Tour of public relations land has taken us from publicity through product pushing to the creation of corporate "images," for the higher up the ladder of public relations you go, the more grandiose becomes its purpose. Indeed, when you arrive at the summit, you can hardly see the customer any more at all. The bait which now dangles from the invisible line is no longer personalities and merchandise, but institutions and ideas.

Thus at the powerhouse of public relations maintained by General Motors, only a fraction of the PR effort is aimed at making people like GM *cars,* and whereas this fraction packs a mighty wallop (the whole idea of Motorama was originally a PR flash of genius), it is hardly central to the company's public relations program. For General Motors —or any large corporation, for that matter—has a more important task for its public relations than the pushing of Chevvies, Buicks, or Cadillacs: Sales Promotion does *that*. What public relations must do is the far more difficult job of selling General Motors itself—as a community asset, a helpful company, a corporation with solid ideas, a big business with its heart in the right place—in a word, as a great institution, and by implication, one which should not be meddled with.

When Paul Garrett arrived in Detroit twenty-five years ago to begin General Motors' public relations program, the first question fired at him was: "How do you make a billion dollars look small?" Garrett said damned if he knew, and furthermore damned if he thought that was his job. Public relations, he argued, was not an "act," but a continuing effort on the part of management to win the confidence of the people with whom it came into contact. Hence you will find General Motors engaged in a host of activities in which altruism and self-interest come together in a creamy blend. Plant City and Field Relations, for example, stimulates local GM participation in the community affairs of the sixty-eight cities where it has factories, thereby helping both the community and itself. Educational Relations works with the schools, providing them with such useful educational material as films on safe driving, and providing itself with a flow of applicants for jobs. The Speakers Bureau is glad to send a company-sponsored lecturer to your club or association to edify it with an inspirational talk—or to educate it with a "sound" economic one. Institutional Advertising tells the story of GM's role in supporting some twenty thousand suppliers, and leaves you with the pleasant impression that what's good for General Motors is good for small business, too. The billion dollars may not look any smaller as a result of the efforts. But it looks much, much nicer.

This same kind of quiet winning of friends and influencing of people is practiced by the biggest public relations firms. At Hill & Knowlton, for instance, which runs neck and neck with Carl Byoir & Associates as the largest PR outfit in the country (H & K's minimum fee $36,000; Byoir's $50,000, but H & K has more accounts), only 6 or 7 per cent of the firm's effort is spent on publicity. The rest is largely concentrated on showing corporations how to do Good Works and how to present their side of the story—which is always known as The Facts.

Thus for its biggest account, the American Iron and Steel Institute (which is incidentally the biggest PR account in the country), H & K provides a whole panoply of services, none of which is calculated to sell a single ton of steel, but all of which are calculated to sell the steel industry and its point of view. It publishes *Steelways,* a magazine which is sent to 100,000 key people, such as editors and educators, who pass along interesting bits of information to an audience estimated at

12,000,000. It puts out booklets on "timely topics of importance" such as the industry's lagging profit rate. It runs a field service which counsels individual companies on such matters as how to conduct plant tours, or how to work with the local school board, or who should go on the Institute's mailing list.

And it runs such interesting services as the Community Resources Workshop. This is a project to acquaint teachers with industry and its potential helpfulness in providing educational material. It also aims at giving teachers an insight into the problems of steel—not on a "propagandistic" basis, but just the way steel executives honestly see them. Dr. Albert L. Ayars, the educator who heads the Workshop, has stated that he would resign if his project were ever used for the propagation of distorted facts. "I suppose you could say," he admits, "that as a result of these experiences the teachers will be more receptive to some legislation which would be of benefit to industry and the public. But again, not because they have been coerced into it. All that we would have done from the standpoint of our client, American Iron and Steel Industry, is to have exposed them to the facts."

For those who picture public relations at the summit as the cunning manipulation of minds, or the subtle exercise of devious techniques, the actual practice of Big PR must look tame indeed. That it is often transparently self-serving, under the guise of serving the public, is perfectly true; and that the motives which prompt it are not entirely spiritual, needs hardly to be pointed out. It is the Invisible Sell on a huge scale, but whereas one may not always particularly like what is being sold, it is hard to get much worked up over the salesmanship.

That goes for nine-tenths of Big PR. Of course there is also the tenth tenth. Witness, for example, the public-relations tactics in the Pennsylvania railroad-truckers fight in 1952. The client here was the Eastern Railroads Presidents Conference; the PR firm was that of Carl Byoir & Associates (Hill & Knowlton's big competitor); and the issue at stake was a bill increasing the size and weight limits for trucks on the state roads. It was not by accident that Byoir was chosen for the task of beating the bill. As the company explained in a letter to one of the railroad vice presidents (in charge of public relations), it was good at that sort of thing, modestly mentioning a chain-store bill it had licked in New York State for the A & P, and a tax reduction it had secured in Louisiana for the Freeport Sulphur company. And so, for a fee of $150,000 it got the job.

And brought home the bacon. In due course the bill was vetoed by the Governor.

Not that the Governor acted out of any but the best interests. He had before him, for example, an early report of the Maryland State

Roads Commission containing very unfavorable data on road damage. He was faced at every turn by newspaper and magazine articles on the evils of trucking, and across his desk passed a succession of interesting studies by institutions such as the New Jersey Citizens Tax Study Foundation. Certainly not absent from the Governor's mind was the opposition of the State Association of Township Supervisors, which had mailed out thousands of postcards protesting the truck bill, and of the State Grange, a politically powerful organization.

When Governor Fine vetoed the bill, it must have seemed to him that he was only expressing the will of the people; but how much of this will of the people was the result of the activities of the Byoir agency who spent several hundred thousand dollars in their campaign?

There is now pending in the United States District Court for the Eastern District of Pennsylvania an anti-trust action entitled *"Noerr Motor Freight, Inc., v. Eastern Railway Presidents Conference et al."* In support of their position the Plaintiff-Truckers introduced through their briefs and supporting affidavits, and by the testimony of witnesses, evidence to the effect that the Maryland Commission's public relations man constantly visited the Byoir offices and later was given a job by the defendant, the Eastern Railway Presidents Conference; that newspaper and magazine articles were planted by the Byoir agency or based upon material supplied by them; and that the New Jersey Citizens Tax Study Foundation was founded and supported by the Byoir agency. Evidence was also introduced that a Byoir man set up headquarters in the Grange and used the Grange stationery and that the postcards mailed in the name of the Township Supervisors were prepared by Byoir.

It is incidents such as this which give rise to alarm over the power of public relations (although it is worthy of note that not a single client left the Byoir firm, and that the Public Relations Society of America—the "standards-setting" organization of the trade—did not suggest that Carl Byoir & Associates should withdraw). But if within the profession most eyes were delicately averted, outside it voices were raised. In a brilliant exposé by Robert Bendiner in the *Reporter*, the question was posed: "Is this what is meant by the engineering of public consent?"

The indignation was natural, and yet the Byoir episode is not a case by which the power of public relations must be judged. For one thing, as is often the way, the success back-fired: Byoir and the railroads are now both entangled in the $250,000,000 suit filed by the truckers. And for another thing, no one has ever denied the power of public relations, in careless or overeager hands, to gain selfish advantage, or to exert legislative influence, on behalf of its clients— whether they are business, labor, farm, or foreign.

All this, however, is aside from the crucial point. It is not the excesses, but the run of the mill of big PR, not its faults but its very virtues which need examination. The basic question is not the power which resides in bad public relations, but that inherent in *good* public relations; not the ability of public relations to subvert, but its capacity to convince. The really important question about the power of public relations is whether it can influence what men *think*.

This brings us to an impressive demonstration concerning the making of public opinion that took place in Cincinnati in 1947.

For six months Cincinnati became the focus for an unprecedented crusade—a powerful, well-planned, and well-financed attempt to teach it what to think. Specifically, Cincinnati was the target of an all-out effort to make a typical American city "United Nations conscious."

The crusade was a thorough and intelligent one. It was launched at every level of city life. On blotters, matchbooks, streetcar signs, and billboards, Cincinnatians read "Peace Begins with the United Nations —the United Nations Begins with You." Local radio stations broadcast UN facts and news daily—one of them on 150 spots a week. The newspapers played up the theme. Every schoolchild in the city was given literature about the United Nations to take home; the PTA, the Council of Churches, and the Catholic Church all climbed enthusiastically aboard the bandwagon. Club women rallied round with letters and telegrams pledging their support to the American delegation to the UN. In the last three months as the campaign reached a crescendo, 225 meetings were held; hundreds of documentary films shown, 59,588 pieces of literature distributed.

Then they took a poll of the results.

At the end of six months only *half* as many people considered the United Nations a means of preventing war as thought so at the beginning.

There was almost no change in the number who thought that the United States should take an active part in world affairs.

There was a drop in the number of those who were in favor of having the United States join an international police to keep peace.

Fewer people thought there should be some sort of international control of atom bombs.

There was almost no change in the numbers who knew what the main purpose of the United Nations was, or who had heard of the veto power, or who knew how the UN worked.

In a word, the campaign was a gigantic frost.

Why? The answer may be shocking, but it is simplicity itself: people in Cincinnati just didn't give a damn about the United Nations, one way or another. For all the matchbooks and the meetings, the UN was something far off, vague, abstract, unconnected with daily life

Hence the propaganda went in one ear and out the other, and save for the pleasant friction stimulated in transit it left no imprint at all.

And the moral, for public relations, seems to be that most people don't give a damn about most things, unless those things are part and parcel of their concrete lives. They just don't listen. For many years, Hill and Knowlton has sought to put across such simple (and true) messages as that the steel industry is not a dangerous place to work, or that steel's profit margins, by comparison with other industries, have been low. The results: slightly *more* people thought steel was dangerous in 1955 than in 1946 or 1943, and there continues to be "considerable belief" (in Hill & Knowlton's own words) that steel's profits are too high.

Or take the case of General Motors. For nearly twenty years, along with seven other large corporations, GM has tested its popularity by means of a continuing opinion poll called the Link Audit. On the face of it, results were excellent: the proportion of people who "liked" General Motors (and all the other companies) rose from less than 60 per cent in the late thirties to over 80 per cent today. The only trouble is, no one quite knows what "like" means. Every time there is a strike in any *one* of the eight companies, the popularity of *all* of them goes down. For some unfathomable reason all the corporations are more popular in fall than spring. And every time there is something to get mad about, the Link Audit "liking" doesn't seem to prevent people from boiling up: when Harlow Curtice, GM's president, testily denied to a Senate Committee last year that there was anything wrong with General Motors' dealer relations, something akin to a whirlwind of angry protest materialized out of the blue. Chastened, Mr. Curtice appeared again in a more conciliatory mood. The whirlwind disappeared. And the Link Audit once again showed that everybody "liked" General Motors.

Hence the public-opinion researchers are, to put it mildly, skeptical about the ability of public relations to engineer the public's consent and dubious about the depth of the affections it arouses. "Give the PR something real and specific—a personality, a product, or even a precise enough idea—and he can usually make an impact," says one professional public-opinion measurer. "But ask him to sell a big fuzzy thing like a 'nice' company or a 'sound' doctrine, and the result is usually an absolutely monumental indifference."

Or worse, skepticism. One opinion researcher, Douglas Williams, measuring the effect of a company's effort to "sell" its employees on Free Private Enterprise, found the net outcome to be an increase in hostility and suspicion. "Those people knew about free enterprise in terms of their own jobs and incomes," he explains. "They didn't like having those realities 'justified' with fancy abstractions. Instead they asked, 'What's really the matter, that they have to sell this thing to me?' "

The wiser public relations men are well aware of these facts. "Make no mistake about it," says Earn Newsom, who counsels, among others, Ford and Standard Oil of New Jersey, "a corporation does not win the confidence of the American people by trying to 'educate' them to its point of view." A case in point is Newsom's client, "Jersey," which has long ago wearily resigned itself to living with the popular opinion that it is still part of the oil trust which broke up some forty years ago. It just doesn't bother to argue any more—because it realizes that it probably wouldn't do any good if it did.

But whereas the public relations men themselves have salutary doubts about the efficacy of their efforts to sell those nice big ideas, their clients share no such hesitations with them. For if there is one part of the public which is really a patsy for the power of public relations, it is that hard-headed pragmatic character, the American big businessman himself. Not content with using public relations to publicize or promote his wares, or to cement his relationships with his employees or stockholders—all of which it can do very well—he is convinced that it can serve to get his "message" across to an eagerly attentive public, and to enshrine his corporation, as well as its products, in their hearts. Nor does he, curiously enough, demand proof of this conviction, for he has swallowed the Invisible Sell hook, line, and sinker.

If the public relations brotherhood is not quite so powerful as its enthusiastic clients think, neither can it be shrugged off as just a collection of publicists, pitchmen, and commercial philosophers. Public relations is more than just an occupation or a bunch of occupations: it is a social force—and as such it has left two indelible marks on our world.

The first mark is its part in the general debasement of communications from which we suffer. It is only a banality to point out the need for effective public communication in today's complex society, but communication has become more of a fetish than a function. Science has a technical term which describes the result of forcing more messages along a carrier than it can accommodate: it calls the result *noise*. We live in a noisy society: one in which everyone talks and few say anything; one in which the spurious, the insincere, the meretricious, and most of all the *empty*, crowd out the meaningful, the useful, the important. People who live in such a society learn not to listen—or worse, when they do listen, they learn to disbelieve what they hear.

In this process of the debasement of communication, public relations must bear its share of the blame. No one can quarrel with the essential function that public relations fills as the purveyor of genuine ideas and information. No one denies that many public relations men, working for corporations as well as for colleges or causes, honestly communicate things which are worth communicating. Nor can anyone absolve public relations for loading the communications channels with noise. We read the news and suspect that behind it lies the "news release." We encounter reputation and ascribe it to publicity. Worst of all, we no longer credit good behavior to good motives, but cheapen it to the level of "good public relations."

It is not *that* bad, of course. But if we step back to view that whole big thing called Public Relations and then attempt to weigh what it has meant to our values and beliefs, it is hard to avoid the conclusion that the net effect of the Invisible Sell has been to further a cynical judgment of the motives behind human behavior.

That is one side of the coin, but there is another, and shinier. If public relations has cheapened the face value of good conduct, at the same time it has enormously increased the prevalence of good conduct. For regardless of its motive or its incessant self-advertisement, good conduct *is* more prevalent on the business scene, and public relations can rightly take much of the credit. The reason is a curious one. It is that something called Good Public Relations has come to be regarded as an indispensable attribute of business—as much a sign that a business is "modern and progressive" as a shiny new glass office building (which is also, of course, a good public relations move). Quite simply, business has sold itself the bill of goods it originally intended to sell the public.

"If you ask me," said one shrewd public relations man, "the aim of a big corporation should be invisibility. But no. It insists on being as visible as possible. Its directors get nervous unless people say what wonderful public relations the company has. So it has to *have* wonderful public relations. It has to *act* lovable. It has to *be* progressive. It has to *become* socially responsible—not because the management necessarily thinks that way, but because that's what Good Public Relations is."

Hence by an unexpected twist, public relations has become a weapon whose recoil is greater than its muzzle blast. Good Public Relations has come to be something very much like the corporate conscience—a commercial conscience, no doubt, but a conscience none the less. If the public relations profession can bolster this role, if it can become the corporate conscience openly, fearlessly, and wisely, speaking not only *for* business but *to* business, then it will have more than redeemed its name.

Suggested Topics

1. A definition of public relations
2. "The engineering of public consent"
3. The role of propaganda in international affairs
4. Government by public opinion
5. Public relations—good and bad
6. Building a presidential candidate
7. Various levels of public relations

THE AGE OF THE THINKING ROBOT   *Robert Bendiner*

> A former editor of the *Nation* and now a contributing editor
> of the *Reporter,* Robert Bendiner has written extensively on a
> variety of contemporary problems. He is the author of *The
> Riddle of the State Department.*

Probably not since Dr. Freud reached the crest of his popularity
has the public been treated to a flow of synthetic words as glittering
and bewildering as those now being poured out by the prophets of
the new industrial technology. Literature on the subject, which is pil-
ing up by the ton, is often rounded out with a glossary for the layman,
and one enterprising firm has actually issued a little dictionary of the
jargon, from "automation," the sacred key word, through "cyber-
netics" to "servomechanism" and beyond.

It is perhaps too much to expect precision in this new argot when
the concepts, especially of automation itself, are still so varied and
the inferences drawn from them are so dazzlingly at odds with each
other. Take automation—at the broadest of its dozen definitions—to
mean the operation of a productive system without human operators
or hardly any, and you will discover from a bewildering day's reading
that "The automatic factory and even the automatic office are coming
nearer to reality [but] as in the past, these changes will of course be
gradual. . . ."—Haldon A. Leedy, Illinois Institute of Technology.
Then again, "Automation will mushroom . . . we want it to mush-

Reprinted from *The Reporter,* April 7, 1955. By permission of *The Reporter*
and the author.

room . . . we couldn't stop it even if we wanted to. It will bring great change to all of us."—Gordon S. Brown, Massachusetts Institute of Technology. Or, more to your taste if you are in a hurry, "The automatic factory is not merely coming. It is already here."—National Association of Manufacturers. But, strangely, "There are no such factories and no such machines, nor will there ever be. . . ." Benjamin F. Fairless, United States Steel Corporation.

You will learn from John Diebold, editor of *Automatic Control,* that automation is "a pattern that will have more meaning for our individual lives and for our collective future than the double-mushroom shape of atomic explosions." You will learn from this same Mr. Diebold, who is something of a high priest in the movement, that its "probable impact upon the economy has been greatly exaggerated." To the United States Chamber of Commerce, the whole thing is just a "bogeyman conjured up by the collectivists to replace an unpromising bogey named 'Economic Collapse.' "

In such swampy terrain it behooves the observer to move with caution, but on the basis of what has already occurred, it takes no unusual rashness to report that major changes are in fact taking place in American manufacturing, processing, and office work. They are changes of such scope and nature that, as we shall see, it is fatuous to regard them merely as extensions of the technological progress we have known for a century. Add to them the imminent introduction of atomic power into private industry, and it becomes startlingly probable that, war or no war, the United States of 1970 will no more resemble our present society than it resembles Andrew Jackson's.

What is there in automation that takes it out of the normal stream of mechanical progress and gives it an entirely new dimension? Unlike individual machines that have revolutionized only their own industries, automation calls for a basic change along the whole productive front. It is comparable, not to the linotype in printing or the Bessemer process in steel, but to such historic concepts as mass production itself, concepts that revolutionized whole economies and made sweeping changes in the social structure.

Where the first Industrial Revolution substituted machinery on a vast scale for human and animal muscle, the second promises on a comparable scale to substitute machinery for the human brain—not at top levels, of course, but in the normal run of the productive process. Since James Watt put steam to work, men have labored at their separate machines, feeding them, guiding them, correcting them, timing their operations, and in general controlling their work at every stage of the procedure. Today automated equipment, given advance instructions by punch cards or recording tape, can process raw materials, assemble the parts, correct its own errors, reject or rework parts that do not measure up to specifications, and even inspect the finished product, the linked chain of machines operating as an integrated whole and controlled by a central electronic brain.

Considering the enormous possibilities in automation, both industry and labor are approaching with a caution that borders on the jitters what an N.A.M. booklet archly calls "the fairyland of the world to come." Captains of industry who fear that the very word "automation" will prompt organized labor to painful demands tend at times to belittle the whole development, while at other times they revel in its promise of low-cost abundance. In the same way, trade-union chiefs have one eye hopefully trained on the coming era of plenty and the other cautiously fixed on the more imminent possibility of technological unemployment.

Mr. Fairless and countless other preachers on the subject never tire of pointing out that, far from being new or strange, automation goes back at least to the flour mill that one Oliver Evans operated near Philadelphia in 1784—a system of conveyors run by water power in which the grain was picked up, carried through several grinding operations, and delivered as finished flour. Punch cards? No newer, they point out, than the player piano and Jacquard's loom.

True enough, these were remarkable devices in their day, but they no more rob of significance this second Industrial Revolution now upon us than the wheel and the lever can be said to have taken the edge off the first. For automation at its fullest is not merely the existence of separate machines, however automatic, but the controlled operation of an entire factory or process in which the machines, as linked units, automatically perform their manipulations in specified sequences, with electronic judgment substituted for the perception of the machinist or foreman. With complete automation, operators disappear from the scene, leaving huge and highly productive plants to be manned only by a maintenance crew and a few engineers to set the equipment and check the dials for trouble signals.

Only a few factories are completely or nearly automated, but even a cursory survey will reveal the deep inroads that have already been made.

Naturally enough, it is in the production of dangerous war materials that automation has had its most complete workout. In Bedford, Ohio, a chemical company turns out a monthly quota of 650,000 pounds of napalm, the jellied gasoline used in incendiary bombs. On any given shift the entire plant, ten thousand square feet in area, is operated by four men and a supervisor, whose jobs consist mostly of maintenance. Automatic-control panels regulate the flow of ingredients, and a sequential interlocking of motors and conveyors does the rest. Production costs are fifty-nine per cent lower than with the conventional method.

Similarly, 155-mm. shells are turned out for the government by United States Industries, Inc., in an automatic factory at Rockford, Illinois. "It is impressive," says the corporation's president, "to watch this tremendous plant operating and to listen to the sounds of the metal being worked in so many ways at such a rapid pace, to see the whole operation being conducted through stations throughout the plant, full of blinking lights and clicking relays, attended by one or two men at each station."

Automation has made most headway in industries most readily reduced to a continuous-flow process—such as oil refining, flour milling, and chemical production.

"A man may work for months on a pipeline or in a refinery or even in the production fields," says an official of the Oil Workers Union, "and never see nor touch oil." To be sure, refineries have been highly automatic for many years, ever since the laborious method of distilling oil in batches was abandoned. But automatic production is not the same as automation, and it might be well at this point to state the most essential difference.

In a word the difference is *feedback*. Not to make a mystery of it, feedback is a technique for self-correction. An outfielder chasing a fly ball constantly corrects his speed and direction as his mind estimates and re-estimates the location at which the ball will descend. That is feedback with a human mind giving the orders. When a ship is set to steer a certain course, the steering mechanism will automatically swing to starboard if the ship veers too far to port, and vice versa. That is feedback with an automatic compass giving the orders. In automated equipment an electronic brain constantly compares variables in the work being done—temperature, speed, thickness, or whatever—with a set of given specifications, continuously correcting the machinery to which it is linked until precisely the prescribed conditions are met, down to the finest tolerances.

It is this tremendous advance that is at the heart of true automation, making it possible in refineries for a few skilled workers to sit at a master-control panel and watch the equipment itself guide crude oil through various intricate steps until it emerges as gasoline or some other petroleum product. An industry spokesman says that a refinery that employs eight hundred people without modern instrumentation could do the same job with twelve people if instrumentation were utilized to the fullest possible extent.

Solids are harder to handle, but some of the most complex problems were solved by the time the Ford Motor Company opened its much-publicized engine plant near Cleveland three years ago. Here six-cylinder engine blocks are turned out by the union of an electronic brain, fed by twenty-seven miles of wire, and forty-two mechanical hands in the form of automatic machine units. Through this giant complex, 1,545 feet long, rough castings are pushed, pulled, turned in every direction, conveyed, and subjected to cutting, drilling, honing, milling, boring, and broaching in more than five hundred manless operations, each one checked and inspected only by the "brain" itself for performance and accuracy. Thoroughly instructed in advance, it decides when a block is ready for the grinder, how fine it is to be ground, and where it is to move when it is done. A block that once took nine hours to complete is now sped through in fifteen minutes.

Where it once took thirty-nine men working twenty-nine machines just to drill the necessary oil holes in a crankshaft, only nine men are needed for that job at the new Ford plant. Most of the small crew lost in the acre of machinery stand by and watch, and replace worn tools whenever a "toolmeter" panel flashes the signal that some particular instrument is approaching the end of its usefulness. "Ours is the only foundry in the world," says the manager proudly, "where the molding sand used to make castings is never touched by human hands except maybe out of curiosity."

Perhaps laboring the obvious, a Ford spokesman is quoted by Walter Reuther as saying, "Automation reduces labor tremendously. Our experience has shown that we can count on a reduction of twenty-five to thirty per cent in what we call 'direct' labor." No men were laid off as a result of this stride in automation simply because it was an addition to existing plant, established in a period of expanding production.

Most automation men agree that the electronic displacement of humans will go farthest and fastest in the office. There, according to a leading accountant, "computers are . . . going to be like bulldozers in the construction industry." It took only a short time to realize that electronic brains which could do a year's astronomical computations in a few minutes or speed an anti-aircraft shell to its moving target could be turned from science and war to the requirements of business. Instead of storing its magnetic "memory" with data on velocities, voltages, temperatures, and the like, one had only to feed it information on payroll rates, income-tax data, overtime, Social Security, etc. The result, as scores of users of I.B.M. and Remington Rand computers can already attest, is that these machines now make up the most complex payroll, perform the necessary accounting operations, and, with their own high-speed printers, run off the pay register and make out the checks.

Insurance companies are particularly ripe for this sort of automation. Three of the largest have already gone electronic, with machines like Univac and I.B.M.'s "701" hired to bill customers for premiums, calculate agents' commissions, figure dividends, and work out all the necessary actuarial data. Prudential is counting on its electronic computer to replace sixty to seventy-five other machines along with their operators—two hundred in one department alone.

What the Ford engine plant represents in the way of robot industry, General Electric represents in the field of office automation. In its Major Appliance Division at Louisville, Univac has been assigned to far more than turning out the payroll. Its chief contribution will be in the highly complex work of inventory control. According to W. W. Smith, who serves as Univac's superior, "If the decision is made to increase the production of appliances from one thousand to two thousand per day, Univac within a matter of hours will be able to show the effect on every item of inventory. . . . To do the same job on a manual basis as one part of total manufacturing planning often requires up to three weeks or longer."

To mention all the types of robots already holding down jobs in American industry and business would tax the reader's patience, but the following items will at least suggest the variety of machine talents to be had on the market today:

Baking: You can "tape" cake or bread now by merely inserting the necessary instructions in a machine.

Radios: Thanks to a system for eliminating wire circuits, which require soldering at all contact points, radios can be and are being turned out automatically. Motorola is reported to have a machine that can spit out complete sets once the components are fed into it. Raytheon Manufacturing Company has a chassis-assembly line, geared to a thousand radios a day, that is operated by two employees where standard methods of production would require two hundred. Admiral, working through a gadget called Robot I, can assemble half a television receiver chassis in a matter of seconds.

Tanning: Automatic controls in a big Milwaukee tannery now mix the acids and oils and regulate the drying temperature while conveyors put the hides through various processing machines. One-third of the men do the work formerly required and turn out a better product in less time.

Electric Power: A conventional plant of the Cleveland Electric Illuminating Company employs a hundred men for 290,000 kilowatt-hours of production, but the company's new push-button plant employs twenty-eight men for 420,000 kwh. This is typical for the industry, which turns out five times the electric power it did twenty years ago with only fifteen per cent more personnel. But what has utility workers far more agitated is the prospect of atom-produced electric power in less than ten years. A pilot plant going up right now is expected to need only six men to furnish electricity for the entire City of Pittsburgh.

Telephones: Even in this industry, where electronic automation is as old as the dial system, the innovations are astonishing. Through Direct Distance Dialing, now available to some subscribers, a caller may by fingering a few digits get the services of an electronic long-distance operator. In fifteen seconds the robot will have located the shortest telephone path from, say, New York to Los Angeles, made the connection, and recorded the call for your bill.

While most of the country still regards such reports as good reading of the "ain't-science-wonderful" variety, the blossoming of these marvels has alerted intelligent industrialists, labor leaders, and sociologists to the prospect of great change, with or without a prolonged struggle.

At this stage, it might be said that a strained air of reasonableness prevails, with a good deal of nervous anxiety showing through on both sides. In the National Association of Manufacturers booklet "An Introduction to the Automatic Machine Age," the future is painted in rosy hues, but there will be responsibilities too, "including the responsibilities of industry for . . . the reallocation of man-power to dry up temporary pools of unemployment."

J. Douglas Elliott, a high official of the Detroit Edison Company, concedes with others that "These new brains are going to replace workers—a lot of workers," though in the long run they will create more jobs, shorten working hours, and increase our standard of living. But in spite of these ultimately fair prospects, he adds, "Management men are somewhat ill at ease, too. . . . They are apprehensive about labor problems resulting from mass layoffs and the problems of hiring and training highly skilled technicians to keep their operations going."

At the same time, sterner voices are being raised on the industrial side of the fence. John I. Snyder, Jr., president of United States Industries, Inc., puts it bluntly: "It often has been thought that automation in its ultimate sense in any industrial plant is a desirable goal because it will reduce labor costs. . . . But reduction of labor costs is only a part of the point. Another highly desirable feature of automation in relation to labor is the fact that machines are easier to control than people (and this is a blessing in our democratic society). The more machines the fewer people, and therefore the easier the control problem." Even assuming that Mr. Snyder is talking strictly about mechanical controls, his point remains that the main trouble with labor today is people.

The same general sentiment was voiced at one of *Fortune* magazine's round tables by Dr. J. J. Brown of Aluminium, Ltd.: "Now men by definition are difficult and tricky things to play around with. You have employee-relations men, time-study men; you have training and educational directors; you have personnel men, washroom men, cafeteria men. That all costs money. My point is this: that if we could take some of the money that we are spending in trying to ease the pain of our assembly-line personnel, and apply that money for some research to get the men out of there entirely, we would be far better off in the long run." A sociological note in another issue of the same journal, by the way, reveals that so many of the employees to be supplanted are young women, at least in offices, that engineers have taken to estimating the new machines in terms of "G.P.'s or girl-power displaced."

But probably it is J. J. Jaeger, a Pratt and Whitney official, who has expounded the hardheaded view most candidly: "I don't think we are consciously trying to ease the burden of our workers nor consciously trying to improve their standard of living. These things take care of themselves. They have a feedback of their own that closes the loop automatically. I don't think it is the part, nor can it be the part, of industry to try to plan the social aspects of this thing."

It is precisely this supposition—that some natural law, some self-regulatory process, will automatically take care of any surplus labor—that rouses the fears and suspicions of trade-union leaders. In the long run, society will no doubt adjust itself to the change, just as it did some generations after the beginning of the first Industrial Revolution. But labor is not willing to buy an eventual boost in living standards for all at the cost of any such prolonged suffering as followed Watt's tinkering with a teakettle. "The long run," in Reuther's view, ". . . is not the consideration, for, as Lord Keynes once said, in the long run we are all dead."

Nevertheless, and in spite of what Fairless professes to see as "a great propaganda campaign which is clearly calculated to discourage and retard technological progress," there is absolutely no sign that labor plans to throw *sabots* into the servomechanisms or even to emulate the vain and foolhardy war against canned music in the 1930's. What most trade-union leaders want, and feel strong enough to demand, is a planned transition, with shock absorbers to soften the bumps on the way to the New Abundance.

So far, automation has been marked by no mass layoffs, and indeed the temperate attitude of leading users of advanced equipment has given the industrialists at least a debater's advantage. They point out that while fifty thousand telephone operators have been replaced by the dial system, net employment in the industry has steadily gone up; that General Motors has about doubled its employment since 1940 in spite of increasing use of automatic machinery. According to *Business Week,* Pontiac executives, knowing that "the saving of manpower is a ticklish subject with labor," kept its working force intact, using its new equipment to increase production by twenty-five per cent.

Those industrialists who uneasily concede the possibility of "displacements" quickly fall back on other defense positions. Where mechanization created hazardous and spirit-deadening tasks, making man a degraded servant of the machine, they say that automation will eliminate these jobs, put a premium on technical skill, and upgrade the labor force all along the line.

What's more, they argue, automation will be limited to the very big manufacturers, processors, and offices that can afford the expensive equipment. And finally, like all technological change in the past, it will create new industries and make additional jobs. The automobile gradually retired the blacksmith and the stableman, but look how many jobs it opened up to mechanics, garagemen, rubber workers, motel-keepers, and roadbuilders!

Obviously there is much that is solid in these arguments, but there is also much that is dangerously hazy and speculative. These weaknesses, which we will consider next, are not lost on those who want to get industry committed now to sharing the blessings of the new technology.

A fifty-seven-year-old hide stripper in a packing house has been relieved of his job, one of the most highly skilled in the business, by a machine that neatly peels off an animal's skin once a semi-skilled workman has made a single incision in the carcass. The veteran employee is not fired. He is simply allowed to work out the few remaining years before his retirement at an inferior job, though his pay may remain the same. Yet the old job classification, with its high rate of pay, is gone from the contract at the next bargaining session with the union, never to reappear. In this year's negotiations with a leading packer, more rates were "bargained out" as a result of new machinery than in the last fifteen years put together. In other industries, too, the individual's chances of being imminently down-graded are greater by far than the reverse prospect, and his eye, reasonably enough, is on the year ahead; not, like that of the sociologist, on the far horizon.

A telephone operator is replaced by a new dial system. She does not show up in the company's statistics as dropped, simply because it had the foresight to hire her as a temporary worker. "For about two years in advance of a particular dial conversion," I was told by Joseph A. Beirne, president of the CIO Communications Workers, "the company will hire new operators only on a so-called 'temporary' basis. They are told they have employment only until the dial cutover is completed." If the operator does have permanent status, the company may offer her a job elsewhere, but, Beirne explains, often this is at a location far removed. "Many take their termination pay, or their pen-sion, and drop out of the labor market or get other jobs" rather than be uprooted.

It is this hidden, creeping type of unemployment that is becoming a source of concern. As one executive candidly concedes, "The person most seriously affected at the moment is the 'employee' not hired."

Just how "seriously affected" is already being indicated in Census Bureau figures. Certainly nationwide *employment,* in terms of the number who hold down jobs, is rising, but the productivity of our factories and offices is rising so much faster, thanks to technological advance, that the yearly additions to the labor market are not being absorbed, and so *unemployment* too is one the rise. *Life* is led to reflect: "With a total of 2.7 million *not* working, we have been able to turn out *and consume* virtually as much goods as at the record heights of the boom. What this indicates is that the U.S. may be able to produce and consume at boom-time levels yet still have a 'permanent reserve' of unemployment, which may increase."

Will the N.A.M.'s "temporary pools of unemployment" be dried up simply by the increased need for technicians and distributors? Or by newly created industries? Ultimately, no doubt, but the evidence is that without countermeasures they will deepen before they evaporate. For a displaced baker who has no chance of becoming an electronic technician, "ultimately" can be a painfully long time.

There is little reason to believe that electronic equipment will long remain exclusively in the hands of the top corporations. On the contrary, competition is expected to force the smaller outfits to adopt modern methods on pain of either going out of business or merging with the giants. Medium and small computers are already being turned out and sold to moderate-size concerns on the theory that they can take the place of big staffs that such employers never could afford. I.B.M.'s "650" rents for as little as $3,750 a month and does far more than could be done by the equivalent ten clerks whose salaries would come to that amount. When the market for computers is thoroughly exploited and displacements mount in geometric rather than arithmetical proportions, will employers still find spots for supplanted workers, even at reduced pay?

As for jobs in those new industries, labor has its fingers crossed. Electronics manufacturing itself, the fountainhead of automation, should be a haven right now, but the fact is that as far as jobs go, it is already contracting as sharply as the industries it serves, and for the same reason. The Bureau of Labor Statistics testifies that in this field also "employment has not kept pace with production during the past seven years. Electronics output in 1952 was 275 per cent higher than in 1947 but was produced by only 40 per cent more workers." At International Business Machines, which with Remington Rand is the chief source of computers, output per employee has more than doubled in a decade.

Until automation actually forces a far greater leisure for Americans, thereby fostering new businesses and services to cater to that leisure, it is not likely to inspire any tremendous wave of secondary investment. Professors Walter S. Buckingham and Sherman F. Dallas, in a paper on the subject presented to the Southern Economic Association, flatly predict that by its very nature automation "will not make the far-reaching investment impression that the introduction and later improvements in automobiles, railroads, and canals, for example, created."

Granted then that there is at least some reason for apprehension, at least in the short run, what can anyone reasonably expect industry to do about a trend as inevitable as taxes? Far from preparing to ram their heads into a stone wall, labor leaders are set to go along with the big shift—but they want a hand in the proceedings. As long ago as 1948, UAW contracts gave the automobile companies a free hand in introducing technological changes. Reuther is, if anything, more lyrical than the NAM itself when he eyes the prospect of "abundance in terms undreamed of before" and of "vast improvements in the living conditions of the American people." And in the AFL George Meany simply renounces the tradition. "The trade union movement does not oppose technological change." What the AFL wants is severance pay for people displaced by machines, the retraining by management of employees so that they can man the new machines, and, sooner or later, a reduction in hours—a thirty-hour week for all by 1980.

The CIO, especially Reuther's Auto Workers, has spelled out the program of demands in more specific detail. Its argument is pitched to the need for keeping purchasing power high enough to buy the ever-increasing volume of goods that the improved technology can provide. This means higher pay for automated jobs, even though the work is less onerous, and it means the guaranteed annual wage.

Actually it did not take automation to give rise to the notion of the guaranteed annual wage, but the demand for it clearly has been stimulated by the new threat to labor's position. It will not only help stabilize purchasing power, the argument runs, but will also "serve as a regulator of the process of technological change, tending to minimize its disruptive consequences. It will affect management's decisions concerning both the timing and the placement of new automation installations."

And, not least, it will tide over the victimized individual, sometimes lost sight of in a mound of statistics, until he either finds a spot at the work he knows or has trained himself for something else.

Not that the unions think this retraining process should be left wholly to the employee. On the contrary, they are in voluble agreement that management has an obligation to retain its veteran employees wherever possible rather than turn them out in favor of young technicians fresh from school.

Unquestionably this "upgrading" of the labor force will present one of the great headaches of the next decade. Take it straight from the National Manpower Council:

"Many of today's electricians will have to learn electronics if they are to retain their skilled status. Pipefitters may have to learn hydraulics. A skilled worker who formerly measured with calipers and now uses a micrometer will soon have to learn to work with tolerances measured with light waves . . . there may be almost no place left for the unskilled industrial worker."

The semi-skilled are in every bit as bad a way, according to the industrial-relations editor of *Factory Management and Maintenance*. "The jobs that are 'duck soup' for elimination by automatic production," he says, "are mainly the semi-skilled ones, such as machine operating and materials handling. Some observers believe the factory of the future will go so far as to wipe out this great 'middle class' of industry."

Some will be fortunate enough to acquire these higher skills and avoid supplanting by trained technicians. All major industrial plants have training programs now and will almost certainly expand them. "The factory of the future," one executive says, "may not be a college, but it's going to look more like one than you might think." For those who make the grade it should be a safe, quiet, white-collar haven where, one engineer told a recent convention of steelworkers, he "would not think it facetious if the workmen wore tuxedos on the job." With somewhat less abandon, a workman in a new Ford plant recently made the same point to a newspaper interviewer. He used to go home every evening jittery with exhaustion, he said, but now "I run a whole battery of machines by pushing buttons and reading dials and go home feeling like talking to my family and reading."

Unfortunately, however, the number who will be needed and trained for button pushing and dial reading will be a small fraction of the total force. The rest will have to pin their hopes on the gradualness of the shift to automation, on preferential hiring at plants slowest to make the change, on pensions or unemployment insurance, and ultimately on drastic reduction of the work week.

In the last analysis it is this steady increase of leisure that will have to be relied on to solve the problem of the technologically displaced. And leisure, of course, means paid leisure—something very different from the happy notion of the oil-equipment executive who recently

announced that, thanks to automation, "We hope to be able to eliminate the overtime pay we're saddled with." For the six-hour day or
the four-day week—ultimately perhaps both—will make a great difference in the way we live and the services we need.

As the number of workers in the productive industries shrinks, the
new leisure should require a steady rise in the number engaged in
facilitating travel, in offering entertainment, in adult education and
cultural activities, in the rebuilding of roads, and in numerous other
activities called for by a people who will have twice as much free time
on their hands as their grandparents.

Not all the burden for the readjustment, of course, will fall on
industry. A drastic overhauling of our educational institutions will be
needed to reduce the unskilled to a minimum, if necessary by new
teaching techniques; to provide the technicians for the new day; to
train the servants of the new leisure; and, not least, to enhance a nation's capacity for leisure, as distinguished from idleness.

Even while the N.A.M. calls for readjustments in curricula to "put
greater emphasis on the electrical, mathematical and mechanical sciences," it suggests that "practical education" is no longer adequate. It
would be a fatal error "if Americans were transformed into highly
specialized cavemen, woefully deficient in the arts and letters." The
concept appears to be gaining among industrial and business leaders
that as our complexities deepen, technology is not enough. Executives
must understand human relations, economics, psychology, and therefore, at last, philosophy, with all that it entails. Witness Bell Telephone's experiment of sending a batch of its top young executives to
the University of Pennsylvania for ten months' exposure to the humanities—from Bhagavad-Gita to Ezra Pound.

Some sociologists feel that the fear of more leisure is acting as a
brake on technological change. In a society rooted in Calvinist doctrine many Americans, David Riesman observes, look upon increased
leisure as "a threat, a problem, a burden, or hazard." Diebold thinks
the gradualness of the change will permit adjustment on this front,
as on others, but he concedes that, barring an all-out war, sooner or
later we will have to face the question, "Are we capable of developing
a culture that does not depend upon work to give meaning to our
lives?"

Depending, again, on the speed of change, government will have to
bear a degree, probably a high degree, of responsibility for salvaging
those unskilled workers who turn out to be a drug in the labor market.
As anti-boondoggle an organ as *Life,* foreseeing trouble, proposes that
government "draw a line—perhaps the present line of 2.7 million—
above which unemployment will not be allowed to go" before public
works now in blueprint are put into concrete. "Fortunately," the

magazine points out, "nearly all such measures can be made in capital improvements—new highways, schools, better housing, etc.—which will eventually pay for themselves by what they add to the income and brain-power of the economy."

To this catalogue might be added airports sorely in need of expansion, city redevelopment, and parks, not to mention the need of government aid to prevent the creation of ghost towns by shifting industries.

How fast is automation moving? Some observers think it is moving at a slower rate of speed than the limitations of either technology or economics dictate. But it is coming swiftly enough for all that. The U.S. Chamber of Commerce, which is far from trying to arouse public concern in the matter, solemnly cites predictions of a three-day weekend within the next decade, as against Meany's ultracautious target of 1980.

According to the Stanford Research Institute, factory sales of data-processing equipment, a good index of the advance of automation, rose from zero in 1940 to $25 million in 1953 and are expected to reach $500 million by 1960. Similarly, instruments for industrial control leaped from $3 million in sales in 1940 to $65 million in 1953 and are expected to hit $150 million in five years.

Want ads plead constantly for engineers and technicians, and investment houses publicly exhort customers to put their money in the booming stocks of automation-equipment makers. Where Ford stamped out four of its car parts automatically in 1947, it now does thirty parts almost without manpower. But perhaps the most striking evidence of the advance comes from the Federal Reserve Board. Its index figure for the manufacturing and mining industries in November, 1953, was 129. In November, 1954, with almost a million fewer people in those industries, the figure was still 129.

No one can say how far the expected "dislocation" may go, how many humans may lose their jobs to Univac, Eniac, and Multra; to Armatrol, Serva, and O-Man; or how many jobs these genies may in turn provide for those they have displaced. Certainly no one with the least sense of history would either want or expect to arrest a trend that will increase the world's wealth and reduce human drudgery. Where the first Industrial Revolution degraded men to the level of a machine part, the second should liberate him from the machine completely.

But if it frees some only to leave as many other stranded, dazed, and for years without the wherewithal to buy what the machines produce, it will hardly have paid its way—at least for a generation that already has all it can stand in the way of large-scale hazards. A measure of coherent planning, a sustained sense of responsibility in industry, labor, government, and education—these are the least we will need to ease us into the second machine age more smoothly than our luckless forebears went into the first.

Suggested Topics

1. Automation—not an unmixed blessing
2. Technological unemployment
3. "The fairyland of the world to come"
4. Reshaping our lives
5. The second machine age
6. The need for higher skills
7. The new leisure

WAYS OF SCIENCE

THE BASIC NEED FOR BASIC RESEARCH   *John Pfeiffer*

Formerly science and medicine editor of *Newsweek* and later science director of the Columbia Broadcasting System, John Pfeiffer is one of the leading free-lance writers on science. His books include *The Human Brain* (1955), *The Changing Universe* (1956), and *From Galaxies to Man* (1959). In 1957 he played a leading role in the preparation of a report by the National Science Foundation urging the Government and private industry to increase their support of basic scientific research. He is a former president of the National Association of Science Writers.

In the continuing stir about the quality and future of American science, two facts stand out. First, no nation can hold its own in the world today unless it provides a favorable atmosphere and generous support for basic research, the undirected search for new knowledge about natural phenomena. Second, we are losing ground to the Russians in basic research—and the sputniks are only a spectacular sign of the trend.

For some time now, members of the President's Scientific Advisory Committee have been urging a wider recognition of these facts. They have emphasized over and over again that basic research, as the source of every single advance in applied science, is vital to the nation's health and prosperity and security. Getting the point across is not easy. Too many people tend to sympathize with the belittling statement of former Secretary of Defense Charles E. Wilson: "Basic re-

Reprinted from *The New York Times Magazine*, November 24, 1957. By permission of *The New York Times* and the author.

search is when you don't know what you're doing." Too many people still regard fundamental science and scholarship in general as a kind of high-grade malingering, a luxury which we might well do without. They feel that the investigator should consider himself lucky indeed to be receiving any support at all.

Where we go from here depends largely on how well nonscientists, including our elected representatives in Washington, understand the values of "purposeless" experiments and theories. Although there has been much talk about basic research recently, relatively little of it has come from basic researchers. What follows is the gist of a reporter's firsthand talks with a number of the most distinguished of them at Columbia University. They represent a variety of interests, from philosophy and physics to biology and medicine. Furthermore, many other investigators share their views on the important question: what good is basic research?

The chief value of such work to the scientist himself is the sort of intense personal satisfaction that accompanies all discovery. In a sense each major advance in fundamental theory represents the equivalent of scaling an Everest for the first time. As far as the layman is concerned the most obvious value of basic research lies in its practical results. It has provided the "raw" knowledge behind the achievement of everything from antibiotics and vaccines to television, transistors and artificial satellites, and we can expect accelerating developments in the future. For example, if applied scientists succeed in controlling the "fusion" forces released in hydrogen bomb explosions—and the odds are that they will, perhaps within a generation—man will have tapped a practically unlimited source of power. The fuel for fusion-type nuclear furnaces is hydrogen, and the seas contain enough hydrogen to take care of the world's energy requirements for the next million years or so.

Dr. Polykarp Kusch is one of the nation's leading nuclear physicists, but his studies have about as much to do with the applications of atomic energy as Stravinsky's compositions have to do with Irving Berlin's. A tall, well-built man, he won a Nobel Prize two years ago for work on the magnetic properties of the electron. Dr. Kusch had been thinking about how to convey an idea of the good of basic research, and began talking rapidly.

"If by 'good' you mean something that will induce the prices of stocks to go up, the prospects are remote. It is certainly true that basic research fathers technology. Science is a way of living in the modern world, propelled by enormous forces and enormous successes. We are aware of our impact. You don't just put electronic circuits and gadgets together to achieve our marvelous communications. Someone had to think deeply. Theories in physics are things of beauty, symmetry and great power.

"They're powerful in two senses. We can use them to make a television set, a guided missile, a nuclear submarine. They are also powerful in the sense that a very limited set of statements describes a very wide range of human experiences. Science as a form of pure inquiry has played a tremendous role in establishing new modes of thought. Our curiosity is conditioned by the belief, the implicit article of faith, that there is order in the world. Otherwise you might just as well count the number of cigarette butts on the street. At first, man didn't know that the whole damn thing wasn't witchcraft."

Dr. Kusch went on to the appeal of fundamental research as a profession.

"We all like to excel in our chosen fields. My ego is satisfied when I see my name in The Physical Review [the leading American journal for reports on basic research in physics]. A reasonable salary is important. I'm not interested in the rewards of Madison Avenue, but I want enough to support my family. These are reasons for going into any field.

"But basic research is a way of making nature talk. I get a great kick out of listening in, out of learning something which has not been known before. A society in which this can occur is a good one. Every morning I look out of my window at the George Washington Bridge, to see if it's still there. It warms me to think that I am a member of the civilization which produced this artistic monument—and I feel the same way about pure inquiry. I came to Columbia after working in industry, and for years I've never entered the university gates without feeling, 'This is wonderful. This is for me.' Millions of people hate going through gates to work."

What about the future?

"There will be continuing technological advances, of course. That's obvious. But the spirit of pure inquiry may act primarily through an evolution of religious attitudes and religious points of view—a religion which will accept the rationality that science has injected into the thinking of men. It will touch on areas of experience about which science has little to say—the death of one's wife or child, human catastrophes. It will give us a sense of unity in facing up to the sort of human experience whose quality is not adjustable by science."

Another Columbia nuclear physicist is Dr. Tsung Dao Lee, who, with his colleague Dr. Chen Ning Yang of the Institute for Advanced Study in Princeton, has just been awarded the Nobel Prize. Their work led to the discovery that there are high energy subatomic particles which do not obey one of the hitherto fundamenal principles of physics, called "parity." By proving that these particles have an intrinsic left- or right-handedness, they have provided important new insights into the structure of the nucleus—and new problems which physicists will be tackling for some time to come. Dr. Lee, Columbia's youngest full professor—he will be 31 tomorrow—devotes himself to those problems rather than to possible applications. "Those of us in fundamental research do not underestimate the importance of practical uses. But the composer is primarily interested in composing, and symphony orchestras could never perform without him.

"Take electricity. Now, every household appliance is related to electrical energy. But when the principle of electricity was discovered, it was a development of pure research. The applications, if any, of our work are completely unclear to me.

"Dr. Yang and I had been working together for many years studying new particles produced by very high energy machines," Dr. Lee went on. "Last year we conducted certain theoretical studies. They took about a month, the month of May. We also suggested specific experiments that might help to check our ideas." The experiments were performed by Dr. Chien Shiung Wu and her collaborators, and proved successful. "These experiments are forgotten now," said Dr. Wu in her Columbia office. "We're looking ahead—that's the excitement of basic research."

Dr. Lloyd Motz is not doing research on the interior of the nucleus, but on the interior of stars thousands of light-years away. "I'm an astronomer without a telescope," he remarked, smiling. "All I have is paper and pencil for theoretical work. We know some things about the surface conditions of stars, and I'm trying to calculate what goes on inside to account for those conditions. We're interested in the evolution of stars. Our sun is fairly young, a second or third generation body made from matter ejected by ancient stars."

That seemed about as remote as one could get from everyday life. "Oh, no. There are applications. Hydrogen atoms are fusing or combining inside the sun and other stars to release enormous quantities of energy. Mankind would have an almost unlimited source of energy if we could duplicate this process in a nuclear furnace. The Atomic Energy Commission is working on that, and one of its projects is headed by Dr. Lyman Spitzer at Princeton. He's an astronomer, you know."

Sooner or later someone always seems to find a use for basic research. Isn't that surprising, since the investigator isn't interested in applications? "It doesn't surprise me. All knowledge is interrelated. It's like learning from a very good teacher. Only in this case the teacher, and sometimes the obscurer, is nature. You never know how fundamental discoveries will be used. In fact, you may be spending your life on something that will never pan out. But nothing is lost. We are rapidly reaching a stage where we have to know all we can about health, disease, our future food supplies, our solar system. Basic research in all fields represents the ultimate difference between man's survival and his death."

The survival of species, including man, is of special interest to Dr. Theodosius Dobzhansky, an internationally known authority on genetics and evolution. One of the tables in his laboratory was crowded with cotton-plugged flasks, containing fruit flies, which are widely used to study heredity-transmitting genes on a "speed-up" basis. (The flies produce about fourteen generations of offspring a year.) "I'm dealing with changes, or mutations, in genes. With a finger in that pie, it's pretty hard not to be interested in the effects of atomic radiations—from the nuclear power plants that will be operating soon all over the world, as well as from medical X-rays and nuclear-weapon fall-out. To measure how much these radiations affect our genes, we must know the natural mutation rate. Fruit flies provide clues to the workings of heredity in men."

Looking ahead to the more remote future, what is likely to be the most important use of genetics? "That's a more than $64,000 question. It may be that some day we will take a more active part in selecting our genes, in improving our hereditary endowment. Nature has no foresight; she is opportunistic. What is good for nature is not necessarily good for us. Although man was produced by the same force that produced every living thing from viruses up, we oppose the idea that he is merely a modified monkey. Some day we may be able to shape our own evolution, but I hope it won't be soon. We don't know enough yet."

Dr. Dobzhansky paused for emphasis. "We're looking for a new concept of man. That's enough and to spare. We want to find out how biological forces have managed to produce such very unusual creatures as ourselves, with all our objectionable and unobjectionable features."

Dr. Teru Hayashi is a biologist studying the chemistry and physics of muscle. His research and that of his colleagues is important in understanding muscular dystrophy and other wasting diseases, as well as certain conditions of the heart, the body's most active muscle. There have also been speculations about the building of a biological machine, using synthetic muscles to do work, instead of gears and levers. But Dr. Hayashi was in no mood to discuss such possibilities.

He was more concerned about the uncertain future of basic research.

"The public doesn't understand science in terms of basic research," he said. "All they see is the applied result. I saw a motion picture on television the other night, and there was the scientist locking himself in a laboratory filled with gadgets and flashing lights. Of course, he was making a monster, or creating life. The public thinks of the basic investigator as if he were one-sided, not a whole man. Actually, he has a far wider range of interests beyond science than most specialists, far

```

wider than people realize." (Dr. Hayashi, by the way, speaks with some authority on this topic. His friends know him as an accomplished tennis and table tennis player, guitarist, folk singer and fisherman, specializing in Cape Cod bluefish.)

Does basic research need more money? "There is a definite need for greater support, particularly from industry. In Denmark, for example, the Carlsberg Breweries give a large share of their profits to basic research and other cultural activities. Not only that, but every man in the street knows this, and respects the company for it. But the problem goes deeper than money. Our society places a stress on material goods as a criterion for success. Abroad, the average man's chances of making a financial killing are practically nil, so science tends to be more highly regarded. Here the public can't get deeply interested in men who work with ideas. This is a problem of education, at all levels, from grammar school through adult life."

The reporter's next visit was to Columbia's Cardiopulmonary Laboratory at the Bellevue Medical Center to see another Nobel Prize winner—Dr. André Cournand. Dr. Cournand shared the 1956 award in medicine with Dr. Dickinson W. Richards, his colleague at the university, and Dr. Werner Forssmann of Germany. They had developed a safe way of inserting one end of a slender tube or "catheter" directly into the chamber of the beating heart (through a vein in the left arm), and measuring internal pressures at the other end. This has now become a standard technique for diagnosing heart trouble and other diseases that may affect blood pressure and circulation. Dr. Cournand was asked about the work that went into this study. He indicated that medical research is always closer to applications than are fundamental studies in the more remote areas of physics and biology.

"But we have intellectual curiosity and pursue our studies whether or not they lead to applications. The man who does medical research must be capable of forgetting the easy life. I spent nearly ten years without practical results, studying blood flow and the distribution of gases in the lungs. During that period my beefsteaks were very small. But we are thinking of human beings, so our research is always close to life and death. There can be no progress in medicine without the work of people in all branches of fundamental biology. They have made penicillin and many other things possible."

Dr. Cournand is chairman of the National Heart Institute Committee, which distributes about $16,000,000 a year in research funds. Is it difficult to find qualified applicants? "My greatest worry for the future is that there are not enough young investigators who can write good English. More and more of them can put together new devices, but many are totally unable to express themselves or to use the devices
```

imaginatively. We must educate people to develop a taste for ideas.

"If you derive satisfaction from seeing how a great literary mind works, that gives you a facility for dealing with great ideas in science and other areas. If you do this early in life, then the taste for ideas becomes like eating and breathing. To provide basic research you must emphasize all human culture."

These views are closely related to those expressed by Dr. Ernest Nagel, a Columbia professor of philosophy. On the desk in his study was a portable typewriter with a sheet of paper in it. "I'm hoping to finish a book on the philosophy of science by next fall," he said. The reporter asked: "Are all scientists aware of the values of science?"

"I don't think so. Some years ago, I was a member of a committee discussing the education of future scientists. We made a report, and of course it was filed away. But we agreed that one thing was particularly important. We should educate the student not only in his specialty, but also in the broader significance of science. Many scientists are illiterate in this sense. Philosophically, basic research has important long-range moral implications. Our values must be related to what we discover about the universe. It is the philosopher's job, his obligation, to teach and to think about such things."

Apparently, there is a great deal to be learned on all sides. The scientists interviewed feel that basic research is, above all, an exciting and creative way of discovering how nature works—and that the question of practical uses is not particularly to the point. Like the rest of us, the basic investigator appreciates applied science. But, again like the rest of us, he generally leaves such matters to other specialists.

The public relations of basic research are in a sorry state. The accent is always on applications. Scientists seeking or giving funds tend to justify their activities in terms of practical benefits to come, chiefly to satisfy the requirements of "practical-minded" boards of trustees and Congressmen. Science writers and advertisers also play up such benefits, and also for strategical reasons. The basic investigator understands this game. But he feels that his cause would be better served if the creative elements of fundamental science received wider attention.

One final word comes from another Nobel Prize physicist at Columbia, and a member of the President's Scientific Advisory Committee, Dr. I. I. Rabi.

"Some people try to tell you that basic research will make you richer, fatter, thinner, more powerful. But the common man, and the young person whom we'd like to interest in science, is more excited about ideas and explorations than they give him credit for. Here we are, living in this world; unless we learn, we are no different from animals. We discover beautiful regularities, the novelty of na-

ture. We discover things far beyond the mind's ability to project
without experiment. That's what every scientist really thinks."

Suggested Topics

1. The practicality of basic research
2. "Basic research is a way of making nature talk."
3. All knowledge is interrelated.
4. Industrial laboratories and basic research
5. The international language of science

THIRD GREAT REVOLUTION OF MANKIND

Charles Frankel

A Professor of Philosophy at Columbia University, Dr. Charles
Frankel has written extensively on contemporary social philosophies and philosophies of history. His books include *The Case
for Modern Man, The Uses of Philosophy,* and *The Faith of
Reason.*

Probably no event in recent years has had a greater impact on the
American mood than the Soviet Union's success in launching artificial
satellites. The sputniks stirred justified anxieties about America's
position in the cold war and upset some of our tenderest assumptions
about our situation. But more than this, the sputniks—and now our
own Explorer—have turned loose some bewildering predictions about
the future.

Trips to the moon and twenty-minute jaunts to Moscow, we are
told, are on the agenda of human "progress"—though no one has yet
said how to make the moon or Moscow more attractive places in which
to land. It is even whispered that mankind may lose one of its oldest
topics of conversation because it will be possible to control the
weather.

But while predictions about man's future career in outer space
have an undeniable interest, the satellites, it may be suspected, also
have a significance that is a bit closer to earth and closer to home.

Reprinted from *The New York Times Magazine,* February 9, 1958. By permission of *The New York Times* and the author.

For they are not merely events in an armaments race or science-fiction stories come true. They are peculiarly dramatic symbols of what has been going on backstage, East and West, during the last fifteen years —a sudden extension of scientific intelligence and technical resourcefulness which represents an extraordinary spurt of human intellect and power. And this spurt of the human mind has social and moral, as well as technological, consequences. The sputniks are signs in the skies that the normal human scene is changing in some of its fundamental characteristics and that we are living in the midst of a fundamental revolution in human affairs.

Some 25,000 years ago an "Agricultural Revolution" took place which changed man from a nomadic hunter and berry picker into a deliberate cultivator of his food supply. In the latter half of the eighteenth century an "Industrial Revolution" began, with results which we have not yet fully absorbed. Both these revolutions began as changes in the ideas and tools men had used to adjust themselves to nature. They ended by changing men's relations to each other, their moral and political outlooks, and the very substance of the things they thought worth seeking in life. It is easy to overestimate the significance of events that happen in one's own day. But the revolution that has taken shape in the last fifteen years must be put in company like this to be seen in its proper perspective.

Indeed, in the natural energies it has released, and in the speed with which it has done so, the present shift in the relation of man to his environment dwarfs either of its predecessors. It is impossible to believe that its other consequences will not eventually be as great. Now that we have had a chance to absorb the first impact of the sputniks, it may be worth while to sit back and reflect on some of the long-range social issues of which the sputniks are a portent.

We can already see some of the more obvious issues. War, for example, has changed its character and has lost one of its traditional functions in international affairs. Leaving all issues of morality aside, large-scale war can no longer be used, as it has sometimes been used in the past, as an intelligent instrument even of national selfishness. While the danger of all-out nuclear war has not substantially receded, such war can only be an instrument of utter desperation.

Similarly, the problem posed by the expansion of population in the world promises to become even more acute as a result of the advances in medicine and technology that are almost surely in prospect. Through most of its history the human race has had to struggle to keep its numbers from declining. But our very success in improving the basic conditions of human existence now threatens to turn back upon us and to lead to incalculable human suffering unless organized measures are taken to control the birth rate.

But war and the growth of the world's population are relatively familiar problems, even though the penalty for failing to solve them has suddenly become astronomically high. The present revolution in human affairs is likely to bring other changes, however, to which somewhat less attention has been paid. And not the least important is a possible change in the way in which human work will be organized with the advent of new industrial processes such as automation.

One possible consequence of automation, for example, is a sharp increase in the ratio of skilled workers to unskilled workers. This means a host of new issues for industrial unions, and new problems for both labor leaders and industrial managers. Of equal significance is the possible impact of the automatic factory on the way in which the working day may be arranged. As the British engineer Landon Goodman has pointed out, the cost of introducing automation may be so high in many cases that it will be uneconomical to operate a plant only eight hours a day. If many industrial plants are going to find it necessary to operate around the clock, obvious consequences will follow for everything from the nature of home life to the way in which cities are organized. Even the old phrase, "as different as night and day," is likely to lose some of its force.

The new way in which work may be organized also affects the attitudes that men may take toward other parts of life. Most of the work that men have had to do in history has been disagreeable; most of the leisure that men have had has been the prerogative of the few. This fact has colored much of our thinking about the way in which life ought to be lived. The democratically-minded have been suspicious of what is "useless"; the aristocratically-minded have regarded the useful as just a bit vulgar. But if leisure becomes everybody's prerogative (and problem), and if automation can be used to make human work less routine and to give more workers the opportunity to exercise their individual skills and discretion, the sharp division between work and leisure will make even less sense than it makes today. The effects will be felt, to take only one example, in our ideals of "liberal" education, which are still primarily leisure-oriented, and in our conception of "vocational" education, which is already anachronistic in its view of what ordinary people need to be "prepared for life."

But the new processes of industrial production are parts of a larger trend which has even deeper implications of its own. During most of the past, developments in technology were largely independent of developments in pure scientific research. To some extent this remained true even in the nineteenth century. But technology has now become almost entirely the child of fundamental theoretical inquiry. This means that we can count in the future on a steady process of technological innovation, and at a steadily more rapid pace.

We come at this point to perhaps the profoundest consequence of the present revolution in human affairs. It is the simple change in the tempo of change. For nothing cuts more quickly or deeply into a society's way of doing things than changes in its technology.

This quickened tempo represents an unprecedented challenge to the human ability to adjust to social change. It took man roughly 475,000 years to arrive at the Agricultural Revolution. It required another 25,000 years to come to the Industrial Revolution. We have arrived at the "Space Age" in a hundred and fifty years—and while we do not know where we go from here, we can be sure that we shall go there fast. Our expectations of change, and the ability of our nervous systems or our social systems to withstand the shock of change, have been formed in the long experience of the race. And this experience, even in the nineteenth century, has not prepared us for the pace of events that lie ahead.

Such an extraordinary change in the basic tempo of human history means that new and deliberate efforts will be needed to control the processes of social change. As the last hundred years of Western history demonstrate, men can learn to change at a much quicker pace than before. But as these same years also suggest, there are limits, and it is difficult to imagine a day when it will not take time for men to adjust to new conditions, to learn new skills and habits, and to get over the nostalgia and resentments that come when old and familiar things are destroyed. There is a conservative in every man and, in the world into which we are moving, he is going to get a harder workout than ever before.

Accordingly, if the things we cherish from the past are not going to be carelessly destroyed, and if the best possibilities of the future are going to be realized, it seems probable that we shall have to have institutions that have been deliberately set up to exercise long-range social forethought. A steady process of technological innovation, for example, can mean recurrent crises of technological unemployment. If this is not to happen, institutions will have to exist to envisage the new skills that will be needed, to undertake the continuing task of retraining workers, and to control the pace at which new techniques are introduced so that we can make a sensible adjustment to them. Given the pace and magnitude of the technical changes that are in prospect, we cannot count on the market place and the price system to do this job alone. Technological innovation means social change; and there is no more reason to introduce such innovations, letting the chips fall where they may, than there is to introduce a new and powerful drug on the market without first making it meet the test of medical examination and control.

The need to exercise more deliberate control over the processes of social change raises, of course, a fundamental issue. It is the issue of freedom and regimentation, the question of the tension between personal liberty and initiative on the one hand, and the obvious and growing necessity, on the other, for an ever larger degree of social organization. This has been the central issue in industrial society for more than a century. In the world which the present revolution is forming it will be equally decisive. But the terms we have habitually employed in trying to solve it will almost certainly need to be revised.

The dangers that a larger degree of social organization can bring are obvious. It can mean, at the very least, a multiplication of the nuisances that exhaust individual energy—administrative forms to fill out, incessant committees, petty bureaucratic tyrannies. It can mean that power will steadily pile up at the center until it is impossible to place an effective check upon it. Perhaps worst of all, our ideals and attitudes can change.

Under the pressure of the need for organization, we can come slowly but painlessly to like the standard and the impersonal, and to prefer the man who fits the system to the man who is difficult to harness. If this happens, we can lose liberties we now cherish and never notice or regret the loss.

But the individual can be crushed just as easily in a subway rush as on an assembly line. When there is more traffic on the streets, more controls are necessary. And when these controls are inadequate or break down, the individual has less freedom to go where he wants to go, not more freedom. The question, in brief, is not whether we shall have a larger amount of conscious social organization or not, but what kind of social organization we shall have. It can be centralized or decentralized; it can be broken up into small units or cover only very large ones; it can concentrate authority up at the top or spread considerable authority down to lower levels. Most important of all, it can have as its conscious object the cherishing of individual differences and the promotion of individual talents. The dangers of a larger degree of social organization are unmistakable. But disorganization will be no healthier a climate for freedom.

The problems of social organization and of controlling the results of technological innovation bring us, however, to a final problem. It is the problem of the use and abuse of science, a problem that is likely to become steadily more acute as our world becomes more steadily and obviously a creature of science. In the future, as in the past, two extreme possibilities confront us. The first is to make an idol out of science. The second is to denigrate its importance on grounds of fixed moral or religious principle.

Illustrations of the tendency to make an idol out of science have suddenly blossomed all around us since the sputniks began their dance in space. With a hopefulness that is somewhat frightening, both scientists and laymen have predicted, for example, that science will soon be able to change human emotions and desires by biochemical means. Others have talked about the coming mastery of the principles of "group dynamics" and the ability that science will give us to choose the right leaders and to get people to work together harmoniously.

Such predictions represent revivals of Plato's ancient dream that, if philosophers became kings, man's political and moral troubles would come to an end. And they rest on precisely the same combination of political innocence and moral arrogance. There is, unhappily, no guarantee that those who dispense the pills that are going to change our desires and emotions will themselves have the right desires and emotions.

But it is a grave mistake to dismiss science as useless in solving moral and political problems. Objective knowledge of the conditions and consequences of our personal desires or our social institutions does help us to realize the actual nature of the ends we choose to pursue; and in this way we can frequently come to choose our ends and ideals more intelligently.

Even more than in the past, the world which the present revolution is creating will be one in which a process of steady re-examination of existing institutions will be a condition, not simply of a decent life, but in all probability of survival as well. Those who take fixed positions in such a world, and who deny the usefulness of scientific knowledge in resolving moral and political dilemmas, will be pleading merely for the rule of dogma or of their own private intuitions. It is unreasonable and unattractive to think that the society of the future should be ruled by a scientific élite masquerading as moral experts. It is equally unattractive to think that it should be ruled by those who make a principle of ignorance, and whose claim to be moral experts rests on their sense of superiority to the processes of sober scientific inquiry.

The attitudes that are aroused by science suggest, indeed, the fundamental educational problem which the present revolution puts before us. This revolution is at bottom the product of ideas and modes of thought which have remained closed secrets to most of the best educated men and women today. As a result, in what is alleged to be the most "scientific" of ages, science has the quality of magic for the popular mind. But while the problem is critical, it is not insurmountable.

The difficulties of acquainting college-trained men and women with the fundamental methods and ideals of contemporary science have been greatly exaggerated. It requires, of course, the imparting of factual information; but it requires, even more, the training of the imagination of the ordinary, educated layman so that he can grasp the general character of scientific problems even if he does not understand all their details, and can appreciate the kind of triumph which the solution of such problems represents.

Such an imaginative grasp of science, which would allow more members of modern culture to share vicariously in the most majestic achievements of their civilization, is possible for a great many more than now have it. And even more than the problem of training more scientists and engineers, this is the fundamental problem of education in the sciences.

As one looks ahead to the unfamiliar world that is emerging, it is possible, of course, to feel overwhelmed by this educational problem or by the other problems which this world puts before us. One can try to retreat from the unfamiliar, either by laughing off artificial satellites as mere basketballs in outer space or by concentrating almost hysterically on just one short-range issue—the military struggle for outer space —to the neglect of all the other issues that artificial satellites dramatize. And one can also take an apocalyptic attitude, and assume that the unfamiliar world that is emerging is also going to be absolutely unrecognizable, whether for the better or for the worse. But human traits like envy, malice and egoism are likely to remain with us no matter what moral medicines the druggist of the future has on his shelves. And once the initial thrill wears off, most honeymooners are probably going to prefer the moon overhead rather than underfoot.

But if utopia is not around the corner, neither is it inevitable that our powers are unequal to the problems that are appearing. In an age whose problems are almost all signs of mounting human powers, this would be a strange moral to draw. Man is now making his own stars and setting his own impress on the solar system. If these stars are as yet minuscule and only a very little way out in space, they still represent something of an achievement for a creature who is built rather close to the ground. The world that is taking shape can preserve old joys and it can also contain many new ones. The scientific imagination of the twentieth century has shown remarkable flexibility and daring. There is no reason in the nature of things why our social imagination cannot show some of the same qualities, or why it cannot escape, as modern science has, from the backyard of its old commonplaces and dogmas. If it did, its achievements could be even greater than the shooting of satellites into the sky.

Suggested Topics

1. Are we too clever for our own good?
2. The quickened tempo of change
3. "Technological innovation means social change"
4. Are we making an idol out of science?
5. Automation and man's future
6. Great revolutions of mankind

PROSPECTS IN THE
ARTS AND SCIENCES

J. Robert Oppenheimer

A scientist, philosopher, and poet, J. Robert Oppenheimer is
the director of the Institute for Advanced Study at Princeton,
New Jersey. He is chiefly renowned as a physicist and moralist
on the responsibility of science to civilization.

The words "prospects in the arts and sciences" mean two quite
different things to me. One is prophecy: What will the scientists discover and the painters paint, what new forms will alter music, what
parts of experience will newly yield to objective description? The
other meaning is that of a view: What do we see when we look at the
world today and compare it with the past? I am not a prophet; and
I cannot very well speak to the first subject, though in many ways I
should like to. I shall try to speak to the second, because there are
some features of this view which seem to me so remarkable, so new
and so arresting, that it may be worth turning our eyes to them; it may
even help us to create and shape the future better, though we cannot
foretell it.

In the arts and in the sciences, it would be good to be a prophet. It
would be a delight to know the future. I had thought for a while of
my own field of physics and of those nearest to it in the natural sciences. It would not be too hard to outline the questions which natural
scientists today are asking themselves and trying to answer. What, we
ask in physics, is matter, what is it made of, how does it behave when
it is more and more violently atomized, when we try to pound out of
the stuff around us the ingredients which only violence creates and
makes manifest? What, the chemists ask, are those special features of
nucleic acids and proteins which make life possible and give it its
characteristic endurance and mutability? What subtle chemistry, what
arrangements, what reactions and controls make the cells of living
organisms differentiate so that they may perform functions as oddly
diverse as transmitting information throughout our nervous systems
or covering our heads with hair? What happens in the brain to make
a record of the past, to hide it from consciousness, to make it accessible

to recall? What are the physical features which make consciousness possible?

All history teaches us that these questions that we think the pressing ones will be transmuted before they are answered, that they will be replaced by others, and that the very process of discovery will shatter the concepts that we today use to describe our puzzlement.

It is true that there are some who profess to see in matters of culture, in matters precisely of the arts and sciences, a certain macro-historical pattern, a grand system of laws which determines the course of civilization and gives a kind of inevitable quality to the unfolding of the future. They would, for instance, see the radical, formal experimentation which characterized the music of the last half-century as an inevitable consequence of the immense flowering and enrichment of natural science; they would see a necessary order in the fact that innovation in music precedes that in painting and that in turn in poetry, and point to this sequence in older cultures. They would attribute the formal experimentation of the arts to the dissolution, in an industrial and technical society, of authority, of secular, political authority, and of the catholic authority of the church. They are thus armed to predict the future. But this, I fear, is not my dish.

If a prospect is not a prophecy, it is a view. What does the world of the arts and sciences look like? There are two ways of looking at it: One is the view of the traveler, going by horse or foot, from village to village to town, staying in each to talk with those who live there and to gather something of the quality of its life. This is the intimate view, partial, somewhat accidental, limited by the limited life and strength and curiosity of the traveler, but intimate and human, in a human compass. The other is the vast view, showing the earth with its fields and towns and valleys as they appear to a camera carried in a high-altitude rocket. In one sense this prospect will be more complete; one will see all branches of knowledge, one will see all the arts, one will see them as part of the vastness and complication of the whole of human life on earth. But one will miss a great deal; the beauty and warmth of human life will largely be gone from that prospect.

It is in this vast high-altitude survey that one sees the general surprising quantitative features that distinguish our time. This is where the listings of science and endowments and laboratories and books published show up; this is where we learn that more people are engaged in scientific research today than ever before, that the Soviet world and the free world are running neck and neck in the training of scientists, that more books are published per capita in England than in the United States, that the social sciences are pursued actively in America, Scandinavia, and England, that there are more people who hear the great music of the past, and more music composed and more paintings painted. This is where we learn that the arts and sciences are flourishing. This great map, showing the world from afar and almost as to a stranger, would show more: It would show the immense diversity of culture and life, diversity in place and tradition for the first time clearly manifest on a world-wide scale, diversity in technique and language, separating science from science and art from art, and all of one from all of the other. This great map, world-wide, culture-wide, remote, has some odd features. There are innumerable villages. Between the villages there appear to be almost no paths discernible from this high altitude. Here and there passing near a village, sometimes through its heart, there will be a superhighway, along which windy traffic moves at enormous speed. The superhighways seem to have little connection with villages, starting anywhere, ending anywhere, and sometimes appearing almost by design to disrupt the quiet of the village. This view gives us no sense of order or of unity. To find these we must visit the villages, the quiet, busy places, the laboratories and studies and studios. We must see the paths that are barely discernible; we must understand the superhighways, and their dangers.

In the natural sciences these are and have been and are likely to continue to be heroic days. Discovery follows discovery, each both raising and answering questions, each ending a long search, and each providing the new instruments for a new search. There are radical ways of thinking unfamiliar to common sense and connected with it by decades or centuries of increasingly specialized and unfamiliar experience. There are lessons of how limited, for all its variety, the common experience of man has been with regard to natural phenomena, and hints and analogies as to how limited may be his experience with man. Every new finding is a part of the instrument kit of the sciences for further investigation and for penetrating into new fields. Discoveries of knowledge fructify technology and the practical arts, and these in turn pay back refined techniques, new possibilities of observation and experiment.

In any science there is harmony between practitioners. A man may work as an individual, learning of what his colleagues do through reading or conversation; he may be working as a member of a group on problems whose technical equipment is too massive for individual effort. But whether he is a part of a team or solitary in his own study, he, as a professional, is a member of a community. His colleagues in his own branch of science will be grateful to him for the inventive or creative thoughts he has, will welcome his criticism. His world and work will be objectively communicable; and he will be quite sure that if there is error in it, that error will not long be undetected. In his own line of work he lives in a community where common understanding combines with common purposes and interest to bind men together both in freedom and in co-operation.

This experience will make him acutely aware of how limited, how inadequate, how precious is this condition of his life; for in his relations with a wider society, there will be neither the sense of community nor of objective understanding. He will sometimes find, in returning to practical undertakings, some sense of community with men who are not expert in his science, with other scientists whose work is remote from his, and with men of action and men of art. The frontiers of science are separated now by long years of study, by specialized vocabularies, arts, techniques, and knowledge from the common heritage even of a most civilized society; and anyone working at the frontier of such science is in that sense a very long way from home, a long way too from the practical arts that were its matrix and origin, as indeed they were of what we today call art.

The specialization of science is an inevitable accompaniment of progress; yet it is full of dangers, and it is cruelly wasteful, since so much that is beautiful and enlightening is cut off from most of the world. Thus it is proper to the role of the scientist that he not merely find new truth and communicate it to his fellows, but that he teach, that he try to bring the most honest and intelligible account of new knowledge to all who will try to learn. This is one reason—it is the decisive organic reason—why scientists belong in universities. It is one reason why the patronage of science by and through universities is its most proper form; for it is here, in teaching, in the association of scholars, and in the friendships of teachers and taught, of men who by profession must themselves be both teachers and taught, that the narrowness of scientific life can best be moderated, and that the analogies, insights, and harmonies of scientific discovery can find their way into the wider life of man.

In the situation of the artist today there are both analogies to and differences from that of the scientist; but it is the differences which are the most striking, and which raise the problems that touch most on the evil of our day. For the artist it is not enough that he communicate with others who are expert in his own art. Their fellowship, their understanding, and their appreciation may encourage him; but that is not the end of his work, nor its nature. The artist depends on a common sensibility and culture, on a common meaning of symbols, on a community of experience and common ways of describing and interpreting it. He need not write for everyone or paint or play for everyone. But his audience must be man; it must be man, and not a specialized set of experts among his fellows. Today that is very difficult. Often the artist has an aching sense of great loneliness, for the community to which he addresses himself is largely not there; the traditions and the culture, the symbols and the history, the myths and the common experience, which it is his function to illuminate, to harmonize, and to portray, have been dissolved in a changing world.

There is, it is true, an artificial audience maintained to moderate between the artist and the world for which he works: the audience of the professional critics, popularizers, and advertisers of art. But though, as does the popularizer and promoter of science, the critic fulfills a necessary present function and introduces some order and some communication between the artist and the world, he cannot add to the intimacy and the directness and the depth with which the artist addresses his fellow men.

To the artist's loneliness there is a complementary great and terrible barrenness in the lives of men. They are deprived of the illumination, the light and tenderness and insight of an intelligible interpretation, in contemporary terms, of the sorrows and wonders and gaieties and follies of man's life. This may be in part offset, and is, by the great growth of technical means for making the art of the past available. But these provide a record of past intimacies between art and life; even when they are applied to the writing and painting and composing of the day, they do not bridge the gulf between a society, too vast and too disordered, and the artist trying to give meaning and beauty to its parts.

In an important sense this world of ours is a new world, in which the unity of knowledge, the nature of human communities, the order of society, the order of ideas, the very notions of society and culture have changed and will not return to what they have been in the past. What is new is new not because it has never been there before, but because it has changed in quality. One thing that is new is the prevalence of newness, the changing scale and scope of change itself, so that the world alters as we walk in it, so that the years of man's life measure not some small growth or rearrangement or moderation of what he learned in childhood, but a great upheaval. What is new is that in one generation our knowledge of the natural world engulfs, upsets, and complements all knowledge of the natural world before. The techniques, among which and by which we live, multiply and ramify, so that the whole world is bound together by communication, blocked here and there by the immense synapses of political tyranny. The global quality of the world is new: our knowledge of and sympathy with remote and diverse peoples, our involvement with them in practical terms, and our commitment to them in terms of brotherhood. What is new in the world is the massive character of the dissolution and corruption of authority, in belief, in ritual, and in temporal order. Yet this is the world that we have come to live in. The very difficulties which it presents derive from growth in understanding, in skill, in power. To assail the changes that have unmoored us from the past is futile, and in a deep sense, I think, it is wicked. We need to recognize the change and learn what resources we have.

Again I will turn to the schools and, as their end and as their center, the universities. For the problem of the scientist is in this respect not different from that of the artist or of the historian. He needs to be a part of the community, and the community can only with loss and peril be without him. Thus it is with a sense of interest and hope that we see a growing recognition that the creative artist is a proper charge on the university, and the university a proper home for him; that a composer or a poet or a playwright or painter needs the toleration, understanding, the rather local and parochial patronage that a university can give; and that this will protect him from the tyranny of man's communication and professional promotion. For here there is an honest chance that what the artist has of insight and of beauty will take root in the community, and that some intimacy and some human bonds can mark his relations with his patrons. For a university rightly and inherently is a place where the individual man can form new syntheses, where the accidents of friendship and association can open a man's eyes to a part of science or art which he had not known before, where parts of human life, remote and perhaps superficially incompatible, can find in men their harmony and their synthesis.

These then, in rough and far too general words, are some of the things we see as we walk through the villages of the arts and of the sciences and notice how thin are the paths that lead from one to another, and how little in terms of human understanding and pleasure the work of the villages comes to be shared outside.

The superhighways do not help. They are the mass media—from the loudspeakers in the deserts of Asia Minor and the cities of Communist China to the organized professional theatre of Broadway. They are the purveyors of art and science and culture for the millions upon millions—the promoters who represent the arts and sciences to humanity and who represent humanity to the arts and sciences; they are the means by which we are reminded of the famine in remote places or of war or trouble or change; they are the means by which this great earth and its peoples have become one to one another, the means by which the news of discovery or honor and the stories and songs of today travel and resound throughout the world. But they are also the means by which the true human community, the man knowing man, the neighbor understanding neighbor, the school boy learning a poem, the women dancing, the individual curiosity, the individual sense of beauty are being blown dry and issueless, the means by which the passivity of the disengaged spectator presents to the man of art and science the bleak face of inhumanity.

For the truth is that this is indeed, inevitably and increasingly, an open and, inevitably and increasingly, an eclectic world. We know too much for one man to know much, we live too variously to live as one. Our histories and traditions—the very means of interpreting life—are both bonds and barriers among us. Our knowledge separates as well as it unites; our orders disintegrate as well as bind; our art brings us together and sets us apart. The artist's loneliness, the scholar despairing, because no one will any longer trouble to learn what he can teach, the narrowness of the scientist—these are not unnatural insignia in this great time of change.

For what is asked of us is not easy. The openness of this world derives its character from the irreversibility of learning; what is once learned is part of human life. We cannot close our minds to discovery, we cannot stop our ears so that the voices of far-off and strange people can no longer reach them. The great cultures of the East cannot be walled off from ours by impassible seas and defects of understanding based on ignorance and unfamiliarity. Neither our integrity as men of learning nor our humanity allows that. In this open world, what is there any man may try to learn?

This is no new problem. There has always been more to know than one man could know; there have always been modes of feeling that could not move the same heart; there have always been deeply held beliefs that could not be composed into a synthetic union. Yet never before today has the diversity, the complexity, the richness so clearly defied hierarchical order and simplification, never before have we had to understand the complementary, mutually not compatible ways of life and recognize choice between them as the only course of freedom. Never before today has the integrity of the intimate, the detailed, the true art, the integrity of craftsmanship and the preservation of the familiar, of the humorous and the beautiful stood in more massive contrast to the vastness of life, the greatness of the globe, the otherness of people, the otherness of ways, and the all-encompassing dark.

This is a world in which each of us, knowing his limitations, knowing the evils of superficiality and the terrors of fatigue, will have to cling to what is close to him, to what he knows, to what he can do, to his friends and his tradition and his love, lest he be dissolved in a universal confusion and know nothing and love nothing. It is at the same time a world in which none of us can find hieratic prescription or general sanction for any ignorance, any insensitivity, any indifference. When a friend tells us of a new discovery we may not understand, we may not be able to listen without jeopardizing the work that is ours and closer to us: but we cannot find in a book or canon—and we should not seek—grounds for hallowing our ignorance. If a man tells us that he sees differently than we or that he finds beautiful what we find ugly, we may have to leave the room, from fatigue or trouble; but that is our weakness and our default. If we must live with a perpetual sense that the world and the men in it are greater than we and too much for us, let it be the measure of our virtue that we know this and seek no comfort. Above all let us not proclaim that the limits of our powers correspond to some special wisdom in our choice of life, of learning, or of beauty.

This balance, this perpetual, precarious impossible balance between the infinitely open and the intimate, this time—our twentieth century —has been long in coming; but it has come. It is, I think, for us and our children, our only way.

This is for all men. For the artist and for the scientist there is a special problem and a special hope, for in their extraordinarily different ways, in their lives that have increasingly divergent character, there is still a sensed bond, a sensed analogy. Both the man of science and the man of art live always at the edge of mystery, surrounded by it; both always, as the measure of their creation, have had to do with the harmonization of what is new with what is familiar, with the balance between novelty and synthesis, with the struggle to make partial order in total chaos. They can, in their work and in their lives, help themselves, help one another, and help all men. They can make the paths that connect the villages of arts and sciences with each other and with the world at large the multiple, varied, precious bonds of a true and world-wide community.

This cannot be an easy life. We shall have a rugged time of it to keep our minds open and to keep them deep, to keep our sense of beauty and our ability to make it, and our occasional ability to see it in places remote and strange and unfamiliar; we shall have a rugged time of it, all of us, in keeping these gardens in our villages, in keeping open the manifold, intricate, casual paths, to keep these flourishing in a great, open, windy world; but this, as I see it, is the condition of man; and in this condition we can help, because we can love one another.

Suggested Topics

1. Increasing knowledge means multiplying questions.
2. The interdependence of science and society
3. Why scientists belong in universities
4. "No man is an island."
5. "This world of ours is a new world."
6. "Knowledge separates as well as it unites."

PARENTS AND CHILDREN

ARE YOU A GUILTY PARENT? — *Jerome D. Frank*

Both a Ph.D. (in psychology) and an M.D., Jerome D. Frank
has written extensively on psychiatric problems for both his professional colleagues and the intelligent laity. He is now associated with Johns Hopkins.

If you are a parent at all, the answer is probably yes. Never before
in human history has there been so much agonized concern over
the raising of children—or so pervasive a feeling of parental inade-
quacy and guilt—as there is in America today. Once all a parent had
to do—when he was faced with a disturbing bit of child behavior—
was to recall how he himself was handled at the same age and repeat
the treatment. Today there is far more apt to be a harried search
through the pages of one or more of the countless books and articles
on child guidance that have flooded the popular press, a desperate
attempt to understand why the child has done whatever he has done—
and a nagging sense that, whatever the reason, the parent is somehow
to blame and may unwittingly make the whole situation worse if he
fails to react properly.

It is tempting to place the whole responsibility for this uncomfort-
able state of affairs on the psychiatrists with their insistence on the importance of childhood experiences to adult behavior. But this would
hardly be accurate. The psychiatrists have played some part, for good
and for bad. But there are more important and general aspects of con-

Reprinted from *Harper's Magazine*, April, 1957. By permission of *Harper's*
Magazine and the author.

temporary American life that have in truth made raising a child more difficult than it used to be.

In the first place, our large family groups with grandparents, aunts, and uncles—all of whom used to take a hand in the rearing of the young—have, by and large, been broken. Mobility is one of the most noticeable characteristics of our present society. A man packs up his wife and children on a few weeks' notice and moves halfway across the continent to take a new job. In a few years he may move again. As a result, the typical modern family unit is a small island.

On such an island, relationships tend to get overheated and hyper-sensitive because the members cannot get away from each other until they cool off. A child who is mad at his mother cannot rush to an aunt or grandparent for consolation. His mother cannot relieve *her* mind talking to *her* mother. The upset child and the upset mother are left facing each other, with no buffers. It is interesting to note that, by contrast, children may do extremely well in societies where many adults act as parents to each child. A fascinating example in American history was the Oneida Community which had no family units. Sexual relations between the adults were on the basis of mutual consent, and all the adults regarded themselves as the parents of all the children. A few years ago the surviving children of the community—all of them by then elderly people—were studied. All looked back on their child-hoods as happy; all had had successful lives.

The isolated, mobile family is only one illustration of the extent to which our whole civilization is changing. And it is doing so with breathtaking speed. Some twenty-five years ago Alfred North White-head observed that his was the first generation in human history that could not use the precepts of its grandfathers as reliable guides. Today we can scarcely count on those of a decade ago. Thrift, for instance, was a basic and unquestioned virtue during the centuries when men lived in an economy of scarcity. In our present economy of abundance it may well prove a vice. As Kinsey amply demonstrated, our patterns of sexual behavior differ widely from those of our parents. How, then, can we raise our children according to the rules of a society that no longer exists? To make it still harder, who knows what our society will be like when these children are grown? Old standards of morality have been shaken, but the new ones are not yet established.

Living in an age of change and cut off from our family clans, many of us have turned instead to the community in which we happen to find ourselves for guidance and have attempted to measure ourselves—and especially our children—in relation to those around us. Herein lies one source of our guilt as parents. Measuring children against others of the same age fosters an inclination to base acceptance of a child on his competitive performance rather than on his attributes as a unique personality. It also leads to unrealistic standards. A parent may come to expect a child who does well at most things to excel at everything, and to feel he himself has failed if the child does not. Now it stands to reason that every child will do worse than most of his contemporaries in something, and a child who is best equipped for one form of activity may, by that very token, be poorly equipped for others. Albert Einstein's magnificent theoretical intellect probably had a lot to do with his feeling of remoteness from his fellow man, and he was a notorious dud at parties.

But suppose a parent turns for help to the professionals—the authors of the child-guidance books and articles? He will find it all right—in bewildering profusion. A copy of a woman's magazine that does not have at least one such article is a rarity indeed; and many of them, like many of the books, perform a real service. But the authors, like everyone else, are influenced by the culture in which we live, and their preachments are changing as fast as the rest of our civilization. All of us have seen the precepts which are looked on with horror today return to favor tomorrow. In one brief span the doctrine of rigid child training and what has been termed "antiseptic neglect" went down before the onslaught of "unconditional love," only to re-emerge as the necessary "setting of limits."

The child experts are influenced by the psychiatrists, and the psychiatrists, too, are influenced by the society. Twenty years ago many psychoanalysts were blaming the ills of their patients on sexual repression resulting from the excessive modesty and prudery of their parents. Today some of the same analysts attribute the difficulties of their current crop of patients to sexual overstimulation in childhood from seeing their parents in the nude. What is a parent to do?

For one thing, he can remember that psychiatrists deal with people who are mentally ill or neurotic. The essence of these conditions is that the individual has failed to profit from experience. Psychiatric patients may, in fact, react in their adult lives in terms of the attitudes and perceptions they had when they were children. But many psychiatrists, who see only such patients, make the mistake of assuming that all people are equally influenced by their various childhood experiences.

This is partly a reflection of the American emphasis—inherent in the democratic philosophy—on the importance of environment over constitution in shaping a personality. Americans too often twist the dictum "all men are created equal" to mean that if a person is unequal in capabilities or happiness it is solely because of what has been done to him, and primarily because of the way he was treated by his parents. A great deal of modern child-guidance literature, as well as some psychiatric thinking, mirrors this point of view and presents the child as if he were a piece of putty to be passively molded by Mom and

Dad. Coupled with this is the implication that the slightest misstep may seriously damage a child for life. The effect on an apprehensive parent can be severe.

A striking illustration of how far it sometimes goes is a well-meaning book on child raising called *The Rights of Infants* by Margaret Ribble. Dr. Ribble did some excellent research on infants and noticed, quite correctly, that newborn babies do not have their breathing machinery under very good control and that handling the baby helps him breathe more regularly. On the basis of this she made the following statement:

> The young baby is never for a moment beyond his mother's reach, for it is vitally important to observe the breathing and to stimulate it by consistent personal attention . . . The importance of mothering in helping a child to breathe . . . can hardly be overstressed.

I know of one intelligent but anxious mother who took this literally and was, for a while, afraid to fall asleep lest she miss some faltering in her first-born baby's respiration with heaven knows what dire consequences. This was obviously hardly the reaction Dr. Ribble had hoped to produce in her readers.

The extent to which the belief that children are infinitely fragile and sensitive objects, to be blighted by a look or a word, has been accepted was recently demonstrated by Dr. Jean Macfarlane. In a study of the behavior problems of normal children between the ages of twenty-one months and fourteen years she found that by far the most common was oversensitiveness which she described as "like the common cold. Almost everybody had it." It seems to stem from two causes. One is the mother's attitude: "I am the understanding, protective mother of a very precious, vulnerable child. While his oversensitiveness complicates living and is hard to deal with, it gives me considerable satisfaction to have produced and to be indispensable to such a child."

The second cause is that children have discovered that "hurt feelings" are their most effective means of dealing with their parents. No other system of control and coercion at their command is half so powerful because no other behavior technique is so subtle or so disturbing to their parents.

Surely this is a peculiarly contemporary problem. Imagine how Clarence Day's father would have reacted if one of his boys had come sniveling to him with hurt feelings!

No one of us today could, of course, transform himself into a Father Day, even if he wanted to. But we may perhaps be able to alleviate some of our guilt feelings if we reconsider exactly what it is that we are trying to do.

Our goal as parents is not to produce adults who are continually serene, but individuals who are able to distill strength and wisdom from the vicissitudes of life. Our remarkable success in this country in achieving an incredibly high standard of living has led some of us to aim at the same lofty goal in our emotional lives. Basking in creature comforts as we do, we are more apt to resent the inevitable hardships and sufferings of life and are perhaps more easily demoralized by them than members of less materially favored societies. The notion that happiness is mankind's due strikes people in most cultures as odd. Europeans are constantly amazed at how readily Americans show resentment in situations of minor inconvenience or adversity, as if these were not the expected thing. And even the Declaration of Independence considered man's unalienable right to be the *pursuit* of happiness, not its attainment.

We have not failed with our children if they are not happy all the time or when they suffer from frustration, fear, and other unpleasant emotions. A cornerstone of mental health, as I see it, is the ability to deal confidently with new experiences and profit from them. A child develops this ability best through having to cope with problems from the start. Far from being as infinitely fragile as some child experts would have us believe, most children are tough, adaptable, and resilient. Given the slightest encouragement, they enjoy surmounting difficulties, and their development is at best only partially influenced by their parents. To be sure, parental mishandling can permanently warp a child, but to do so it must be long continued and severe. A single mistake, or even a series of mistakes, is never fatal. It is not underestimating the significance of childhood patterns in determining adult attitudes to point out that a salient fact about human beings is the capacity to learn. Brain damage or severe, prolonged emotional stress can impair this capacity, but the ordinary child can always modify his early patterns in terms of later experiences.

Raising a child is a two-way street in which the child, too, plays a part. We must ask ourselves not only how we are coping with our child, but also, with Dr. Macfarlane, how our child is coping with his parents. Since no two human beings are alike, relationships in each family will be different. It is ridiculous to think that what is good for one child and one parent is good for all. An active, aggressive parent and child will work out quite a different pattern from a passive, thoughtful pair. Trouble starts when a parent tries to fit a pattern to which neither he nor his child is suited. It is not necessarily wrong to spank a child, if spanking comes naturally. But it is not necessarily right either. If a parent, when his child is on a rampage, will try to understand what is going on in himself as well as in his child and then do what seems natural, he will be better off than if he tries to remember what Gesell or some other authority has to say.

The authorities' main service is making available to each parent the accumulated experience of many others, filtered through the mind of a specialist. A parent is constantly facing problems he has never met before. In such circumstances it is comforting and useful to learn how others have handled similar difficulties. But it is not a final answer. There is still the individual child—and the individual parent.

The most important thing is the state of mind in which we approach our children. If we are constantly aware that what we are trying to do is to produce adults who can deal competently with a vastly complicated, continually changing world, we will cease to concern ourselves so much when we fail to provide them with a perfect home life—which is impossible anyway. And we will realize that, no matter how many books to the contrary, negative emotions are not always bad. They can clear the air on both sides, and they most certainly simulate the conditions which the child will find in later life.

Anger, for one, can reinforce the parent's instructions so that they really make an impression. A furious shout can stop a baby dead in his tracks before he touches the hot stove, and make him think twice about approaching the stove in the future, where no amount of sweet reasonableness would. Anger directed at a child's shortcomings is good for his self-esteem and contributes to his emotional growth: it implies that he *can* do better.

Beyond this, it is almost always preferable to let a child know how you really feel than to pretend that you don't feel that way. Children are not easily deceived. If an angry mother insists she is filled only with loving thoughts for her child, the child, who probably senses her anger, becomes confused and distrustful. If he and his mother agree she is angry, he knows where he is.

For example, I once heard a four-year-old who was on excellent terms with her mother remark, "Mother is giving me a hard time this morning." She used exactly the same slightly aggrieved tone as she would in saying, "This soup is too hot." Both were temporary inconveniences of life which one had to accept. On the other hand, a schizophrenic patient, describing her mother, said: "Mother always said the opposite of what she meant." And it seemed clear that this had contributed importantly to the patient's intense distrust of others, so characteristic of schizophrenics.

Conflict, too, is good for emotional growth. Sibling rivalry is generally regarded as a terrible thing to be avoided or forestalled whenever possible. And, of course, fixed, unresolvable tensions between members of a family are harmful. But such tensions rarely occur unless one or both parents, to satisfy hidden needs of their own, make a practice of playing off the children against each other.

To take an extreme case, I know of a psychiatric patient who had suffered all her life from feelings of sibling rivalry with an older sister who had died when both were babies. The sister had caught an infectious disease from the patient, and the mother had somehow made the child feel this was her fault. Still worse, she had hung a framed lock of the dead child's hair in the other child's room. Here, clearly, the patient's feelings of rivalry reflected a disturbed relationship with her mother. In families where each child feels he has reasonable access to his parents' attention and affection, sibling rivlarly is not only inevitable but desirable.

It is inevitable because every child, at least initially, wants to be his parents' favorite. It is desirable because every child is bound to meet conflict sooner or later, at school if not before, and there is no better place in which to learn how to cope with it constructively than in the home where there is love and concern for both parties. Sibling rivalry is one of the major ways by which children can develop a sense that the world is, within limits, a trustworthy place in which they can feel reasonably secure.

Conflict increases strength of character in various ways—through victory, through learning how to handle defeat, through the discovery of hidden reserves of strength, or the realization that one has convictions worth fighting for. In conflict a child learns to withstand the pressure of other personalities and to keep his head in the face of such powerful emotions as anger, fear, and elation. Defeat, if not too drastic, strengthens his capacity for self-discipline or may lead to a beneficial change of attitude. When two children fight over the possession of something that both want and end up deciding to take turns, they are developing the sense of fair play, justice, and keeping one's word that is so basic to the individual's sense of personal security and his ability to inspire this feeling in others.

And finally, it is conflict that teaches the invaluable skills of compromise—for if there were no disagreements there would be nothing to compromise about—and develops the quality of empathy—the ability to feel with another person, to put oneself in his shoes even when one disagrees with him. The importance of both these abilities does not need to be underlined.

We will never get rid of all our guilt as parents. It is part of the price of *being* parents in mid-twentieth century America. But if we will bear in mind that every child's development depends at least as much on his own characteristics and potentialities as on how his parents handle him, we may make a better job of raising our children. Certainly we will get more fun out of it.

Suggested Topics

1. The consequences of overprotection
2. Reasoning and spanking
3. Innocent victims in the broken home
4. Family relationships in the mobile family
5. "Let's look it up in Spock."
6. My own guide for parent behavior
7. Sibling rivalry

WHETHER, HOW AND WHY TO SPANK   *David Dempsey*

For ten years editor of the "In and Out of Books" page of *The New York Times Book Review*, David Dempsey is now a successful free-lance writer who contributes frequently to publications like *Harper's*, the *Atlantic*, *The New Yorker*, *Saturday Evening Post* and *The New York Times Magazine*. He is also the author of a novel, *All That Was Mortal*, and of a study called "Flood."

Not long ago Governor Harriman vetoed a bill that would have permitted New York City school teachers to spank their pupils, a right at present denied them. The Governor's action was regarded by many as a blow in favor of more enlightened forms of discipline—or a blow against blows. Proponents of the bill, however, are not so sure. What is enlightened, they ask, about tying the hands of the teacher when a good whack, in the right place at the right time, might forestall more serious problems later on?

A lack of corporal punishment—the so-called woodshed treatment —pro-spankers contend, is one of the things wrong with modern youth. In their view, juvenile delinquency is at least partly the result of too much leniency in dealing with the disobedient child. A generation ago, it is argued, Father sat at the head of the table, where he belonged, and a paddle hung in every school principal's office. Both were symbols of authority, effective even when not in use. Today, Father has abdicated his position as stern parent for the more socially ap-

Reprinted from *The New York Times Magazine*, July 6, 1958. By permission of *The New York Times* and the author.

proved role of big brother, and the paddle, in many city school systems, has been outlawed.

Despite this trend, 70 per cent of the nation's parents, according to a Gallup poll made last year, believe that teachers should be permitted to discipline their students more strictly, including the use of force. The fact that two-thirds of rural and small-town schoolmarms can—and do—crack down on the unmanageable boy (girls seldom seem to need it) is often cited as evidence that the "get tough" policy works: delinquency, in these areas, runs considerably lower than in cities. (This argument, of course, overlooks other social, economic and home factors that influence youthful crime.)

Even more persuasive, to the public in general, is the number of successful men who have come out in favor of "spanking," "birching," "caning" and "switching" as a solution to the problem of delinquency. Pro-spankers have included former President Truman, the late Mayor LaGuardia, former Brooklyn Magistrate Abner C. Surpless (he called for "a spanking machine to be attached to each court"), the late Dr. Alfred E. Stearns, headmaster of Phillips Andover Academy ("I was whipped as a child, thank goodness"), and Field Marshal Viscount Montgomery.

Lecturing at Teachers College, Columbia University, in 1945, the man who led the British Army to victory remarked that "a good beating with a cane can have a remarkable sense of awakening on the mind and conscience of a boy."

As a parent who spanks—in moderation—I am well aware of the arguments against it. I agree, moreover, that corporal punishment is not only ineffective in dealing with the really difficult youngster, but that too much will only make him more difficult. To seek solutions to juvenile misbehavior solely in terms of punishment or its lack—as the extremists are inclined to do—is to simplify the problem beyond hope of solving it.

I am aware, too, that many child psychologists, social workers (and nearly all children) are against spanking. The authorities contend, for example, that (1) the child is defenseless and is, therefore, being treated unfairly; (2) spanking creates hostility in the child and encourages violence as a means of "getting even"; (3) too often it takes the place of finding out why the child misbehaved; (4) it is a form of punishment based on fear, and (5) it does no good.

"At best, punishment may stop undesirable conduct," writes Mrs. Sidonie Matsner Gruenberg, former director of the Child Study Association, "but it does not improve a child's attitude and relationships; nor does it teach a boy or girl the positive things he ought to do."

Thus the highly disciplined "little angel" at home may become the "little hellion" at school or play. He has learned to be good, not because of any positive motivations, but rather through fear of disapproval. As adolescents, these youngsters often find it hard to make the difficult adjustment into an adult world. One student of delinquency, Dr. Edward Joseph Shoben of Teachers College, Columbia, found that parents of problem children, in 80 per cent of the cases he studied, were strict disciplinarians—a finding contrary to the widely held view that the troublemakers come from homes that are too lax.

A basic question, members of this "permissive" school believe, is not whether the child is "well behaved," but whether he grows up to be "well adjusted." Their evidence indicates that no child ever had "sense beaten into him," and that, on the contrary, the mistreated boy or girl is the more likely to become a social outlaw.

While agreeing with this, we spankers say that such examples do not cover the average home situation. Most children are not "problems" and a majority of fathers are not psychologists. In addition, we deny that "freedom" for the child is incompatible with reasonable discipline. To have rules for behavior without the threat of physical punishment is like having laws without jails.

Refusal to make the child face up to his responsibilities, under the guise of unlimited "permissiveness," we say, is simply parental neglect. Better to punish children than to be indifferent to them, since it is the neglected child who is more likely to grow up to be a problem. A father who spanks can at least be said to care.

Perhaps the most impressive argument that we advance—although not necessarily the most logical—is that nearly all parents spank at some time, even those who are in theory opposed. Recently, to find out how true this might be, I polled the second-grade pupils of our local school. All eighteen had, with some degree of frequency, experienced corporal punishment. Did it do any good? Most agreed that because the spanking hurt, it kept them from repeating "the bad thing."

Some would have preferred other forms of punishment, although one child insisted that he would rather have a spanking and get it over with than be deprived of something for a week. Seventeen of the group thought their parents had a right to spank, and eleven out of the eighteen declared that when they grew up and had children, they, too, would spank.

I cite these figures because ours is an enlightened and, generally speaking, "permissive" community. Our rate of juvenile delinquency is low. It would seem that "permissiveness" and some degree of discipline (including corporal punishment) are no longer as incompatible as we once thought. The lenient parent no longer believes that anything goes, nor does the rod wielder exact the fealty from his children that was common in the nineteenth century.

Rearing children today is understood as an art rather than a dis-

cipline, albeit an art in which physical punishment is sometimes necessary. In the words of Prof. Goodwin Watson, a psychologist who
recently completed a study of the comparative behavior of "permis-
sively" vs. "strictly" reared children, "it is not the form of punishment
that matters so much as the attitude behind it." "Humane" punishment, administered with a lack of understanding, may leave more emotional scars than anything inflicted with a strap or the flat of the hand.

On this point, I stand with George Bernard Shaw in his admoni-
tion, "Never strike a child except in anger." Were it not so, I would
be a coldblooded brute, something I believe no parent should be.

For the sooner a child finds out that his mother and father are
human—that they are capable of the emotional retaliations that society
will administer later on—the better prepared will he be to adjust to a
realistic world. And at the risk of seeming banal, may I say that life
spanks us all for mistakes which, had they been caught in time by a
parent who cared enough to correct them, need never have happened?

Unfortunately, our society has indoctrinated the spanking parent
with feelings of guilt—so much so that it has compounded the error by
also making him a liar. Far from "hurting me more than it does you,"
spanking makes the average parent feel considerably better. Indeed,
this is frequently the best reason for doing it—tensions that might
otherwise remain bottled up are given a therapeutic release. While it
is true that the child is not happy about this, he might be far less happy
with a father who restrains his temper at the cost of continued
irritability.

"A good spanking clears the air" is a phrase that is commonly used
by mothers who resort to it in moments of desperation. Many psychiatrists agree, pointing out that to build up a sense of guilt in children
by long-term forms of punishment can be permanently harmful.

"A youngster understands the righteous wrath of his parent," one
of these men writes, and adds that spanking "is no worse than yak-
yakking and explaining all the time." It certainly may be less harmful
than confining children to their rooms, putting them to bed early, cutting off their allowances and following other methods that suggest
calculated reprisal rather than the reasonable exercise of authority.

It is frequently argued that spanking too often takes the place of
finding out why the child misbehaved. I am inclined to doubt this,
because I believe that a child does not always have a specific reason
for misbehaving. He wants, at a certain age, to "defy" authority (i.e.,
to be himself). This is a healthy sign, up to a point, but it becomes
dangerous (to himself and society) if he goes too far. Better to define
the limits as they are reached—with reason, when possible; with the
flat of the hand, if necessary.

In this respect, I believe that the modern parent has a tougher time
of it than his forebears. The symbols of authority, once so widely dis-

tributed through our society and implicit in the community mores, have been largely dispersed.

An easy-going and prosperous America no longer finds it necessary to indoctrinate its young with the "old-fashioned" attitudes of obedience, respect for one's elders and belief in an arbitrary moral code— rules for survival that are the product of a poor and pioneering, rather than a rich and sophisticated, nation.

The child cannot be blamed for this, although it is unhappily a fact that he is one of its victims; punishment of the individual can never be made to fit the collective crime of society. The basic compensations must be positive, for it is the emotionally healthy home atmosphere that produces well-adjusted children. Within this context, spanking is simply a means of achieving compliance with the needs of the family group when all else has failed. In a genuinely democratic home environment, where everyone has rights as well as responsibilities, it will not often be necessary.

But when it is, parents need not feel guilty. To those who do, the approach recommended by some family guidance authorities may be helpful:

(1) Spank only as a last resort, never as a routine measure. As the *only* discipline, it loses its effectiveness.

(2) Don't use physical punishment as a means of taking out hostilities that are carried over from causes outside the home. The child should not be a victim of the parents' frustrations.

(3) Don't spank in public. This arouses resentment and creates a feeling of shame.

(4) Discipline is best divided between both parents. The child should not grow up to think that father is the villain and mother his protector—or vice versa.

(5) Discipline should be "firm, consistent and fair." Don't spank for petty infractions. Don't exempt one child from rules that his brothers and sisters are expected to follow. If the rules are reasonable, children will not resent being punished for breaking them.

(6) If you must spank, love, too.

Suggested Topics

1. My parents' rules for spanking
2. I will (or will not) spank my children.
3. "This hurts me more than it does you."
4. Permissive and prescriptive parents
5. Should teachers be permitted to use force?
6. Rearing a child is an art, not a discipline.
7. Cycles in fashions of bringing up children

TEEN-AGERS MIRROR THEIR PARENTS   *Russell Lynes*

Managing Editor of *Harper's Magazine* since 1947, Russell
Lynes has effectively displayed his talent in the field of popular
sociology as a commentator on Americans and their cultural
tastes. His books include *Snobs* (1950), *Guests* (1951), and *The
Tastemakers* (1954).

The number of 13-year-olds is increasing at a rate twenty times
faster than the rest of the population. "Between 1958 and 1960," a recent report of the David L. Babson Company of Boston says, "the number of children crossing the 13-year-old threshold will rise by nearly
40 per cent. By 1965 there will be a 35 per cent increase in the 14-17
age group." The total population grows by a comparatively sluggish
2 per cent a year. We are obviously reaping the whirlwind of post-
World War II romance.

One of the specters that haunt our time is the sprawling expansion
of the population, and it is more and more difficult not to picture the
future as though it were going to be life in a sardine can. If the figures
on the teen-age population are correct (and they must be), it's going
to be a boisterous, noisy, squirming can indeed.

There are those who view this prospect with alarm for they fear
that civilization, as we know it, will be swept away by juveniles—if not
entirely delinquent, then at least objectionable. Others, who have a
hand in the teen-ager's pocket, consider the explosion the best sort of
news. It seems to me unlikely that civilization is doomed, at least not
by teen-agers, and I would like to suggest that if we want to know
what the teen-agers will do to us, we should look at ourselves.

In all the brouhaha about teen-agers we are inclined to forget, it
seems to me, that they are primarily reflections of us, of our foibles
and fumblings and aspirations, our fears and frustrations, our hopes
and our beliefs. They are, in effect, a magnifying mirror of their elders
—like a shaving mirror in which our eyes seem to bulge, our pores to
be extinct volcanoes, and our eyebrows thickets of thistles.

Consider their rebellious natures. Of a New York Times Youth
Forum last year it was reported: "A group of high school students
said . . . that teen-agers were increasingly rebellious toward authority

Reprinted from *The New York Times Magazine*, June 28, 1959. By permission
of *The New York Times* and the author.

—especially parental authority. And the tension behind teen-agers'
attitudes comes from a lack of close understanding with their parents."
The students also blamed this rebelliousness on "the terrible age we
live in" and the "looseness of family ties."

This is where we come in. These are not things the teen-agers
thought up for themselves; they are ideas that have been impressed
on them by the rest of us. We have drummed into their heads their
"need to be understood," and they would be less than human not to
use this ready-made excuse as an escape hatch for their natural high
spirits.

A few years ago two revealing studies of teen-agers appeared, one of
them something of a shocker, the other reassuring. They both throw
some light on ourselves. The first was a book called "The American
Teen-ager," a summary for the general reader of the findings of a
fifteen-year investigation of teen-agers made at Purdue University
under the direction of Dr. H. H. Remmers. The second was called
"Adolescent Girls" and was a study made for the Girl Scouts by the
Survey Research Center at the University of Michigan.

From "The American Teen-ager" one gets the superficial impression that our youngsters are monsters. (One also gets this impression
from the newspapers, of course.) Teen-agers believe, the book says, in
wire-tapping, in search without warrant, in "censorship of books, newspapers, magazines and other media as protection of the public against
improper ideas." Furthermore, they believe that "most people aren't
capable of deciding what's best for themselves," and they "see no harm
in the third degree." Not all of them, to be sure, but a good many
more than half of them.

I find this rather chilling, less because of what it says about the teen-
agers than what it says about their parents. But the Girl Scouts' report
takes a somewhat more optimistic view.

Their study found that by and large the youngsters of this era are
"conservative." Far from being rebellious, the study exposed them as
idealistic and practical, more eager than their mothers had been for
advanced education, but not, in general, wanting to be high-powered
executives or movie stars. Fewer than a fifth of them has a good thing
to say for "going steady." In many respects they are more independent
than their mothers were at the same age. They have weekly allowances
that give them more freedom to choose their fun; they have part-time
jobs, and they play a larger role in making family plans. The attitude
of the family has come a long way since the "children should be seen
and not heard" era. No one would now say, as my wife's grandmother
used to, that there was nothing to do with children but "put them in a
barrel and feed them through the bunghole until they're 21."

Somewhere along the line we stopped thinking of teen-agers as just young people in transition between childhood and the state of being "grown up," and we began to regard them as a minority pressure group in our society. We now look on them not as just "kids," as we used to, but as a sub-culture with a powerful effect on the culture as a whole.

You will look in vain (or at least I have looked in vain) for references to "teen-agers" in the literature of my parents' day. You will find "youngsters" and "schoolboys" and "schoolgirls," but you will not find teen-agers as a group, treated as though they were something between menaces and the hope of the world, a class by themselves, a threat to adult sanity.

The change came during and after the second World War, the result of the dislocation of families both physically and spiritually. Children were asked to adjust to change rather than to continuity, to pulling up stakes rather than to putting down roots. They began to look more than ever to their contemporaries for security, and they began to look for their own set of rules, to live by. The practice of "going steady," for example, was an attempt to establish formal relationships that promised some sort of continuity and sense of belonging to some one person.

The songs popular with youth, you may have noticed, belie the old Tin Pan Alley cliché that a hit can't be made on the theme of married love. As Arnold Shaw has pointed out, "Honeycomb" and "Kisses Sweeter than Wine," both songs of marriage, have been taken to the hearts of teen-agers whose popular hits are "a growing literature of . . . protest." "Born Too Late," they sing, and "Why Won't They Understand?"

At the same time they want to be a self-sufficient and rebellious group, they reach out for a hand to guide them. Their accusation that adults "fail to understand" them is a reflection of our "wanting to understand," and their "rebelliousness" is, in part at least, a reflection of our fairly new belief in "permissiveness" and in our encouraging them to make up their own minds. They seem to be in a terrible hurry to be grown-up, to have grown-up respect paid to them, at the same time that they resent the group they most want to be part of— a not uncommon human condition.

They have reason to resent us, and if the reflection of ourselves that we see in them is not a pretty one, we should not be surprised. Let's look a little deeper into the mirror of our society and see theirs.

There was a time not long ago when parents not only preached the virtues of work but practiced them. The work week was ten or fifteen hours longer than it is now for father, and his day off each week was a restorative to enable him to do a better job on the other six days. Now leisure has become a kind of job in its own right, and it is going to become still more of a job. When the work week shrinks, as economists say it will, to twenty hours, it is going to be difficult indeed for father to preach to his children the old gospel that "the devil finds work for idle hands." There is plenty of evidence around us now of what happens to young people deprived of the opportunity to work and without the resources, either cultural or social, to put their time to good use.

But time on parental hands has still further effects. At its worst it is corrosive and it is stultifying. It passively accepts what is put before it. It wallows in ways to make time pass—hours of sitting before the television or in aimless puttering. Or it can be dangerously aggressive against society, or against self, as in dope addiction or alcoholism.

Less spectacular, but also corrosive, undirected leisure takes itself out in consumption for consumption's sake, in buying gadgets that save time, when time is the thing that least needs saving for the already time-ladened. It shows itself in ostentation and in competition with one's neighbors. Everyone wants to be the biggest Jones in the block. These are the lessons that the young learn when leisure is not constructive and does not enrich the spirit. It can, of course, be otherwise, but it is the parents who show the direction.

There is another direction they show. A good deal of journalistic space is occupied these days by articles about the number of young people who cheat on exams. Is this, after all, very different from padding an expense account or, more important, shading the truth on an income-tax return? If colleges and universities promote gifts in such a way that it is sometimes possible for a donor to make money by giving gifts to them, doesn't the line of academic honesty become a little blurred?

Or take another matter that is related to schools. It is not uncommon today to find youngsters who, when they have graduated from high school, wish they had been made to work harder. Why? Suddenly adults have been spurred into believing that only education will save us from lagging behind the Russians; suddenly bright students have a new status which a few years ago they sadly lacked—often to the point of being ostracized by their contemporaries. The "grind" and the "brightie" were looked down upon, a reflection of intellectual distrust on the part of parents. Now the winds blow in a different direction.

Or take the shibboleth of "conformity" with which the critics of our society plague us. (In my opinion this is a convenient tag that has been greatly overused to describe one aspect of a highly industrialized nation.) How is the teen-age custom of "going steady" a reflection of our own insecurity? To what extent is it, as I have suggested, an attempt to inject a kind of formality into relationships among young people that they miss in this age of informality?

The Girl Scouts may say that they are against it, but it has become a tribal custom of the young that they observe with almost universal respect all the same.

We are inclined to be indulgent about the hero-worship of the teen-ager for the movie glamour boys, for the Presleys and the James Deans and Eddie Fishers and Ricky Nelsons. We should be. We are hero-worshiper ourselves. It is evident in our political attitudes, in the numbers of us who don't even bother to vote, presumably because we are willing to "leave it to the boss." It is evident in our reverence toward leaders of business and industry, toward scientists, toward anybody who we think can lead us by the hand through the maze of complications that beset us.

To what extent is our fear of the Russians, for example, responsible for the teen-ager's belief in censorship, in wire-tapping, in search without warrant? If we are worried, as we should be, about their attitudes toward personal liberties, hadn't we better look to our own?

It is easy to take this subculture, this minority group, the teen-agers, and read our characters and future in them as though they were tea leaves. We can seen adumbrated in them our attitudes toward religion, toward the arts and toward education more clearly than we can by looking at ourselves. We are likely to be more indulgent in looking at ourselves than at them; we smooth over our own exaggerations while we view theirs with alarm.

But I can see no reason why the simple statistical fact that there are going to be a great many more teen-agers in the next few years should be cause for anything more than the usual alarm. Unquestionably they will cause problems, just as we caused problems when we were teen-agers. But they will also give delight. There will be more noisy households than we are accustomed to, more telephones endlessly tied up, more records strewn around the living-room floor, more starry-eyed young lovers, more hard questions to answer, more nonsensical fads to throw up the hands about.

There will be something that will take the place of rock 'n' roll, bobby socks, and hot rods, something that will seem ludicrous to those who will have recently grown out of their teens into adulthood, and alarming to the parents who have to put up with it.

Possibly I am lucky. I have just lived through the teen-ages of a son and a daughter. There were moments when I thought murder was too good for them; there were moments when they thought murder was much too good for me. Sometimes their angish was my anguish; sometimes their cussedness was my fury; occasionally their pleasure was my despair. But I saw myself sometimes distorted, sometimes all too clearly, in them as a mirror. I suspect I learned from them as much as I taught them, and I wouldn't have missed it for anything.

Suggested Topics

1. The insecurity of teen-agers
2. The decline in individuality
3. Constructive leisure activities for teen-agers
4. Are parents firm enough with their children?
5. The problem of juvenile delinquency
6. Cheating—in school and on expense accounts

JOB OF THE CHILDREN'S MOTHER'S HUSBAND   Margaret Mead

> A world-famous anthropologist, Margaret Mead is Associate Curator of Ethnology at the American Museum of Natural History in New York. Her books include *Male and Female, Coming of Age in Samoa, Sex and Temperament in Three Primitive Societies,* and other works that illuminate the bases of not only primitive societies but also our own society.

After a decade of attacks on Mom, the guns are being shifted to Father. Not Pop or Dad—he's all right. But Father, the solemn, public label for the paternal parent or, to put it another way, the children's mother's husband.

On every side Father encounters fusillades, and significantly the attacks are contradictory and irrational, as they were on mothers in the Nineteen Forties. Fathers are criticized both for neglecting their children and for spending too much time in the nursery; for being wedded to the rat race in business and for putting their families ahead of their careers; for a lack of interest in their sons and for forcing their sons into following in their footsteps.

Similarly in the Forties, mothers simultaneously were berated for having spoiled and babied their sons, who were found unready for

Reprinted from *The New York Times Magazine,* May 10, 1959. By permission of *The New York Times* and the author.

army life at 18, and exhorted to spend every living minute with their children.

The latest blast on the subject was contained in a few remarks attributed to a young anthropologist who insisted that Father must make up his mind to being "odd man out, coexisting as a third party." If he consents to this gracefully, and limits his role to that of an "objective, friendly, informal solver of interpersonal problems," he may never become "obsolete or expendable."

Caught on one side or the other of this barrage—damned if he does and damned if he doesn't—the young father may well feel exposed and confused, wondering what his role really should be in such a rapidly shifting world. A little history may help.

From our pioneer days, we have preserved the myth of a self-sufficient farm household in which Father farmed, hunted, built and was home all day to keep the boys' and girls' minds on their chores and their schooling; a home in which the division of labor between Father and Mother was clear but both were strong and self-reliant, and if Father was away when the Indians attacked, Mother could defend the children. To the same general period of mythology belong the widowed mothers who reared their children on the farms or in the growing cities, where they took in washing while their sons delivered newspapers and rose to be millionaires.

These two Americans myths contradict each other superficially but not actually: on the farm the father provided a model for the son, who in all probability would not stay on that farm nor depend upon his father's bounty and goodwill, but one day would strike out for himself, leaving the meager acres of the East for the wide plains of the West. The fatherless boy who helped support his mother simply stepped early into his dead father's shoes, as a responsible hard-working man before his time—and he succeeded, and became a folk hero.

Then came a second period of father-images, the fathers of the late nineteenth and early twentieth centuries. If they were rich self-made men, they ruined their sons, who had been born with silver spoons in their mouths and thus could come to no good; if they were men just getting along they neglected their sons, devoting themselves to making money, while the mothers raised the children; if they were poor, they were thought of as immigrants who, ignorant of the culture, had to accept low-paying jobs for which their sons could not respect them, and who left the whole management of their homes to their wives.

The father who sent his children to expensive schools and his wife to Europe, while he slaved in the heat; the father who never saw his children, who came home from the office when they were fast asleep; the father who was too illiterate and inexperienced to control or appreciate his American-born or city-born children—these were the father figures of the early part of this century.

There were a few other facets to the stereotype. In the hurly-burly of settling a new country, the finer things of life were left to the women while business became a man's career, with money its measure. Women were the custodians of social class, and leisure activities which were masculine also were "common"—fishing and playing poker in one's shirt sleeves and politics.

A good woman had to watch out that her boy didn't follow his father to the corner saloon; if he was to go up in the world—and everyone was to go up in the world—he had to adopt the proprieties which his mother, who traditionally had "taught school," was able to teach him. The politician's maxim, "All that I am and all that I hope to be I owe to my angel mother," was often a literal truth.

Such a mother's son married a woman who, like his mother, would help him control his low, masculine impulses and keep his mind on his career. In each generation, however, the women carried along the image of the masculine side of their fathers, of which their mothers had disapproved, and in daydreams wished they themselves had chosen the Sheik of Araby to marry instead of the successful bank president. Each generation of children was exposed to the contrast: the masculine man who drank, fished and gambled and, by implication, beat his wife and neglected his children; and the emasculated man, Mr. Milquetoast, who did just what his wife wanted him to do—made a business success, bought her a new hat and supported her plans for their children.

Then women went to work, and the single clear sign that a man was really a man—the pay envelope—was clouded over. Sometimes, particularly in depressions when men's whole sense of themselves as responsible heads of families was threatened anyway, women made more than their husbands. The simple division of labor, so clear in the eyes of children, that father went *out,* and mother stayed *in,* disappeared. Men demonstrated their sense of loss of manhood by refusing to give any woman—old, young, pregnant or with a baby in her arms— a seat on a bus.

The worry that American men weren't masculine grew stronger. It persists today in the form of an adolescent's concern about proving his sexual prowess or his ability to perform crudely symbolic acts such as driving a car like a demon or messing about with firearms. Tales from the Korean war of how unprepared young men were to fire guns or to stand up under imprisonment have not improved this picture, but only intensified the game of "chicken" played at all levels of society.

Meanwhile, after World War II, something did happen to men as fathers. The G. I.'s came home to be the best fathers—from the standpoint of their young children—that any civilized society has ever known. In the Australian deserts and the mountains of New Guinea, fathers hold their little babies in their arms and limit their demands on their wives to protect the health of their infant children. But in all the known civilizations of the world, as soon as a society has become complicated with governments and armies, merchants and ships, nobles and serfs, men have no longer cared for small children.

An important man in most such societies was protected from the night cries of his children by many walls between his bedchamber and the nursery, and an army of women—nurses, pensioners, female relatives—stood between him and even the sight of a diaper. His children were brought to him occasionally, well washed and prettily dressed, to be admired and whisked away again. Such fathers saw very little of their children until they were partly grown, and then more in a disciplinary or didactic relationship than in a companionable and loving one.

But now, for the first time in their history, the United States, North America and parts of Northern Europe and the British Commonwealth are experimenting with a new kind of fatherhood. Now the élite of our societies, the statesmen and scientists, the financiers and entrepreneurs, the judges and the legislators, are helping their servantless wives take care of little children.

This new style in fatherhood crept up on us gradually, with the G. I. Bill, life in trailers, early marriage and the currently fashionable large family. It is a very extreme contrast to anything we have known before, and we don't know yet what the effects are going to be. In the past little boys have learned that childbearing and child care were for women, while their job was to go out into the world and do things —farm, fight, build, invent, govern. Now for the first time, men are being given a chance to enjoy their children.

There seems to be a real danger that the care of young children will prove both so time-consuming and so fascinating that many men will skimp their careers in order to get more time with their families. In the past, dedicated scientists, artists who starved in garrets and explorers of strange places either postponed having children or left their care to women. We have known for a long time that being a mother of several children was a full-time job, and definitely interfered with a woman's career. Now it looks as if we were turning being a father into a full-time job, too, with all a man's best energies going into the home, and too little left over for work outside.

From the whole sweep of human history, it is possible to trace the growing responsibility of men for their children, and women for the wider world. At the beginning of history—if we may judge by the very simple primitive people living today—women stayed close to home, burdened by their children, while men ranged abroad. The sexes envied each other even then, and men invented ceremonies in which they pretended to bear children, and women borrowed their husbands' head-hunting regalia to pretend they were men.

Then, thousands of years of experimenting with civilization brought us to the kind of world where men had become highly specialized and far removed from their children, while women, although occasionally developing airs to grace a court, or competence in running a plantation or a manor, remained essentially as housebound as their primitive forebears.

Next we experimented with educating women, and permitting them to venture out into a man's world. Now we are experimenting with letting men into woman's world. Both moves involve drastic changes in the relationships between the sexes.

These are upsetting changes, when men feel less like husbands because their wives work outside the home, and women feel less like wives because their husbands do so much work inside the home. They are dangerous changes because we don't know what effects they will have on men's sense of themselves as men, as well as husbands.

In attempting to judge what the consequences of these new styles may be, and especially what kind of fathers this new generation will make, we can examine the traditional ideals for an American father. The ideal American father does not expect his son to follow in his footsteps, to be what he is, but to go on to better things, to get a better education, earn a better salary, have a better career.

True, many fathers have insisted on their sons going to their own colleges, and taking up their occupations, especially when their colleges or their occupations were at the top of the heap. But these are not ideal fathers. The ideal father leaves his son free to choose, cheers him on when he does well, encourages him when his spirits flag, expects him to live his own life—not his father's life.

At the same time, the American father is expected to hold enough of his children's respect so that they will care about having him as an appreciative supporter. The stereotype immigrant father who doesn't know enough about the new culture to recognize his son's success loses his son's allegiance altogether.

The ideal American family is like the American two-party system at its best, in that parents are expected to be strong, yet different, and each is expected to be a responsible part of the whole. So the ideal American father is strong, but does not have to demonstrate his strength by dominating his wife and children, or to live out his own sense of inferiority by pushing his son in the Little Leagues.

The American ideal for strength without domination, encourage-

ment without trying to live through one's children, is a difficult one.
It is more difficult when fathers are still supposed to represent the
outside world—to know more than mothers about what is going on
in the whole field of male achievement, from baseball to international
politics, from mending the furnace to explaining a satellite, from running a savings account to explaining the World Bank, from electing
the school board to evaluating the U. N. No matter how small a section of the outside world a father commands, it remains his expected
role to encourage his son to move out of the home, into the world.

Much of the concern about Father's supposedly diminishing masculinity may not be so much the result of the fluctuations and uncertan-
ties of his new role—as a father— but rather the result of an increased
confusion about the difference between being masculine and being a
man. Masculinity is that part of a male's behavior which distinguishes
him from a female—in his sex relations, in fighting and in sport. Stress
on masculinity means stress on *not* being like a woman. But manhood
is that part of a male's behavior which makes him a responsible human
being, able to control his sexuality, bridle his aggression, protect and
provide for his wife and children and make some positive contribution
to the world.

If taking care of children is seen as playing a woman's part, being
a sucker, being dominated by women, it will be looked at one way.
If it is seen as an extension of manhood, as an exercise of strength,
imagination and tenderness, it will be looked at the other way.

Suggested Topics

1. Mothers as bread-winners
2. Changing stereotypes of fathers and mothers
3. "A new kind of fatherhood"
4. Early marriage and parenthood
5. The American ideal: strength without domination
6. Masculinity and manhood

THE ANALYST'S COUCH AND THE CREATIVE MIND

Roger Burlingame

Roger Burlingame, who graduated from Harvard in 1913, has written a number of novels, articles, and factual works on inventions and technology, including *March of the Iron Man, Engines of Democracy,* and *Backgrounds of Power.*

I have not called myself an artist though in much of my writing I have worked with artist's materials and in the artist's framework. I believe, therefore, that I have what is known as a creative mind and though circumstances have not always permitted it, I like to write from the inside out. And, from my own long and kaleidoscopic experience and from the experiences of some true artists whom I have known closely I am convinced that, however much good it may do the business executive, the physician, the politician, or the housewife, the psychoanalyst's couch is not for the creative mind. In testimony I offer case history.

If, for instance, the theses of the psychiatrists and psychoanalysts are applicable to me, I should be, if not a gibbering idiot, at least a model of chronic maladjustment. According to late theory, my parents —indeed my entire family including my Irish Nanny—did everything wrong from the moment the doctor shook the breath into me.

First of all, I was an afterthought. I came along eleven years after my parents had apparently decided that enough was enough. Later, when it was supposed that I could understand such things, I was told that I was planned and I believe it. A year or so before my birth, the family's economic condition improved and this, added to Mother's nostalgia for babies, moved the uninstructed parental minds toward the belated impulse. And, in those primitive days, insufficient exploration had not yet proved how dangerous afterthoughts can be—especially when the progenitors are past forty.

During the fateful years zero to five, my nurse indoctrinated me with every variety of morbid fancy. She had, for example, a passion for funerals. Often when she took me walking in the city she would detect a funeral blocks away and seizing me by the hand would run me

Reprinted from *Harper's Magazine*, May, 1959. By permission of *Harper's Magazine* and the author.

breathlessly to the scene so that she could count the carriages behind the hearse. I became so fascinated with the pomp of death that once, when asked what I wanted for Christmas, I replied a toy cemetery, please, complete with plumed hearse, corpse, and practicable coffin.

Nanny also exploited my precarious constitution. Born in what was known as "the grippe year," I was frequently on the threshold of death, from which I was saved by a series of miracles. In the intervals between the crises, Nanny surrounded me with fears. Everything that I must not do I must not do "for fear" of the consequences: bronchial pneumonia, for example, if I went out in the rain. Nanny was entranced by the long names of diseases and I too grew to mouth and love their resonant beauty. Starting with the sonorous "pneumonia," my sallies into the poetry of medicine have led me into rapture over the rhythm and melody of "insomnia," "arteriosclerosis," and, best of all, "electrocardiogram."

The "sentence of silence" so abundantly condemned in the paleo-Freudian days was strictly imposed upon me. Every scrap of information about sex was withheld from me notwithstanding my insistent questioning and the fact that my mind was, from my first consciousness, profoundly occupied with the subject.

Far from the teachings of "progressive" upbringing, my behavior was geared to a set of absolutes. Reason rarely intervened between me and parental authority. I did things because they were right and they were right because Mother or Father or my grown-up brother or sisters or Holy Scriptures said so. (Nanny also got in on this act.) In my consciousness, moral relativity was a stranger though I know now that it governed much of my father's thinking.

Finally, my strenuous religious training brought me into a vivid and daily awareness of sin. I don't think the reality of sin would have impinged much upon Mother's clean and extrovert mind except that her prayer book was so jam-packed with it. But to me the abstraction inherent in all the resounding Anglican prayers was troubling indeed and, in my introspective hours, as I grew older, I even became fearful that I might have sinned without knowing it. On my knees in church, my small head buried in my folded arms, I sometimes put the question to my Maker but I was never quite sure of any response.

My earliest memory is of weaving my way through a forest of legs. Unlike most children, I had five parents instead of two. All—even my still adolescent sister—had equal authority, at least when the others weren't around. They could all say Don't to me and they all did. Sometimes there were jurisdictional disputes conducted in whispers which I heard or in French which I understood. I hugely enjoyed the conflicts between my sisters, sometimes involving slammed doors

or ending with that final thrust, "All right for you," which was so
popular in those days among the young.

The only time no one said Don't to me was when I was sick. Then
they hovered silently near my bedside so imbued with the belief that
I was going to die, I wonder they did not kill me with their thoughts.
I did, indeed, sometimes suspect the incidence of my demise. I was
deeply impressed by that macabre prayer they used to teach children
to say:

> If I should die before I wake
> I pray the Lord my soul to take . . .

I could see the Lord's hand coming through the darkness and grab-
bing my small soul. I then thought myself into a white coffin with
my disembodied spirit hovering over my bereaved family and happily
observing their tears.

When it wasn't too painful, I really enjoyed being sick. To lie in
a darkened room with Mother's countless petticoats rustling about and
a fragrant inhalant cooking over an alcohol lamp was quite pleasur-
able. I liked the taste of the paregoric—the universal remedy for
everything that could not be cured by castor oil—the frequent doses
of which, by another miracle, I survived. Nanny, in these times, was
relegated to the background and Mother took full charge. It is surprising, then, that I acquired that most devastating of all fixations
for the growing male, a "silver cord" attachment?

Could a combination of Doctors Freud, Jung, and Adler—not to
mention John Dewey and the progressive educationeers—imagine a
more blighting background? Yet I have eluded breakdown, compulsive criminality, perversion, and the Death Wish. I have spasms of
self-pity but so do my younger acquaintances whose psychiatrists are
just around the corner. My suicidal impulses are rare and fleeting—
subject to diversion by almost any bright object. Rape, homosexuality,
and sadism have appeared interesting but not compelling. My impulses toward murder have usually had rational motivation. It is
true that I often treat my wife with extreme mental cruelty but so do
the graduates of the progressive schools.

I take no credit for having licked, with my heroic character, all of
the grim conditioners I have described. Indeed, I have never wanted
to lick them. On the contrary, I exult in every one. Far from frustrating me they have been largely responsible for every worthy thing I
have done.

Take, for example, the reticence about the so-called facts of life.
The silence was highly stimulating to what I like to think was my
incipiently creative mind. Had I been told, I should have been deprived of the delight as well as the constructive exercise of discovering

them for myself. Does the child from whom nothing is hidden get more fun out of life? Will the creativeness of new generations be enhanced by absence of mystery? Is the imaginative child whose stories are all told him on the television screen any better equipped than one who devises his own plots and people, albeit with a certain creative agony? No; I cherish the secrecy to which I was so early introduced and I have practiced it happily.

What I have withheld has given me more joy than what I have expressed because it has helped build a storehouse, a potential of great pregnancy. Secret after secret I can now give birth to in sublime pain. The confessional to priest or analyst is abhorrent to me. If you keep your hopes or fears, your chimeras, the tantrums of your conscience inside you, you can still make use of them; told, they leave you empty, sterile, and impotent. Confession, except in creation, is exceedingly bad for the creative soul.

And how about the other mental and emotional ingredients of my child life? To the artist, morbid thought is a pigment. To be there ready at any moment to be dipped into for the creation of a painting or a story it must be squeezed early on the palette of the child's mind. If the child is an incipient artist, it will not stand there alone. Brighter colors will probably be juxtaposed. The child need not be preoccupied by morbid thought but if he is to be an artist he must be aware of its existence. It is cruel to protect an imaginative child from the sense of death or the taste of grief. To an artist a Nanny with her funerals may be immensely useful.

Nor are the feminine pressures hurtful to the male artists. If he is a novelist he must be, in himself, man, woman, and child. The mother who runs frightened by the shadows of Oedipus had better consider carefully whether her son is a potential artist or bond broker.

As to the unreasoned dicta about right and wrong, these established a code like the multiplication table which catches you up when you make a mistake. Yet it may also, to change the metaphor, be a springboard from which to take off. Of course I have departed from some of the formulas but how could I have departed if there was nothing to depart from? The shore you leave stays in your mind however far you swim away, but how about the child who has known no shore, who has been taken out in a boat in the dark and dropped into an unbounded sea?

There is a truism which says you must know the rules in order to break them, and who breaks more rules than the writer unless it be the painter or composer?

I have left behind most of the religious concepts that were so important to my mother and I have sometimes said that my strict religious bringing up threw me, on maturity, into agnosticism, yet in my heart, I also value that memory. Once the sin ingredient evaporated there was a residue of beauty. My doubts about a personal God cannot filter that out. But how constructive that knowledge of faith, of the faith of others if not my own, of the intellectual fact of God, however skeptical I may be of his tangible existence! The best book by far that I ever wrote was based on what I heard in those solemn hours when Mother prepared me for confirmation.

I once knew a true artist—a painter of transcendent talent—who had been brought up on an austere New England farm, a desire-under-the-elms sort of place where morbid thought abounded. His own ran to cows. For hours, as a child, he would sit on a fence and reflect on the sufferings of cows. The cow, to him, was a symbol of exploited femininity; her entire existence was by necessity dedicated to being a female. She was bred, gave birth, and began to nurse her child; then both child and milk were stolen from her. When the milk stopped, the whole sad sequence was repeated. What my friend supposed to be the other enterprises in which the cow might have engaged had she been relieved of the urgency imposed upon her was never quite clear to me or perhaps to him; the point was that the grief about the cows developed into other griefs as he matured and he became, so he said, an exceedingly unhappy man. Yet all this time he was painting pictures which were the wonder of the art world. Everything he did had that nostalgic trace essential to any real work of art.

One day he heard about a Swiss psychoanalyst who could treat those grim neuroses which were a legacy from a morbid childhood. So he laid his painting aside and spent a year in Zurich. I had lunch with him the day after he returned. "I am," he said, "completely happy. The nightmares are gone. I can look back on my obsessions and laugh at them. My slate has been washed clean."

Unfortunately his palette had also been washed clean. From that moment his pictures were commonplace or pretty. He lost his place in the top rank. Perhaps he would have been restored in time because I am inclined to believe that a true artist is, in the long run, indestructible, but not until he had put back some of the things that the doctor had erased. For that he died too soon.

But this is only one story. I could tell others as true and as sad of men and women who have confessed too much. Some have survived because, once on the couch, they have instinctively kicked and screamed or slyly, with tongue in cheek, defrauded their expensive doctor.

I am far from believing that there is pain in all creativity; I have touched the fringe often enough to be aware of its joys—even when they are merely the joys of cool sweat after fever, but I am certain that therapy designed to eliminate suffering from the creative mind is more often destructive than otherwise. I think certain honest analysts have become aware of this. At least two of them who are more interested in the truth than in their bank account told me that certain artists have so resisted the treatment—as if they were being robbed— that the doctors have had to abandon the cases.

Now if all this be true, why is it that psychoanalysis may still be good for the industrial executive, the lawyer, the government worker, or the secretary of the woman's club? It is, I think, because these people have no machinery for sublimating their childhood "disasters." They cannot *use* their traumas as the painter, the writer, or the composer may. Use is the great anodyne for these wounds. The use may be painful, but when the chagrin is painted or written it is often gone or its combination with its product mellows it. At any rate something has resulted, the rotary motion has ceased, a tangent has been struck. The frustration has been embodied in something which may partake of immortality; at least it may transfer the artist's hurt to the multitude of those who see or read it. A neurosis is better expressed, I think, than confessed.

But it has now become fashionable to turn adolescents or even children—whose talents may still be unsuspected—over to persons who practice under the general name of psychiatrist. "Send her to a psychiatrist," or, "Let Doctor X see him," say parents at the drop of a tantrum. In many cases neither parent nor child knows what creative potentials may be in Dick's or Mary's make-up.

My advice to parents would be: Try to find out if your child has leanings toward graphic or literary or musical creation before you call in the doctor. And to the doctor, I would say, impertinently, make sure you are not removing something valuable in your attempt to ease your patient's pain or his family's inconvenience. If you detect a foreshadowing of the art that may come, forgo your fee and send the patient home. Usually even the child, if he be an embryonic artist, will quickly show his allergy to the analyst's methods.

In days past, there was a synthetic treatment of non-creative patients which was known as occupational therapy. This is still practiced I believe in the rehabilitation of mentally wounded veterans and in various old-fashioned establishments. Here, patients are made to express their troubles in some medium of art if it be only a string of beads. This, I am told, is looked down upon by "modern" practitioners. Yet does it not suggest that the man or woman dedicated— one might almost say addicted—to some all-absorbing creative endeavor is in little danger from his neurosis and, perhaps, even cannot do without it?

Suggested Topics

1. Creativity and social adjustment
2. The "Dale Carnegie" personality
3. "My parents did everything wrong."
4. Everybody is neurotic.
5. The pleasure of being a non-conformist
6. What makes a great artist?

PEOPLE AND PLACES

GO EAST, YOUNG MAN
Thomas Griffith

> Now Foreign News Editor of *Time,* Thomas Griffith was a
> Neiman Fellow at Harvard University in 1942-1943. After his
> graduation from the University of Washington he joined the
> staff of *The Seattle Times* as a reporter. *The Waist-High Culture*
> (1959) is his first book—an excellent example of sociology not
> for the specialist but for the educated and thoughtful layman.

Long aware that an American boyhood was different from a Dane's,
from an Italian's, or from a Hottentot's, I naturally assumed that it
was they who must be odd. Only gradually did it dawn on me that
though a public-school upbringing in a medium-sized American city
was an experience shared with hundreds of thousands, it was not
every American's lot, and that there were inevitable disparities between my own outlook and that of boys raised on an Iowa farm, in
a small Vermont town, on the crowded sidewalks before a New York
tenement, or in the atmosphere peculiar to the South. I was a
Westerner, a species of patriotism which if not loudly asserted is
strongly felt.

We thought that something in our surroundings and in our in-
heritance made us more open and generous than the rest of the
country. "Welcome, *Stranger*," was a friendly greeting in the West: a
newcomer must be made to feel at home. After that he was on his
own, but the assumption was that he was as goodhearted as we, until
proven otherwise, and would do as much for us. This was so instinc-

tive with us that I remember the shock of first experiencing another kind of behavior in those businesslike pit musicians who came to Seattle with road-show musicals. Recruited from New York City or Chicago, they were Jewish or Italian, had sallow complexions and long black hair and obviously felt superior to their present surroundings. But what really set them apart was that on seeing someone unknown to them *they did not smile*. Years of living in the East have not yet completely erased from my face an expression of indiscriminate amiability, of smiling whenever I catch someone's eye, though I am well aware that in the East, and even more so in Europe, this is regarded as forwardness, an uninvited attempt to establish acquaintanceship. I had to learn the impassive subway stare, neither hostile nor friendly, and to recognize the right to make an unapproachable island of oneself in the midst of a crowd. Rudeness is the privacy of New Yorkers. It saves them from intrusions; it reflects their consciousness— so alien to a Westerner—of economic and social distinctions, and their refusal to be involved with one another.

We in the West detected that people elsewhere spoke our language a little differently—through the nose if from Indiana, having trouble with *a*'s and *r*'s if from Boston, slowly and with marshmallow softness if from the South; and from having seen haughty butlers on the screen we could all mock the way Englishmen talked. We were convinced that only our own speech was natural, and anything else a variant. For all I know, this may be everyone's experience, just as our pride in salmon and oversized apples is matched by the New Englander's pride in his chowder and his Indian pudding, the Southerner's in those odd leavings he eats.

As Westerners, we felt ahead of the times, having already discovered a place and a way of life that others would in time find, for we knew it to be a certainty, and considered it progress, that our countryside would fill up (it was only when it did so with an onrush, during and after World War II, that misgivings began to be heard over whether fast growth was improvement and larger population a gain). We lived stretched out, with room for lawns between our houses, and within easy driving of quiet, green places. Beyond us, when the days were sharp and clear enough to see them, loomed white mountains, cold and noble. Lakes and bays surrounded us, edged by forests of evergreens broken only by occasional clearings and modest cottages. No walls of estates locked us from the best views. Fishermen had the meandering rights to any stream; nearby were lakes to sail on and mountains to ski down. I was as proud of these advantages as anyone else, though inclined as a city boy to consider the countryside an empty space between two towns. To fortify our complacency in what we had, our newspapers spread eight-column headlines to report every heat wave in the Midwest or blizzards in the East. (Patriotism in weather, fed by local newspapers, is perhaps an American trait.) We were happy in our temperate climate, and objected only occasionally to the frequent not-too-insistent rain. This was God's country.

This was also man's country, and somewhat abused by him. The timber companies no longer plundered the forests, leaving ugly patches of stumps and debris: they were learning to replenish what they took, but their past greed still disfigured the land. Highways slashed through hills, leaving naked scars; the second growth of trees spread in thin monotony, and the roadsides were cluttered with gas stations, hamburger joints, and roadhouses shaped like chickens, derbies, or lemons, competing in garishness for attention. Faded campaign posters were left on trees, billboards obscured the views, and stray signs littered the fields. Cottages beside the road were often unpainted, and innocent of any proportion or style; old bedsprings and abandoned automobiles had come to rest in the weeds in the back yard. We either did not see all of this, our eyes on the hills beyond and editing the view in our minds, or made allowances. There was a squatter mentality about those times; we recognized that the people in these ugly shacks had little, and we admired them for making a new start here; in time, as they prospered, they might feel like sprucing up. We would not have thought of indicting them for defacing the land, yet that is what they were doing, along with those who had less excuse—the billboard industry and the proprietors of ramshackle roadhouses and used-car graveyards. Western man made little demand on himself to match the grandeur about him. When I later discovered the tilled New England countryside, with its white houses, black shutters, and red barns, its relative immunity from signs, its neat stone fences and its respect for trees, I realized (as I was to come to realize in France) the pleasure and pride of a country settled for centuries, and the serenity to be found in homogeneity of structure and color. Not all the newness of the West, nor its easygoing license, deserved celebrating: they spoke rightly who talked of its *natural* beauty.

But I can be severe only out of an exacting love of what is my home country, and, even in deploring, understand. When one enthuses on his home town to someone unfamiliar with it, he stresses what is distinctive about it (in Seattle's case, the hillside streets coming down on one side to fresh lakes and on the other to salt water, and the view of distant peaks), yet the appeal of a home town is what is ordinary about it, not the grand panorama but the familiar street corner. Even the shop fronts, hideously universal as they may be, are a litany of remembered names.

Nor can I be neutral about the people. In a French village one sees people so plainly themselves and *making no effort,* as an American would say, to be otherwise. This making an effort has its wrong side, but it also accounts for that good-tempered American hospitality, which is a matter not of manners (and sometimes lacking in them) but of a genuine desire that everyone feel included, at home. There was not one world, in Seattle, of doormen and elevator operators and taxi drivers, and another of those served. We sought an equality with them all, and would have thought ourselves snobs had we not. We made a point of seeing something in everyone, and usually found something to see: the milkman might not have read Chaucer but might have a better knowledge of flowers, or be wiser in rivers, than you, and perhaps had gone to the same school. We were not taught to regard him politely but to keep a distance: we naturally accepted him as a human being like ourselves. A few people in Seattle might be recognizably distinct—an occasional Greek or Pole with an odd name—but they did not clot in communities and accent their separateness.[1]

Occasionally someone would be so unregeneratively unattractive that we had to concede that his unattractiveness reflected not a quirk of personality but a defect in his origins: we would concede a little guiltily—and still affirming our belief in equality—that he *hadn't had all the advantages* we'd had. This charitable Western assumption of equality may have no justification in reality; it is not universally felt even there, and may disappear as the West fills up, but it is nonetheless a heart-warming trait, whose absence throughout much of the world accounts for many of the world's needless hatreds.

But this Western attitude of considering no man better than you, and yourself no better than anyone else, has its drawbacks too. It generates much worthy community activity and some that is only

[1] There were, of course, Negroes, Chinese, Japanese and Filipinos, who lived apart from us because of their lower income and seemingly of their own volition, as I thought at the time. The Japanese labored in truck gardens on the outskirts of town, had the cleanest stalls in the public market, and their bright children— as American of speech and thought as any of us—often became our high school valedictorians and salutatorians. The Chinese ran the laundries and chop suey joints; in the eyes of the police they got in trouble as the Japanese never did— mixing in narcotics, gambling, and secretive tong behavior. The Filipinos made sunny houseboys for the well-to-do, but the rest of us too often knew them only through the headlines: since only Filipino boys were imported, they would often figure in the news as attempting to rape a white woman, or running amok, knife in hand. Proper white girls did not go out with Filipinos, and once a year our paper ran without explanation a picture of a crowded pier as a cannery ship came in from Alaska. The swarm of women who greeted the Filipino cannery workers would have all their season's wages within a few days, and after that no further interest in them.

Pearl Harbor, among its other effects, compelled a hasty revaluation of which among Asian peoples we were supposed to admire most.

pleasant and harmless, but it inclines to a suspicion of those who would set themselves apart in any way. It is all right to have odd interests, so long as you are careful to depreciate them. But if your separate pursuit demands privacy and concentration it is apt to be regarded as an attempt to set yourself off from, and therefore above, your fellow man; one becomes defiant or apologetic, but in either case unnatural, or abandons his private disciplines and settles into the general ease. Skills which are spontaneous and communal are much appreciated: the ability to dash off a parody, but not the exacting solitude required to write a good poem; the capacity to entertain at the piano but not to play well, which compels too silent and respectful a hearing; and a talent for home decorating and a dabbling in paint will get you acclaimed as artistic—so long as you paint recognizable likenesses. There is, of course, a substantial minority whose standards of appreciation are considerably higher, but in the West one is apt to live not only among them but among everyone else—which may be why so many visitors from the outside world return cheering the Western setting, acclaiming its generous hospitality and casserole informality, but muttering about its intellectual sterility.

So deep in myself lies the Western attitude that a monitor inside my head wants to moderate the indictment, but it cannot be done. If a Westerner wants to pride himself on the generosity of his attitude, commending the good intentions that went into fashioning a pot, a painting, or a piano solo, instead of risking the unpleasantness of judging by severe enough standards, he runs the risk of getting second-rateness in what is done. Asked to choose between what Yeats called perfection in the work or perfection in the life, the Westerner will usually settle for what makes him more sociable as a man. This elasticity of standards has the effect in a Westerner's personality of giving him an unforced assurance, even when his achievements are few. It gives him a serenity of countenance that is not blighted by a discovery of any inferiority of station or of worth; his self-confidence (that most precious intangible) is not destroyed too soon, as it might be in a more fixed and demanding society. He lives a combination of work and play and is perhaps not even conscious that this, too, was to have made a choice.

Sometimes, sitting with friends beside a campfire on the beach, enjoying the night stillness, the salt air, the lapping of the water, the sweet fragrance of the cedars, and hearing the odd cry of a loon far off, we would ask each other contentedly why anyone would ever want to leave the West. I did not think that I would be the one ever to do so; and yet it was I who left, feeling the cramp of a limited future there in my chosen trade of newspapering, forced by something inside myself not to be content with what did not engage my whole heart, and prepared to work wherever my imagination would be compelled to stretch itself, even if it meant living in surroundings less amiable and agreeable.

We Americans have developed an odd passion for crisscrossing our country at great speed, taking in sweeping views, finding a pleasure in sheer movement, reckoning up proudly how many miles we drive in one day, seeing everything to be seen but little of it intensely, absorbing impressions but palavering idly all the while, enjoying a family intimacy, seeing of other people only those who man the gas pumps or fellow motorists at roadside motels. The hours we spend on such motoring trips may account for the size of our cars: at these times we live in them. In this way many see quite a bit of the United States, taken as panorama, and enjoy a soporific realization of its expanse, while indirectly acknowledging that only an occasional national park, colorful cities like New Orleans and San Francisco, or historic ones like Philadelphia and Boston, are worth slowing down for, to study by foot. Americans feel at home wherever they see an A & P store or a Coca-Cola sign, and develop the sensation that they understand each other perhaps better than they do.

I have often been part of this aimless caravan, going everywhere in vast loops of motoring, and coming to have a feel for many American places if intimate knowledge of few. First came a great circle of the West's geographic splendors—the waterfalls, the deserts, the mountains—then a discovery of the flat inland horizons of the Middle West. Later there were forays into the Deep South—but since most of what was different about it I found myself unsympathetic to, I am quite prepared to accept the Southerner's insistence that only he is entitled to discuss the subject.

To be fair, only after putting down roots into a place (as I have not, in the South) does one come to know its soil, its rocks and its winds, and the rub of disasters on its character. I have come to know only one other American region well: a year in New England, with repeated visits since, and fourteen years in New York City, have made me sharply aware of American qualities there that either disappear or become diluted before reaching the Pacific Coast—and I also became aware that other qualities I had thought universally American were unique to the West.

I came from a land where Indians abandoned their Sears, Roebuck denims and old Fords whenever they saw a dollar to be made by putting on war paint, getting on a horse and coughing over a peace pipe; suspicions of tourist-conscious local atmosphere, I suspected the storied New England character, cranky and frugal, to be an attitude preserved in aspic, like colonial Williamsburg. New Englanders themselves are fond of telling nasal Calvin Coolidge stories that either delight in, or burlesque, their reputation. But I learned that New England thrift was stinginess only when set against the voluptuous waste that prevails in much of the rest of the country, and discovered that New England's political conservatism—though I did not share it—could be conservative of the best in the classic American attitudes of dissent and independence. The New Englander takes knowing, and will not be taken by storm, has a dignity in his plainness that is immovable by that artful gregariousness which is the false excess of the open American nature. His dislike of all that New York stands for is no peevish regionalism: he would hew to an older set of values even at his own expense. I found his character a welcome tributary to the American mainstream.

This was my first discovery. The second was, to a Westerner naïve in his mid-twenties, more shattering: I discovered the Eastern world of privilege, and what must accompany it, the world of those without privilege. In the East were barriers that set off a world all its own, to a degree that was inconceivable in the West. In its extremer manifestations, in Virginia, in the orbits around Philadelphia and around Boston, lived those staunch old families so pleased by their heritage and regarding themselves as so favored by nature that admittance could only be by birth. Even in the outer rings of this circle, where the credentials were hardly of long standing, there was a tendency to prefer an insider's outlandishness to an outsider's merit. If this were all, it would be no bad thing, for it was easy to be content to be excluded from what one regarded as effete, stagnant, and undemocratic.

But there was a wider area of Eastern exclusivity where the outsider could recognize, and reluctantly concede, criteria he respected. These are people with a quietness in dress that amounts to a uniform, who would sooner be out at the elbows in what they deem acceptable than all dressed up in something they would not be caught dead in. At home and at school they have been taught values that do not depend on the approval of the crowd but only of their own set; they get a good education and rub up against art and music as a matter of course; they learn restraint of taste and considerateness in manners, without undue damage to their virility. They have an enviable ease and sureness about them; the best of them—like the best in England—are very good indeed. The poorest of them have an unassailable conviction of their superiority. In their way of life is much that I could wish for everybody; it is a pity that its benefits are unequally conferred.

These people were hospitable to those with the same interests, but the outsider soon learned the disadvantage of being late to class: the pattern was set in childhood, in the segregation—but also the discipline—of good private schools. Higher income may first have set this group apart but was not its chief characteristic, for many who no longer had the income made do with less but still lived by the values: the touchstone is not money but upbringing.

The chief defect of these people was that their preoccupation with the canons of agreed good taste isolated them from some of the spontaneity as well as from the vulgarity of American life. They found it hard to separate the good from the rough in those who were not like them in upbringing. They did not so much dismiss the rest of Americans as fail to understand them.

When Westerners and Midwesterners gravitate to New York City, their first shocked reaction is to deplore the Eastern compounds of privilege, and to vow that their own children will go to a public school. In time, this noble resolution fades as they discover that Eastern public schools do not represent a full spectrum of the community as their own public schools did. It is only necessary to watch twelve-year-old toughs bursting out of New York City schools, cigarettes already lit, to know what these parents are being fastidious about. To send one's own child among them is not to immerse him in the diversity of American life but to confine him in something unrepresentative. How much easier it was to be democratic out West!

If national and racial prejudices are unevenly spread in America, it may be because groups which are well assimilated minorities in one area of the country dominate another, and where unchallenged exhibit a quite different personality. I came to realize this in Boston, the first Eastern city I lived in. I was prepared for the cold, grey Eastern mill towns inhabited by Poles, Croats, Hungarians, and the big-city pockets of Jews and Italians, but nothing in my lifetime of romanticizing my Irish ancestors as a gay and fey people had prepared me for the dour and resentful qualities to be found in that singular cluster known as the Boston Irish. Anyone who has read into the history of nineteenth-century immigration knows the frightful poverty the Irish left behind; concedes the depths of a justified hatred of the English and a scorn for those of their people who during the Famine "took the soup" in submission to the Protestants; realizes the shabby welcome the Irish got in the New World, what hovels in the back alleys of Boston they were cramped into, and how defeating were the NO IRISH NEED APPLY signs; yet, knowing all this, can be saddened to see a people so victimized by intolerance become so intolerant themselves, so ready to vote for those of shoddy charm who stir their spite and flatter their grievances, so ready to give houseroom to McCarthyism, anti-Semitism, or any other ill wind of hate. Their resentments I understood, but not their persistence in them, which was marking their own characters but achieving little else.

A Westerner's simple solution was that the Boston Irish should drop their old antagonisms and become "like the rest of us." But on second thought, did we want the American melting pot replaced by a bland bouillon cube, ready made, edges squared off, slickly packaged —wasn't it better for us as a nation to be a simmering *pot au feu* tasting sharply of contesting savors? Here we were, only half a century after the widespread alarm over the unassimilable millions debarking at Ellis Island, and already worried that Americans were becoming too much alike, and on guard against homogenized Americanism! Very well, let us have a society for the preservation of Old World ingredients, but not in cellophane: it must come to more than getting oneself up in *Lederhosen,* singing "Santa Lucia" or dancing the Highland Fling once a year. But if each group was to contribute to America something out of its own heritage, was there nothing better than hatred in their legacy to inspire the Irish?

After Boston, almost unwillingly I settled down in what called itself the greatest city in the world. Not the city, but the work to be found there, drew me. The jagged towers forming an asymmetrical harmony out of a thousand individual decisions had their celebrated post-card beauty, but the streets below needed a new Dante to bring hell up to date. New York is a city where millions are forced to work in the center, piled high in skyscrapers, borne up and down in crowded elevators in close body contact. ("Make room for one more.") They must be taken there and removed each night through underground tunnels of lurching subway cars, where they stand packed, dull-eyed with fatigue and noise, self-concentrated and hostile, hurrying home to steel shelves where on unpaid furniture they spend their evenings watching the grey glare of the television screen. It is a city whose towers house businessmen who hire psychologists to study human fears which can be exploited to sell deodorants or toothpaste, and where glamor is set by synthetic personalities trained to appear relaxed and natural before hot lights and stop watches, so that they can create the right air of conviction about products they themselves never use. It is a city where people do not do, but watch: crowd stadiums to see others play baseball or football, go to galleries to see what others paint or concerts to hear others play, and pay comedians to bring them laughter.

Wipe the soot from your eyes and examine the city about you. Travel the trains, out to the shining suburbs which are neither city nor country, where rows of empty automobiles beside the railroad platform reproachfully, wastefully await their owners, away in the city until dark making a living. Those who live in these bedroom towns—people with sufficient salaries to command a place with clean air and a plot of green, along with the patience to make a long journey to enjoy it—realize the artificiality of any community where people do not work among those they live with, but what else can they do? As the commuter train makes its slow, dull, interrupted passage, peer out at the platforms where people lean resignedly against pillars as they wait for their trains: their eyes buried in newspapers or staring out and seeing nothing, their numbness apparent not only in their faces but in their elbows, their slouching hips, the way their feet are flatly planted in the concrete, and in the way they barely hear, and seem not to resent, the racket and roar of the express train hurtling by on the center tracks. Or come back to the city itself, past the abandoned brick buildings with windows empty, across the industrial river hedged by oil stations and warehouses and gravel pits—the only life stirring in the river below the slow shunting of barges. Now come the large housing projects all alike, geometrically sterile, with apartment buildings scientifically placed to catch the light yet somehow designed to keep out the life that agitated the slums they replaced. And beyond are the older places: fire escapes with laundry hanging out; grimy brick façades with upper windows open and fat women, leaning elbows on dirty pillows, looking torpidly out, or calling petulantly down to their children in the streets below—black, Puerto Rican, or white—who play among ash cans and parked cars, or sometimes flee to a concrete playground beside the river. Where is the equality of opportunity here?

Not from them, but from among the ambitious all over the country must the big city draw constantly to replenish its talent and vitality, for the big city is not, as those who dream of it imagine it to be, a creator, but only an assembly point and consumer of talent. Ignore the multitudes about you, those Italians and Puerto Ricans with the look in their eyes of expecting a hurt; ignore too the well-to-do ladies for whom the city is the place where everything can be done for those who can pay; look instead at the city's most virile people—the successes. And what do you see? Too often it is marriage without communication; insatiable search for what, if found, will not satisfy; people who read detective stories or lending-library romances to pass the time; who otherwise read reviews, not books; who do not express thoughts but repeat remarks; who read magazines, hear music, and tour museums not so much in pleasure as out of a felt need to keep up; who judge by dress and not by character; who shun the unexpected encounters of living for fear other human beings will make demands on them; who even spend vacations in places where they know the other guests will have been screened to be like them— polite, decent, and facile in talk that says nothing and will not disturb. These are the kind that fill the apartment buildings on the desirable streets, who crowd the proper cafés and fill the bars. Those who come from outside the city have to learn to draw on their accumulated capital of tolerance, for something in the city dries one up, killing instinctive sympathy, and substituting a conscious and detached politeness which is not at all the same.

But as the seasons turn, as the static heat of summer, lodged oppressively between the tall buildings, turns to wind-swept autumn days when people walk head down against the wind, each with his mind only on his own purposes, self-centered and melancholy, oblivious of the gutter sight of collapsed ribs of abandoned umbrellas blown inside out by the storm, indifferent to the frail city trees shivering and shedding their gold leaves—on these days, one discovers a community of shared frustrations with his fellow New Yorkers, a common pride in resistance to the harassments about one: noise, dirt, crowds, hurry, rain, the slam of brakes, fume of buses and chatter of riveting. It must be easy to be well-behaved in heaven, we think to ourselves; but we have learned adaptability and even a mutual forbearance on the cliffsides of hell. Civility breaks but rarely through the prevailing rudeness of New York. When it does, it makes no profession of sympathy, fears to be identified as softness, and does its good deed gruffly as if half-expecting to be rebuffed. And then one comes to contrast his own lot—his advantage in having been brought up in the confident open spaces; having a job that stimulates, and the opportunity to get away from it; having the price of good restaurants and theaters to escape the turmoil of the city streets—and marvels at any good nature at all in people whose whole lives have been spent here, condemned to work at tedious jobs and live in squalid quarters.

Out of the congested streets of New York comes a toughness and resilience of character that knows what it wants and is unsentimental in demanding it. Its most familiar product is that pushing, fast-talking, ruthless fellow who will step on faces to get where he wants. The quality manifests itself also in that mordant, unsparing wit that is the style of those big-time comedians who honed themselves on hecklers on the borscht circuit in the Catskills; it is also to be heard among thousands of New Yorkers, cab drivers and delivery boys, who pass off their daily complaints in the same rhythm of caustic wisecrack and deadpan response, as if wit would be spoiled if given too good a reception. Economy of words, and those slurred, is the New York speech; courtesy, consideration and sympathy are carefully rationed: "So what? We all got problems."

The unsentimental, demanding metropolitan quality that is New York's gift to the rest of the country has its origins in harsh circumstances and European beginnings. Here there is none of the West's sunny benevolence conferred on all but on none deeply: Old World families, a unit to themselves, are capable of strong feeling within it, but against everyone else are armored like armadillos. Among these people—the Italians, the Poles, the Russians, but above all the Jews—humor is never far from melancholy. They seem to have been born generations ago, and never to have passed through naïveté. They know the price of things, and think you a fool if you do not. They demand value. They know that they must work to get ahead, and are not indulgent of those who plead their charm to escape being judged on their merit. It is not only the poor who have this severity of judgment; among Jewish intellectuals, among wealthy Jews, among other European groups in New York are inherited standards in music, in art, in medicine, in science: if you would claim a special distinction, then deserve it. I do not mean that all Jews, all Europeans, have good taste (any more than all Negroes have rhythm) and if it is tawdriness they want, they can be just as demanding of value. But there is in New York City a sophisticated nucleus centering around them that makes for exacting critics and appreciative audiences. This is not the world of the Western United States, pleased to have heard an evening of chamber music at all: New Yorkers insist that the performance must measure up, and from their ruthlessness come the big city's standards of quality, the seeming heartlessness that sets it off from the rest of the country.

I came to like even New York.

Suggested Topics

1. God's country vs. man's country
2. Is New York heartless?
3. "Homogenized Americanism"
4. The combination of work and play
5. Are people the same all over?
6. Billboards and the American landscape
7. Types of American speech

CONFESSIONS OF AN IRISH REBEL   *Brendan Behan*

> Regarded as "Ireland's most impressive new dramatist," Bren-
> dan Behan has made a reputation for himself as a "bedeviled
> elf," a rebel—and a writer of top rank. His autobiography, *The
> Borstal Boy,* attracted considerable attention, as did his plays,
> *The Quare Fellow* and *The Hostage.*

I was born in Holles Street, Dublin, on Feb. 9, 1923, while my
father was a Republican prisoner in a camp holding 10,000 prisoners,
including the now President of the Republic, Sean T. O'Kelly.

All my family were strong Republicans and were active in the
movement to free Ireland from English rule for centuries. Unlike
many good Nationalists, they were doctrinaire Republicans in direct
descent from Tone (who lived and plotted in the Rue de Bac, and was
captured in Ireland with a French expeditionary force in 1798). My
father, Stephen Behan, is President of the House and Ship Painters
Union of Ireland.

My mother's brother, Peadar Kearney, wrote the "Soldier's Song,"
the now national anthem, and many other revolutionary songs. He also
was a house painter.

My father's and mother's families were involved in the early days
of the Abbey Theatre, but before that my mother's sister, Margaret,
was married to P. J. Bourke, whose family ran music halls for generations. The Bourkes are the best-known theatrical family in Ireland
and one of the biggest suppliers of theatrical costumes, make-up and
accessories in Europe. They have dressed films for British companies
—"Odd Man Out," "Captain Boycott," "Henry V," etc. The present
head of the family, my cousin, Lorcan Bourke, was Deputy Lord
Mayor two years ago when the Lord Mayor of Dublin, Robert Bris-
coe, T. D., was touring the United States and my brothers were the
leaders of the Dublin unemployed struggles of the same year.

Like most emerging countries, Ireland still has these strange family
connections of solid citizen and working-class agitator. Our new
bourgeois have already started to wear top hats. Alas!

In religion, my family have been Catholics always, and anti-clerical.
It is a strange thing, I do not know of any priest in any generation of

Reprinted from *The New York Times,* November 16, 1958. By permission of
The New York Times and the author.

my family, and I do not know of one member of it who died without a priest, Deo Gratias.

I was reared in the slums of the north side of Dublin. Big Georgian houses with sometimes one family living in one room, although we had two rooms. The kitchen and the back parlor. The kitchen had a huge range in it, and we ate and lived there during the day. My father and mother and whoever was the baby—there were eight of us, seven boys and one girl—slept there at night, and the children slept in the back parlor, which was separated from the front parlor by a folding door. There was a small brothel conducted in the front parlor.

The main business of the place did not interest us at all, but I enjoyed the conversation, which we could easily overhear, and the singing when they got drunk. And it was all very homey and comforting on a dark winter's night.

I went to school with the French Sisters of Charity at North William Street and liked that. I was a great pet with them. When I was 11, I was sent to the Christian Brothers on the North Circular Road.

The Brothers threw me out in 1936, and I went to the Technical School as a house-painter's apprentice.

The next year the Dublin Corporation moved us to a house in a huge housing scheme in Dublin.

We had electric light, a bath, a fine lavatory and plenty of fresh air.

I hated it. Not that I dislike being clean, but I missed my companions and I missed the street.

It was O. K. for my younger brothers and my little sister, but I was 14 and knew no one in this wilderness, and I like cities. I think a day is a long time in the country, though I love the sea.

I was in the Fianna Eireann, which is the Republican Boy Scouts, since I was 9, and in 1937 I was transferred to the Irish Republican Army as a messenger boy.

When I was 16, I was transferred to the I. R. A. itself and in 1939 was arrested in Liverpool and sentenced to three years at Borstal (reform school) for having explosives.

I was released in 1942 and deported and subsequently sentenced to fourteen years by a military court in Dublin for the attempted murder of two detectives.

I was released in a general amnesty in 1946, but was arrested in Manchester in 1947, having assisted in the escape of an I. R. A. man from jail. They could not prove any connection between me and the escape so they sentenced me to four months for breaking my expulsion order.

I was arrested in 1952 at Newhaven, fined £25 and deported to France.

I went to France first in 1947.

Everyone admires Paris for the artists. I equally loved Paris of the barricades. Delacroix is my man, for he married the two. I worked for a while as painter (peintre en batiment) in Paris at the Air Exposition at the Fare des Invalides and at Saint Gratien.

The only disadvantage Paris has is its distance from the sea.

Recently I had a dispute at Orly Airport. I have seen reports in France Soir and Paris Presse that I said I did not wish to die for France.

I do not wish to die for France, or for Ireland, or at all, if I can help it, but the inference in their reports was that I am anti-French. What I did say was that I did not wish to die for Air France.

I love France, but my own France. Republican France. I love Ireland, Republican Ireland.

I did not relish being brought to Choisy le Roi and put in a cage for the night.

I am not fond of police anywhere. In Ireland or in France. In England, either. I have heard no good reports of the New York police, though most of them are of Irish descent.

I do not hear any good of the Russian police or of the Germans.

They are mostly peasants and are delighted to be let loose on towns in uniforms and with guns, through whose streets they crawled in dumb wondering fear when first they left the bog.

Police are a necessity of course—if you've got any money.

So when I say I love France I do not include the cops because they are peasants and mental invalids, just as they are anywhere else.

The world being a madhouse, who is more fitting to patrol its wards than armed idiots?

As I cannot write about my writing without putting on some sort of an act, I would prefer to leave it at that.

As regards drink, I can only say that in Dublin during the depression when I was growing up, drunkenness was not regarded as a social disgrace. To get enough to eat was regarded as an achievement. To get drunk was a victory.

Lately, however, I have discovered that hangovers are getting worse. So is the post-booze depression. Worst of all, I get some sort of rheumatism in the back that nearly cripples me. Proust remarks: "We obey no doctor but Doctor Pain." Maybe I'll reform my habits. Maybe.

P.S. I am married to Beatrice Salkeld, a painter—an artist-painter this time. We have no children, except me.

Suggested Topics

1. An autobiographical sketch
2. The plays of Brendan Behan
3. The anticlerical believer
4. The rebel in many artists
5. Can Behan be called a "beatnik"?
6. "We have no children—except me."

THE HAUNTING DRAMA OF
DYLAN THOMAS
Harvey Breit

Formerly Assistant Book Review Editor of *The New York Times,* Harvey Breit is now a free-lance writer and playwright. With Budd Schulberg he is the co-author of a successful play, *The Disenchanted,* based on the life of F. Scott Fitzgerald.

When Dylan Thomas came here for the first time seven years ago at the age of 35, he was quite obscure. Few Americans outside the little-magazine orbit had heard of him or had read his verse. When he died in New York on a dreary November day four years later, he had become one of the most talked-about literary figures in our time. Many thousands had flocked to hear him in person. Many more thousands had bought his recordings. And nearly everyone had a Dylan Thomas story, whether true or untrue. This seemed fame enough; certainly more fame than Thomas had been prepared to reckon with or bargain for.

But his posthumous fame has grown even greater. A few short years ago, unknown. A few years after that, dead. And now, three years after he did "go gentle into that good night," this broadened recognition of his gift, this tribute to his appeal as well as to his talent, this calculated risk on his popularity at the box office with its grosses, its percentages and its intimidating minimums. How are we to understand such a turn-about? What are we to make of the posthumous evolution of a little-magazine poet and coterie darling into a mass-audience playwright?

Reprinted from *The New York Times Magazine,* October 6, 1957. By permission of *The New York Times* and the author.

Without distorting or oversimplifying the various knockabout nuances of Thomas' life, his activities as a poet can be divided into two parts—the English and American phases, the totality perhaps to be titled (ironically, even bitterly) "The Two Triumphs of Dylan Thomas." The first triumph was literary; it was relevant to the poet's aims, labors, concerns and anxieties. The second triumph was extra-literary; it was more relevant to the human-all-too-human Dylan, but not to the poet who asked that his images roar and rise on heaven's hill. Triumph in England was the poems, mainly that; triumph in America was an ensemble of poems and voice and rhetoric and behavior and personality—an intricate ensemble that the man Thomas was partially intrigued by and that the poet Thomas probably feared.

Thomas was born in a Welsh town near Swansea and went through the Swansea Grammar School, the extent of his formal education. He was never burdened by erudition, perhaps a lucky thing for his poems. But knocking around Wales as a youth, going on drinking parties and careless picnics with the old men of the village, trying his hand at journalism and hack-writing, taking odd jobs of one sort or another— these left their mark. Though he never lost an essential innocence, these constituted his sentimental education. The Welsh landscape is ubiquitous in the poems; the gallivanting elders, the stay-at-home wives, the gossip and the drinking are at the core of his play and his stories. In his teens he began writing poems, strange, wild things written in a childish scrawl on scraps of paper—gifted, bewildering items for magazine editors in those early days.

In 1932 The Sunday Referee, edited by Mark Goulden (now chairman of the publishing house of W. H. Allen & Co., Ltd.), who had for contributors such distinguished writers as Aldous Huxley, Bertrand Russell, Richard Aldington and Wyndham Lewis, awarded Thomas its poetry prize (a grand 150 quid). For the first time, Thomas made the awesome journey to London to collect his prize and meet the famous—he was 18—and it echoes that momentous and fateful meeting of some sixty years before when the youthful Rimbaud first journeyed to Paris. Attracted and repelled, they made violent enemies as well as friends; but their poems captivated the Bohemian habitués of the cafes and pubs. Thomas would thereafter flee London, as Rimbaud fled Paris, but, unlike Rimbaud (who fled permanently), mainly for bursts of work and fits of required isolation.

Thomas' poems were extraordinary for any time. They were particularly so for their time. The important English poets of the Thirties were writing unambiguous political poems, were quoting Marx and Lenin. Thomas roared in, wrote mainly about his subterranean self: *I dreamed my genesis in sweat of sleep. . . . I, in my intricate image, stride on two levels. . . . When all my five and country senses see. . . .*

As John Sweeney wrote, Thomas was Freudian rather than Marxian. He was Welsh and his verses contained ritual, magic, folklore, the Bible, John Donne, Herbert and Vaughan, Hopkins—but above all himself, with his theory that a poem was a moment of peace wrested from the clash and conflict of images within him.

His verse attracted such disparate poets as Stephen Spender and Roy Campbell. Critics declared he was the most original poet since Auden, since Eliot, since Hopkins. Herbert Read wrote that the poetry "was the most absolute poetry of the time." The magazines bought his verses, the B. B. C. bought a few talks, the publishers began to sell his books. But a published poet is still a poor poet. He made many good friends, among them the brilliant critic and editor, Geoffrey Grigson, who helped Thomas by feeding him books to review, mostly dreadfuls.

According to Grigson, when Thomas first came down to London he was a Rossetti boy, with curling locks, flowing ties and a tongue dripping with esthetics. Not for long, though. He gradually arrived at a role more natural to him, more truly himself, that of the Roaring Boy, the Young Tough, the Poet of the Pub. Grigson and his friends called Thomas, affectionately, Dirty Dylan, Ditch Dylan, the Ugly Suckling. "When he disappeared," writes Grigson, "it was a relief; when he reappeared, a pleasure."

His arrival here in 1950 was a great pleasure. Like a rare if perverse wine, Dylan Thomas not only traveled well across the corrupting seas; he improved. The sparks he had set off in England leaped into conflagrations here. Everywhere he went to read his poems—on his first visit he toured the country with stop-overs at forty university towns and campuses—audiences were stunned by the dazzling performance of the actor on the stage. Half of it was improvisation anyway—sardonic, wicked comments on the poems, on himself for commenting on the poems, on himself for being a public figure and standing where he was. Last and least of all it was the poems—though many of them glowed with a new beauty.

And the performances after the stage performances, those Roaring Boy parties at which he offended genteel ladies and even semi-sophisticated college girls; but best of all was the titillation for those at the various parties who had gotten off scot-free, only because Thomas had a limited amount of energy to expend. And for friends of friends and for people twice and thrice removed: "Did you ever hear what he said when she said . . . ?" and "Did you see what he *did* when she was standing next to him . . . ?"

As against the gossip and the titillation over the half-true myth that was springing up around the man, there were genuine admirers, people who loved the poems and who loved people and things and

who made no demands on the poet's time and who did not even need
to know him. Poems like "Do Not Go Gentle Into that Good Night,"
"Poem to October," "Ceremony After a Fire Raid," "Fern Hill," "And
Death Shall Have no Dominion," or "In My Craft or Sullen Art," in
which Thomas writes that he writes

> *Not for the towering dead*
> *With their nightingales and psalms*
> *But for the lovers, their arms*
> *Round the griefs of the ages,*
> *Who pay no praise or wages*
> *Nor heed my craft or art.*

Placed alongside the poems of Blake and Wordsworth and Keats,
these do not distort or outrage that order.

In the American triumph the poems are almost beside the point;
if they are to the point they are only to the degree that they permitted
the poet the better to conform to an ideal public image—the Pure
Genius, the Romantic Anarchist. The camp-followers, the hero-wor-
shipers and the art zanies (as Grigson calls them) are rarely interested
in the work as such; they are far more interested in an image that
impels them, a constellation of elements (of which the work is a small
part), something less than the poem and more than the man. The
myth of Dylan Thomas in America lent itself to just such a following
and accounts far more than the poetry can for the perverse glamour
that attached itself to the poet.

In our time there are few contenders for the Pure Genius type.
Today poets are respectable. They hold down jobs, are the backbones
of universities, share responsible political opinions, wear overcoats
against the weather. Not Thomas: no overcoat in the winter (he wore
an *invisible* overcoat, he said), no job, no opinions except aloof and
paradoxical ones ("A hero? More likely a Nero") or, when possible,
shocking ones. His gifts, always at hand, were summoned up at seemingly impossible times (when he'd had too much to drink just before
going on), and they appeared inexhaustible, like a God-given spring.

His language was so imaginatively concrete as to make it seem that
there had emerged out of another time a sullen prophet, a bard from
the dark ages—all wooded and misted and cemeteried and foxgloved
and blooded (some of his favorite words). His voice with its magnificent quiver could register the tremolos of tragedy as well as the *sec*
scrapings of drollery, tomfoolery, irony, obscenity. And the drinking—
the scotch, the bourbon, the beer, the black velvet—it was the final
100 proof, if proof was ever needed, that in Thomas the Pure Genius
Type could not have found a more ideal contemporary lodging.

In this mixture of the bewildering poetry and the bewildering man and the bewildering game the man played, in this whole consort dancing together did the American triumph consist. Not, in short, by poetry alone did Thomas muster his vast and ill-assorted army of the States. It is more than probable that at first Thomas was awed by the phenomenon; that, gradually, he toyed with it and even exploited it; and, ultimately, was sickened by it. At the conclusion of a public reading there was always a loyal band of poets waiting for him to shake loose from the encircling battalions of the army. But could he, at those seldom times when he wanted to, shake himself loose from both his army *and* his inner echelon? He seldom wanted to and he seldom could.

It was nobody's fault. It is a mistake for poets and critics to write that Thomas was killed in America by Americans. He died of illness, of drink, maybe even of desire and despair. But to say that it was our way of life, our capacity to adore and worship and fete and feed that killed Thomas is to insult him. Besides, too many people cared about him in America, cared about his verse. Those who came to know him, who saw him enter a room and observed the muscular, lumpy, squat sack of potatoes shuffle in, clothes disheveled, hair awry, the features of his face askew (yet touchingly lit by quizzical eyes and the gentlest flick of a smile)—as they tick off these comic horrors they know how endearing the man was, how unworldly, and how dreadfully missed.

Thomas once said, "I like to think of poetry as statements made on the way to the grave." One can let his end go at that. What his friends and critics worried about in Thomas was his future as a writer. What would he do when he finally exhausted the well of his youth, those basic, exclusive materials of his poems and stories? In "Under Milk Wood" it is probable that he had found the way out of the potential impasse. He delighted in drama of every sort. And in spite of the brooding self-sufficiency, his eyes squinted in awareness of people and their behavior and their areas of pride and sensitivity. In "Under Milk Wood," which is a day's cycle in a Welsh village, all of Thomas' gifts are present, far more so than in the poems—his sense of drama, his knowledge of people, his language, his slyness, his wit and humor, his seriousness at play, his profound and intimate proximity to the heart of tragedy.

And so in October, a birthday month, Thomas will traffic with large audiences who will pay the steepest prices to view his essentially private labors. He would have been amused. One may speculate that alive and kicking, he would perhaps have hung about the lobby for the intermission crowds and made nasty and noisy remarks about the pretentiousness of the playwright. Though it would not have been that simple. Conceivably, he would have on that opening night

managed to be alone at a bar where he could buy expensive champagne, perhaps a vintage Moët et Chandon (instead of the usual cheap
sort) to blend with the good stout for his favored Black Velvet.

Finally, he could have been fearful, he could have undergone that
terrible moment of self-scrutiny and self-condemnation. Perhaps only
because he did not yet know how to cope with a public triumph. His
words uttered at the end of his alarmingly successful first American
tour ring a little like a sad bell. "Success is bad for me," he said. "Before, I was arrogant and lost. Now I am humble and found." And the
bell sound again, both smaller and yet more bravado: "I prefer that
other—what I was before."

Do Not Go Gentle Into That Good Night

Dylan Thomas

Do not go gentle into that good night,
Old age should burn and rave at close of day;
Rage, rage against the dying of the light.

Though wise men at their end know dark is right,
Because their words had forked no lightning they
Do not go gentle into that good night.

Good men, the last wave by, crying how bright
Their frail deeds might have danced in a green bay,
Rage, rage against the dying of the light.

Wild men who caught and sang the sun in flight,
And learn, too late, they grieved it on its way,
Do not go gentle into that good night.

Grave men, near death, who see with blinding sight
Blind eyes could blaze like meteors and be gay,
Rage, rage against the dying of the light.

And you, my father, there on the sad height,
Curse, bless, me now with your fierce tears, I pray.
Do not go gentle into that good night.
Rage, rage against the dying of the light.

Suggested Topics

1. The haunting drama of a) Brendan Behan, b) Alexander Pushkin, c) Paul Verlaine, d) Tennessee Williams, *or* e) some other writer of your choice
2. The irony of posthumous fame
3. The college poet (or artist, composer, novelist) in residence
4. What makes a genius?
5. Why I read (or don't read) poetry

OUR UNEASY WORLD

AN OBLIGATION TO TOMORROW *Albert Schweitzer*

One of the world's great figures, Dr. Albert Schweitzer has
gained fame as a man of extraordinary scope—as a theologian,
musicologist, philosopher, and medical missionary. He and his
wife maintain a hospital at Lambaréné in the Gabon Republic
(formerly French Equatorial Africa). In 1952 he won the Nobel
Peace Prize.

Part I

In April of last year I raised my voice, together with others, to
draw attention to the great danger of radioactive poisoning of the
air and the earth, following tests with atomic bombs and hydrogen
bombs. With others, I appealed to the nuclear powers to come to a
workable agreement to stop the tests as soon as possible, at the same
time declaring their genuine desire to renounce the use of nuclear
weapons.

At that time there appeared to be reasonable hope that this step
would be taken. It was not. The negotiations in London last summer
achieved nothing. The conference arranged by the United Nations
in the autumn of last year suffered the same fate when the Soviet
Union withdrew from the discussions.

The question of nuclear arms control, however, cannot be put
aside. Any discussions among the major nations will have to consider
this problem.

As a first step in any comprehensive plan for workable arms con-

Reprinted from the *Saturday Review,* May 24, 1958. By permission of the
Saturday Review.

trol, the proposal for a cessation of nuclear tests has frequently been advanced.

One might have thought that it would be comparatively simple for all those involved to agree on this first step. No nuclear power would have to sacrifice any of the atomic weapons in its possession. The disadvantage of not being able to try out new bombs or nuclear devices would be the same for all.

The United States and Great Britain have been reluctant to take the first step. They spoke against it when the matter was discussed in the Spring of 1957. Since then many statements have been issued claiming that the radioactivity resulting from nuclear tests is not dangerous. For example, in an official statement coming from the United States, we read the following:

> The necessary steps should be taken to correct the present confusion of the general public [with respect to the effects of testing]. . . . The present and potential effects on heredity from the gradual increase of radioactivity in the air are kept within tolerable limits. . . . The possibility of harmful effects which people believe to be outside control has a strong emotional impact. . . . The continuation of nuclear tests is necessary and justified in the interests of national security.

Despite these assurances, however, people are becoming increasingly apprehensive concerning the possible dangers resulting from nuclear tests.

The reasoning behind the somewhat obscure statement that "the effects on heredity from the gradual increase of radioactivity in the air are kept within tolerable limits" is that the number of deformed children that will be born as a result of the harm done to the sexual cells supposedly will not be large enough to justify the stopping of the tests.

During this campaign of reassurance, a prominent American nuclear physicist even declared that the luminous watchdials in the world represent a greater danger than the radioactive fall-out of nuclear tests until now.

This campaign of reassurance sets up anticipations of glad tidings to the effect that science has succeeded in making the prototype of a hydrogen bomb with a considerably reduced dangerous radioactive fall-out. The new explosive is called a "clean" hydrogen bomb. The old type is being designated as the "dirty" bomb.

The so-called "clean" hydrogen bomb differs from the other in having a jacket made of a material which does not release immense quantities of radioactive elements at the enormous explosion temperature. That is why it is less harmful, as regards radioactivity, than the usual ones.

However, the new, highly-praised hydrogen bomb is—let it be said in passing—only relatively clean. Its trigger is an uranium bomb made of the fissionable uranium-235—an atomic bomb as powerful as the one dropped over Hiroshima. This bomb, when detonated, also produces radioactivity, as do the neutrons released in great numbers at the explosion.

Earlier this year, in an American newspaper, Edward Teller, the father of the "dirty" hydrogen bomb, sings a hymn of praise to the idylic nuclear war to be waged with completely clean hydrogen bombs. He insists on a continuation of the tests in order to perfect this ideal bomb.

Here are two stanzas from Edward Teller's hymn to idylic nuclear warfare:

"Further tests will put us into a position to fight our opponents' war machine, while sparing the innocent bystanders."

"Clean weapons of this kind will reduce unnecessary casualties in a future war."

The idea of limited nuclear war is a contradiction in terms. Each side will use all the power at its disposal in an attempt to annihilate the enemy. The U.S. Department of Defense has quite recently declared that the irradiation of whole areas has become a new offensive weapon.

The "clean" hydrogen bomb may be intended, I fear, more for display-case purposes than for use. The intention seems to be to convince people that new nuclear tests will be followed by less and less radiation and that there is no real argument for the discontinuation of the tests.

Those who think that the danger created by nuclear tests is small mainly take the air radiation into consideration, and persuade themselves to believe that the danger limit has not yet been reached.

The results of their arithmetic are not so reliable, however, as they would have us believe. Through the years the toleration limit for radiation has had to be lowered several times. In 1934 it was 100 radiation units per year. At present the limit is officially put at 5. In many countries it is even lower. Dr. Lauriston Taylor (USA), who is regarded as an authority on protection against radiation, holds—like others—that it is an open question whether there is anything called a harmless amount of radiation. He thinks that we can only speak of an amount of radiation which we regard as tolerable.

We are constantly being told about a "maximum permissible amount" of radiation. What does "permissible" mean? And who has the right to "permit" people to be exposed to these dangers?

When speaking about the risk of radiation we must take into consideration not only the radiation coming from the outside, but also the radioactivity that gets into our bodies.

What is the source of this radioactivity?

The radioactive materials put into the air by nuclear tests do not stay there permanently. In the form of radioactive rain—or even radioactive snow—they fall to the earth. They enter the plants through leaves and roots and stay there. We absorb them by drinking milk from cows or by eating the meat of animals which have fed on it. Radioactive rain contaminates our drinking water.

The most powerful radioactive poisoning occurs in the areas between the Northern latitudes 10° and 60°, because of the numerous nuclear tests conducted mainly in these latitudes by the Soviet Union and the United States.

The radioactive elements absorbed over the years by our body are not evenly distributed in the cellular tissue, but are deposited and accumulated at certain points. From these points internal radiation takes place, causing injuries to particularly vulnerable organs. What this kind of radiation lacks in strength is made up for by its longevity, working as it does for years, day and night.

It is a well-known fact that one of the most widespread and dangerous elements absorbed by us is strontium-90. It is stored in the bones and emits from there its rays into cells of red bone marrow, where the red and white corpuscles are made. If the radiation is too great, blood diseases—fatal in most cases—are the result.

The cells of the reproductive organs are particularly sensitive. Even relatively weak radiation may lead to fatal consequences.

The most sinister aspect of internal as well as external radiation is that years may pass before the evil consequences appear. Indeed, they make themselves felt, not in the first or second generation, but in the following ones. Generation after generation, for centuries to come, will witness the birth of an ever-increasing number of children with mental and physical defects.

It is not for the physicist, choosing to take into account only the radiation from the air, to utter the final word on the dangers of nuclear tests. That right belong to the biologists and physicians who have studied internal as well as external radiation, and to those scientists who pay attention to the facts established by the biologists and physicians.

The declaration signed by 9,235 scientists of all nations, handed to the Secretary General of the U.N. by Dr. Linus Pauling on January 13, 1958, gave the campaign of reassurance a serious blow. The scientists declared that the radioactivity gradually created by nuclear tests represents a grave danger for all parts of the world, particularly serious because its consequences will be an increasing number of deformed children in the future. For this reason they insist on a international agreement putting an end to the nuclear tests.

The declaration signed by the 9,235 scientists did well in stressing the danger of the harmful effects of nuclear tests on future generations which, according to biologists and physicians, will be the result of the radiation to which we are being exposed.

We must not disregard our responsibility to guard against the possibility that thousands of children may be born with the most serious mental and physical defects. It will be no excuse for us to say later that we were unaware of that possibility. Only those who have never been present at the birth of a deformed baby, never witnessed the whimpering cries of its mother, should dare to maintain that the risk of nuclear testing is a small one. The well-known French biologist and geneticist Jean Rostand calls the continuation of nuclear tests "a crime into the future" (le crime dans l'avenir). It is the particular duty of women to prevent this sin against the future. It is for them to raise their voices against it in such a way that they will be heard.

No longer can we take any comfort from the fact that the scientists do not agree on the question of the danger of radiation, or that we must await the decision of international bodies before making positive statements about radiation. Despite all the claims of safety, the truth about the danger of nuclear explosions marches imperturbably along, influencing an ever-increasing section of public opinion. In the long run, even the most well-organized propaganda can do nothing against the truth.

It is a strange fact that few people have taken into consideration that the question of nuclear testing is not one which concerns the nuclear powers exclusively, a question for them to decide at their pleasure. Who has given these countries the right to experiment, in times of peace, with weapons involving the most serious risks for the whole world? What has international law—enthroned by the United Nations and so highly praised in our time—to say on this matter? Does it no longer look out on the world from its temple? Then take it out, so that it may face the facts and do its duty accordingly.

International law should consider at once the compelling case of Japan. That country has suffered heavily from the effects of nuclear tests. The radioactive clouds created by the Soviet tests in Northeast Siberia and by the American tests in the Pacific Ocean are carried by the winds over Japan. The resultant radioactive poisoning is considerable. Powerful radioactive rainfalls are quite common. The radioactive poisoning of the soil and the vegetation is so heavy that the inhabitants of some districts ought to abstain from using their harvest for food. People are eating rice contaminated by radioactive strontium, a substance particularly dangerous for children. The ocean surrounding

Japan is also at times dangerously radioactive, and thereby the very food supply of the country—in which fish has always played an important part—is being threatened.

As every new nuclear test makes a bad situation worse, the Japanese ministers, when hearing of plans for new tests to the north or south of Japan, have presented their country's urgent appeal in Washington or Moscow, beseeching the American or Soviet authorities to give up their plans.

We generally learn about these appeals and the refusal through short newspaper items. Unfortunately, there have been few responsible editorials drawing our attention to the stories behind the news—the misery of human beings who are now in jeopardy. In that way, we and the press are guilty of a lack of compassion. Even guiltier, however, is international law, which has kept silent and indifferent on this question, year after year.

It is high time to recognize that the question of nuclear testing is a matter for world law to consider. Mankind is imperiled by the test. Mankind insists that they stop, and has every right to do so.

If anything is left of international law in our civilization, then the nations responsible for nuclear tests must renounce them immediately, without making this dependent on agreements with respect to the larger questions of general disarmament. Nuclear tests have nothing to do with disarmament. The nations in question will continue to have those weapons which they now have.

There is no time to lose. New tests must not be allowed to increase the already existing danger. It is important to realize that even without new tests the danger will increase during the coming years: a large part of the radioactive elements flung up in the atmosphere and stratosphere at the nuclear experiment is still there. It will come down only after several years—probably about fifteen.

The immediate renunciation of further tests will create a favorable atmosphere for talk on controlling the stockpiles of nuclear weapons and banning their use. When this urgently necessary step has been taken, such negotiations can take place in peace.

That the Soviet Union has announced its willingness to stop its tests is of great importance. The world now looks to the United States and Great Britain for the kind of moral initiative and action that go along with great leadership.

Part II

Today we are faced with the menacing possibility of an outbreak of an atomic war between Soviet Russia and the United States. It can only be averted if the two powers decide to renounce atomic arms.

How did this situation arise?

In 1945 America succeeded in producing an atomic bomb with uranium-235. On August 6, 1945, this bomb was dropped on Hiroshima. Another atomic bomb was dropped on Nagasaki on August 9.

When America came into the possession of such a bomb it held a military advantage over other countries.

In July 1949 the Soviet Union also test-exploded its first nuclear bomb. Its power was approximately equal to the American bomb then existing.

On October 3, 1952, England exploded its first atomic bomb on the Isle of Montebello (situated on the northwest coast of Australia).

In the quest for nuclear supremacy, both the Soviet Union and the United States moved towards the development of a nuclear weapon many times more powerful—the hydrogen bomb. A series of tests was undertaken by the United States in the Marshall Islands beginning in May 1951, and culminating in a successfully exploded hydrogen bomb in March 1954.

The actual power of the explosion was far stronger than had been originally calculated.

At approximately the same time, the Soviet Union also started its experimentations, exploding its first hydrogen bomb on August 12, 1953.

Today, guided missiles can be launched from their starting points and directed with accuracy at distant targets. The larger explosives are carried by missiles containing the fuel necessary for their propulsion. The gases from this fuel rush with tremendous velocity through a narrow opening. Science is in the process of discovering a fuel which is similar and more efficacious to deal with.

It is said that the Soviet Union already has available rockets with a range up to 600 miles. Soon to come are rockets with a range up to 1,080 miles—if they are not already in use.

It is said that America is attempting to develop rockets with a range of 1,440 miles.

Whether the intercontinental ballistic missile, with its range of 4,800 miles, already exists cannot be ascertained. The Soviet Union has claimed it already has such a missile.

Even without respect to intercontinental ballistic missiles, submarines could launch nuclear attacks on the United States.

The long-range rockets attain unbelievable speed. It is expected that an intercontinental rocket would not take more than twenty minutes to cross the ocean with a payload of nuclear explosive weighing from one to five tons.

How could an atomic war break out today? Not long ago there was talk of local or limited wars that could be contained. But today there is little difference between a local war or a global war. Rocket missiles will be used up to a range of 1,440 miles. The destruction should not be underestimated, even if caused only by a Hiroshima-type bomb.

It can hardly be expected that an enemy will refrain from using atomic bombs or the most devasting hydrogen bombs on large cities at the very outset of a war. One hydrogen bomb now exists that is a thousand times more powerful than the atomic bomb. It will have a destructive radius of many miles. The heat will be 100 million degrees. One can imagine how large would be the number of city-dwellers who would be destroyed by the pressure of the explosion, by flying fragments of glass, by heat and fire and by radioactive waves, even if the attack is only of short duration. The deadly radioactive contamination, as a consequence of the explosion, would have a range of some 45,000 square miles.

An American general has said to some Congressmen: "If at an interval of ten minutes 110 hydrogen bombs are dropped over the USA there would be a casualty list of about 70 million people; besides, some thousands of square miles would be made useless for a whole generation. Countries like England, West Germany, and France could be finished off with fifteen to twenty hydrogen bombs."

President Eisenhower has pointed out, after watching maneuvers under atomic attack, that defense measures in a future atomic war become useless. In these circumstances all one can do is to pray.

Indeed, not much more can be done in view of an attack by hydrogen bombs than to advise all people living to hide beneath a very strong wall made of stone or cement, and to throw themselves on the ground and to cover the back of their heads, and the body if possible, with cloth. In this way it may be possible to escape annihilation and death through radiation. It is very important that the immediate survivors are given non-radioactive food and drink, and that they be removed immediately from the radioactive district.

It is impossible, however, to erect walls and concrete ceilings of adequate thickness to cover an entire city. Where would the material and the means come from? How would a population find time even to run to safety in such bunkers?

In an atomic war there would be neither conqueror nor vanquished. During such a bombardment both sides would suffer the same fate. A continuous destruction would take place and no armistice or peace proposals could bring it to an end.

When people deal with atomic weapons, it is not a matter of superior arms which will decide the issue between them, but only: "Now we want to commit suicide together, destroying each other mutually . . ."

There is a reason for an English M.P. saying: "He who uses atomic weapons becomes subject to the fate of a bee, namely, when it stings it will perish."

Radioactive clouds resulting from a war between East and West would imperil humanity everywhere. There would be no need to use up the remaining stock of atomic and hydrogen bombs now running literally into the thousands.

A nuclear war is therefore the most senseless and lunatic act which could ever take place. This must be prevented.

When America had its atomic monopoly, it was not necessary to equip its allies with nuclear weapons. Owing to the end of the monopoly, however, this situation is changing. A whole family of nuclear weapons now exists that can be fitted into the military capability of smaller nations.

As a result, the United States is considering a departure from its stated principle not to put atomic weapons into the hands of other countries. If it does so, this could have the gravest consequences. On the other hand, it is comprehensible that the United States wishes to supply the NATO countries with such new weapons for defense against the Soviet Union. The existence of such arms constitutes a new cause of war between the Soviet Union and the U.S., one that did not exist before. Thus, the ground is laid open for a nuclear conflict on European soil. The Soviet Union can be reached with long-range rockets from European soil, as far as Moscow and Kharkov, up to 2,400 miles away. Similarly, London, Paris, and Rome are within easy reach of Soviet rocketry.

Rockets of an average range may be used for defense purposes by Turkey and Iran against the Soviet Union. They could penetrate deeply into its country with arms accepted from America.

The Soviet Union is countering those measures. Both America and the Soviet Union may now seek alliances with the Middle East by offering those countries various kinds of financial support. Therefore, events in the Middle East could endanger the peace of the world.

The danger of an atomic war is being increased by the fact that no warning would be given in starting such a war. Indeed, it could erupt merely on the basis of some incident. Thus, the time factor enters— the side that attacks first would have the initial advantage over the attacked. At the very start, the attacked would find himself sustaining losses which would reduce his fighting capacity considerably.

As a result, one has to be on the alert all the time. This factor constitutes an extreme danger in the event of a sudden outbreak of an atomic war. When one has to act with such speed, he has to reckon with the possibility that an error may occur on what is registered on the radar screen, and that this could result in the outbreak of an atomic war.

Attention was drawn to this danger by the American General Curtis LeMay. Quite recently the world found itself in such a situation. The radar station of the American Air Force and American Coastal Command indicated that an invasion of unidentified bombers was on the way. Upon this warning, the general who was in command of the strategic bomber force ordered that reprisal bombardment should be made. However, realizing that he was taking a great responsibility, he hesitated. Shortly afterwards, it was pointed out that the radar stations had committed a technical error. What could have happened if a less balanced general had been in his place!

In the future such dangers are likely to increase. Owing to the fact that small rockets exist which pass through the air with terrific speed and are over the target within a few minutes—defense possibilities become very limited. Only seconds remain to identify the markings on the radar screen, so that the counter-attack can spring into being. The theoretical defense consists in sending out missiles to explode the attacking missiles of the enemy before they complete their job, and also in releasing bombers with a view to destroying the ramps from which they are launched.

Such split-second operations cannot be left to the human brain. It works too slowly. The job has therefore been entrusted to an electronic brain.

Such are the heights of our civilization that a cold electronic brain rather than the moral conscience of many may decide human destiny. Are we so certain that an arithmetical or mechanical decision is really superior? The mechanism of the electronic brain may become faulty. It is dependent on the absolute reliability of its complicated functions. Everything has to click to the minutest detail.

Under the circumstances, the greater the number of countries, large or small, that become part of the nuclear arms terror the greater the terror. Naturally, America must assume that the weapons it entrusts to other nations will not be used irresponsibly. But accidents can happen. *Who* can guarantee that there may not a be a "blacksheep" acting on his own, without troubling about the consequences? Who is *able* to keep *all* countries under a situation of rational control? The dam is punctured and it may break down.

That such worries have become very real is shown by the reasoning of the 9,235 scientists on January 13, who petitioned the United Nations regarding the cessation of atomic tests. The statement says: "As long as atomic weapons remain in the hands of the three great powers, agreement on control is possible. However, if the tests continue and extend to other countries in possession of atomic weapons, the risks and responsibilities in regard to an outbreak of an atomic war becomes all the greater. From every point of view the danger in a future atomic war becomes all the more intense, so that an urgent renunciation of atomic weapons becomes absolutely imperative."

America has wisely declared that its objective is to outlaw nuclear weapons. Yet, at the same time, America seems to be moving away from the measures necessary to achieve it. America insists that the missiles it offers to other countries be accepted as quickly as possible. It wishes to hold such a position as to be able to maintain peace by nuclear deterrent. It happens, however, that most of the NATO countries are not in any hurry to acquire such weapons. An increasingly strengthened public opinion is the cause of this.

Public opinion in Europe has been convinced during recent months that under no circumstances should Europe be allowed to become a battlefield for an atomic war between the Soviet Union and America. From this position it will not deviate. The time is past when a European power could plan secretly to establish itself as a big power by manufacturing atomic weapons exclusively for its own use. In view of the fact that no public opinion would agree to such an undertaking, it becomes senseless even to prepare secretly for achieving such a plan.

Gone, too, is the time when NATO generals and European governments can decide on the establishments of launching sites and stockpiling of atomic weapons. In view of the fact that the dangers of atomic war and its consequences cannot be avoided, political procedure as employed hitherto can no longer be considered.

Only agreements that are sanctioned by public opinion are now valid.

Part III

What about the negotiations that could lead to the renunciation of nuclear weapons?

One reads and hears that the success of the projected Summit Conference must depend entirely on its every detail being diplomatically prepared beforehand. The best diplomacy is objectivity. One good way of preparing for a conference (if a respectful and well-meaning criticism is permissible) would be for the statesmen and other representatives to make a change from their present undiplomatic way of dealing with each other and to become diplomatic. Many unnecessary, thoughtless, discourteous, foolish, and offensive remarks have been made by both sides, and this has not been advantageous to the political atmosphere.

It would be fitting if those who have the authority to take the responsibility, and not those who have only nominal authority and who cannot move an inch from their instructions, would confer together.

It would be fitting to go ahead with the conference. For more than five months East and West have talked and written to one another, without any conclusions as to the date and the work program being reached. Public opinion everywhere is finding it difficult to accept this state of affairs and is beginning to ask itself whether a conference which comes into being so limpingly has any hope of really achieving anything.

It would be fitting to hold the conference in a town in some neutral European country, for example, Geneva, as was the case in 1955.

It would be fitting that at this conference only questions that have to do directly with the control and renunciation of nuclear weapons should be discussed.

It would be fitting if not too many people were present at the summit meeting. Only the highest personalities of the three nuclear powers together with their experts and advisers should take their seats there.

Attendance could also be opened on a consultative basis to the representatives of those peoples who—like the NATO countries with America—have connections in nuclear matters; they could then state their opinions on the decisions that hold such grave consequences also for them.

Apart from this, experience teaches us that unnecessarily large attendance brings no advantage to a conference.

The Summit Conference, therefore, is in no way an international or half international one, even though its decisions are of great importance to the whole of mankind.

The three nuclear powers and they alone must decide, in awareness of their responsibility to their peoples and to all mankind, whether or not they will renounce the testing and the use of nuclear weapons.

In regard to the planning of the conference, impartiality may justify one remark, which is that to date such planning has not been done objectively, and has therefore led nowhere. This leads to the thought that the outcome of a Summit Conference is bound to reflect what went into it.

What is the difference between the partial and the impartial; the fitting and the unfitting in this matter? It lies in the answer to the question on what basis the three nuclear powers decide whether or not to renounce the testing and the use of nuclear weapons.

The unobjective reply would be that the decision will depend on

whether an agreement is first reached on comprehensive disarmament
or not.

This is a false logic; it presumes that there could be an agreement
acceptable to both the East and the West on this issue. But previous
negotiations have shown that this is not to be expected; they became
stalled right at the start because East and West have been unable to
reach agreement even on the conditions under which such discussions
should take place.

The anticipated procedure itself is by its very nature not impartial.
It is based on false logic. The two vital issues so essential to the very
existence of mankind—the cessation of tests and the disposal of
nuclear weapons—cannot be made dependent on the Heavens performing the impossible political miracle that alone could insure that
none of the three nuclear powers would have any objections to a
complete agreement on disarmament.

The fact is that the testing and use of nuclear weapons carry in
themselves the absolute reasons for their being renounced. Prior agreement on any other conditions cannot be considered.

Both cause the deepest damage to human rights. The tests do harm
to peoples far from the territories of the nuclear powers—endangering
their lives and their health—and this in peace time. An atomic war,
with its resultant radioactivity, would make the land of peoples not
participating in such a war, unlivable. It would be the most unimaginably senseless and cruel way of endangering the existence of
mankind. That is why it must not be allowed to happen.

The three nuclear powers owe it to themselves and to mankind to
reach agreement on these absolute essentials without first dealing with
prior conditions.

The negotiations about disarmament are therefore not the fore-
runner of such agreement but the outcome of it. They start from the
point where agreement on the nuclear issues has been reached, and
their goal is to reach the point where the three nuclear powers and the
peoples who are connected with them must agree on guarantees that
will seek to avert the danger of a threat of a non-atomic nature taking
the place of the previous danger. Everything that the diplomats will
have done objectively to prepare the preliminaries to the conference
will keep its meaning even if it will be used not before renunciation,
but as the result of it.

Should agreement be reached on the outlawing of nuclear weapons,
this by itself will lead to a great improvement in the political situation.
As a result of such an agreement, time and distance would again become realities with their own right.

Nuclear weapons, used in conjunction with missiles, change a distant war to a war fought at close range. The Soviet Union and the

United States have become next-door neighbors in the modern world but live in constant fear of their lives every minute.

But if nuclear arms should be abolished, the proximity factor would be made less explosive.

Today America has her batteries of nuclear missiles readily available in Europe. Europe has become a connecting land strip between America and Russia, as if the Atlantic had disappeared and the continents had been joined.

But if atomic missiles are outlawed on the basis of effective and enforceable control, this unnatural state of affairs would come to an end. America would again become wholly America; Europe wholly Europe; the Atlantic again wholly the Atlantic Ocean.

The great sacrifices that America brought to Europe during the Second World War and in the years following it will not be forgotten. The many-sided and great help that Europe received from her and the thanks owing for this will not be forgotten.

But the unnatural situation created by the two world wars, that led to a dominating military presence in Europe, cannot continue indefinitely. It must gradually cease to exist—both for the sake of Europe and for the sake of America.

Now there will be shocked voices from all sides: What will become of poor Europe if American atomic weapons no longer defend it from within and from without? Will Europe be delivered to the Soviet? Must it be prepared to languish in a Communist-Babylonian imprisonment for long years?

What Europe and the Europeans have to agree about is that they belong together for better or for worse. This is a new historical fact that can no longer be by-passed politically.

Another factor that must be recognized politically is that it is no longer a question of subjugating peoples, but learning to get along with them intellectually, culturally, spiritually.

A Europe standing on its own has no reason to despair.

Disarmament discussions between the three nuclear powers must seek the guarantees that can bring about actual, total and durable disposal of nuclear weapons. The question of control and safeguards is a vital one. Reciprocal agreement will have to be reached about allowing international commissions to inspect and investigate on national soil.

One talks of giving aircraft belonging to a world police the right to fly at medium and high altitudes for purposes of aerial inspection.

One asks to what extent a state would be willing to subject itself to such control? It may be said that unfortunate incidents could easily occur as a result. And what about the power that should be entrusted to such a world control? Even the widest form of such control could never insure that everywhere and all the time war could be avoided. But it represents a reasonable basis on which, given time and some relaxation of tension, a workable world system of security might be built.

The same applies also in another matter. As a result of renouncing nuclear arms, the Soviet Union's military might insofar as Europe is concerned would be less affected than that of America. There would remain to the Soviet the many armed divisions with conventional weapons; with those divisions it could easily over-run the NATO states in western Europe—particularly Western Germany—without it being possible for anyone to come to their aid. With this in mind, the Soviet Union should agree in the course of disarmament negotiations to reduce her army, and to commit herself not to undertake steps against Germany. But here, too, no manner of detailed agreements and internationally guaranteed disarmament agreements would be enough. Therefore, we must strive continually to improve the situation, building brick by brick.

We live at a time when the good faith of peoples is doubted more than ever before. Expressions putting into doubt the trustworthiness of the next nation are bandied back and forth. They are based on what happened in the two world wars when the nations experienced dishonesty, injustice, and inhumanity from one another. How can a new trust come about?

We cannot continue in a situation of paralyzing mistrust. If we want to work our way out of the desperate situation in which we find ourselves another spirit must enter into the people. It can only come if the awareness of its necessity suffices to give us strength to believe in its coming. We must presuppose the awareness of this need in all the peoples who have suffered along with us. We must approach them in the spirit that we are human beings, all of us, and that we feel ourselves fitted to feel with each other; to think and to will together in the same way.

The awareness that we are all human beings together has become lost in war and politics. We have reached the point of regarding each other as only members of a people who is allied with us or against us, and our attitudes, prejudices, sympathies, or antipathies are all conditioned by that fact. Now we must rediscover the fact that we—all together—are human beings, and that we must strive to concede to each other what moral capacity we have.

That way we can begin to believe that also in other peoples there will arise the need for a new spirit, and that can be the beginning of a feeling of mutual trustworthiness towards each other. The spirit is a mighty force for transforming things. Let us have hope that the spirit can bring people and lands back to an awareness of enlighten-ment.

At this stage we have the choice of two risks. The one consists in continuing the mad atomic arms race with its danger of unavoidable atomic war in the near future. The other is in the renunciation of nuclear weapons, and the hope that America and the Soviet Union, and the peoples associated with them, will manage to live in peace. The first holds no hope of a prosperous future; the second does. We must risk the second.

In President Eisenhower's speech of November 7, 1957, we find the following: "What the world needs more than a gigantic leap into space is a gigantic leap into peace."

This gigantic leap consists in finding the courage to hope that the spirit of good sense will arise in all peoples and in all lands, a spirit sufficiently strong to overcome the insanity and the inhumanity.

Once agreement on renunciation of nuclear arms has been reached it would be the responsibility of the United Nations to undertake to see that now, as in the future, they would neither be made nor used. The danger that one or another people might attempt to manufacture nuclear weapons will have to be kept in mind for a long time.

The future holds many difficult problems. The most difficult of these will be the rights of access of overpopulated countries to neigh-boring lands.

But if in our time we renounce nuclear arms we will have taken the first step on the way to the distant goal of the end to war itself. If we do not do this we remain on the road that leads to atomic war and misery in the near future.

Those who are to meet at the Summit must be aware of this, so that they can negotiate with propriety, with the right degree of seri-ousness, and with a full sense of responsibility.

The Summit Conference must not fail. The will of mankind will not permit it.

Suggested Topics

1. Co-existence or co-extinction
2. The sinister isotopes
3. The dangers of chemical spraying of crops
4. Let's outlaw nuclear weapons.
5. "Clean" and "dirty" bombs
6. "Neither conqueror nor vanquished . . ."

KEY QUESTIONS FOR AWAKENING AFRICA

Tom Mboya

A member of the Legislative Council of Kenya, General Secretary of the Kenya Federation of Labour, and Chairman of the All-African People's Conference, Tom Mboya, who was born in 1930, is prominent among the new leaders of Africa in this era of awakened African nationalism and independent self-rule.

At the invitation of the American Committee on Africa, I recently visited the United States for a six-week lecture tour in an effort to explain the new Africa—its problems and aspirations—to the American people. I spoke in every section of the country, and met people of widely varied interests: Congressmen and Senators, State Department officials, labor leaders, Governors and Mayors, college and university students and teachers, newspaper men and broadcasters and Negro leaders. I think, therefore, that my impressions are fairly representative of a cross-section of the American people.

Having visited the United States in 1956, I was much impressed with the increase in knowledge about Africa. The questions I was asked were based more on interested understanding than on detached curiosity. Four questions in particular which seemed to trouble Americans came up at almost every meeting. I should like to answer them here.

(1) Are Africans ready for self-government?

I was often reminded of the lack of adequate numbers of educated personnel to run the new governments which we in Africa have been demanding. I was told that the high illiteracy rate in many dependent territories would make it impossible for Africans to operate a democracy successfully.

While conceding that Africa has a long way to go toward creating a generally literate community, I answered that this was a common argument used by colonial powers in defense of their continued rule. Often my questioners assumed that the colonial powers were primarily concerned with the education of our people, and that there were deliberate training programs looking toward the day of independence.

In fact, however, colonial systems give priority to—and indeed are based upon—such activities as permit or promote the human and material exploitation of the people and territories concerned. Effort is concentrated on extractive industries and quick profits. In every case, investment in education, public health and other social development programs lags behind.

Ghana's recent history clearly illustrates what I mean. When the all-African Cabinet took over the Government, about 20 per cent of the country's children were in school. In five years, this Government has raised the figure to 85 per cent and continues to open a new school every other day. There had been nothing to equal this in eighty years of colonial rule.

In areas with a European settler community the problem is even worse. Not only does African education lag behind, but African political rights are subordinated to European domination. Thus, while France has ultimately conceded freedom for Tunisians and Moroccans, she refuses to recognize that Algerians—a people with similar aspirations, history and background—are entitled to the same status. The British concede the rights of Africans on the West Coast, in Somalia and Uganda—and soon in Tanganyika—but refuse to go all the way in Kenya, and certainly dispute these rights in the Central African Federation of Nyasaland and the Rhodesias.

In Africa, Britain has adopted various formulas of qualitative franchise, not based on any training program for independence, but aimed at preserving the position of the white settlers. Thus, in Uganda, where there is a comparatively small settler community, literacy in the vernacular is the minimum qualification for the vote. But in Kenya, where adult suffrage is granted settlers and Asians, the African franchise is limited by such qualifications as an income of £120 or eight years of education. In Central Africa, in addition to rigid control of the number of Africans allowed in the Parliament, the initial qualification for the vote is a £750 income.

In Portuguese areas there is not even a pretense at development or training for future self-government. The Portuguese maintain that Angola and Mozambique are integral parts of Portugal, and insist that all indigenous people may be assimilated as Portuguese citizens, but less than 1 per cent of the African population has been. Slave labor, forced labor and brutal treatment of Africans is common. No freedom of assembly, association or the press exists and schools are rigidly controlled by the state with the apparent sanction of the church.

In these so-called multi-racial areas, representation in the Legislatures is based on communal divisions—i.e., fourteen elected members for 60,000 Europeans and an equal number for 6,000,000 Africans in Kenya, ten elected members for 20,000 Europeans and an equal number for 8,000,000 Africans in Tanganyika. In Kenya, the per capita expenditure on the education of a European child amounts to £32 a year, while that for an African child is £5.

This, then, is my answer to those who ask us to wait until we are prepared by the colonial powers for self-government. While we are appreciative of the benefits we have derived from our contacts with Europe and other parts of the world—especially in the post-war period —we are convinced that if we are to develop rapidly and effectively, as indeed we must if we are to meet the technological and scientific challenges of the twentieth century, we must not only have an effective voice in the government of our countries, but become masters of our own fate. To suggest that this would lead to an overnight reversion to barbarity shows an utter disregard for history and the fact that Africa, despite her many temporary handicaps, lives in the twentieth century, receptive to all the influences of the attitudes and developments of the present.

The question is not whether African freedom will come, but how and when. Even in areas where there is white settlement it must come, and it is futile to think otherwise. In this context, all one can say about South Africa is that her prospects look blacker each year.

(2) *Is the African independence movement democratic?*

African nations, like all others, enjoy the right to experiment, and above all the right to make mistakes. It is true that a lot depends on the personality of the leadership, especially during the early days of independence. There does not seem to be, however, any alternative to this period of youth and adventure. To think that continued colonial rule would offer a solution is not only to be unrealistic but to indulge in the highest degree of wishful thinking.

If honest mistakes are made we should not be apologetic, for this is part of the process of operating a democracy the world over. It is ironic—and, indeed, flattering—that the older powers should ask us to guarantee perfection when they have not, even after hundreds of years, reached perfection themselves.

Some non-Africans are concerned about the development of opposition parties and others about the forms that governmental institutions will take. Many people seem to expect that Africa must keep what she inherits from her former colonial masters. Africa cannot, however, for very obvious reasons, adopt a blueprint of European or American institutions. Her governmental institutions must recognize Africa's cultural and social background and must move away from the forms used by the colonial powers—fitted for indirect rule—to a representative system.

Opposition parties are a desirable and healthy development, but they must not merely point accusing fingers at the party in power when difficulties arise. Both sides must play the game according to certain rules.

It is unrealistic to expect effective opposition parties in the early days of independence, when the momentum and personality of the liberation movement is still strong and popular, and when genuine differences are usually lacking. To suggest that the popular leaders who combine during the struggle for liberation should break up and form different parties because the book so requires is not only reckless but is to ignore the urgent problems that a new state faces. The solution to these problems requires a stable Government that can also offer security for expanded economic growth. The responsibility thrust on the shoulders of both the party in power and the often weak, ineffective opposition party is tremendous and one which requires strength of character, honesty of purpose and, above all, a deep conviction in the service of the country and the people.

(3) Does the policy of nonalignment adopted by Africans mean that they are falling victim to Communist propaganda?

In so far as the African struggle is one against colonial rule, and since all leaders have publicly committed themselves to freedom and universal suffrage, Africa is essentially committed to the democratic tradition. In this common identity the free world has a position of advantage over the Communists.

But, although African leaders do not take a neutral position in their choice of democracy and freedom, I doubt whether this is the position the West truly represents in the eyes of the uncommitted world today. Inconsistencies between standards preached and actual practices based on expediency, and the priority given alliances over the basic human rights of peoples in Africa, Asia and the Middle East have contributed to a loss of faith and confidence.

The West has friendly embraces for the Union of South Africa, despite her racist policies and denial of human rights to 11,000,000 non-white people. Why, our people ask, doesn't the West put South Africa in the same category with the Soviet Union? Why is Portugal's use of slave labor not classified with the Siberian slave labor camps? France uses NATO arms supplied by the United States against Algerians. The British shoot more than fifty unarmed demonstrators in Nyasaland and their agents beat to death eleven Kenyans in the Hola detention camp. The free world raises not a finger. Contrast this with the reaction to Hungary and Tibet! The Africans wonder why double standards are used where human rights are involved, and naturally suspect the motives of some of the nations in the free world.

It should be understood that we feel a special kinship with American Negroes, and that we see our struggles as closely related. Segregation robs the United States of the moral standing she needs if she is to give effective leadership to the free world. All the good that she does—even the existence of Supreme Court judgments and other efforts to secure integration—is hardly noticed, whereas Little Rock or a Mississippi lynching receives front-page publicity.

One cannot overlook the fact that conditions exist in all underdeveloped areas that provide fertile ground for Communist propaganda. As I look at this situation, I have come to the conclusion that if the free world is to be effective it must concern itself with how best to remove these conditions—poverty, disease, ignorance and racism. It should devise a freedom offensive rather than merely engage in a negative opposition to communism. Too often the free world moves only in emergency situations, pouring in money and guns too late. It is the compromise with principle to accommodate colonialism and racism practiced by countries in the West that undermines the moral capacity of the free world.

(4) What is the future of the white settlers in Africa?

The fear of possible victimization of immigrant groups or of anti-white racism on the part of Africans is often expressed. On the contrary, experience in the independent states so far has shown a deliberate policy of assuring foreign investors of their safety.

The problem really is one for the immigrants themselves. They have come to regard as a right the position of privilege and domination they have always enjoyed. They refuse to adapt themselves to change, and regard equality for all as injustice.

When Europeans emigrate to America they are content to be called Americans; equally they are content to be called Canadians when they go to Canada. They insist on democratic equality there. But in Africa, they are ashamed to be called Africans. How then can we solve this problem for them?

In conclusion, one thing that I must emphasize is that no country can afford to ignore the emergence of new nations in Africa. Each year new states will be born, and with these changes must be established new relationships. Above all, it must be recognized that emergent Africa must not only claim but assert her right to interpret and speak for herself.

Suggested Topics

1. Are Africans ready for self-government?
2. Racism in the Union of South Africa
3. Colonial rulers and second-class citizens
4. The effect of segregation in the United States on African opinion
5. Is the free world handling Africa correctly?
6. "Fertile ground for Communist propaganda"

WHO ARE THE FORMOSANS?   *J. Raymond Dyer*

A graduate of Princeton University and of Harvard Law School, J. Raymond Dyer is an attorney in St. Louis. His interest in Formosa began when he was a Naval Reserve officer during World War II. After serving in the Pacific, he received special training in the economy, geography, and history of Formosa at the Navy Military Government School at Princeton, and later studied the Japanese language and the Far East in general at the Army Military Government School at Stanford.

For the past five years, we have heard a great deal about Formosa but very little about the Formosans. Yet if we are to talk about the "vital stake of the free world in a free Formosa," as President Eisenhower did in his January 24 Message to Congress, we should first know what we are talking about when we say "free Formosa."

Formosa was a Japanese colony from 1895 until the close of the Second World War. Today, Chiang Kai-shek's Nationalist Government occupies it and exercises *de facto* sovereignty over it, but no *de jure* recognition of Nationalist sovereignty over Formosa and the Pescadores has even been accorded by the United States government or any other.

When President Roosevelt and Prime Minister Churchill met with Generalissimo Chiang at Cairo during the war, they pledged themselves and their governments to "restore" to the Republic of China Formosa and the Pescadores, which had been "stolen" from China by Japan. But although Great Britain recognizes the Communist govern-

Reprinted from *The Reporter*, March 10, 1955. By permission of *The Reporter* and the author.

ment, Sir Winston has recently declared that the Cairo declaration is out of date. We, of course, do not recognize the Communist Chinese régime. The peace treaty with Japan finally signed in 1951 did no more than abrogate the sovereignty of Japan over Formosa without bestowing that sovereignty anywhere else. We have signed and ratified a Mutual Defense Treaty with the Nationalist Republic of China. In this treaty the territories referred to in respect of the Republic of China were specified as Formosa and the Pescadores. But in passing the treaty, the Senate declared that this did not in any way affect the legal status of these islands. At the present time, no one has sovereignty over Formosa.

The issue of Formosa has become an international problem. Certainly we would not be interfering in a civil war if the Communist Chinese invaded Formosa and we entered the conflict to hold them off. But neither would we be interfering in an internal matter if we concerned ourselves with the kind of government which the Nationalists on Formosa are in fact imposing on the Formosans. We have the right to ask that the wishes of the Formosans themselves be considered.

Historically, the Formosans are no more Chinese than the Mexicans are Spanish. The original settlers who came to Formosa some two thousand years ago were of proto-Malay stock. Before most of them became assimilated among themselves and with later comers, they comprised numerous tribes. At present there are only seven tribes of pure aborigines. The peoples of two of them bear direct relationship, respectively, to the Tagalog and Igorot peoples of the Philippines. The people of one of the tribes closely resemble the Dyaks of Borneo. Those of another, the Tsuo tribe, closely resemble both in culture and features the North American Algonquin tribes. The Ami, another tribe of Formosan aborigines, are, according to ethnologist Carl von Hoffman, a Polynesian people. That all came from the south, and not from the Chinese mainland, is accepted by anthropologists as undisputed.

Not more than 160,000 of them remained on Formosa at the time of the last Japanese census. But the others had not died off, as had the aborigines of Tasmania; through the centuries they had blended with peoples coming to their island.

These different proto-Malay tribes settled different parts of the island. The Taiyals and the Paiwans on the west coast were the tribes with which the Chinese first came in contact. The name "Taiwanese," by which the Chinese called these people, was a contraction of the names of these two tribes. The Japanese adopted the Chinese name Taiwan for the island.

The first recorded Chinese incursion against the Formosan aborigines was in A.D. 605, over a thousand years before Jamestown was settled.

The Taiwanese in turn raided the Fukien coast of China opposite and such raids and counter-raids went on for centuries. In an age when rape was considered a legitimate practice in war and slave concubinage an accepted way of Oriental life, many of the west coast Taiwanese began to look like the Chinese.

Early in the sixteenth century Japanese trading settlements were established on the north coast. But Japanese women did not come to Formosa; it was too dangerous. So the women of the Japanese settlements were all aborigines, and another ingredient was added to the racial strain. In the south, Chinese pirate traders held sway over most of the ports, subject to constant harassment by the Formosans. But on the east coast and in the mountainous interior, the Formosan aborigines continued unmolested by outsiders. Some of the tribes intermingled freely with each other and also with the Japanese, who were racially somewhat akin, but some did not. At that time it was the Chinese pirate looters who were hated by the Formosans and not the Japanese traders.

Counting on that and expecting that the Formosans would become his allies, the Japanese governor of Nagasaki, Toan Murayama, attempted the conquest of Formosa in 1615. He did not have much difficulty in ousting the Chinese, but he completely misjudged the temper of the Formosans. He was beaten, and on his return to Japan was executed for disrupting Japanese commerce. The Japanese trading settlements, though temporarily abandoned, were soon re-established with the sanction of the Formosans. The Chinese pirate traders came back too.

It was the Portuguese in the sixteenth century who became the first Europeans to sight the island. They christened it Ilha Formosa, "beautiful island." The Spanish came to Formosa in 1626. They settled in the north, established Christian missions, drove out the Japanese traders, set up schools, and converted many Formosans to Christianity.

Early in the seventeenth century, the Dutch came to Formosa. In 1622, having established a small depot on Formosa at what is now Anping, the Dutch seized the Pescadores. This meant that the Chinese pirate traders, sailing those waters in their none too seaworthy junks, no longer had the harbors and leeward shelters of the Pescadores to put in to. To regain them, the Chinese officials of Fukien Province obligingly "ceded" the Japanese settlement of Anping to the Dutch, and with it all Chinese claim to Formosa. The Pescadores meant little to the Dutch, whose ships were more seaworthy, once the harbors of Formosa were open to them.

The Dutch who came there were primarily traders and exploiters. backed by soldiers, but they were also good organizers, and they organized the Formosans with whom they came into contact. They also taught some of them to speak Dutch, and added some Dutch blood to the Formosan bloodstream. In 1642 the Dutch drove the Spanish out.

But the Dutch, who had been permitted to retain their trading stations in Japan, never organized their various holdings on a centralized colonial basis. That later proved their undoing. Commencing in 1642, a series of crises in China during the Manchu invasion of that country drove many Chinese to Formosa, some as Ming loyalists (like the Nationalists some three hundred years later), some merely as refugees in economic distress. For the first time the Chinese coming to Formosa were not merely pirate traders but agricultural settlers. Between 1623, when the Dutch first came in any number, and 1662, when they were driven out, the Chinese population on Formosa increased to nearly fifty thousand. The permanent Dutch inhabitants numbered only some three thousand, mostly soldiers.

This presented an opportunity the Formosans, augmented by the Chinese newcomers, were not slow to grasp.

There arose a remarkable Formosan national hero named Koxinga. Born in Japan of a Fukien Chinese pirate-trader father, nominally Christian, and a Japanese mother (who, Formosan legend has it, was really an aboriginal Formosan), Koxinga inherited from his rich father a fleet of some three thousand junks. His father had served the Portuguese at Macao and from him Koxinga learned the art of European warfare. In 1651, after being ousted from Amoy by the Manchus, he took the Pescadores from the Chinese, whose garrison had been called to the mainland. There he gathered a sea force of some twenty-five thousand. He trained it for eleven years and then, in 1661, descended on the Dutch forts of Providentia at Tainan and Zeelandia at Anping. After nine months of fighting the Dutch capitulated, completely overwhelmed. Next year they tried to recapture their strongholds, but were beaten off.

The kingdom of Koxinga was formed and the first independent government of Formosa came into being in 1662. Koxinga soon died, but his son carried the rebellion to the north. Both had managed to weld the conflicting Formosan factions together. In 1668 the last of the Dutch left for Java. For the first time in history, an Asian war lord had wrested an Asian territory from a strong European power and had set up an independent government in its stead. That is the heritage of freedom the Formosans cling to.

It was not the Chinese who, in the seventeenth century, drove the Japanese out of Formosa. It was the Spaniards and the Dutch. And it was not the Chinese who drove the Dutch out, after the Dutch had driven out the Spaniards. It was Koxinga. That gave to the Formosans a distinction no other Asian people could claim.

But Koxinga's son was not satisfied with his Formosan kindom. Like the Nationalists today, he wanted to reinvade the mainland. His forces made frequent invasions of the China coast, and went up the Yangtze as far as Nanking. These expeditions frittered away much of the strength of the Formosan kingdom.

Then, in 1683, the Manchus, through bribery and guile, enticed Koxinga's twelve-year-old grandson, who had succeeded to the Formosan throne on the death of his father, to Peking. There he was forced to give up his throne, receiving in return the high-sounding title of Sea-quelling Duke. The Manchus took over Formosa. However, they took it over by infiltration rather than by conquest.

Much of the Chinese immigration to Formosa ceased in 1683, with the fall of the kingdom of Koxinga and the infiltration of the island by the Manchu overlords. The Manchu overlords discouraged immigration, a policy the Japanese copied more than two hundred years later. Formosan Chinese were in a constant state of rebellion, and the Manchus did not want to have anything more on their hands than they could cope with.

That the Formosan Chinese were disaffected is not surprising when it is remembered that most of them, at that time, were Ming loyalists, and that Ming loyalists hated the Manchus. Furthermore, their spirits, like those of the aborigines, were fired by the memory of Koxinga. In common cause they rebelled against the Manchus.

Twice they threw off the Manchu yoke, once in 1722 and again, for three years starting in 1786, during the period known in Formosan history as the Great Rebellion. After that there were many unsuccessful rebellions—the last in 1884, when, seizing the opportunity afforded by a French naval victory over the Chinese at Keelung, the Formosans struck, only to be repulsed by their Chinese masters with bloody losses.

There was one other period in their history besides Koxinga's when Formosa was free: That was for a dramatic five-month period in 1895, as the Republic of Formosa. It is strange that so little has been said about it. At the time of its formation the New York *Tribune* for May 26, 1895, carried the announcing headlines on its front page: A RE-PUBLIC IN FORMOSA—FOREIGN POWERS INFORMED OF THE ISLAND'S INDE-PENDENCE. Indeed, for five months that "Butterfly Republic," as it was later called, was the *de facto* government of Formosa, reported as such in the log of the old U.S.S. *Concord,* which was lying off Tansui at the time. The postage stamps of the Republic of Formosa are collectors' items, and its flag is an even rarer museum piece.

The Formosan Declaration of Independence, on May 23, 1895, came about as the result of the Treaty of Shimonoseki, which had been ratified by China fifteen days earlier. That treaty ended the Sino-

Japanese War. In it China relinquished all claim of sovereignty over Formosa and undertook to cede the island to Japan. It did so as the price it had to pay to keep the Japanese Army away from Peking. Since the armistice excluded Formosa from its terms, the treaty left Japan free to carry on its war there. To conquer Formosa, the Japanese had to fight the Formosans, not the Chinese. And when China "ceded" Formosa to Japan, just as the Chinese officials of Fukien Province had "ceded" it to the Dutch 272 years earlier, China gave up what did not belong to China, at least in large measure.

True, the Chinese government exercised what in international law is called a "sphere of influence" over the island, and by the Treaty of Shimonoseki "ceded" that, but as far as actual jurisdictional sovereignty was concerned, China's ownership of Formosa was limited to the north, west, and south coastal cities and their contiguous agricultural hinterlands. In the mountainous interior and on the east coast, China exercised no sovereignty whatever.

Indeed, from 1867 onward, China had officially disclaimed jurisdiction over the peoples of the east coast and the mountainous interior. These, very much like the Indians of our own West at that time, harassed travelers and menaced foreign shipping with their raiding. Admiral Bell of the U.S. East Asia Fleet proposed that our government should require China to extend its protective jurisdiction over east Formosa. But nothing came of the proposal. China continued right down to the Treaty of Shimonoseki to disavow all responsibility for the actions of the east-coast Formosans. Nor was China ever successful in subduing the mountain people of the interior.

The Republic of Formosa's Declaration of Independence, a curious document in this day, and one that seems to have been lost sight of by our government, was made public to the people of Formosa and cabled to the European and American powers and to the Emperor of Japan on May 23, 1895. By it the "literati and people of Formosa" expressed their "determination to resist subjection to Japan" and "declared themselves an independent Island Republic."

The Republic of Formosa came into being because of the resentment of the Formosans at having been sold down the river to Japan, and because of their deep-rooted desire to be free from all overlordship. It was a comic-opera republic in some respects, with a former Montana bartender as Minister of War, and former Chinese officials as its leaders. But the Formosan population supported it and Formosan soldiers died for it, and it succumbed only to the overwhelming superiority of the Japanese.

Then followed fifty years of Japanese rule. The Formosans were suppressed, but they were pushed together—by, among other things, being made to learn Japanese. They clung to such of their old customs as were permitted, but they could not help adopting many of the forcibly imposed customs and much of the culture of their conquerors.

During the period when Formosa was a Japanese colony, Japanese nationals held all key government posts and were the executives, foremen, and teachers. They transformed the Formosans into a people even more distinct from the mainland Chinese than they had previously been. They instilled in them an appreciation of the order and security of life and property achieved by the Japanese adminstration. Freed from the pulling and hauling of Chinese politics and the extortions of Chinese officialdom, the Formosans were welded into one people—a far more homogeneous people than the mainland Chinese.

The Japanese occupation brought relative economic prosperity to the Formosans. Japan imposed a technological revoltion in both industry and agriculture that put Formosa well ahead of the Chinese mainland. Nevertheless, the Formosans wanted freedom, and the Japanese knew it. When, following the "China Incident," the first Chinese bomber came over the Formosan capital on February 18, 1938, the Japanese alerted their anti-aircraft guns around the public buildings before they sounded the air-raid alarm, and then trained the guns not at the sky but on the Formosan population in the streets.

When Japan surrendered in 1945 the Formosans thought they would at last get the self-government they wanted. They welcomed the Chinese, who came to their island as liberators. But their hopes were soon dashed.

In the fall of 1945, Chiang Kai-shek sent a general, Chen Yi, to occupy Formosa. Chen Yi and his entourage took over the entire economy, and within a year it went to pieces. Unemployment was rampant; most middle-class Formosans were reduced to bankruptcy. Chinese from the mainland arrived in droves and plundered whatever they could get.

The Formosans grew more and more rebellious. In early 1947, riots broke out. Conservative Formosans pleaded with Chen Yi to make some reforms. But at the very same time that Chen Yi was promising not to bring more troops into Taipei, Nationalist troops were marching toward the city.

A small committee of leading Formosans then appealed directly to Chiang Kai-shek and drew up a list of demands. They got their answer the night they presented their proposals for reform. Nationalist troops swarmed into Taipei and machine-gunned the crowds there. A systematic effort was made by the Nationalists to eliminate all Formosans of standing. In this famous massacre of March, 1947, ten thousand Formosans were killed.

In 1949 the Nationalist Government in China fled to Formosa, and the waves of Chinese coming there from the mainland increased. All together 2.5 million Chinese Nationalists, military and civilian, have been added since the Second World War to a Formosan population that by now numbers nearly eight million.

With the coming to Formosa of the Chiang Government itself, the Formosans expected some improvement in their lot. But in January, 1950, native leaders warned that the Formosans might revolt against the Nationalists. A group working for Formosan independence addressed a memorandum to the President of the United Nations General Assembly pleading for U.N. relief against the Nationalist régime of "carpet baggers" and "highway robbers" on Formosa.

Now the island of Formosa and the life of the people—indigenous or immigrant—have become the stake in a colossal battle of principle. Should the principle of Race prevail and the Formosans be united to the Chinese mainlanders under Mao, or should Strategy have the last word, and in that case whose strategic interests? Or should the principle of Sovereignty be upheld—but represented by which Chinese Government?

As there is no prospect for any fair answer to all these questions, and since the answer should not be left to the caprice of war, perhaps it would not be a bad idea to let the Formosans themselves, old and new, have their own say on where they belong and how they would like to be ruled.

Suggested Topics

1. Communist China and the United Nations
2. A solution to an international dilemma
3. Occupied lands in the world today
4. Nationalism and the Formosa problem
5. The struggle for power in Asia

THE AMERICAN SCENE

SHOULD AMERICAN HISTORY
BE REWRITTEN? A Debate by Allan Nevins and
Matthew Josephson

One of the nation's leading historians, Allan Nevins is Emeritus Professor of History at Columbia University, a two-time winner of the Pulitzer Prize, a biographer of note, and one of the guiding spirits in the "Oral History" project to record the voices of prominent contemporary figures.

A former editor of *New Republic* and other publications, Matthew Josephson is best known for *The Robber Barons* (1934), a study of the major American capitalists; his other books include perceptive studies of Victor Hugo, Zola, and Stendhal. His biography of Edison appeared in 1959.

YES   *Allan Nevins*

One curious thing about history, as Philip Guedalla said, is that it really happened. Another curious fact about history is that while it was happening nobody really understood its meaning.

John Fiske, pausing one day in his young manhood before the window of Little, Brown & Co. in Boston, saw a volume within entitled "Pioneers of France in the New World" and noted that its author was identified as the man who had written "The Conspiracy of Pontiac." He remembered that when that earlier volume appeared he had wondered whether Pontiac was a barbarous chieftain of

Reprinted from *The Saturday Review*, February 6, 1954. By permission of *The Saturday Review* and the authors.

medieval Europe. He recalled also that some teacher at Harvard had once expressed the view that the French and Indian War was a dull squabble of no real significance to students of history. Passing on, Fiske wondered why any one should write about French pioneers in America. He lived to pen an essay on Francis Parkman which not only placed that author at the head of American historians (where he yet stands), but recognized that the epic significance of the struggle of Britain and France for the mastery of North America—a significance which Parkman had first expounded—could hardly be overstated. An interpretation of our continental history which nowadays we assume no child could miss had been beyond the grasp of the brilliant young John Fiske in the 1860's.

The idea that history can ever be so well written that it does not need rewriting can be held only by those foolish people who think that history can ever ascertain exact truth. It cannot. We can go further than the assertion of that truism: we can say, "Fortunate for history that it cannot ascertain exact truth!" If history were a photograph of the past it would be flat and uninspiring. Happily, it is a painting; and, like all works of art, it fails of the highest truth unless imagination and ideas are mixed with the paints. A hundred photographs of London Bridge look just alike and convey altogether a very slight percentage of the truth, but Turner's Thames and Whistler's Thames, though utterly different, both convey the river with a deeper truth.

All parts of our history are always being rewritten; no segment of it, from 1492 to 1952, is not now in need of vigorous rewriting. Whenever an expert applies himself to the scrutiny of a special area he at once sounds a lusty call for more searching exploration of the terrain. Douglas Freeman, carrying Washington through the Revolution, agreed with Bernard Knollenberg, writing a history of that war, that every part of the Revolutionary struggle needs the most searching reexamination and the boldest reinterpretation. Merrill Jensen states in the preface to his study of the Confederation that the entire period 1783-1789 demands a study that will embrace every state and every act of Congress. There are men who believe that the historical study of the Civil War period has only just begun—and they are right. Margaret Leech, now completing a study of the McKinley Administration, is convinced that a hundred research workers should be set to exploration of the dark nooks and secret crannies of the time.

"In vain the sage, with retrospective eye," wrote Pope, "would from the apparent what conclude the why." The three main reasons why history constantly needs reinterpretation include something more than the impossibility of ever learning all the truth about all the motives and actions of the past.

The chief of the three reasons is the need of every generation for a reinterpretation to suit its own preconceptions, ideas, and outlook. Every era has its own climate of opinion. It thinks it knows more than the preceding era; it thinks it takes a wider view of the universe. Every era, too, is affected by cataclysmic events which shift its point of view; the French Revolution, the Metternichian reaction, the movement for national unification in Italy, the United States, and Germany, the apogee of Manchester Liberalism, and so on down to the multiple crisis of our atomic age. We see the past through a prism which glows and sparkles as new lights catch its facets. Much of the rewriting of history is a readjustment to this prism. George Bancroft's spectrum was outmoded a few years after his laborious "last revision"; Charles A. Beard's begins to be outworn today, for we now possess what Beard would have called a new frame of reference.

As a second reason, new tools of superior penetrative power are from time to time installed in the toolshed of even our rather unprogressive race of historians. Our council for research in the social sciences (it should be studies) justly emphasizes the value of overlapping disciplines. Much could be said for the contention that the best historians nowadays are prepared in some other field than that of history. Thus Wesley Clair Mitchell, the historian of the greenbacks, of business cycles, and of the ebb and flow of economic activity, whose National Bureau of Economic Research inspired so much fruitful historical writing, was trained as an economist. (He also was trained by John Dewey, who gave courses under all sorts of titles, but "every one of them dealt with the same subject—how we think.") Beard was trained as a political scientist. Parrington was trained as a student of literature. Carl Becker was trained in European history but wrote in the American field. James Henry Breasted was first trained in theology, a fact which stood him in good stead when this pioneer of Egyptology in America began to trace the development of conscience and religion in the Ancient East. Not one historian in fifty knows as much as he should of the tool called statistics, or of psychology, or of economic geography, or of ecology. The kinship between Halford J. Mackinder, the geographer, and Frederick J. Turner, the historian, in loosing seminal ideas showed what the geographer could learn from history, and the historian from geography.

But the third great reason why history is rewritten is simply because the constant discovery of new materials necessitates a recasting of our view of the past. We might think that this would one day cease, but it never does. Everyone who has laboriously mapped any historical subject appreciates the impact of new facts upon that map, blurring some lines and defining new ones. Happy are those who live to rewrite their books, as Parkman rewrote one of his—"LaSalle and the Great

West." One would have said that all the materials for a history of the Revolution had been assembled in print by the innumerable agencies, local, state, and national, devoted to that effort, but Freeman assures us that the great archives like the Massachusetts Historical Society, the American Philosophical Society, and the main state libraries bulge with unstudied documents. One would have said that all the material for the history of the Confederate War Office had been studied and restudied; but behold!, the diary of the third officer of that department, Kean, is suddenly deposited in the University of Virginia, and we find it possible to make a sweeping reassessment of the Southern military administration.

Thus, the idea that history is photography is set at naught. It is art; it constantly requires a new mixture of pigments, new points of view, new manipulation of light and shade; and as an art it presents an endless challenge to the writer who perceives that the highest truth of history will always transcend a statement of fact; that, indeed, historical fact is but a foundation for the truth won by imagination and intellectual power.

The best history is always interpretive, but this does not mean that the best history is consciously or ostentatiously interpretive. The work of the historical masters, from Thucydides to Trevelyan, illustrates the fact that interpretation is most effective when implicit rather than explicit. The true historical attitude is a search for truth about a situation, force, or event—the War of 1812, the Abolitionist impulse, Pearl Harbor—which slowly, painfully, accurately dredges up an unforeseen interpretation. That is, history properly operates by the inductive, not the deductive, method. The merit of an Olympian historian like Parkman is that he says in effect: "Let us collect and collate all the relevant facts and find what conclusions emerge from their impartial analysis." The cardinal weakness of a controversial historian like Beard is that he repeatedly gave the impression—perhaps falsely —of having said to himself: "Let us take this provocative theory of the truth, and see how impressive an array of facts we can collect in its support." Ideas in history, that is, should be applied in subordination to the ascertainment of all the facts, and not in control of the ascertainment of one picked body of facts. Hence it is that nothing could be more absurd than to try to predict in advance the interpretations to be applied to our history by future writers—who will certainly go their own way. But we may legitimately make some guesses—they are not prophecies, but mere guesses, offered with due modesty—as to the drift of some of the new interpretations.

As American history lengthens and the past falls into longer perspective, we tend not so much to discard major interpretations entirely as to place new ones beside them; not so much to substitute one simple synthesis for another as to embrace old monistic views in a new and complex synthesis. During the first century of our national history, 1775-1875, three great dominant developments lift themselves above all others. They are the establishment of American Independence, political, economic, and finally cultural, from Europe; the westward movement for the conquest and development of the continent; and the abolition of slavery and a Southern way of life in a civil war which vindicated national unity. Some students, to be sure, would select other elements in our historical fabric, but three special students out of five and nine lay readers out of ten would, I believe, choose these. Now it is evident to a cursory view that each of the three lent itself at first to a simple monistic interpretation, expounded in the work even of subtle historians; and that within one or two generations this simple view of the past was replaced by a dual or multiple interpretation. What had been a flat telescopic image was given depth and reality by a stereopticon lens.

Thus it was that the old simple view of the Revolution as a politico-military struggle was amplified and enriched by subsequent views of the Revolution as a great movement for social and institutional change of a purely internal character. The old simple view of the conflict of North and South as centering in the slavery struggle was widened and deepened by later treatments of that collision as arising also from the increasing moral, social, economic, and cultural differences between the two sections. The old simple view of westward expansion as significant for what the pioneer did in changing the wilderness was immensely enlarged by Turner's thesis that a greater significance lay in what the wilderness did in changing the pioneer.

Nowadays the character of a fourth great development, accomplished and sealed in the last fifty years of our national life, can hardly be missed. On that new phase of our history, too, general agreement will perhaps be found. We have become first a great world power, and then *the* great world power. We have moved first into the open arena of world affairs, and then into the very center of that arena. We now view our national past from the vantage-point of this new turn, and with the changed perspective which it gives us.

Just as John Fiske saw our history from 1607 to 1789 as an evolutionary preparation for the gift of practical democracy and the Anglo-American principle of self-government to the world in the shape of our Constitution and Federal system; just as Von Holst saw the whole period from 1776 to 1861 as a preparation for the vindication of human liberty and national unity; so now we have historians who view our whole national life as an unconscious preparation for the time when we should become Protector of the Faith for all democratic peoples; when, having turned away from Western European affairs until we gained first place among the nations, we returned to them as the pivot and support of Western European civilization. These writers regard American history not in terms of the Western continent, but in terms of an Atlantic community. We find, indeed, that we never left that community; that the Seven Years' War was our first world war, the Revolution our second; that we have but awakened to our consciousness of a global role. And when these historians write of our national future they speak not of short-term objects, but of what Lincoln called "man's vast future."

This tremendous change of the past forty or fifty years—this emergence of America to the leadership of the Western World—will undoubtedly affect our children's children, and the long generations to come, in the most sweeping way. It will loom up in time to come as tremendously as the great changes which preceded it—as the Revolution internal and external, the American conquest of the frontier and the frontier's conquest of the American, the death of slavery and the birth of machine industry. But the full significance of this development will not become evident until it, too, is given the dual or multiple interpretation that historians gave these older developments. We shall not understand its essential character until all the accompanying phenomena, social, economic, and intellectual, have been analyzed, and some mind as electric as Parrington's and as penetrating as Turner's has pierced nearer its heart. What then will be its significance? That is a question we cannot answer; it is for the oncoming generation of historians.

My own guess is that this great development by which America has been projected into world leadership, with all the exhilarations and perils, the opportunities and costs of that position, may in some fashion be connected by future interpreters with the advent of an age of mass action, mass production, and mass psychology in American life. From being one of the most unorganized, the most invertebrate of nations in 1860 we have grown into the most powerfully and efficiently organized people on the globe. Our population of 160,000,000 disposes of its resources through such mass combinations, political, social, and economic, as mankind never saw before. Our thinking in 1865 was still individual thinking; today it is largely mass thinking, shaped and colored by mass media of unparalleled and sometimes dismaying potency—press, radio, television, cinema. No one can go to what were recently primitive frontier communities in America—say Texas and California—without being struck, and a little appalled, by the complexity and efficiency with which they have organized their life. It was our mass production which won the two last world wars; it was our genius for making big organizations work which has built the means for saving Western democracy since the latest world war. Our

ALLAN NEVINS

national outlook, once that of the individualistic pioneer, has become a social outlook. Without this pervasive internal change our new position in the world would have been impossible.

The striking shift in our character and our world position in the last half century, of course, has some direct results, already visible, in our interpretation of history. We are evincing a greater militancy in asserting the virtues of our political and social system. The apologetic attitude of the years of the Great Depression is gone. We can henceforth be more confident, and more energetic, in asserting that our way of life, called decadent by our enemies, has proved itself historically to be freer, more flexible, and more humane than any other in history. We can be as emphatic and frank as ever in describing our past weaknesses, from slavery to slums, but we shall insist more rigorously on the fundamental healthiness of our system and on its proved ability to mend its defects and give us a constantly self-regenerating society.

We shall also evince, I think, a tendency to insist more emphatically on the fundamental unity of the United States with Western Europe and the various other nations sprung from Western Europe. All kinds of Western institutions and virtues now find their principal stronghold in the United States. The literature written in the English tongue increasingly has its main center of vitality in America, a fact well recognized by the London *Times Literary Supplement*. The Roman Catholic Church, like the Protestant churches, finds its chief springs of wealth and power in the United States. The Atlantic Community, as many publicists term it, has taken the place of the former division between Europe and the Americas. Oldtime quarrels between America and Western Europe have lost a great part of the significance which was once attached to them. What does the War of 1812 count for compared with the maintenance and growth of the political, social, and cultural ties that have made the English-speaking nations so nearly a unit? The nationalistic view of our history will increasingly be replaced by the international view, treating America as part of a great historic civilization with the Atlantic its center, as the Mediterranean was the center of the ancient world; the tides of population, power, and influence first moving from Europe to America, and then beginning to flow in the opposite direction.

We may look forward, also, to a more appreciative attitude toward our material strength, and to a more scientific treatment of the factors which have created this material power. In the past our historians were apologetic about this. They condemned our love of the dollar, our race to wealth, our interest in material objects; they deprecated our worship of size, and deplored our boastfulness about steel tonnage, grain production, and output of machinery. Clio, with her tradition of devotion to moral values, was scornful of any others. Our writers in

general—for the historians but followed the poets, the novelists, and
the dramatists—intimated that America had grown too fast, too
coarsely, too muscularly; they exalted the rural virtues as against industrial might, the rarefied air of the study as against the smoky atmosphere of the mill.

Without denying that some accompaniments of our swift industrialization were atrociously bad we can now assert that this historical
attitude was in part erroneous. The nation grew none too fast. We
can see today that all its wealth, all its strength were needed to meet a
succession of world crises—and we still dwell in a crisis era. Had we
applied restrictions to keep our economy small, tame, and timid we
would have lost World War I. Had the United States not possessed
the mightiest oil industry, the greatest steel industry, the largest automotive factories, the most efficient machine-tool industry, the best
technological schools, and the most ingenious working force in the
world, we would indubitably have lost World War II.

Were we significantly weaker today in technical skills, in great mills
and factories, and the scientific knowledge which gave us priority with
the atomic bomb and hydrogen bomb, all Western Europe would perhaps be cowering—we ourselves would perhaps be cowering—before
the knout held by the Kremlin. The architects of our material growth
—the men like Whitney, McCormick, Westinghouse, Rockefeller,
Carnegie, Hill, and Ford—will yet stand forth in their true stature as
builders, for all their faults, of a strength which civilization found
indispensable.

That Jay Gould deserves the unscientific term "robber baron" is
doubtless true. Nobody can object if similar malisons are heaped on
such other disreputable businessmen as Collis P. Huntington, Bet-a-
Million Gates, and Frenzied-Finance Lawson. Industry, like politics, has
its bad men and dark chapters, and it has long been easy to get a spurious reputation for "courage" by dilating on them. The *real* courage,
however, is required by those who argue that we should approach our
business history with discrimination, balance, and a concern for scientific analysis of all the evidence. The forthcoming multivolumed history of the Standard of New Jersey by members of the Harvard School
of Business Administration will show that Rockefeller and his successors were guiltless of many of the charges flung at them, and in
organizing the incredibly chaotic oil business performed a work not
destructive, but essentially constructive. Andrew Carnegie, who did so
much to build the nation's steel industry, cannot be dismissed with
the term "robber baron." Nor can James J. Hill, whose Great Northern
contributed so much to Northwestern growth. Nor can Henry Ford,
who lowered prices, raised wages, and in 1911-1914 brought to birth at
Highland Park the complex creative process called mass production,

which, widely applied, has done so much to make life richer and Western democracy stronger. As the era of muckraking fades the era of a true history of our industrial growth—not apologetics, not abuse, but scientific appraisal, giving blame and credit where each is due—can open. And the credit side of the ledger far outweighs the debit.

It will yet be realized that the industrial revolution in the United States came none too soon, and none too fast; and that the ensuing mass production revolution as yet so little understood by Americans was not born a day too early. We shall also come to realize that the turmoil and human suffering which inescapably accompanied the industrial revolution and the mass-production revolution were not, after all, a tremendous price to pay for their benefits. The price was smaller in the United States than in foreign lands. The industrial revolution cost less in human travail here than it did in England, where it first came to birth; less than in Germany or Japan; far less than it is costing in Russia. Here is a wide field for the rewriting of American history, and for the re-education of the American people, who should have a fair presentation of the facts in place of tendentious writing.

Our material might, to be sure, is valuable only as it supports, and carries to victory, great moral ideas; only as it buttresses a civilization in which spiritual forces are predominant. But the fundamental difference between the democratic world and the totalitarian world lies precisely in the superior position which we give to moral and spiritual values. It is we, not our enemies, who have the right to talk about what Lincoln called man's vast future, for we really value men as individual souls. Behind our dreams of man's vast future we mobilize an unconquerable strength. In time, when future historians look back on this period, which to us is so full of struggle, sacrifice, and anxious uncertainty, they will perhaps give it an interpretation of no mean character. They may say: "The era in which the United States, summoning all its strength, led democracy in winning the First World War, the Second World War, and the ensuing struggle against the Communist tyranny, was one of the imposing eras of history. It stands invested, in its own fashion, with something of the radiance of the Periclean era, the Elizabethan era, and the era of Pitt and the long struggle against Napoleon."

NO   *Matthew Josephson*

When Professor Nevins read the foregoing paper before the Society of American Archivists in Dearborn, Michigan, the newspapers rose to the significance of certain passages in it as foreshadowing a new fashion in our historical writing. These were quoted very widely, in some cases, under fairly alarming headlines, such as that in *The New York Times* for September 20, 1953:

REWRITING HISTORY IS URGED BY NEVINS

Our writers and scholars had been growing a bit edgy at reports of the banning and burning of books and of the predations of Senator McCarthy and his "literary department" in the republic of letters. Now came news that Professor Nevins was out to "rewrite" some of our recent history and it gave many persons quite a turn. He has been saying much the same thing for several years and with less reservation or prudence than in the Dearborn lecture. In the 1953 edition of his biography of John D. Rockefeller ("A Study in Power"), as earlier, in August 1951, before a meeting of history teachers at Stanford University, he had asserted that many of our contemporary writers had done grave injustice to

. . . the leaders of our material growth—the Rockefellers, Carnegies, Hills, and Morgans . . . In the past our historians tended to a feminine idealism. They were apologetic about our dollars, our race to wealth, our materialism. . . . They spoke scornfully of the robber barons who were not robber barons at all; they intimated that America had grown too fast.

Professor Samuel Eliot Morison, president of the American Historical Association, sounded the same notes last year in an address before that learned body. He assailed the tendency to the "economic interpretation" of our history as exemplified by Charles Beard, and he went to great lengths to castigate the "debunkers" who in the 1930's and 1940's, by their excessively critical spirit, as he argued, often insulted our "folk-memories," stripped America's "great figures" of all virtue, all nobility, and in fact of their greatness. Mr. Morison, therefore, urged that our damaged heroes should be salvaged from the historical junk heaps where they had been consigned, that they be patched up, varnished, and made to look like real antiques. At the same time *Fortune* magazine, which candidly glorifies our large corporate enterprises, in April 1952 published a long article by E. N. Saveth surveying the many injuries done to the repute of our business class by American historians old and new, from Parkman and Prescott, down to Henry Adams, Beard, and the other so-called "muckrakers." All this had made for "bad" public relations and needed much correcting, *Fortune* noted, if businessmen were to avoid new reform measures by the Government.

These facts are mentioned to indicate the context in which Professor Nevins dropped his latest remarks on how our history should be rewritten. It has all added up to quite a campaign. Assuredly, "every era has its own climate of opinion," as he observes. The present (though by a narrow electoral margin) has assumed some of the character of a Restoration, with our own Stuarts and Bourbons coming in again where they left off. The "revisionists" of history are now much concerned that our masters of heavy industry and finance be given their due.

How different was the climate of 1933 when, as it happened, I wrote my own study of our nineteenth-century industrialists and, in a spirit of good clean fun, entitled it "The Robber Barons." There were some fifteen millions unemployed in our cities; our farmers were up in arms literally; our most prominent financiers were being investigated or tried or were in flight abroad. Never were the creative contributions of our big business leadership rated so low. As for the term "robber barons," it was not of my own coinage, but was drawn from the folklore of the Kansas Greenbackers and Populists of the 1880's who had their experience with the Jay Gould type.

Today is a different day, and the prevailing trade winds in this country drive us toward mental conformity. Our university scholars are but made of flesh. Even the Justices of the Supreme Court, it has been long said, "follow the election returns" in handing down their opinions. Should historians lag far behind in judging the shift of political power to conservative hands? Reflecting upon Mr. Nevins's timely advice that we assume "a more appreciative attitude" toward the architects of our prosperity and progress, we can imagine whole flocks of historians, large and small, hastening to change their old liberal lights for new. Where only a decade or two ago they, like Mr. Nevins himself, were fairly strong for the New Deal, we may fancy them, henceforth, writing panegyrics on the wisdom, courage, and moral beauty of FDR's enemies, the economic royalists.

The talk of rewriting our history inevitably brings to mind the nightmare vision of George Orwell's "Nineteen Eighty-Four," with its regiments of poor intellectual helots in the labyrinthine skyscrapers of the Ministry of Truth retouching records, destroying old documents, removing all trace of liberal and democratic ideas. Orwell's anti-utopian fantasy was, of course, based on the Nazi creation of a Federal Institute for the History of the New Germany and on the revision of the history of Soviet Russia under Stalin's direction. Will the New History of this country, too, be rewritten as crude propaganda for the party in power? Will Franklin Roosevelt be trimmed down to size—say that of Calvin Coolidge—and Henry Ford be given wings and a harp? Will the art of Tacitus, Voltaire, and Gibbon be reduced to a public-relations job?

Perish the thought. The last person to recommend such a program would be Allan Nevins, who has long conducted himself as a sincere democrat. But his proposals for "revision" have been to my mind ill conceived and ill timed. Ill timed because these are days when the works and ideas of some of our most creative thinkers, such as Oliver Wendell Holmes, Veblen, and John Dewey, have come under suspicion and attack by overheated patriots. Ill timed because history books long esteemed and profitably studied have been banned; because many writers and teachers of history show increasing fear to use their faculties on the materials and lessons of the past. Mr. Nevins's example, termed in some university circles "a harbinger of coming revisionism," will scarcely spread courage.

To be sure, history is always being rewritten. As Benedetto Croce said: "All true history is contemporary history." We write not for the dead but for the living. Yet in the past, change in the art has been a slow alembic process carrying it away from myth, romance, and superstition toward an ever more rational chronicle of the past. Thucydides vowed that he would eschew romance. Gibbon, as a man of the Enlightenment, rewrote the early Christian historians; and the men of the "scientific" school of Ranke in the next century tried to correct Gibbon. But seldom before have serious historians come with proposals to lay aside the tools of exact knowledge and place important figures of the past in the setting of romance or myth.

The revisionists have singled out Beard for punishment, because he was stubbornly unromantic about our tycoons and, as they contend, contributed more than almost any other to the formation of a skeptical attitude toward our institutions among the intellectuals of the 1930's and 1940's. His highly documented "Economic Interpretation of the American Constitution," as Dr. Morison would now say, "debunked" the Founding Fathers. Here, by a semantic device, the word "debunk" is used in the pejorative sense. But is it not honorable to eliminate bunk or buncombe? Is America not great and strong enough to do without Washington's cherry tree and Sheridan's fictitious ride? Beard's best-known work, "The Rise of American Civilization," done in collaboration with his wife, described the industrial revolution after the Civil War and the coming of the great monopolies in a coolly critical spirit. Most intelligent Americans of that era generally regarded the men of the trusts and the railway combinations with intense fear and said, with Henry Adams, that Rockefeller, Morgan, and the trusts were "doing their best" to bring on a social revolution. The masters of industry and finance were, after all, hauled into court year after year as "conspirators" against the rights of other American businessmen and farmers to engage in competitive enterprise; and the politicians of both major parties vied with each other in enacting laws regulating the monopolists. Nevins does not deny all this, but holds that Beard was not "objective"; that he wrote of the "barons" of pork, oil, or sugar with the *partipris* of an economic determinist; that the Rockefellers were "better" than Beard and his intellectual kin believed, or worked better than they knew to build up empires in industry or mass-production plants that transformed an agrarian America into the world's most powerful industrial nation.

To be sure, Charles Beard began his studies during the spectacular industrial and political conflicts of the 1890's; he was influenced, moreover, when he studied at Oxford, by the Fabian Socialists, as well as by the reading of Marx. In those days the concept of economic determinism, broadly speaking, was embraced even by scions of banking families like Professor E. R. A. Seligman. It seemed to be embodied in the career of John D. Rockefeller himself, as even Nevins pictures it. By means regarded as "morally indefensible," he relates, by use of secret railroad debates and espionage, the "anarchy" of small, competitive oil producers was ended and order and efficiency introduced into their field. A business world of small weak units was made "inevitably" to give way to a world of concentration and highly organized power. "Great business aggregations are not built without frustrating, crushing, or absorbing multitudinous small enterprises," concludes the modern apologist of Rockefeller. The historic concepts of Marx—aside from his advocacy of Socialism—have permeated our culture so generally for a hundred years that one finds Nevins unconsciously echoing one of the most familiar of Marxian doctrines: that which sees the rising capitalist class as an agency of progress leading to the triumph of "scientific" and large-scale industry.

Our Rockefellers, then, were not "morally worse" than their contemporaries of the Gilded Age, in Nevins's view, and above all should not be judged by the ethical standards of the present era. By their very ruthlessness in business, terrible even for that "loose period," he holds, they were enabled to build with all the greater speed a vast oil empire that would one day, in wartime, help save our country. Here one finds a philosophy of economic materialism in no way different from that which Beard, in earlier life, embraced—save that Beard preserved always a moral balance somewhat wanting in our current crop of revisionists. And if Dr. Nevins is going to teach us to "appreciate" or condone the moral ruthlessness of our older captains of industry, if he is going to let the end always justify the means, then I fail to see what arguments we can bring to bear against the Russian Communists. Reinhold Niebuhr was quite right in his recent observation (in "The Irony of American History") that our conservative apologists for unbridled monopoly, for the American way of materialistic life, are little better than the Communists.

There was nothing "effeminate" about Beard's idealism. That, incidentally, was the kind of accusation usually directed at reformers by the old corrupt political bosses of the General Grant era, like Roscoe Conkling. Beard was a prodigious worker, forever mining for his facts. He was not "any one thing" in his beliefs, and with time his views changed. But in writing the history of a country where most people had come to improve their material lot he would have been a dull-witted historian indeed if he had ignored the economic motive. In the long run his work stands in the mainstream of the modern pragmatists and sociologists. He desired to turn historical writing away from the mere chronicle of "past politics" or the doings of "great men" or famous diplomats and write of the people, of man in society, of the many-sided growth of a national culture or "civilization." And, far from belittling the role of those who, for private gain, usurped natural resources, acquired or built railroad nets, and organized huge industries, he insisted that they were in truth the prime actors, the dominant figures in the post-Civil War scene, beside whom Presidents and Senators were but animated shadows. Long years before Nevins approached the oil or automotive industries Beard asserted that the rise of a House of Rockefeller or Morgan was as important a subject for American historians as that of the House of Howard or Burleigh for the English.

Nevins's books, like his article urging the rewriting of our history, are after all but the expressions of his own partiality for the "leaders" of our industrial progress. In truth, they were never beloved or popular as folk-heroes as were our military leaders, great inventors, famous preachers, silver-tongued orators, and picturesque newspaper editors of the Horace Greeley type. If we would return to our folklore then the real American tradition is after all reflected by our earlier "literary" historians as well as by the later social-minded ones who expressed habitual distaste rather than adulation for the men of fortune. Charles Francis Adams, Jr., who as a railroad president saw a good deal of them, wrote in his autobiography: "Not one that I have ever known would I care to meet again either in this world or the next . . ." And in these days of the "businessmen's Administration" in Washington it is well to recall the statement of one intensely American historian of half a century ago who said: "In no other country was such power held by the men who had gained these fortunes, the mighty industrial overlords. . . . The Government was practically impotent. . . . Of all forms of tyranny the least attractive and the most vulgar is the tyranny of mere wealth." Was it a Socialist who spoke? No, it was a Republican, a President of the United States, Theodore Roosevelt. He preferred as his heroes men like Peary, the explorer, or Bury, the historian, not the financial magnates. It was Roosevelt who said: "I am simply unable to make myself take the

attitude of respect toward the very wealthy men that many persons
show nowadays . . ."

Beard, the chief target of the revisionists, maintained in his later
years, in quite un-Marxist fashion, that the writing of completely
"objective" history was an impossibility in view of the problem of
selection, proportion, and emphasis that came into play. History thus
became something like an "act of faith." The historian began always
with an "assumption" or a "scheme of reference." One might fix upon
the theme of the struggle of church and state as the *leitmotiv* of the
period studied; another upon the clash of great interest groups and
institutions. But we can never reproduce the past, in Ranke's words,
"as it really was."

Nor does Allan Nevins. In the concluding part of his article one
finds a series of historical guesses or "assumptions" about the past and
future that seem as visionary or speculative as anything in George
Bancroft or Parson Weems. In his closing vaticinal phrases everything
comes out all white or all black. On the one side are the plumed
knights of business who were "the architects of our material progress";
on the other the dragons of totalitarianism, German, Russian and
Chinese. Had we applied "restrictions," that is, state controls, upon
the masters of industry, he writes, we should have lost World War I.
And but for the men who organized "the mightiest oil industry, the
greatest steel industry, the largest automotive factories . . . we would
indubitably have lost World War II." Thus, he paints a picture all
dripping with glamour of the Rockefellers, Carnegies, and Fords, con-
juring up the industrial arms with which to defend democracy and
lead the "Atlantic Community" in a crusade against the totalitarians
of the East. This is a fairly *simpliste,* big-business version of the
American Century. And this, he tells us, is the direction in which the
rewriting of our history is to be carried out.

But what does the corpus of ascertainable facts reveal? To those
who were in a position to study the defense program being launched
in 1940–1941 it was plain that all too many leaders of our industry
for two years after war had come to Europe stubbornly resisted the
conversion of their plants for the manufacture of arms, or delayed
providing added plant capacity, until the Government, under Franklin Roosevelt, agreed to subsidize a large part of such conversion or
expansion by allowing very rapid depreciation rates for tax purposes.
Today even conservative economists, such as Galbraith of Harvard
University, acknowledge the truth that the swiftest and greatest expansion of our industry and our labor productivity took place *not* under
the free-enterprise rules of peacetime, but in wartime under the
indispensable Government planning, control, and priority restrictions.

Was "Uncle Henry" Ford thinking of the American Century when

—prior to Pearl Harbor—he flatly refused to build aircraft engines for the hard-pressed British? One wonders what Ford's idea of history was. "The bunk," he said.

Suggested Topics

1. History as an art form
2. Are there valid reasons for rewriting history?
3. The need for a frame of reference
4. "You can't see the forest when the trees are in the way."
5. "All true history is contemporary history."
6. The climate of American opinion today
7. The new conformity vs. the old dissent

WHERE GOVERNMENT MAY NOT TRESPASS

Henry Steele Commager

> Since 1956 Professor of History at Amherst College, Henry Steele Commager is one of the nation's keenest and most prolific writers on America's constitutional and intellectual history. He taught at New York University and Columbia, and has lectured extensively both in this country and abroad. He is the author of a score of books and is now engaged in the preparation of a 40-volume study of "The Rise of the American Nation."

The climate of freedom has cleared, to some degree at least, in the last two years—thanks in good part to the integrity and wisdom of our courts—and the nightmare of McCarthyism is receding into the past to join similar aberrations ranging from the Alien and Sedition Acts of 1798 to the Red hysteria of the Twenties.

But while the overt threat to freedom is less urgent, a new and, in some ways, more serious threat has developed. This is the threat of governmental control over ideas. It is more serious because it is less ostentatious and does not therefore excite alarm. It affects groups and interests unorganized and unable to protect themselves. It threatens not merely a temporary departure from sound constitutional

Reprinted from *The New York Times Magazine*, November 24, 1957. By permission of *The New York Times* and the author.

practices but a fundamental revolution in the constitutional system itself; it also threatens the most precious of all our interests, our intellectual and spiritual integrity.

The framers of our constitutions, state and national, differed on the question of what authority government should exercise, but they were almost unanimous on the question of what authority government should not exercise. All of them—Jefferson and Hamilton, Madison and John Adams, Paine and Wilson—agreed that there were some things no government could do. And if we ask what were these things—what was the area over which government had no authority whatsoever—the answer is plain. It is the answer written into bills of rights, state and Federal alike. Government had no authority over the realm of ideas and their communication—religion, speech, press, assembly, association and so forth.

The reason that control over these matters was denied to government is equally plain. It was not out of any peculiar tenderness for preachers or writers or editors or critics. It was because the kind of governments that the framers were setting up—governments resting on the consent of the people and run by the people—simply could not work unless churches, press, universities, political parties and private associations were free to inquire, discuss and criticize. This is not a sentimental consideration, but a tough-minded one. If government controls access to and dissemination of information, there is no true freedom, and without freedom we will fall into error that may be irremediable.

What we have witnessed since the second World War, and more particularly in the last four or five years, is the entry of government into areas heretofore thought immune from governmental invasion. The danger is not—as the President and many state Governors argue —that the Federal Government has taken on new responsibilities in the realms of social security or hydroelectric power, public health or housing. These developments we can take in our stride. If they prove to be mistaken or misguided, they can be reversed. What is ominous is that government—chiefly, though not exclusively, the Federal Government—has invaded the area of ideas and their communication. It has moved, steadily and stubbornly, into control of activities traditionally—and constitutionally—immune from such control.

This is not, let it be said at once, the result of a conspiracy, or of lust for power, any more than the growth of Federal control over such matters as conservation, agriculture, banking and transportation was the product of a conspiracy or lust for power. Nobody, apparently, wants it this way, and nobody in authority is prepared to admit that it is happening. Almost everybody talks about the necessity of less control in certain areas and, for example, the return to the states of oil lands goes on apace. But in the realm that really counts—the realm that will be decisive of the kind of government we have in the future—Federal assumption of authority increases.

Let us look at this process of growing controls in the realm of ideas, and let us note the way in which local governments and private groups, ordinarily hostile to controls, supinely acquiesce in and adopt Federal practices and standards. First, there is the approval of the "security" program, which President Truman inaugurated, and which has expanded under Mr. Eisenhower. I am not concerned here with the wisdom or the ethics of the program itself, with its monstrous abuses, with its palpable inefficiency. What I am concerned with is, rather, the way in which its operation puts control over political and social ideas in the hands of government. The Attorney General's list, for example—a list to which the Wright Commission on Government Security would now give clear legality and permanence—establishes Federal standards of desirable and undesirable organizations. It is a list which state after state has adopted—and expanded; it is a list which local communities, and even private organizations, have hastened to accept as a standard for employment, or even for the purchase of library books or of works of art.

Thus New Yorkers who look with dismay on the invasion by the Federal Government of slum clearance are quite prepared to accept a list prepared by some bureaucrat in Washington as a valid test for the hiring of teachers. Thus Texans who are ready to fight at a new Alamo against Federal control of tidelands oil or of natural gas are quite ready to accept what amounts to Federal standards of what books should be in their libraries and what pictures should hang in their art museums.

Consider the furor over those who take refuge in the First or Fifth Amendment, or who refuse to "cooperate" with Congressional committees. Some states require by law that all those in public employment "cooperate" with investigating committees; others punish by deprivation of their jobs those who, for one reason or another, take refuge in the First or Fifth Amendment, thus punishing where the law itself does not punish. Everywhere the result is the same: local standards are influenced or determined by decisions, or merely attitudes, radiating from Washington.

A second example of the growth of Federal authority in the realm of ideas is the exercise of control over foreign travel. Time was when Americans did not need passports for travel abroad. Then they came to be used purely as statements of identification and formal requests for courtesy from other nations. The use of the passport and the visa as a mark of approval or disapproval is something new in our history, and it is fraught with danger.

If the right to travel abroad is to depend on the subjective judgment of some subordinate in the State Department as to whose travel is "in the interests of the United States," there is an end—in theory, at least—to freedom of travel. Who determines what are the interests of the United States? Who determines whether a particular passport applicant meets these murky criteria? If everyone who expects to travel must so comport himself as to satisfy the notions of Federal bureaucracy about political ideas, associations and activities, control over travel may well become a powerful instrument for Federal control of thought.

Nor does this principle operate only in the *denial* of passports. When the State Department assumes responsibility to decide that it is, or is not, in the interest of the United States for a particular person to go abroad, it follows in logic that those who are permitted to travel travel in the interests of the United States. This is, perhaps, the logical assumption behind Mr. Dulles' recent announcement that newspaper men are, in a sense, instruments of national policy.

A third area of Federal control is science. We know from our own experience, and from the experience of Germany and Italy, how important it is to national security and progress that science be free. But we know, too, that the pressures on science and scientists to be "instruments of national policy" is heavy, and growing. The concern of the Government with the whole area of nuclear physics, for example, is too obvious to elaborate, and it is obvious, too, that the Government must maintain security regulations in such areas of scientific investigation. This in itself assures extensive Federal control over important realms of science.

Another factor making for governmental control of science is, of course, the power of the purse. It is in the interest of the Government to subsidize research in university and private laboratories; such subsidy almost inevitably carries with it some measure of direction and supervision.

But what this means is that in large and important areas scientists are no longer free agents, but subject to governmental pressure. They are committed to projects not always of their own choosing, and sometimes to the neglect of pure research of the greatest value. Universities that accept Federal subsidies find themselves accepting, too, Federal supervision over their faculty members, their research assistants, even over the uses to which their findings may be put. This is not only the negation of the function of the university, it is an enormous accretion to Federal authority. Those who oppose Federal aid to school construction but accept Federal supervision of scientific research are indeed straining at a gnat and swallowing a camel.

A fourth major area of Federal authority is education. An important part of American nationalism has been the absence of statism, and one thing that has contributed most powerfully to this is that education has never been subject to national control. Even those who advocate Federal aid to school building or to school lunch programs, or Federal scholarship aid, balk at suggesting Federal control over the content of education itself. Yet, indirectly, the Federal Government is moving steadily toward the exercise of such controls, and many state and local governments are enthusiastically supporting the policy. Thus teachers who belong to organizations on some Congressional "list" are in danger of dismissal; teachers who refuse to "cooperate" with Congressional committees lose their jobs; teachers who advocate policies currently unacceptable to the State Department—the recognition of Communist China, for example—find themselves in hot water— though the water is not quite so hot now as it was a year or two ago.

Students, too, must be careful what organizations they join, and even what books they read. Those who expect to enter the civil service or who are candidates for officer training have had fair warning: their careers may depend on obscure standards established by obscure officials in Washington.

There is a drift toward Governmental control even in the field of religion, long thought immune. This has come indirectly, in the pressures of the Velde committee, the operation of the security program, the activities of the customs and post office censors. The spectacle of the Velde committee attacking Bishop Oxnam because it disapproved a pamphlet sent out by the Methodist Church to its missionaries, or of the Customs Office holding up literature advocating pacifism, is one to give grave concern to those who cherish the traditional separation between church and state in America. Even more ominous is the attempt of a Congressional committee to dictate policy to the Religious Society of Friends, the Quakers.

Closely connected with education and religion is the work of the foundations, and here the pressure of Federal control is peculiarly dangerous. The argument advanced by the Cox, the Reece and the Walter committees to justify their investigations into the operations of the Ford and other foundations is at once simple and delusive. It is that because they enjoy tax exemption Government has a right to inquire into their activities—into the substance, as well as the administration and financing, of their work. On the basis of this theory the committees saw fit to inquire into the social and political philosophies of recipients of awards, into the interest and direction of scholarly programs.

No more specious theory has ever been advanced than that tax exemption authorizes government to inquire into the ideas of foundations. If this is true, it is equally true that tax exemptions to religious bodies authorizes Government agencies to pass on the content of every sermon preached in every church, or into the doctrines taught in theological seminaries. If it is true, it is equally true that tax exemption authorizes government to investigate what is taught in the classrooms of state and private universities—a theory actually advanced by the Attorney General of New Hampshire, only to be rejected by the Supreme Court with the contempt which it merited. Once establish the theory that tax exemption authorizes Federal supervision of ideas, as distinct from overt actions, and there is an end to freedom for intellectual or spiritual activities.

One of the most dangerous areas of Federal control is that occupied by the press: a term which embraces books, magazines and newspapers alike. No one in America needs to be convinced of the quintessential importance of freedom of the press, yet in recent years we have witnessed a series of developments which, collectively, seriously curtail our access to information through the press.

These pressures are exercised in many ways, some subtle, some ostentatious. There is the kind of pressure that was implicit in the effort to intimidate Mr. James Wechsler of The New York Post. There is the kind of pressure involved in the prolonged denial of passports to newsmen who wish to go to China, a policy now at last reversed. There is the pressure that comes from denial of information, or from classification of information as secret.

This policy of the denial of information is one that has grown to ominous proportions in recent years. It has, indeed, been elevated into a principle, which we may designate, after its formulator, the Philip Young Doctrine of "the inherent non-availability of information." Not only sensitive Government departments—the Department of Defense or the Atomic Energy Commission—now have censorship officers, but almost every department; even the Civil Service Commission and the Department of Agriculture find it necessary to establish internal censorship. If agencies of the national Government can influence or intimidate the press, or can control the flow of information through the press, we will have taken a long, and dangerous, step toward authoritarianism.

These examples by no means exhaust the list. There is pressure for Federal supervision, direct or indirect, over the films, the theatre, the radio and television. There is pressure—through the policies of the State Department—on art and music. Refusal to underwrite a traveling art exhibit or symphony orchestra because of the political beliefs of the artists involved, squints toward what we have hitherto escaped: official standards of orthodoxy in the arts. All these developments are not only threats to freedom; they are threats to local autonomy and to grass-roots democracy.

The most notable example of centralization in the realm of civil liberties is, of course, the Fourteenth Amendment of 1868. This, the most important amendment ever added to the Constitution, worked a revolution in the relations of state and Federal governments to the rights of persons. In effect, it nationalized the liberties of men, throwing over them the protective mantle of the Federal Government. For, whereas the original Bill of Rights had been designed to protect men against Federal tyranny, the Fourteenth Amendment was designed to protect men against state tyranny. For a long time ineffective, this function of the Fourteenth Amendment took on vitality in the Nineteen Twenties, when the Supreme Court began to hold that its due process clause in effect incorporated the guarantees of the first eight amendments, and began to apply it energetically to state denial or impairment of civil and political liberties.

Recent civil rights legislation is designed to give effect to the guarantees of the Fourteenth Amendment and—where voting is involved—of the Fifteenth as well.

This is, of course, Federal centralization, and it is a centralization that affects the realm of ideas and their communication. The Fourteenth Amendment is not a recent development, but constitutionally almost ninety years old, and almost venerable; only its more energetic application is relatively new. It differs fundamentally from recent legislative and administrative invasion of the realms of civil and personal rights in that it is designed to enlarge, not to circumscribe, the exercise of those rights; to facilitate, not to hamper, the communication of ideas. Its application is not, in short, centralization of the control of ideas, but the use of the Federal authority to frustrate such control.

Those who fear the Leviathan state direct their fears, and their defenses, almost entirely to the political and economic realms, just as those who are determined to maintain private enterprise think of it almost entirely in economic terms. But the growth of economic centralization, mistaken as it may be, is of *relatively* minor importance, as the concept of private enterprise as an economic institution is of *relatively* minor importance. The real danger is not to economic enterprise, but to intellectual enterprise. And the real danger of governmental authority is in the intellectual realm.

Once allow the state to invade the areas of thought—scholarship, science, the press, the arts, religion and association, and we will surely have statism. It will be too late, then, to protect invasion of the economic realm. Those who fear the Leviathan state—and all who are steeped in the American tradition must fear it—should resolutely oppose it where it is most dangerous—namely, in the realm of the mind and spirit of men. Once we get a government strong enough to control men's minds, we will have a government strong enough to control everything.

Suggested Topics

1. What is McCarthyism?
2. The threat of "government control of ideas"
3. The Attorney General's list
4. The right to travel abroad
5. Science as an "instrument of national policy"
6. Tax exemption and government influence
7. Pressures on the press

IS DEMOCRACY POSSIBLE?   *Robert M. Hutchins*

Now President of The Fund for the Republic, Dr. Robert Maynard Hutchins was President of the University of Chicago and before that Dean of the Law School at Yale. He has written extensively on education and has been a leading and outspoken defender of the freedom to teach and to learn. In 1959 he received the Sidney Hillman Award for Meritorious Public Service.

Last Saturday was the anniversary of an event I have sometimes regretted. Sixty years ago last Saturday, on the other side of the River, near the fire station on Herkimer Street, I was born. Another of the nineteenth century's last gifts to Chicago, Alphonse Capone, was born on the same day. Readers of the Chicago *Tribune* may remember that that newspaper often seemed confused about which one of us capricorns it was talking about. I have always felt that the *Tribune*'s astrologer had in those days a strong influence on its policies.

Sixty years is a long time, and naturally I have been thinking about what has happened in this period. I must tell you that the award of the Hillman prize is one of the pleasantest things that has happened to me. To be associated in this way with the name of Sidney Hillman,

An address by Dr. Hutchins on receiving the Sidney Hillman Award for Meritorious Public Service, January 21, 1959. Reprinted from The Fund for the Republic *Bulletin*, February, 1959. By permission of The Fund for the Republic.

whom I knew and admired, to hear that I have been thought worthy
of this association by those who knew him best, this is a consolation
and an encouragement. The people who really need and deserve this
consolation and encouragement are those who in spite of many appeals to their better judgment gave me the opportunity to do whatever
I have done and who thereafter instructed me in private and supported me in public: the faculty of the Yale Law School, the trustees
and faculty of the University of Chicago, the directors and staff of
the Fund for the Republic. To them for their guidance, confidence,
and long-suffering patience, and to you for recognizing them through
me, my grateful thanks are due.

My earliest memories of my childhood in Brooklyn are of the horse
cars, the ice wagon, the cruller wagon; of yelling git-a-hoss, in the
quaint dialect of the region, at an occasional automobile, and playing
one-o-cat in front of our house on Dean Street, where we had moved
to be near my father's church on the corner of Nostrand and Dean.
The faith in which I was brought up was simple. Democracy was the
answer to everything, including the ills of democracy. These ills would
be cured by more democracy. The ideal toward which we were moving
was the civilization of the dialogue, where everybody talked with everybody else about everything, where nobody tried to get his way by
force or fraud, where everybody was content to abide by the decision
of the majority as long as the dialogue could continue. Democracy
meant self-government, and self-government meant primarily participation by the individual, at least through the selection of his representatives, in decisions affecting his life and happiness. Since decisions
affecting his life and happiness were taken not merely by his government, but also by many other institutions, corporations, trade unions,
and political parties, for example, the thing to do was to democratize
them, as well as the government.

In this view the great crime is to try to prevent other people from
speaking up, or to say that there are certain things you won't talk
about, or certain people you won't talk to, either at home or abroad.
In this view education and communication are of prime importance,
because if you can't hear what the others are saying, or can't understand it, or if they can't hear or understand you, there can't be any
dialogue, and democracy becomes meaningless.

The democratic faith is faith in man, faith in every man, faith that
men, if they are well enough educated and well enough informed,
can solve the problems raised by their own aggregation.

One advantage of this faith is that it is practically shock-proof.
Industrialization can sweep the world. Nationalism and technology
can threaten the extinction of the human race. Population can break
out all over. Man can take off from this planet as his ancestors took

off from the primordial ooze and try to make other planets to shoot from. Education can be trivialized beyond belief. The media of communication can be turned into media of entertainment. The dialogue can almost stop because people have nothing to say, or, if they have something to say, no place to say it. And still it is possible to believe that if democracy and the dialogue can continue, if they can be expanded, if they can be improved, freedom, justice, equality, and peace will ultimately be achieved.

Some shocks I have received lately have bothered me a little. The first came when during the excitement of last year I was recommending my democratic panacea as a remedy for the troubles of the labor unions to the people on the trade union project of the Fund for the Republic. They informed me that the idea of government by the people had little application to labor unions and that in any event democratic forms in unions were no safeguard against anti-social behavior on their part. In fact, they said, some of the unions in which democratic forms were most conspicuous were the most anti-social.

The second shock came when at the conclusion of my usual tirade against the wild irrationality of our foreign policy I explained to the people on the common defense project of the Fund for the Republic that we should subject that policy to democratic control. My colleagues pointed out to me that in addition to being impossible this was unconstitutional, and had always been regarded as such, and that whatever I might think of the policies followed by the President and the Secretary of State, and however much I might dislike being blown up or suffocated as a result of these policies, the Founding Fathers intended that I should be in precisely this position. In any event, they said, there was no way, particularly in view of the enormous technical problems of modern warfare and international relations, in which the citizens could actually participate in the decisions upon which their lives depended.

The third shock came when I was proposing my usual remedy to the people on the project on political parties, which deals with the political process in a free society. Participation was my watchword. Get out the vote. Or, as the Advertising Council has it, Vote as You Please, but Please Vote. My associates indicated to me that getting people out to vote when they did not know what they were voting for was not helpful, and might be harmful, to the objects I had in view. Under modern conditions, they said, it might be that responsible political participation and decision by the citizens would prove to be impossible, anyway.

Somewhat shaken, I went to the conference on the Island of Rhodes on Representative Government and Public Liberties in the New States. The basic problem of the conference turned out to be whether government by the people is possible, or even desirable, in the modern world. The sense of relief with which members from the new states welcomed military dictatorships in their countries and with which the Frenchmen present welcomed de Gaulle was a measure of the current disenchantment with democracy. These men saw no way of adjusting democratic institutions to contemporary realities. What they hope for is a period of order in which the most acute problems, like Algeria in France and corruption in Siam, may be solved; after which they may, or may not, try government by the people again.

Eminent European philosophers and political scientists present reassured the members from the new states, three of whose governments turned into military dictatorships while the conference was in session, by telling them that democracy was an illusion in both old and new states, for different reasons. In the new states we could not expect government by the people because they lacked education, communication, organization, and law. In the old states it had been out of date since the Peloponnesian War, and even then it was not what we mean by democracy now. Pericles, a leader of the Left, struck thousands of voters from the rolls because they could not prove that both their parents were native-born Athenians. Greek democracy was based on a uniformity of ideas and practices appropriate to an extended family group. The kind of government by the people that may be said to have worked in Athens and in the New England town meeting could not possibly work in a large, heterogeneous, industrial, bureaucratic society. The most we could hope for was order, efficiency, and the maintenance of civil liberties, those rights historically carved out against governmental interference with private life. Alexander Pope, whose celebrated lines had always seemed to me as false as they were celebrated, was justified at last:

For forms of government let fools contest;
Whate'er is best administered is best.

I came away from Rhodes with the foreboding that we might be at the beginning of something new in the last hundred years—a world-wide anti-democratic trend that had little or nothing to do with the intimidations or seductions of the Kremlin. (It was significant by the way that in eight days of discussion no member from any new state said a word about communism or Russia.) This anti-democratic trend would reverse the aspirations of all men of good will at least since 1848 for government by the people. It would have alarming connotations for the United States in the realm of foreign policy. It should force us to re-examine the assumptions and slogans by which we have lived in the light of the actual operation of our institutions in the new industrialized, polarized, bureaucratic world.

If you ask how my democratic faith is doing,

Whither is fled the visionary gleam,
Where is it now, the glory and the dream?

I reply that it is still here. Perhaps the gleam is not quite as bright as it used to be, and somewhat more visionary, but it is still here. Yet, even at my age, I cannot long sustain a position to which my reason will not assent. The shocks I have received are recent; and I cannot claim that I have absorbed them or that I know how to repel others in the future. Perhaps what I can do is to communicate the sense of crisis that I feel and to ask you, since you have all shared my faith (and most of you were born in Brooklyn), to join in thinking for a moment how that faith can be defended.

The faith rests on the propositions that man is a political animal, that participation in political decisions is necessary to his fulfillment and happiness, that all men can and must be sufficiently educated and informed to take part in making these decisions, that protection against arbitrary power, though indispensable, is insufficient to make either free individuals or a free society, that such a society must make positive provisions for its development into a community learning together; for this is what political participation, government by consent, and the civilization of the dialogue all add up to.

If we are to become a community learning together, as I insist we can, the first thing we have to do is to make up our minds that we want to learn. We have lived on a note of triumphant philistinism. Here is a characteristically triumphant proclamation made by Carl D. Becker, perhaps the most celebrated American historian of his day, in 1931. He said,

Our supreme object is to measure and master the world, rather than to understand it . . . Viewed scientifically, it appears as something to be accepted, something to be manipulated and mastered, something to adjust ourselves to with the least possible stress. So long as we can make efficient use of things, we feel no irresistible need to understand them. No doubt it is for this reason chiefly that the modern mind can be so wonderfully at ease in a mysterious universe.

At ease, indeed! Anybody who feels at ease in the world today is a fool. And anybody who would say now that he was content to master and manipulate the environment without bothering to understand how it worked or what to do with it would show first that he did not know what science was, for science is organized understanding, and second that he had no grasp of the kind of problems we now confront. The great overwhelming problems of our country are how to make democracy a reality, how to survive in the nuclear age, and what to do with ourselves if we do survive. None of these problems is technological, though technology has helped to create all of them, and none of them will yield to the kind of measurement, manipulation, or mastery that Professor Becker had in mind. We may, in fact, reverse his statement of 1931 and come nearer the truth of 1959. Then it would go like this: no doubt it is because we have felt no irresistible need to understand the world that the modern mind can be so wonderfully ill at ease in a mysterious universe.

The next question is, how are we going to learn? History will have trouble with American education in the twentieth century. It will see a people who say they are dedicated to education and who are the richest in the world indifferent to education and unwilling to pay for it. It will see an educational system that delivers less education per dollar than any I can think of saying that all it needs is more money. The people and the educators are united only in this: they both want education without pain, either intellectual or financial. History will find it hard to explain how a nation that *is* one, a nation in which the political subdivisions have no relation to social or economic life and little to political life, can entrust its future to these subdivisions by relegating education to them. History will smile sardonically at the spectacle of this great country getting interested, slightly and temporarily, in education only because of the technical achievements of Russia, and then being able to act as a nation only by assimilating education to the Cold War and calling an education bill a defense act.

We might as well make up our minds to it. If our hopes of democracy are to be realized, every citizen of this country is going to have to be educated to the limit of his capacity. And I don't mean trained, amused, exercised, accommodated or adjusted. I mean that his intellectual power must be developed. A good way to start finding the money that is needed for education would be to kick out of it the subjects, the activities, and the people that make no contribution to the development of intellectual power. Such an operation would produce vast sums.

I suggest that two things might be done with this money and with any more that may be needed: first, we should double teachers' salaries, not because all the teachers we have deserve twice as much as they are getting, but because we want to attract the ablest people into the profession; and second, we should establish a national system of scholarships that makes it possible for every citizen of this country to be educated to the limit of his mental capacity, regardless of the financial capacity of his parents.

If life is learning, and I think it is, and if our object is to become a community learning together, education ought to continue throughout life. Here is the great educational opportunity and obligation of the next generation. The education of adults is not only indispensable to the continuation, expansion, and improvement of the dialogue, but it is also an answer to the question of what we are going to do with ourselves if we survive. As automation advances, as new sources of energy are applied in industry, as the hours of labor decline, we have the chance to become truly human by using our new and disturbing leisure to develop our highest human powers to the utmost. Here we can build on the experience of such organizations as the Great Books Foundation, which has succored tens of thousands of refugees from television.

This brings me to the media of mass communications. If our hopes of democracy are to be realized, the media must supply full and accurate information on which the people can base their judgment on public affairs, and they must offer a forum for the discussion of those affairs. I doubt if there are six cities of any size in the United States in which the newspapers come anywhere near meeting these requirements. As for radio and television, with a few distinguished exceptions now and then, they make no attempt to meet them. The so-called "extended news coverage" supplied by radio and television during the recent newspaper strike in New York was a bad joke. A dozen years ago the Commission on the Freedom of the Press recommended the establishment of a continuing independent agency, privately financed, to appraise and report periodically on the performance of the media. Everything that has happened since, and especially the use of the most marvelous electronic methods of communication for the communication of the most insignificant material, makes the adoption of this recommendation more urgent every day.

If we were well educated and well informed, could we make ourselves felt in the realm of political action? In the Republic as I have described it every act of assent on the part of the governed is a product of learning. Could we learn by doing in politics? Or would the archaic aspects of our governmental structure and the vast bureaucratic machine that goes creaking on, following the right procedure instead of seeking the right result, prevent us from using our newly won education and information as active, deciding, responsible citizens?

Today the dialogue is impeded by obsolescent practices and institutions from the long ballot to the presidential primary, from the electoral college to the organization of cities, counties, and states. In too frequent elections unknown persons by the hundreds running for insignificant offices, and numerous improper questions, like the dozens submitted at every California election, are presented to the electorate. This is not democracy, but a perversion of it. The political anatomy is full of vermiform appendices, many of them, like Arkansas, inflamed.

Some of these obsolescent practices stop the dialogue in its tracks, like the failure of the FCC and Congress to develop any concept of the public interest, convenience, and necessity. Some of them distort the dialogue by throwing false weights into it, as the electoral college gives a false weight to the large states and the laws on campaign expenditures give money an overwhelmingly false weight in elections. One thing is certain, and that is that if our hopes of democracy are to be realized, the next generation is in for a job of institutional remodeling the like of which has not been seen since the Founding Fathers.

Well, suppose we got this remodeling done. Could we then turn ourselves into active, responsible, participating citizens? Wouldn't the bureaucracy, though better, and administering better laws, still have us by the throat? The answer depends partly on our capacity for political invention, which in 1787 was quite large, and partly on what participation means. If we can be equipped for the dialogue and then invent the means by which the bureaucracy can hear it and be made responsive to it, we shall have come a long way from where we are now in relation, for example, to the State Department and the Atomic Energy Commission. Then political participation would mean not only what it too often means exclusively now, the ballot, but also participation in the dialogue about the ends and means of the political society. We would be a community learning together, and the bureaucracy would be learning, too.

The notion that the sole concern of a free society is the limitation of governmental authority and that that government is best which governs least is certainly archaic. Our object today should not be to weaken government in competition with other centers of power, but rather to strengthen it as the agency charged with the responsibility for the common good. That government is best which governs best. Mr. Hoover could see no constitutional way of coping with depression, as Buchanan before him could see no constitutional way of coping with secession. We started out to show in 1932 that our institutions were sufficiently flexible to care for the welfare of all the people. The demonstration was never made. We have got instead the pressure group state, which cares for the welfare of those who are well enough organized to put on the pressure.

The genealogy of this development is strange. When I was a boy, we knew what stood between us and freedom, justice, and equality: it was special privilege. Get rid of special privilege, we said, and the common good will be achieved. In our time pacification has been attained not by getting rid of special privilege but by extending it, by extending it to those well enough organized to threaten the special privileges under attack.

Is the tariff hurting the farmers? Retain the tariff and subsidize the farmers. Are administered prices hurting labor? Let's have administered wages, too. Is industry demoralized by expense accounts and tax dodges? Let's have featherbedding in labor, too. Is something done by some group anti-social? Let's all of us—all of us who can put on the pressure—be anti-social, too. And if a federal agency is established to regulate us, never fear: we have the pressure that will shortly make the agency the servant and mouthpiece of the interests it was intended to control. And as we laughingly count our gains at the expense of the public, we can reverently repeat the solemn incantation that helped to make them possible: that government is best which governs least.

The Constitution must protect the citizen against the government. The government must protect him against society, and the rapacity of organizations in it by seeing to it that these organizations pursue purposes and programs consonant with the common good.

The stresses and strains in our society are obscured for us partly by our preoccupation with Russia, which plays a curious double role as the devil in our world and as the standard by which we measure our progress. If we weren't getting ahead of Russia, or falling behind her, how could we tell where we were?

Our real problems are also concealed from us by our current remarkable prosperity, which results in part from the production of arms that we do not expect to use, and in part from our new way of getting rich, which is to buy things from one another that we do not want at prices we cannot pay on terms we cannot meet because of advertising we do not believe.

But beneath these superficial manifestations, beneath our fantasies of fear on the one hand and wealth on the other, are moving those great, fundamental, historic forces which will put our institutions and our democratic faith to the test. This is the basic fact of our life as a people.

I have never subscribed to the proposition once debated in the Oxford Union, that in the opinion of this House Columbus went too far. Nor can I bring myself to refer to man as he is now referred to in military technology, as a "biomechanical link." If Columbus had not gone so far, man might never have had the chance to become anything more than a biomechanical link. America is still the hope of mankind. It is still our responsibility, now more than ever, to see to it that government of the people, by the people, and for the people does not perish from the earth.

Suggested Topics

1. "The civilization of the dialogue"
2. Is "government by the people" possible?
3. Education ought to continue throughout life.
4. "Our new and disturbing leisure"
5. The inadequacies of our mass media
6. "That government is best which governs least."
7. "America is still the hope of mankind."

OUTLOOK FOR OUR CIVIL LIBERTIES   Walter Millis

A former editorial writer for *The New York Herald-Tribune* and before that on the staffs of the *Baltimore News* and *The New York Sun,* Walter Millis has been an articulate observer of political, economic and military developments in this country. His books include *The Road to War* and *Arms and Men.* He also edited the diaries of the late Secretary of Defense James Forrestal.

Are the civil liberties and democratic freedoms of Americans in danger? It is not a simple question. In a society with its normal quota of ambitious, fanatically dedicated, power-hungry or violent men, civil liberties are always in a sense in danger. Civil liberty is in essence the protection of the dignity and just rights of the individual against the repressions and conformities which such men, utilizing the apparatus of the state or the force of public opinion, seek always to impose upon him. In some important areas of our life such pressures seem in the last few years to have risen to new heights. At the same time, in a society of constantly increasing complexity, the individual's reciprocal rights and duties are bound to grow more complex. The state is now making many demands upon him which a half century ago would have seemed quite insupportable in a free society. While recently there has been some relaxation in the more outrageous manifestations of these tendencies, many feel that they have not lost their dangerous underlying force.

On the other hand, it is possible to point to a fairly steady progres-

Reprinted from *The New York Times Magazine,* April 28, 1957. By permission of *The New York Times* and the author.

sion in popular acceptance of the concepts which underlie our civil liberties and popular respect for their principles. Since they were enshrined in the Declaration of Independence, the Constitution and its Bill of Rights (as well as the state constitutions which were forerunners of or modeled on these documents), there has been a rather continuous expansion in the scope and application of these principles. Chief Justice Warren, who once said that he doubted that the Bill of Rights could be enacted today, also delivered the school desegregation opinion which gave to the Bill of Rights one of its most significant extensions. The original Constitution, although establishing a nation "conceived in liberty," to use Lincoln's famous phrase, "and dedicated to the proposition that all men are created equal," could accept and provide for chattel slavery; today the Constitution cannot allow even that degree of unequal treatment represented by racial segregation in public schools.

The basic civil liberties in our society may be simply summarized. Aside from the guarantee of political liberty—representative popular government—they are three: equal opportunity and equal protection of the laws for all; freedom of speech, press and belief (with no state-established church); assurance that none will be deprived of life, liberty or property save by due process of law. This guarantee of due process includes certain other more specific guarantees—such as the right to jury trial, the protection against self-incrimination, the protection against unreasonable searches and seizures—which experience had taught the authors of the Constitution were essential if the legal system was to work duly and justly. To the men of 1789 these seemed the minimum guarantees, as it were, prerequisite if their bold and then novel experiment in free popular government was to succeed.

While one may point to certain notable setbacks in the application of these principles in recent years, it is hard to deny that all or most of them are more practically effective in our daily lives than they were half a century ago. The Negro and other racial minorities have made great advances toward more equal treatment; there is a far wider general acceptance of the idea that all men, regardless of race or status, possess an equal human dignity and an equal claim to opportunity. There is certainly much less mob violence, less police illegality, more generally improved access to more efficient courts, perhaps a greater tolerance of eccentric or dissenting religious faiths. There is probably more censorship and suppression of dissenting or "seditious" political belief than formerly; but the extravagant vigilantism, terrorization and illegality which characterized the suppression of Communists and anarchists at the end of the first World War were not repeated in the attack, savage though it was, on domestic communism after 1945.

With this observable progress in the general acceptance and application of the underlying principles of civil liberty, one might question the Chief Justice's remark that the Bill of Rights could not be enacted today. It might seem extreme to suggest that there is anything seriously wrong; or that the problem, if there is a problem, goes beyond the perennial task of vigilance against specific instances of injustice or discrimination, of publicizing our great charters of civil liberty and furthering popular education in their significance. It was, for example, with some such concept of the problem that the Fund for the Republic began its career four years ago as the first large-scale foundation established to work exclusively in the field of civil liberties. Its subsequent experiences are but one indication that the issues, unfortunately, run much deeper than that.

The most difficult current challenge to those interested in civil liberty has been presented by communism and the intensive war which has been waged upon its domestic manifestations. This was clearly inevitable. While the American Communist party is indisputably a political party, it is also in many aspects a political conspiracy. It has promoted espionage and possibly sabotage; it has sought clandestinely to infiltrate into positions of power in Government and in trade unions. But worse than that, it is a political heresy. It is a root-and-branch denial of all the fundamental tenets of faith, of belief, on which our political system operates.

It denies that our first loyalty is to our own state, substituting a loyalty to a world proletarian revolution. It denies democratic majority rule, substituting the idea that only a class dictatorship in the hands of a few all-powerful men can provide "democracy." For our faith in "a government of laws and not of men" (itself a somewhat metaphysical concept) it substitutes an even more mystic and less provable faith in economic determinism. Here is a clash, not of fact or even of philosophical interpretation, but of fundamental beliefs. It is irresolvable by the Jeffersonian appeal to rational debate, under which "errors cease to be dangerous when it is permitted freely to contradict them." Error can be contradicted; faith cannot be. Here is a problem in heresy.

I feel that our approach to domestic communism has been dictated much less by fear of its menaces—of violent overthrow (which is ridiculous to contemplate in the present economic and political context) or of espionage, sabotage and infiltration (all dangers which, if real, have been grossly exaggerated)—than by hatred of the heretical challenge to our deepest political convictions. The main drive behind the many anti-Communist measures of the past few years has not been a timid search for "security"; it has been an angry thirst for extirpation. The anti-Communist crusade may fairly be called a heresy hunt; and as such it has raised within our free society many of the issues which in the sixteenth and seventeenth centuries were raised within evolving popular government by religious heresy and heterodoxy.

Most of the prohibitions of our Bill of Rights arose from the experiences of those times. In the sixteenth and seventeenth centuries matters of religious belief and affiliation had a critical political importance. To Protestant England in the days of James I the Catholic Gunpowder Plot represented an alien menace of much the same kind, and perhaps almost as great in degree, as the Communist atomic espionage plot represented to our society in 1950. English Catholics were thereafter pursued by much the same methods as have recently been employed here in the harrying of Communists and the extirpation of communism. These are the methods not only appropriate but doubtless unavoidable in the extirpation of heresy of any kind—the self-incriminatory oath, the trial for belief rather than for acts, the condemnation on secret police report, the punishment for associations, the suppression of speech of "ill tendency."

The eighteenth century rationalists who wrote our Declaration of Independence and our Federal and state bills of rights sought to forbid the use of such methods. In so doing they were making a double judgment. Not only were they saying that these methods were violative of natural right; that they were contrary to justice and due process, involving as they did too many of the innocent together with the guilty, and incompatible with the successful operation of free popular government. They also were saying that heretical belief was no longer of serious political significance; that its extirpation was no longer a necessary object of the state or, indeed, any business of the state whatever. This latter judgment—and the Bill of Rights which embodies it—could stand unimperiled only so long as no substantial body of opinion believed that heretical belief *was* of vital significance to the state and its security.

So far as religious issues are concerned, the judgment has stood substantially to this day. But the Federal Bill of Rights was not ten years old before it was challenged by the rise of a political heresy, French Jacobinism, which to a great many did seem to represent the same kind of menace to our free institutions as does communism today.

One result was the Alien and Sedition Acts of 1798, which closely resembled the anti-Communist measures of today, which were defended by the same arguments and occasionally enforced with the same rigor as are the current measures, and which also carried many of the same implications in domestic politics. To Jefferson and his Democratic-Republicans, against whom the Sedition Act was largely aimed (just as anti-communism in its heyday was in considerable measure a political weapon against the Truman Administration), it was "palpably unconstitutional." But it was on the books, and in the climate of the day no mere appeal to Constitutional principle could remove it.

Again a political heresy has become a matter of concern to substantial numbers of our citizens. It is probably inevitable that again, as in 1798, the methods necessary to the extirpation of heresy should be invoked against it. Men have been convicted, as in the Smith Act trials, for their beliefs and utterances. Men have been required to testify against themselves, or heavily penalized if they do not. Men have been severely punished, through loss of reputation or livelihood, because of alleged associations, this often without fair trial, opportunity to confront their accusers or the other safeguards of due process. Men have been punished in various ways for voicing, or even entertaining or being suspected of entertaining, opinions of "ill tendency."

No doubt many of those who have suffered in these ways (certainly not all) were Communist true believers, genuinely dedicated to the destruction of our freedoms and therefore without moral right to appeal to their protection. Yet that only accentuates the dilemma.

Despite the many arguments and devices which have been used to keep anti-Communist measures beyond the letter of the Constitution, it is, I believe, indisputable that they are prohibited by its spirit. It is indisputable that, as always happens in wars upon heresy, many in fact quite innocent of the heretical beliefs have been mangled along with the guilty. Nevertheless, the civil libertarian (an awkward phrase, but there seems no good substitute) is in a difficult position. If he insists that the spirit as well as the letter of the Constitution must be scrupulously upheld and that no heresy-hunting is permissible under any circumstances, he immediately becomes a pro-heretic, or at best an "anti-anti-Communist," subject to the charge—and it is not wholly illegitimate—that in his defense of liberty he is exposing it to its heretical destruction.

About his only means of escape is to argue, as the eighteenth century rationalists would have done, that the heresy is of no real political importance; that the actual dangers are slight, and readily controllable by other means—less costly in the human values of justice, tolerance and decency—than the extirpation of the belief out of which these dangers are assumed to grow. In this case he is still pro-heretic; he invites the further charge of being a fool or a blind man while, even worse, he compromises his own position. He is forced into what amounts to an admission that if the dangers were really as great as they are represented, or if another and actually dangerous heresy should appear, then he would suspend the civil liberties upon the integrity of which he sets so great a value.

Fortunately, our political life does not proceed in absolutes. In the past two or three years the civil libertarian has taken both lines of argument; he has met with both forms of attack, but whether he has been consistent or not he seems in general to have had rather the better of the debate. The anti-Communist crusade has considerably abated. The public has come to regard the perils of domestic communism in a calmer perspective; the problem has come to seem less the problem of a dangerous heresy and more a practical problem in protection against whatever limited but specific perils of espionage and infiltration it may present.

In this changing climate court decisions have recalled us more closely to the spirit as well as the letter of the Constitution, and the Congress and the Executive have not been unmindful in their own spheres. The Communist true believer has been thrust perhaps too effectively beyond the pale of the Constitutional guarantees; and some grievous damage to Constitutional principle may survive. In upholding the Smith Act, the Supreme Court seems only further to have confused the already baffling issues raised by the free speech clause of the First Amendment.

When Jefferson took office it was easy for him to allow the Sedition Act to lapse; today there remains a good deal on the statute books (and in popular attitudes), equally contrary to the spirit of the Constitution, which will not lapse. But communism and the crusade against it no longer appear to present many practical threats to justice and liberty, and it seems probable that we shall survive the episode without serious impairment of the basic principles of free speech and belief, equal treatment and due process.

Yet grave issues of theory do remain; they are both troubling and troublesome. The civil libertarian's dilemma has not been solved, and it is likely to arise again in other areas. The Communist-anti-Communist problem may be regarded as only a special case of a general issue posed by the ever-increasing complexity of the individual's relationship to his state and his community. If the basic eighteenth century principles of civil liberty survive in our affairs, the difficulty of applying their simple eighteenth-century formulations to a society grown inordinately more complex becomes constantly greater.

It was the greater intricacy of our internal and international society which made the Communist heresy seem more dangerous to a larger part of the population than did the Jacobin heresy in 1798. It was the rise of a developed public school system (nonexistent at the end of the Civil War) which created the issues leading to the Supreme Court's desegregation decision; while the growing complexity of the Deep South's economic and social organization have had something to do with the violence of the reaction against it.

In the resistant states desegregation has become a political heresy, and is being fought by methods many of which directly imitate those applied against communism. Here the principles may not be in danger, since the Southern view is not shared elsewhere, but their application, in theory as well as in practice, has been complicated by the problem of Federal as against state power.

The Constitution with its Bill of Rights was an attempt to establish the just and due relationship of the free individual to ordered government. It was made at a time when government and church were almost the only major organized institutions affecting the individual's life, and when government's claims upon him were of the simplest. There were no great standing armies into which he had to be drafted in peacetime, no elaborate economic rules and restrictions of complex tax structures. There were no labor unions, no massive industrial corporations, no highly organized private pressure groups, no huge and quasi-monopolistic media of communications.

Today the price of freedom is not simply the establishment of a just relationship between the individual and the state, but the establishment of a just relationship between the individual and these many institutions, and among the institutions themselves, all of which serve the individual as well as encroach upon him. In this maze of intertwining rights and duties the civil libertarian faces problems whose answers can no longer be read in the simple, if sublime, phrases of the Constitution.

The outlook for civil liberties, especially if you define them in the simple terms of free speech and belief, equal treatment and due process, is good. In all of them, even the first, we have made enormous strides over the last century and a half; and, barring major catastrophe, the trend should continue, I think much more than the classic "eternal vigilance" in defense of eighteenth-century principles is required. A lot of popular (not merely legal) re-examination, reinterpretation and reapplication, comparable to that which led the court to reverse itself on school segregation, seems necessary if we are to preserve the essential liberties, the essential spirit, of our free society.

Suggested Topics

1. Could the Bill of Rights be enacted today?
2. The Fund for the Republic
3. Our "basic civil liberties"
4. The anti-Communist crusade
5. The letter and the spirit of laws
6. The Fifth Amendment
7. "Trial for belief rather than for acts"

THE EGGHEAD LOOKS AT HIMSELF

Seymour Martin Lipset

A Professor of Sociology at the University of California, Seymour Martin Lipset is the author of a number of articles on
social problems and of such books as *Union Democracy,
Agrarian Socialism, Social Mobility in Industrial Society,
Political Man,* and *The Social Base of Politics.*

The American intellectual has for some time been resentful of his
status in American society. Often during the last decade he has felt that
he was nothing more than a convenient target for a great number of
people who are openly and aggressively anti-intellectual. He has been
variously labeled "long-hair," "egghead" and "doubledome." Conservatives and the "radical Right" represented by McCarthyism have
termed the "intellectuals" a threat to American tradition. How accurate are these images of the politics and status of the American intellectual?

First, it is desirable to define the intellectuals. They are all those
who create, distribute and apply culture—the symbolic world of man,
including art, science and religion. Within this group, three different
levels can be set out. There is the hard core who are the creators of
culture—authors, artists, philosophers, scholars, editors, some journalists. Second, there are those who distribute what others create—performers of various arts, most teachers, most reporters. Third, and the
most peripheral group, are those who apply culture as part of their
jobs—professionals such as physicians and lawyers.

When Europeans speaks of the intelligentsia they mean all those
in all three categories. In America, however, the tendency is to include only the first two categories—the creators and distributors of
culture.

This definition I will use here, even though the broader category
has been used by some Americans. The journal Facts Forum, in the
days of McCarthyism, charged intellectuals as a group with being most
vulnerable to communism and described them as "lawyers, doctors,
bankers, teachers, professors, preachers, writers, publishers." And in

Reprinted from *The New York Times Magazine,* November 17, 1957. By permission of *The New York Times* and the author.

more general terms the targets were described as "the American respectables, the socially pedigreed, the culturally acceptable, the certified gentlemen and scholars of the day, dripping with college degrees . . ."

The extent of anti-intellectualism, its sources and its reasons bear some examination.

In the case of the "radical Right" the attack on the university-educated was an attack on precisely those professional groups which were the most effective opponents of McCarthyism. Furthermore, evidence demonstrates that the better educated individuals are the more they favor all forms of "non-economic liberalism," such as civil liberties for unpopular political minorities, equal rights for Negroes and other ethnic minorities, foreign aid and internationalism, the end of national immigration quotas.

In less extreme circles, many business men and other adherents of economic conservatism have sought to reduce the political effectiveness of American intellectuals by ridiculing their supposed lack of practical know-how, or by making scapegoats of them because they erred in the past. Anti-intellectualism has been a useful, even a natural, weapon of conservatives, and to some extent of Republicans, simply because there have been few conservative intellectuals until very recently.

Just where do the intellectuals, taken as a group, stand?

During the twentieth century the great majority of social science academicians, of significant literary figures and the leading intellectual journals of opinion have been on the Left politically. A study of a systematic sampling of academic social scientists by Paul Lazarsfeld of Columbia University reveals that three-quarters are Democrats, and that two-thirds voted for Stevenson in 1952. In the South, most university communities are citadels of the liberal wing of the Democratic party. In the solidly frozen Republican states, universities have often supplied the leadership for the minority Democratic party. The largest chapters of Americans for Democratic Action have existed in university communities.

One 1948 survey of a national sample of librarians, an occupation closely associated with intellectual activities, indicated that not less than 20 per cent backed the Progressive Henry Wallace, the Socialist Norman Thomas, or the Communist Earl Browder (who was on the sample ballot, but did not run). Studies of the "élite corps" of journalists—the Washington and foreign correspondents—indicate that the majority of them are Democrats, and that during the depression of the Thirties a small but significant minority were Socialists. Indicative of the liberal bent of American intellectuals is the fact that most intellectual groups organized to combat Communist influence among intellectuals have invariably been led by Socialists and fairly Leftist liberals.

The general Leftist political bias of the American intellectual happens to be a fact, whether one shares it or detests it. And the attack by the Right on intellectuals is, after all, no more "unsporting" than the attack by the Left on the propensity of corporations or wealthy individuals to contribute money to conservative political groups.

As a matter of fact, the attacks on specific parts of the academic community in America have seldom been purely "anti-intellectual." They have usually been against the opinions held by the group. In the late nineteenth and early twentieth centuries, economists openly critical of capitalism were likely to have a hard time getting promoted; a few were reported to have lost their jobs. However, when the Populist movement was successful in some states, economists who approved of the gold standard were fired from the state universities. When intellectuals are on the side of labor, the unions and their leaders accept them; when they oppose labor, they are called "bourgeois" or middle class," starry-eyed and impractical theorists. The point is that men in politics find it necessary to demolish the strength of the opposition's views.

The matter of the sources of the historic leftism of American intellectuals is obviously a much more complex problem than the phenomenon itself. Two factors, both resultant from our equalitarian ideology, have been important. First, historically, the ideology most easily available to American intellectuals has been the equalitarian dogmas of the Declaration of Independence, which are fundamentally the values of the Left; and, second, the very intellectuals who completely accept the equalitarian implications of the American Creed have felt themselves to be underprivileged, as a class, because they have not been accorded the symbols of high status which their brethren in Europe receive.

On the first point, it is a curious fact that there is no real conservative tradition in America, a condition common to many former colonial countries. American democracy was born in a revolution against a foreign oppressor and it rejected the claims of inherited privilege. Americans, regardless of party, class, or religious persuasion, do believe in their revolutionary creed—unlike those Europeans who live in societies with ancient aristocratic class structures and established churches, where the forces of conservatism never really accepted the legitimacy of equalitarian democracy even when imposed by revolutions.

This means that conservative ideologies which look back to a golden age have never held sway in this country; consequently, no conservative "utopia" has even been counterposed to the equalitarian utopias that have guided our political struggles. The political intellectual, the man of ideas, is nowhere very interested in defending inconsistencies, and every *status quo* is full of inconsistencies. Only by attacking the limitations of this political and social order can he feel himself playing a fruitful creative role. In Europe, he has been able to do this either by supporting a reformist utopia, an image of the good society of the future, or by advocating a conservative utopia, usually in the image of a society with traditional values.

This restriction of possible ideological choices for American intellectuals has meant that even conservatively disposed men have been forced to espouse Leftist or liberal political goals in periods of social stress which called for political action or writing. Conservative politicians have not had an ideology, they have simply attempted to prevent change, or, like the current-day modern Republicans, competed with liberals in seeking equalitarian reforms which they could espouse.

A second major source of the political leftism of American intellectuals derives from their seemingly almost universal feeling that they are an underprivileged group, that they are not high on the scales of social recognition (prestige), income and power, as compared with businessmen and professionals. And with this feeling of being undervalued and underpaid goes the common response of deprived groups the world over: support for those political parties that attack the existing distribution of privilege, and an antagonism toward those who are "overrewarded"—the business classes.

It is a surprising fact, however, that the American intellectual's image of himself is quite different from that held by his fellow citizens.

In one study of the ranking of ninety-six occupations conducted by the National Opinion Research Center of the University of Chicago, college professors rank above every non-political position except doctors. Artists, musicians, and authors rank almost as high. A second national opinion survey conducted by Professor Richard Centers of the University of California in Los Angeles reported similar results.

Since the intellectual's self-image seems to be one major source of his leftism and since the facts contradict this appraisal, the question naturally follows: why then does the American intellectual feel that he is looked down upon?

I suspect that, in large measure, his feelings of inferiority derive from his glorified opinion of the European intellectual's status.

Now, it is certainly true that there is a difference between the European and American treatment of the intellectual. This difference is no more or less than the difference between a fairly rigid class society and a society which emphasizes equality. In Europe, open deference is given to all those with higher status, whether engineers, factory owners, or professors, while in this country it is not given to anyone in anything like the degree obtaining abroad.

What the American intellectual who envies his European brother fails to see is that he is really objecting to the equalitarianism of the United States. In this country a worker will argue the judgment of engineers, and a worker's son will "tell off" his teacher at a university. American employers and engineers find this code of manners natural, but intellectuals object to it. Unconsciously, they think in European terms.

Many American intellectuals see in the supposedly greater dominance of "low-brow" popular culture in America as compared to Europe further evidence of the lower prestige of genuinely creative endeavor in this country. Yet in recent years, as Europe has become more like America in its economic and class structure, many Euorpean intellectuals, including a number of Leftists, have been in despair at the rapid increase of similar popular patterns of culture in their own countries. Perhaps the growth of mass culture in Europe is a result of the fact that for the first time the lower classes have enough money and time to make their own demands in the culture market felt.

There are some other sources of the low self-appraisal and Leftish politics of American intellectuals which do not follow as directly from American equalitarian values—their lack of political power, as compared with that of European intellectuals; their income, as contrasted with that of business executives and professionals.

It is true that the average American intellectual has less direct contact with political power and the men who wield this power than the average European intellectual. But the fact is that, in number, there are far more intellectuals in America than in any other country. This matter of number can be quite important indeed.

For example, in 1929 all ten professors of economics in Australia met and told the Government they believed it would be disastrous for the country to go off the gold standard. The Labor Government of the day was not happy about this, but it felt it should not move against the "experts." But there are far too many experts in the United States for them to have such a unified corporate influence.

The Government of the United States even when the Republicans are in office, does employ and consult professors and other intellectuals —as many as if not more than in most European nations. It is only when you make a comparison in terms of the proportion of intellectuals who are effective that America scores low—there are just so many more of them.

Even in the field of party politics intellectuals do not do badly. In the United States Senate there are five former academicians (Senators Douglas, Humphrey, Fulbright, Morse and Mansfield). Considering the fact that the American electoral and party system makes it difficult for men to get nominated unless they come up the road of machine-politics, and get the backing of local party bosses, the ability of so many intellectuals to win high office at all is rather impressive.

Another point, and a very sore one, in the figure the American intellectual presents to himself is his income. Compared with business men and independent professionals, he is threadbare. His argument goes like this: people are paid according to what they are worth; consequently lower pay implies that one is valued lowly.

This syllogism omits the important fact that there are really two income structures in modern Western countries—the private one and the public one. A public position is always more poorly paid than a corresponding private one. A lawyer at the peak of his profession, that is, as a justice of the Supreme Court of the United States, earns a good deal less than many a corporation lawyer in private practice.

To consider a comparable group among intellectuals, leading professors at major American universities earn salaries which compare favorably with those paid for high-level posts in government. (And many of them make considerably more on the side—in consulting fees from corporations and government, in fees for articles, lectures and books.) A professor who complains that he could be earning much more in private industry is forgetting that this very assertion disproves his contention that his talents are not valued. The truth of the matter is that he, like the lawyer who becomes a judge or politician instead of a corporation counsel, really believes the non-economic rewards of his job are better than monetary gains.

The analysis of the sources of political anti-intellectualism in America has involved some curious paradoxes. I have argued that attacks on intellectualism have been a necessary weapon of conservatives because intellectuals have not been distributed more or less equally among the different political parties and that the reformist spirit of the American intellectual was in turn related to the equalitarian ideology of the United States. The latter not only eliminated conservatism as a real intellectual alternative but also led many intellectuals to regard themselves as underprivileged because equalitarian America did not give them the same overt deference that their continental brethren received. Thus the very success of the liberal ideology which most American intellectuals espouse reinforces their feelings of deprivation, which is one source of their reformist zeal, and that zeal in turn has stimulated political attacks on intellectuals by conservatives, which furnishes further support for left-of-center intellectual politics.

This self-supporting cycle, which seemingly would keep the American intellectual on the Left, and the Right on the offensive against him indefinitely, has shown some signs of breaking down in the last few years. American intellectuals as a group have shifted sharply toward the Center, though most of them probably remain to the left of that imaginary line, and a significant minority have actually become Republican in their party affiliation and conservative in their thinking.

There are many factors underlying this shift, but one of the most important seems to be the general recognition that communism is the main threat to freedom. The recognition of the Communist menace has meant that for the first time Leftist intellectuals in America and other countries have been forced to recognize that revolutions claiming to fulfill the values of the American and French revolutions actually can create a far worse society than the one which now exists in the West.

Such intellectuals find it necessary to defend an existing or a past society against those who argue for the future utopia. Like Burke, they look for sources of stability rather than of change. The very social classes which the reformist intellectual saw as the carriers of the good society, the lower classes, especially the workers, back the new despotism, and not only the despotism of the Left, but—as McCarthyism and Perónism have shown—they can even be foundations of threats to freedom from the "radical Right."

Furthermore, the very success of non-authoritarian forms of leftism —the New Deal in this country and democratic socialism in the British Commonwealth and Scandinavia—has served to remove programs for economic reform from the category of utopia to that of reality, with imperfections and inconsistencies.

The American intellectual today has worked himself into the unhappy position of knowing that he should like and defend his society, but feeling that in so doing he is betraying his obligation as an intellectual to attack and criticize. His solution to this dilemma is to continue to feel himself a man of the Left, to vote Democratic, to describe his politics as liberal or surprisingly often as Socialist, but basically to withdraw from active involvement in or interest in politics, and concentrate on his work, whether it be writing poetry or scholarly articles.

As a final word on the sources of these changes in the intellectual's attitudes, it is important to note that the evidence does not support the assertion by the few who remain in the extreme Left that McCarthyism and other forms of intimidation have silenced the radicals and created a frightened or "bought" group of conformists. The same changes toward moderate politics and toward withdrawal from politics have been occurring among Left-minded intellectuals in other countries as well.

In Britain, the London School of Economics, once regarded as a stronghold of the Labor party, now contains a Conservative voting majority among its faculty, according to a number of reports. In

Canada, the Canadian Forum, organ of Socialist writers and academics for three decades, ceased being a Socialist magazine within the last five years. In Scandinavia, one can point to similar changes. Only in Catholic Europe, where leftism of all varieties has meant anti-clericalism, where conservatism has been linked to Catholicism, has the drift of reformist intellectuals toward the Right been slowed.

The existence of a vicious Leftist totalitarianism which bases itself on the working class, together with the varied effects of prolonged prosperity, has challenged the strength of reformist utopias among American intellectuals. And this change in political attitudes may reduce sharply the expressions of anti-intellectualism. Only time will tell whether we are in for a permanent change in the relation of the American intellectual to his society.

Suggested Topics

1. Who are the intellectuals?
2. Anti-intellectualism in the United States
3. Is the intellectual becoming conservative?
4. Differences in treatment of the intellectual in America and Europe
5. The "radical" Right and the "radical" Left

WHERE IS THE BEAT GENERATION GOING?   *Norman Podhoretz*

A writer, critic and teacher, Norman Podhoretz is editor of *Commentary* magazine. He was a Pulitzer Scholar at Columbia College and holds Bachelor's and Master's degrees in English from Cambridge University, England, where he was a Fulbright Scholar and a Kellet Fellow.

Americans are very fond of rebels, at least at a distance and provided they aren't too subversive, so it was probably to be expected that the Beat Generation would become the object of a lot of journalistic ballyhoo. In the last year or two, Jack Kerouac, Allen Ginsberg & Co. have been more intensively interviewed ("Tell us, Jack,

Reprinted from *Esquire*, December, 1958. © 1958 by Esquire, Inc.

why do you hate the suburbs?"), more glamorously photographed (always looking spiritual as hell, of course), and more earnestly analyzed ("In this Age of Conformity when the Individual is Crushed . . .") than all the Lost Generation writers put together. They have been advertised as the spokesmen for all the hipsters, all the junkies and all the juvenile delinquents in America—as though it were some kind of special virtue to speak for a vicious tendency. They have also been related to the Angry Young Men in England, to the loosely connected group of under-thirty artists (made up of the novelist Françoise Sagan, the painter Bernard Buffet, and the director Roger Vadim) in France, as the American branch of an international movement of Youth rising up to protest against the Conformity, Collectivism, and Despair of the postwar years. Almost everything, in fact, has been done with the Beat Generation except to ask what its existence reveals about the state of our culture and what the pernicious spread of hipsterism, juvenile violence, and drug addiction among the young can be expected to lead to. In England and France, where the literary rebels have no Teddy-boy nonsense in them, no taste for violence and criminality, no *mystique* of "free," instinctual self-expression, and where they are fighting not against civilization but against a strong traditional social and cultural order, the situation (both in life and literature) is not so alarming. But in America, we are witnessing a revolt of all the forces hostile to civilization itself—a movement of brute stupidity and know-nothingism that is trying to take over the country from a middle class which is supposed to be the guardian of civilization but which has practically dislocated its shoulder in its eagerness to thrown in the towel.

There isn't any question, I think, that the rebels in America, England, and France are products of a similar mood, but we can't begin to understand what in fact has been happening throughout the world until we look behind the slogans that have been flying so noisily through the air since Allen Ginsberg's *Howl* brought the Beat Generation into public view. The best way to begin is to ask what attitudes the Beat boys, the Angry Young Men, and the French group have in common, and since it is in literature rather than music or painting or the movies that these attitudes are most explicitly expressed, the best place to look is in the books they have produced. Probably the most general thing we can say is that they show very little interest in, and want as little as possible to do with, the public world—the world of politics, social problems, and large-scale action. Where the Cold War is concerned, for instance, they tend to be apathetic and resigned, or to take a more or less pacifist position. John Osborne, both in his plays and in an essay he contributed to the symposium of Angry Young Men called *Declaration,* denounces Britain's hydrogen tests without so much as considering whether they may be a hideous political necessity. Kingsley Amis, whose first novel *Lucky Jim* has become the classic source-book of the Angries, stigmatizes devotion to anything other than self-interest in politics as "romantic," and says that intellectuals have no interests as a class and therefore no "respectable" motive for being politically active. And Françoise Sagan— in sharp contrast to all the older French writers—never even glances sideways at the political turmoils of her time.

What the young rebels mainly care about is the private life—love, personal relations, problems of the self. The same emphasis on love and the same attribution of supreme importance to personal relations mark every word written by Kerouac, Ginsberg & Co., and love is, of course, the only subject that Françoise Sagan ever bothers with. For her, the alternatives seem to be ennui or a grand passion, and for Jack Kerouac it is always a choice between boredom and kicks. A kick is anything that stimulates sensation and therefore enables you to get into contact with others. The great thing is contact, communication, intimacy, sex, and let the rest of the world go by, preferably at ninety miles an hour.

It's easy enough to understand why this mood of retrenchment, this impulse to shrink back into oneself, this feeling that any involvement in the affairs of the great world is bound to corrupt a decent man, should have become so powerful in the writing of young people everywhere. In itself it is a perfectly sensible reaction to a political stalemate on the international front and the absence of any deep social disturbances on the domestic scene. Being apathetic about the Cold War is to admit that you have a sense of utter helplessness in the face of forces apparently beyond the control of man—for all we know the guided missiles will start firing themselves one of these days of their own malignant volition and save our governments the trouble of declaring war. And it is both reasonable and justifiable to feel that there is no point in getting overly ambitious and competitive in a world where the possibility for great careers in the old style is so severely limited by the Welfare State or the American Organization, and where action on a heroic scale has become inconceivable and even a little ridiculous ("I suppose people of our generation aren't able to die for good causes any longer," says Jimmy Porter, the hero of Osborne's play, *Look Back In Anger*. "If the big bang does come, and we all get killed off, it won't be in aid of the old-fashioned, grand design. It'll just be for the Brave New-nothing-very-much-thank-you").

This increasing apathy was forecast by the writers of the so-called "Silent Generation," who were supposed to be the conformists, express pretty much the same impulse to wash their hands of the world of affairs and to concentrate on love, friendship and self. The novels and poems of the "Silents" exhibit the same indifference to politics and society, the same bias against ambitiousness and competition, the same inclusive concern with personal relations and love. And to make matters still more curious, the sociologists tell us that, for the same reasons, even the junior executives in industry these days suppress the urge to go after power and wealth, settling instead for modest careers that do not engage their deepest responses and giving themselves over whole hog to problems of marriage and family. In what sense, then, are the rebels rebellious? What are they protesting against? What do they stand for? And most important, what do they mean for the future?

At this point we have to look more closely at the particular situation in each of the three countries under discussion. France presents the interesting case of a society in a state of unprecedented economic boom that continues to produce an art of despair and bitterness. There is the "nausea" of Sartre's work, the deserts and plagues that dominate Camus' fiction, the grim, emaciated figures of Buffet's paintings, the stark amoralism of Sagan's novels. There are, too, Vadim's movies in which his former wife Brigitte Bardot often stars and in which she has become the very incarnation of unbridled sexuality and the attempt to intensify every passing moment by a pursuit of pleasure without regard for consequences. (Incidentally, one of those rare moments of symbolic history was made some months ago when Bardot offered to act as godmother to Vadim's illegitimate daughter by another woman a day after her divorce from him became final.) But the melancholy of the older writers should be distinguished from the mood of the younger group. In the bitterness of Sartre, Camus, Simone de Beauvoir, and others of their generation we can detect a reaction to the cultural decline of France since World War II, the loss of its age-old position as the leader of Western civilization—a reaction so powerful that it remains unaffected by the new optimism of the general population. And here we have the link between the Sagan-Buffet-Vadim group and the economic boom. One of the main effects of this modernization of France's economy has been to create a mass of young people who have grown up in an atmosphere very unlike the curious combination of national self-esteem and wartime demoralization of their elders, and who, as one observer has put it, are "almost un-French" in their interest in technology and their indifference to the ideological passions of their parents. The young generation, that is, have been "Americanized," and not only because it cares more about machines and technology than witty conversation and a glorious national destiny. Along with the modernization of the economy, a mass popular culture similar to our own and perhaps based on it has begun to emerge—cars, jazz, movies, picture magazines, and the like. If Françoise Sagan and her circle are rebels, it is in the sense that they participate in and support this invasion of French life and culture by a kind of Americanizing spirit. Sagan's novels, in fact, are full of the feeling that traditional French education is irrelevant—Bergson is a bore because as a philosopher he demands close attention and mental discipline, Stendhal is someone once read in school, intellectual discourse is tiresome.

Actually England is involved in a process of Americanization, but the causes are social and cultural rather than economic. As a result of legislation passed by the Labor Government after 1944 which opened the doors of the universities to more and more children of the lower classes, the upper-class monopoly on education has been broken, and a new type of Englishman (born in the provinces, raised in a relatively poor milieu, educated, if he was bright enough to win a scholarship, at Oxford or Cambridge or one of the "red-brick" universities, and typically holding down a job as a teacher or a librarian somewhere in the Midlands) has come into prominence and begun to demand his cultural rights. The Angry Young Men are either of this class themselves or spokesmen for it. In general, they welcome the forces that are turning England into an egalitarian society, and they have directed their wrath against the upholders of the established culture, who are known simply as "The Establishment." The Establishment includes the rich and fashionable who live in Mayfair and make the rounds of Epsom and Ascot: the graduates of the old public schools like Eton and Harrow and Oxford and Cambridge, the people who control the BBC, *The Times,* and *The Observer.* In the style and tone of The Establishment, the Angry Young Men hear the voice and see the values of an obsolete ruling class, the class that proved its bankruptcy in the Suez fiasco of 1956. When John Osborne denounces the "posh" Sunday papers, or when Kingsley Amis sneers at "filthy Mozart" and T. S. Eliot and says that he would be happiest if the low-brow picture magazines could come out "once an hour instead of once or twice a week, without impairing the rigor of their standards," we know that they are attacking the effete highbrows of The Establishment in the name of something more honest, more vigorous, and more masculine in British life.

The Establishment more or less dismisses America and Americans as vulgar, but John Osborne and Kenneth Tynan are forever praising American movies and plays and books (whose excellence, they seem to think, is America's reward for believing in equality), and Kingsley Amis intimates that his real interests in life are "films, drinking, women's breasts, American novels, jazz, science fiction."

But here again, as in France, the pull of the established culture is

strong enough to keep the rebels from flying off into space. Amis, for
instance, stays strictly within the main tradition of English social
comedy; even his theme—the rise of a new class into "polite society"
—is the theme of much eighteenth-century English fiction which
was preoccupied with the effects of the growing power of the *bour-
geoisie* as against the aristocracy. The point to remember about
Lucky Jim Dixon is that he has a pathetic desire to make it in a world
where Mozart and T. S. Eliot and elegant manners are necessary,
and because he really is an intellectual himself, we can imagine him,
ten years after the novel closes, beginning to sneak off into a secret
room where he can listen to records of *Don Giovanni* without being
exposed to the charge of artiness and affectation from one of his drinking buddies in the pub down the road. As for John Wain, he was
attacked not long ago by the Angry movie-director Lindsay Anderson
for saying that The Establishment, after all, has the virtue of having
acted as a bulwark against the corruptions of "the entertainments industry and the cheap press." "At this rate," Anderson comments, "he
will soon be writing speeches for the Queen."

If the rebels in France and England both represent and stand
for the "Americanization" of their native countries and are critics of
the traditional social and cultural order, what about the Beat Generation? Does it represent and stand for anything comparable over here?
Only, I think, superficially. Like the Angry Young Men, who are
attacking the kind of airy-fairy gentility that passes for cultivation
in The Establishment and who are asserting that there is nothing
"crude" or "vulgar" about the tone and attitudes of provincial lower-
class life, the Beat boys have turned their fire on the standards and
style of the educated American middle class and they have claimed
to be introducing a new vigor, based on the language and experience
of the mass of the people. To some extent, it would be accurate to
say that the San Francisco writers represent an attempt to challenge
the cultural dominance of the big cities (or, rather, of New York)
and the major universities. But what is the challenge founded on?
Who are the grass-roots constituents of the movement? What social
forces are being expressed in Kerouac's novel, in Ginsberg's and
Philip Lamantia's and Lawrence Ferlinghetti's poems? The answer
they themselves would probably give is: all the economic failures
(poor farmers, bums, vagrants, and the lumpen of the cities), all the
victims of social injustice (colored people and people who can't
find work), and especially the suffering adolescent, the juvenile
delinquent, and the hipster. As usual in such movements, the underprivileged, the dispossessed, and the snubbed—the types who
haven't for one reason or another been able to make it in the world
—are declared to be the source and fountainhead of all things

good and true, including (in this particular case) culture itself. Do the outcasts and the adolescents have trouble in articulating their feelings and ideas? This must mean that there is something wrong with the power of articulation; to speak and think coherently isn't "true" intellectuality but "pretentiousness"; "true" intellectuality is in the soul and since the outcasts and the adolescents are considered in our culture to have greater purity of soul than the so-called intellectuals, they must be the "true" intellectuals. Or again—does the stuff Kerouac writes seem to you careless, confused, and chaotic? This must mean that you are a conformist, upholding the standards and values of those creeps who (in Ginsberg's image) are burning to death in their grey flannel suits on Madison Avenue. The Beat Generation writers, it seems, are trying to redefine culture so as to include themselves in. You can't criticize their work by calling it careless and confused, banal and aesthetically undernourished, because they don't admit that coherence and careful thought and precision are virtues. They are like a baseball team that has no hitters and therefore insists on changing the rules so that to swing at the ball three times and miss will be scored as a home run.

Listen to Jack Kerouac's prose:

I was coming down the street with Larry O'Hara old drinking buddy of mine from all the times in San Francisco in my long and nervous and mad careers I've gotten drunk and in fact cadged drinks off friends with such "genial" regularity nobody really cared to notice or announced that I am developing or was developing, in my youth, such bad freeloading habits though of course they did notice but liked me and as Sam said "Everybody comes to you for your gasoline boy, that's some filling station you got there" or say words to that effect—old Larry O'Hara always nice to me, a crazy Irish young businessman of San Francisco with Balzacian backroom in his bookstore where they'd smoke tea and talk of the old days of the great Basie band or the days of the great Chu Berry—of whom more anon since she got involved with him too as she had to get involved with everyone because of knowing me who am nervous and many leveled and not in the least one-souled—not a piece of my pain has showed yet—or suffering—Angels, bear with me—

And so on and on for another twelve lines until the sentence ends. You certainly need the patience of an angel to "bear with" this prose. Not only does it fail to "break through" into new vitality, but it is a style a thousand times more "literary" and derivative and academic than the writing produced by the most anemic instructors of English in our colleges. It is an inept imitation of Faulkner and Joyce done by a man who thinks that to be a Faulkner or a Joyce all you have to do is sit back and pour out anything that pops into your head—and the more mixed-up the better.

But the Beat Generation is a significant phenomenon for all that, and it can't be disposed of by showing up its literary fakery or even by pointing out that its "protest" finally comes to nothing because it stems from nothing and leads to nothing (except perhaps the irresponsible Western interpretation of Zen Buddhism). There *is* meaning in the fact that these writers have attracted so much attention. The San Francisco "renaissance" and the spread during the last few years of hipsterism, juvenile delinquency, and drug addiction among the young arise from the same central cause: the flabbiness and spinelessness of contemporary American middle-class culture. What I mean by middle-class culture here is not only the books written by respectable people and for respectable people, but the way of life, the values, and the attitudes shared by the majority of college-educated Americans. For all practical purposes, this is the class that runs America, just as surely as the aristocracy ran France before the revolution of 1789: it controls industry, dominates the best universities, and has a monopoly on the professions, and because it is a prosperous group, it also embodies the American notion of how to be "high class." Anyone moving up in American society has to learn how to fit into this group: he has to like Martinis (very dry), he has to be interested in (but not too earnest about) good books, good music, serious ideas. Most sociologists agree that this class is largely liberal and "enlightened" in its view of the world. On the whole, it tends to believe in reason and science as opposed to dogmatic authority and churches, and increased social justice as opposed to preserving the *status quo*; unlike the lower-middle and working classes, it sets great store by civil liberties and "Internationalism"; it is indifferent or even hostile to religion; it favors greater freedom in sexual matters than the older middle class did (in principle it has nothing against premarital affairs for men or women, and though its members get jealous like anyone else, most tolerate the idea of infidelity in marriage or at least don't absolutely condemn adultery, and of course they have a much higher rate of divorce).

When I say that middle-class culture is flabby and spineless, I mean that it has grown defensive and timid about its (liberal and "enlightened") values and has therefore proved unable to assert its authority over the young. The causes are too complex to go into here, but we can see the kind of timidity I am talking about almost anywhere we look. Take the much-publicized religious revival, for example. What has actually been revived is not piety and spirituality (even most clergymen are willing to admit that), but the influence of the anti-secularist forces in our society who were temporarily routed during the Thirties and Forties.

Today we inhabit a society where parents are only too happy to let the children "decide for themselves" because they don't have enough faith in the soundness of the principles and values that are the driving force of their own way of life—I mean their *real* principles and values, not the pieties they mouth. And what has come along to fill this power vacuum? Only the conservative drivel that the fears and insecurities of the Cold War period have dredged up again—the slogans of rugged economic individualism preached incessantly by politicians and propagandists who themselves know perfectly well that the day of rugged individualism is long since gone; the pretense that we are a pious God-fearing nation, when every ten-year-old recognizes that religion plays about as important a role in the actual way of life of this country as the regulations of medieval chivalry; worst of all, perhaps, the insidious attempt by clerics in psychiatric clothing to make the freer sexual mores of a whole population seem disreputable and unhealthy by calling them "immaturity." Does anyone expect the obsolete morality—disguised or not—of the new Victorians who have come to the fore in the Eisenhower era to impress a creature even so impressionable as a child? We are not so different, really, from those Englishmen who go around pretending (in Lindsay Anderson's phrase) that "it's *Great* Britain" still, or who (as John Osborne describes it) suggest that "fatuity, so long as it is hallowed by tradition, is acceptable and admirable." No wonder that young writers everywhere and of every stripe are so obsessed with hypocrisy and so sure that to be an adult is to be a phony. The combination of hypocrisy with a paralysis of parental authority is beautifully contrived to turn the children loose to make their own rules. And the rules they make are invariably the rules of the street.

The disobedience of a child with a weak father often takes the form of a tantrum, an explosion of undirected, incoherent, inarticulate rage and aggression. This, plus the need to organize the world by setting up authoritative standards in the absence of any provided by adults, is what much juvenile delinquency amounts to. And what juvenile delinquency is to life, the San Francisco writers are to literature—howling at random against they don't know what and making up aesthetic rules of their own that are a rough equivalent in literary terms of the rules of the street gang, where control and discipline are "chicken," and subtle or complicated ideas are a lot of bull. Exactly the opposite is true of England, where The Establishment plays the role of a very strong parent indeed, and where the young rebels are forced to *argue,* rationally and passionately, instead of simply whining and then being patted on the head.

Where will it all end?

The pall of conservatism and hypocrisy that has been hanging over America for the past decade can only get blacker and fouler in the next few years, and the liberal middle class will probably react by sticking its head deeper into the sand and by growing mushier and globbier by the hour. This means that American youth will perisist in believing that the only two alternatives in life are Zen Buddhism and drug addiction on the one hand, and wholesome suburban boredom on the other. We already have some of the results before our eyes, and anyone who isn't screaming in horror at them deserves whatever he gets—which will be plenty. The main result so far has been the development of what Robert Brustein (one of the few effective screamers-in-horror around) has called "America's new culture hero." This hero appears in many guises: he is the brutal Stanley Kowalski in Tennessee Williams' *A Streetcar Named Desire,* whose vicious animality and mindlessness (especially as Marlon Brando played the role) have become the image of masculinity and—God help us—sensitivity for the rank-and-file of the Beat Generation; he is also Jimmy Dean, whose inability to speak is taken as the mark of spiritual superiority, just as inarticulateness in Jack Kerouac is proof positive of saintliness and virtue; and he can be heard in the orgiastic mumblings of every Elvis Presley record ever made. All these phenomena, to quote Brustein, "prophesy the ruin of culture. . . . In the hero's inarticulacy, we find represented the young American's fears of maturity, for to speak out—to be a speaker —is to be a man."

Exactly.

There you have the whole point.

Isn't the Beat Generation a conspiracy to overthrow civilization (which is created by men, not boys) and to replace it *not* by the State of Nature where we can all romp around in free-and-easy nakedness, but by the world of the adolescent street gang? Maybe our own civilization demands too high a price in repression from the individual spirit, but it is sheer madness to think that the answer lies in never getting beyond the age of seventeen. The San Francisco writers, in their hatred of intelligence, their refusal to respect the requirements of artistic discipline, their contempt for precision and clarity are a perfect reflection of "the fear of maturity," the fear of becoming a man that Brustein finds in American youth at large. We all know what happens when a human being grows up without achieving maturity—he continues to need someone to make decisions for him, to run his life, to lead him. If the guardians of our civilization allow themselves to be bamboozled and intimidated by the arrogant clamor of the crippled young, what will be the political consequence? For what begins as culture always ends in politics, and it is dreadful to contemplate a situation in which nothing exists to stand up against the Beat brigades except the fuddy-duddies informing us that "a family that prays together stays together."

Suggested Topics

1. Why do Beatniks look like that?
2. "To hell with everything"
3. The difference between England's "Angry Young Men" and America's Beatniks
4. A review of a book by Jack Kerouac
5. What are they protesting against?
6. Conformists and non-conformists
7. The "fear of maturity"

WHAT'S AMERICAN ABOUT AMERICA?

John A. Kouwenhoven

A former editor of *Harper's Magazine*, John A. Kouwenhoven is now a professor of English at Barnard College. He is the author of *Adventures of America, 1857-1900; Made in America;* and *The Columbia Historical Portrait of New York*.

The discovery of America has never been a more popular pastime than it is today. Scarcely a week goes by without someone's publishing a new book of travels in the bright continent. The anthropologists, native and foreign, have discovered that the natives of Middletown and Plainville, U.S.A., are as amazing and as interesting as the natives of such better known communities as the Trobriand Islands and Samoa. Magazines here and abroad provide a steady flow of articles by journalists, historians, sociologists, and philosophers who want to explain America to itself, or to themselves, or to others.

The discoverers of America have, of course, been describing their experiences ever since Captain John Smith wrote his first book about America almost 350 years ago. But as Smith himself noted, not everyone "who hath bin at Virginia, understandeth or knowes what Virginia is." Indeed, just a couple of years ago the Carnegie Corporation,

Reprinted from *Harper's Magazine*, July 1956. Reprinted by permission of the author.

which supports a number of college programs in American Studies, entitled its Quarterly Report "Who Knows America?" and went on to imply that nobody does, not even "our lawmakers, journalists, civic leaders, diplomats, teachers, and others."

There is, of course, the possibility that some of the writers who have explored, vicariously or in person, this country's past and present may have come to understand or know what America really is. But how is the lay inquirer and the student to know which accounts to trust? Especially since most of the explorers seem to have found not one but two or more antipodal and irreconcilable Americas. The Americans, we are convincingly told, are the most materialistic of peoples, and, on the other hand, they are the most idealistic; the most revolutionary, and, conversely, the most conservative; the most rampantly individual-istic, and, simultaneously, the most gregarious and herd-like; the most irreverent toward their elders, and, contrariwise, the most abject wor-shipers of "Mom." They have an unbridled admiration of everything big, from bulldozers to bosoms; and they are in love with everything diminutive, from the "small hotel" in the song to the little woman in the kitchen.

Maybe, as Henry James thought when he wrote *The American Scene,* it is simply that the country is "too large for any human con-venience," too diverse in geography and in blood strains to make sense as any sort of unit. Whatever the reason, the conflicting evidence turns up wherever you look, and the observer has to content himself with some sort of pluralistic conception. The philosopher Santayana's way out was to say that the American mind was split in half, one half symbolized by the skyscraper, the other by neat reproductions of Colonial mansions (with surreptitious modern conveniences).

"The American will," he concluded, "inhabits the skyscraper; the American intellect inherits the Colonial mansion." Mark Twain also defined the split in architectural terms, but more succinctly: American houses, he said, had Queen Anne fronts and Mary Ann behinds.

And yet, for all the contrarieties, there remains something which I think we all feel to be distinctively American, some quality or char-acteristic underlying the polarities which—as Henry James himself went on to say—makes the American way of doing things differ more from any other nation's way than the ways of any two other Western nations differ from each other.

I am aware of the risks in generalizing. And yet it would be silly, I am convinced, to assert that there are not certain things which are more American than others. Take the New York City skyline, for example—that ragged man-made Sierra at the eastern edge of the continent. Clearly, in the minds of immigrants and returning travelers, in the iconography of the ad-men who use it as a backdrop for the bourbon and airplane luggage they are selling, in the eyes of poets and of military strategists, it is one of the prime American symbols.

Let me start, then, with the Manhattan skyline and list a few things which occur to me as distinctively American. Then, when we have the list, let us see what, if anything, these things have in common. Here are a dozen items to consider:

1. The Manhattan skyline	7. Mark Twain's writing
2. The gridiron town plan	8. Whitman's *Leaves of Grass*
3. The skyscraper	9. Comic Strips
4. The Model-T Ford	10. Soap operas
5. Jazz	11. Assembly-line production
6. The Constitution	12. Chewing gum

Here we have a round dozen artifacts which are, it seems to me, recognizably American, not likely to have been produced elsewhere. Granted that some of us take more pleasure in some of them than in others—that many people prefer soap opera to *Leaves of Grass* while others think Mark Twain's story telling is less offensive than chewing gum—all twelve items are, I believe widely held to be indigenous to our culture. The fact that many people in other lands like them too, and that some of them are nearly as acceptable overseas as they are here at home, does not in any way detract from their obviously American character. It merely serves to remind us that to be American does not mean to be inhuman—a fact which, in certain moods of self-criticism, we are inclined to forget.

What, then, is the "American" quality which these dozen items share? And what can that quality tell us about the character of our culture, about the nature of our civilization?

Skylines and skyscrapers

Those engaged in discovering America often begin by discovering the Manhattan skyline, and there as well as elsewhere they discover apparently irreconcilable opposites. They notice at once that it doesn't make any sense, in human or aesthetic terms. It is the product of insane politics, greed, competitive ostentation, megalomania, the worship of false gods. Its products, in turn, are traffic jams, bad ventilation, noise, and all the other ills that metropolitan flesh is heir to. And the net result is, illogically enough, one of the most exaltedly beautiful things man has ever made.

Perhaps this paradoxical result will be less bewildering if we look for a moment at the formal and structural principles which are involved in the skyline. It may be helpful to consider the skyline as we might consider a lyric poem, or a novel, if we were trying to analyze its aesthetic quality.

Looked at in this way, it is clear that the total effect which we call "the Manhattan skyline" is made up of almost innumerable buildings, each in competition (for height, or glamor, or efficiency, or respectability) with all of the others. Each goes its own way, as it were, in a carnival of rugged architectural individualism. And yet—as witness the universal feeling of exaltation and aspiration which the skyline as a whole evokes—out of this irrational, unplanned, and often infuriating chaos, an unforeseen unity has evolved. No building ever built in New York was placed where it was, or shaped as it was, because it would contribute to the aesthetic effect of the skyline—lifting it here, giving it mass there, or lending a needed emphasis. Each was built, all those now under construction are being built, with no thought for their subordination to any over-all effect.

What, then, makes possible the fluid and everchanging unity which does, in fact, exist? Quite simply, there are two things, both simple in themselves, which do the job. If they were not simple, they would not work; but they are, and they do.

One is the gridiron pattern of the city's streets—the same basic pattern which accounts for Denver, Houston, Little Rock, Birmingham, and almost any American town you can name, and the same pattern which, in the form of square townships, sections, and quarter sections, was imposed by the Ordinance of 1785 on an almost continental scale. Whatever its shortcomings when compared with the "discontinuous street patterns" of modern planned communities this artificial geometric grid—imposed upon the land without regard to contours or any preconceived pattern of social zoning—had at least the quality of rational simplicity. And it is this simple gridiron street pattern which, horizontally, controls the spacing and arrangement of the rectangular shafts which go to make up the skyline.

The other thing which holds the skyline's diversity together is the structural principle of the skyscraper. When we think of individual buildings, we tend to think of details of texture, color, and form, of surface ornamentation or the lack of it. But as elements in Manhattan's skyline, these things are of little consequence. What matters there is the vertical thrust, the motion upward; and that is the product of cage or skeleton, construction in steel—a system of construction which is, in effect, merely a three-dimensional variant of the gridiron street plan, extending vertically instead of horizontally.

The aesthetics of cage, or skeleton, construction have never been fully analyzed, nor am I equipped to analyze them. But as a lay observer, I am struck by fundamental differences between the effect created by height in the RCA building at Radio City, for example, and the effect created by height in Chartres cathedral or in Giotto's campanile. In both the latter (as in all the great architecture of the past) proportion and symmetry, the relation of height to width, are constituent to the effect. One can say of a Gothic cathedral, "This tower is too high"; of a Romanesque dome, "This is top-heavy." But there is nothing inherent in cage construction which would invite such judgments. A true skyscraper like the RCA building could be eighteen or twenty stories taller, or ten or a dozen stories shorter without changing its essential aesthetic effect. Once steel cage construction has passed a certain height, the effect of transactive upward motion has been established; from there on, the point at which you cut it off is arbitrary and makes no difference.

Those who are familiar with the history of the skyscraper will remember how slowly this fact was realized. Even Louis Sullivan—greatest of the early skyscraper architects—thought in terms of having to close off and climax the upward motion of the tall building with an "attic" or cornice. His lesser contemporaries worked for years on the blind assumption that the proportion and symmetry of masonry architecture must be preserved in the new technique. If with the steel cage one could go higher than with load-bearing masonry walls, the old aesthetic effects could be counterfeited by dressing the façade as if one or more buildings had been piled on top of another—each retaining the illusion of being complete in itself. You can still see such buildings in New York: the first five stories perhaps a Greco-Roman temple, the next ten a neuter warehouse, and the final five or six an Aztec pyramid. And that Aztec pyramid is simply a cheap and thoughtless equivalent of the more subtle Sullivan cornice. Both structures attempt to close and climax the upward thrust, to provide something similar to the *Katharsis* in Greek tragedy.

But the logic of cage construction requires no such climax. It has less to do with the inner logic of masonry forms than with that of the old Globe-Wernicke sectional bookcase, whose interchangeable units (with glass-flap fronts) anticipated by fifty years the modular unit systems of so-called modern furniture. Those bookcases were advertised in the 'nineties as "always complete but never finished"—a phrase which could with equal propriety have been applied to the Model-T Ford. Many of us remember with affection that admirably simple mechanism, forever susceptible to added gadgets or improved parts, each of which was interchangeable with what you already had.

Here, then, are the two things which serve to tie together the otherwise irrelevant components of the Manhattan skyline: the gridiron ground plan and the three-dimensional vertical grid of steel cage construction. And both of these are closely related to one another. Both are composed of simple and infinitely repeatable units.

The structure of jazz

It was the French achitect, Le Corbusier, who described New York's architecture as "hot jazz in stone and steel." At first glance this may sound as if it were merely a slick updating of Schelling's "Architecture . . . is frozen music," but it is more than that if one thinks in terms of the structural principles we have been discussing and the structural principles of jazz.

Let me begin by making clear that I am using the term jazz in its broadest significant application. There are circumstances in which it is important to define the terms with considerable precision, as when you are involved in discussion with a disciple of one of the many cults, orthodox or progressive, which devote themselves to some particular subspecies of jazz. But in our present content we need to focus upon what all the subspecies (Dixieland, Bebop, Swing, or Cool Jazz) have in common; in other words, we must neglect the by no means uninteresting qualities which differentiate one from another, since it is what they have in common which can tell us most about the civilization which produced them.

There is no definition of jazz, academic or otherwise, which does not acknowledge that its essential ingredient is a particular kind of rhythm. Improvisation is also frequently mentioned as an essential; but even if it were true that jazz always involves improvisation, that would not distinguish it from a good deal of Western European music of the past. It is the distinctive rhythm which differentiates all types of jazz from all other music and which gives to all of its types a basic family resemblance.

It is not easy to define that distinctive rhythm. Winthrop Sargeant has described it as the product of two superimposed devices: syncopation and polyrhythm, both of which have the effect of constantly upsetting rhythmical expectations, André Hodeir, in his recent analysis, *Jazz: Its Evolution and Essence,* speaks of "an unending alternation" of syncopations and of notes played *on* the beat, which "gives rise to a kind of expectation that is one of jazz's subtlest effects."

As you can readily hear, if you listen to any jazz performance (whether of the Louis Armstrong, Benny Goodman, or Charlie Parker variety), the rhythmical effect depends upon there being a clearly defined basic rhythmic pattern which enforces the expectations which are to be upset. That basic pattern is the 4/4 or 2/4 beat which underlies all jazz. Hence the importance of the percussive instruments in jazz: the drums, the guitar or banjo, the bull fiddle, the piano. Hence too the insistent thump, thump, thump which is so boring when you only half-hear jazz—either because you are too far away, across the lake or in the next room, or simply because you will not listen attentively. But hence also the delight, the subtle effects, which good jazz provides as the melodic phrases evade, anticipate, and return to, and then again evade the steady basic four-beat pulse which persists, implicitly or explicitly, throughout the performance.

In other words, the structure of a jazz performance is, like that of the New York skyline, a tension of cross-purposes. In jazz at its characteristic best, each player seems to me—and has the sense of being—on his own. Each goes his own way, inventing rhythmic and melodic patterns which, superficially, seem to have as little relevance to one another as the United Nations building does to the Empire State. And yet the outcome is dazzlingly precise creative unity.

In jazz that unity of effect is, of course, the result of the very thing which each of the players is flouting: namely, the basic 4/4 beat—that simple rhythmic gridiron of identical and infinitely extendible units which holds the performance together. As Louis Armstrong once wrote, you would expect that if every man in a band "had his own way and could play as he wanted, all you would get would be a lot of jumbled up, crazy noise." But, as he goes on to say, that does not happen, because the players know "by ear and sheer musical instinct" just when to leave the underlying pattern and when to get back on it.

What it adds up to, as I have argued elsewhere, is that jazz is the first art form to give full expression to Emerson's ideal of a union which is perfect only "when all the uniters are isolated." That Emerson's ideal is deeply rooted in our national experience need not be argued. Frederick Jackson Turner quotes a letter written by a frontier settler to friends back East, which in simple, unself-conscious words expresses the same reconciling of opposites. "It is a universal rule here," the frontiersman wrote, "to help one another, each one keeping an eye single to his own business."

One need only remember that the Constitution itself, by providing for a federation of separate units, became the infinitely extendible framework for the process of reconciling liberty and unity over vast areas and conflicting interests. Its seven brief articles, providing for checks and balances between interests, classes, and branches of the government establish, in effect, the underlying beat which gives momentum and direction to a political process which Richard Hofstadter has called "a harmonious system of mutual frustration"— a description which fits a jazz performance as well as it fits our politics.

The aesthetic effects of jazz, as Winthrop Sargeant long ago suggested, have as little to do with symmetry and proportion as have those of a skyscraper. Like the skyscraper, a jazz perforance does not build to an organically required climax; it can simply cease. The "piece" which the musicians are playing may, and often does, have a rudimentary

Aristotelian pattern of beginning, middle, and end; but the jazz performance need not. In traditional Western European music, themes are developed. In jazz they are toyed with and dismantled. There is no inherent reason why the jazz performance should not continue for another 12 or 16 or 24 or 32 measures (for these are the rhythmic cages which in jazz correspond to the cages of a steel skeleton in architecture). As in the skyscraper, the aesthetic effect is one of motion, in this case horizontal rather than vertical.

Jazz rhythms create what can only be called momentum. When the rhythm of one voice (say the trumpet, off on a rhythmic and melodic excursion) lags behind the underlying beat, its four-beat measure carries over beyond the end of the underlying beat's measure into the succeeding one, which has already begun. Conversely, when the trumpet anticipates the beat, it starts a new measure before the steady underlying beat has ended one. And the result is an exhilarating forward motion which the jazz trumpeter Wingy Manone once described as "feeling an increase in tempo though you're still playing at the same tempo." Hence the importance in jazz of timing, and hence the delight and amusement of the so-called "break" in which the basic 4/4 beat ceases and a soloist goes off on a flight of rhythmic and melodic fancy which nevertheless comes back surprisingly and unerringly to encounter the beat precisely where it would have been if it had kept going.

Once the momentum is established, it can continue until—after an interval dictated by some such external factor as the conventional length of phonograph records or the endurance of dancers—it stops. And as if to guard against any Aristotelian misconceptions about an end, it is likely to stop on an unresolved chord, so that harmonically as well as rhythmically everything is left up in the air. Even the various coda-like devices employed by jazz performers at dances, such as the corny old "without a shirt" phrase of blessed memory, are harmonically unresolved. They are merely conventional ways of saying "we quit," not, like Beethoven's insistent codas, ways of saying, "There now; that ties off all the loose ends; I'm going to stop now; done; finished; concluded; signed, sealed, delivered."

Twain and Whitman

Thus far, in our discussion of distinctively "American" things, we have focused chiefly upon twentieth-century items. But the references to the rectangular grid pattern of cities and townships and to the Constitution should remind us that the underlying structural principles with which we are concerned are deeply embedded in our civilization. To shift the emphasis, therefore, let us look at item number 7 on our list: Mark Twain's writing.

Mark's writing was, of course, very largely the product of oral influences. He was a born story-teller, and he always insisted that the oral form of the humorous story was high art. Its essential tool (or weapon), he said, is the pause—which is to say, timing. "If the pause is too long the impressive point is passed," he wrote, "and the audience have had time to divine that a surprise is intended—and then you can't surprise them, of course." In other words, he saw the pause as a device for upsetting expectations, like the jazz "break."

Mark, as you know, was by no means a formal perfectionist. In fact he took delight in being irreverent about literary form. Take, for example, his account of the way *Pudd'nhead Wilson* came into being. It started out to be a story called "Those Extraordinary Twins," about a youthful freak consisting, as he said, of "a combination of two heads and four arms joined to a single body and a single pair of legs— and I thought I would write an extravagantly fantastic little story with this freak of nature for hero—or heroes—a silly young miss [named Rowena] for heroine, and two old ladies and two boys for the minor parts.

But as he got writing the tale, it kept spreading along and other people began intruding themselves—among them Pudd'nhead, and a woman named Roxana, and a young fellow named Tom Driscoll, who —before the book was half finished—had taken things almost entirely into their own hands and were "working the whole tale as a private venture of their own."

From this point, I want to quote Mark directly, because in the process of making fun of fiction's formal conventions he employs a technique which is the verbal equivalent of the jazz "break"—a technique of which he was a master.

When the book was finished, and I came to look round to see what had become of the team I had originally started out with—Aunt Patsy Cooper, Aunt Betsy Hale, the two boys, and Rowena, the light-weight heroine—they were nowhere to be seen; they had disappeared from the story some time or other. I hunted about and found them—found them stranded, idle, forgotten, and permanently useless. It was very awkward. It was awkward all around; but more particularly in the case of Rowena, because there was a love match on, between her and one of the twins that constituted the freak, and I had worked it up to a blistering heat and thrown in a quite dramatic love quarrel [now watch Mark take off like a jazz trumpeter flying off on his own in a fantastic break] wherein Rowena scathingly denounced her betrothed for getting drunk, and scoffed at his explanation of how it happened, and wouldn't listen to it, and had driven him from her in the usual "forever" way; and now here she sat crying and broken-hearted; for she had found that he had spoken only the truth; that it was not he but the other half of the freak, that had drunk the liquor that made him drunk; that her half was a prohibitionist and had never drunk a drop in his life, and, although tight as a brick three days in the week, was wholly innocent of blame; and, indeed, when sober was constantly doing all he could to reform his brother, the other half, who never got any satisfaction out of drinking anyway, because liquor never affected him. [Now he's going to get back on the basic beat again.] Yes, here she was, stranded with that deep injustice of hers torturing her poor heart.

Now I shall have to summarize again. Mark didn't know what to do with her. He couldn't just leave her there, of course, after making such a to-do over her; he'd have to account to the reader for her somehow. So he finally decided that all he could do was "give her the grand bounce." It grieved him, because he'd come to like her after a fashion, "notwithstanding she was such an ass and said such stupid, irritating things and was so nauseatingly sentimental"; but it had to be done. So he started Chapter Seventeen with: "Rowena went out in the back yard after supper to see the fireworks and fell down the well and got drowned."

It seemed abrupt, [Mark went on] but I thought maybe the reader wouldn't notice it, because I changed the subject right away to something else. Anyway, it loosened up Rowena from where she was stuck and got her out of the way, and that was the main thing. It seemed a prompt good way of weeding out people that had got stalled, and a plenty good enough way for those others; so I hunted up the two boys and said they went out back one night to stone the cat and fell down the well and got drowned. Next I searched around and found Aunt Patsy Cooper and Aunt Betsy Hale where they were aground, and said they went out back one night to visit the sick and fell down the well and got drowned. I was going to drown some of the others, but I gave up the idea, partly because I believed that if I kept that up it would arouse attention, . . . and partly because it was not a large well and would not hold any more anyway.

That was a long excursion—but it makes the point: that Mark didn't have much reverence for conventional story structure. Even his greatest book, which is perhaps also the greatest book written on this continent—*Huckleberry Finn*—is troublesome. One can scarcely find a criticism of the book which does not object, for instance, to the final episodes, in which Tom rejoins Huck and they go through that burlesque business of "freeing" the old Negro Jim—who is, it turns out, already free. But, as T. S. Eliot was, I think, the first to observe, the real structure of *Huck Finn* has nothing to do with the traditional form of the novel—with exposition, climax, and resolution. Its structure is like that of the great river itself—without beginning and without end. Its structural units, or "cages," are the episodes of which it is composed. Its momentum is that of the tension between the river's steady flow and the eccentric superimposed rhythms of Huck's flights from, and near recapture by, the restricting forces of routine and convention.

It is not a novel of escape; if it were, it would be Jim's novel, not Huck's. Huck is free at the start, and still free at the end. Looked at in this way, it is clear that *Huckleberry Finn* has as little need of a "conclusion" as has a skyscraper or a jazz performance. Questions of proportion and symmetry are as irrelevant to its structure as they are to the total effect of the New York skyline.

There is not room here for more than brief reference to the other "literary" items on our list: Whitman's *Leaves of Grass*, comic strips, and soap opera. Perhaps it is enough to remind you that *Leaves of Grass* has discomfited many a critic by its lack of symmetry and proportion, and that Whitman himself insisted: "I round and finish little, if anything; and could not, consistently with my scheme." As for the words of true poems, Whitman said in the "Song of the Answerer"—

> They bring none to his or her terminus or to be content and full,
> Whom they take they take into space to behold the birth of stars, to
> learn one of the meanings,
> To launch off with absolute faith, to sweep through the ceaseless rings
> and never be quite again.

Although this is not the place for a detailed analysis of Whitman's verse techniques, it is worth noting in passing how the rhythm of these lines reinforces their logical meaning. The basic rhythmical unit, throughout, is a three-beat phrase of which there are two in the first line (accents falling on *none, his,* and *term . . . be, tent,* and *full*), three in the second and in the third. Superimposed upon the basic three-beat measure there is a flexible, nonmetrical rhythm of colloquial phrasing. That rhythm is controlled in part by the visual effect of the arrangement in long lines, to each of which the reader tends to give equal duration, and in part by the punctuation within the lines.

It is the tension between the flexible, superimposed rhythms of the rhetorical patterns and the basic three-beat measure of the underlying framework which unites with the imagery and the logical meaning of the words to give the passage its restless, sweeping movement. It is this tension, and other analogous aspects of the structure of *Leaves of Grass* which give to the book that "vista" which Whitman himself claimed for it. If I may apply it to T. S. Eliot's idea about *Huckleberry Finn,* the structure of the *Leaves* is open at the end. Its key poem may well be, as D. H. Lawrence believed, the "Song of the Open Road."

As for the comics and soap opera, they too—on their own frequently humdrum level—have devised structures which provide for no ultimate climax, which come to no end demanded by symmetry or proportion. In them both there is a shift in interest away from the "How does it come out?" of traditional story telling to "How are things going?" In a typical installment of Harold Gray's *Orphan Annie,* the final panel shows Annie walking purposefully down a path with her dog, Sandy, saying: "But if we're goin' why horse around? It's a fine night for walkin'. . . C'mon, Sandy . . . Let's go . . ." (It doesn't even end with a period, or full stop, but with the conventional three dots or suspension points, to indicate incompletion.) So too, in the soap operas, *Portia Faces Life,* in one form or another, day after day, over and over again. And the operative word is the verb *faces.* It is the process of facing that matters.

America is process

Here, I think, we are approaching the central quality which all the diverse items on our list have in common. That quality I would define as a concern with process rather than with product—or, to re-use Mark Twain's words, a concern with the manner of handling experience or materials rather than with the experience or materials themselves. Emerson, a century ago, was fascinated by the way "becoming somewhat else is the perpetual game of nature." And this preoccupation with process is, of course, basic to modern science. "Matter" itself is no longer to be thought of as something fixed, but fluid and ever-changing. Similarly, modern economic theory has abandoned the "static equilibrium" analysis of the neo-classic economists, and in philosophy John Dewey's instrumentalism abandoned the classic philosophical interest in final causes for a scientific interest in "the mechanism of occurrences"—that is, process.

It is obvious, I think, that the American system of industrial mass production reflects this same focus of interest in its concern with production rather than products. And it is the mass-production system, *not* machinery, which has been America's contribution to industry.

In that system there is an emphasis different from that which was characteristic of handicraft production or even of machine manufacture. In both of these there was an almost total disregard of the means of production. The aristocratic ideal inevitably relegated interest in the means exclusively to anonymous peasants and slaves;

whaṫ mattered to those who controlled and administered production was, quite simply, the finished product. In a mass-production system, on the other hand, it is the process of production itself which becomes the center of interest, rather than the product.

If we are aware of this fact, we usually regard it as a misfortune. We hear a lot, for instance, of the notion that our system "dehumanizes" the worker, turning him into a machine and depriving him of the satisfactions of finishing anything, since he performs only some repetitive operation. It is true that the unit of work in mass production is not a product but an operation. But the development of the system, in contrast with Charlie Chaplin's wonderful but wild fantasy of the assembly line, has shown the intermediacy of the stage in which the worker is doomed to frustrating boredom. Merely repetitive work, in the logic of mass production, can and must be done by machine. It is unskilled work which is doomed by it, not the worker. More and more skilled workers are needed to design products, analyze jobs, cut patterns, attend complicated machines, and co-ordinate the processes which comprise the productive system.

The skills required for these jobs are different, of course, from those required to make handmade boots or to carve stone ornament, but they are not in themselves less interesting or less human. Operating a crane in a steel mill, or a turret lathe, is an infinitely more varied and stimulating job than shaping boots day after day by hand. A recent study of a group of workers on an automobile assembly line makes it clear that many of the men object, for a variety of reasons, to those monotonous, repetitive jobs which (as we have already noted) should be—but in many cases are not yet—done by machine; but those who *like* such jobs like them because they enjoy the process. As one of them said: "Repeating the same thing you can catch up and keep ahead of yourself . . . you can get in the swing of it." The report of members of a team of British workers who visited twenty American steel foundries in 1949 includes this description of the technique of "snatching" a steel casting with a magnet, maneuvered by a gantry crane running on overhead rails:

In its operation, the crane approaches a pile of castings at high speed with the magnet hanging fairly near floor level. The crane comes to a stop somewhere short of the castings, while the magnet swings forward over the pile, is dropped onto it, current switched on, and the hoist begun, at the same moment as the crane starts on its return journey. [And then, in words which might equally be applied to a jazz musician, the reports adds:] The whole operation requires timing of a high order, and the impression gained is that the crane drivers derive a good deal of satisfaction from the swinging rhythm of the process.

This fascination with process has possessed Americans ever since Oliver Evans in 1785 created the first wholly automatic factory: a flour mill in Delaware in which mechanical conveyors—belt conveyors, bucket conveyors, screw conveyors—are interlinked with machines in a continuous process of production. But even if there were no other visible sign of the national preoccupation with process, it would be enough to point out that it was an American who invented chewing gum (in 1869) and that it is the Americans who have spread it—in all senses of the verb—throughout the world. An absolutely non-consumable confection, its sole appeal is the process of chewing it.

The apprehensions which many people feel about a civilization absorbed with process—about its mobility and wastefulness as well as about the "dehumanizing" effects of its jobs—derive, I suppose, from old habit and the persistence of values and tastes which were indigenous to a very different social and economic system. Whitman pointed out in *Democratic Vistas* more than eighty years ago that America was a stranger in her own house, that many of our social institutions, like our theories of literature and art, had been taken over almost without change from a culture which was not, like ours, the product of political democracy and the machine. Those institutions and theories, and the values implicit in them, are still around, though some (like collegiate gothic, of both the architectural and intellectual variety) are less widely admired than formerly.

Change, or the process of consecutive occurrences, is, we tend to feel, a bewildering and confusing and lonely thing. All of us, in some moods, feel the "preference for the stable over the precarious and uncompleted" which, as John Dewey recognized, tempts philosophers to posit their absolutes. We talk fondly of the need for roots—as if man were a vegetable, not an animal with legs whose distinction it is that he can move and "get on with it." We would do well to make ourselves more familiar with the idea that the process of development is universal, that it is "the form and order of nature." As Lancelot Law Whyte has said, in *The Next Development in Man:*

Man shares the special form of the universal formative process which is common to all organisms, and herein lies the root of his unity with the rest of organic nature. While life is maintained, the component processes in man never attain the relative isolation and static perfection of inorganic processes . . . The individual may seek, or believe that he seeks, independence, permanence, or perfection, but that is only through his failure to recognize and accept his actual situation.

As an "organic system" man cannot, of course, expect to achieve stability or permanent harmony, though he can create (and in the great arts of the past, has created) the illusion of them. What he can achieve is a continuing development in response to his environment. The factor which gives vitality to all the component processes in the individual and in society is "not permanence but development."

To say this is not to deny the past. It is simply to recognize that for a variety of reasons people living in America have, on the whole, been better able to relish process than those who have lived under the imposing shadow of the arts and institutions which Western man created in his tragic search for permanence and perfection—for a "closed system." They find it easy to understand what that very American philosopher William James meant when he told his sister that his house in Chocorua, New Hampshire, was "the most delightful house you ever saw; it has fourteen doors, all opening outwards." They are used to living in grid-patterned cities and towns whose streets, as Jean-Paul Sartre observed, are not, like those of European cities, "closed at both ends." As Sartre says in his essay on New York, the long straight streets and avenues of a gridiron city do not permit the buildings to "cluster like sheep" and protect one against the sense of space. "They are not sober little walks closed in between houses, but national highways. The moment you set foot on one of them, you understand that it has to go on to Boston or Chicago."

So, too, the past of those who live in the United States, like their future, is open-ended. It does not, like the past of most other people, extend downward into the soil out of which their immediate community or neighborhood has grown. It extends laterally backward across the plains, the mountains, or the sea to somewhere else, just as their future may at any moment lead them down the open road, the endless-vistaed street.

Our history is the process of motion into and out of cities; of westering and the counter-process of return; of motion up and down the social ladder—a long, complex, and sometimes terrifyingly rapid sequence of consecutive change. And it is this sequence, and the attitudes and habits and forms which it has bred, to which the term "America" really refers.

"America" is not a synonym for the United States. It is not an artifact. It is not a fixed and immutable ideal toward which citizens of this nation strive. It has not order or proportion, but neither is it chaos except as that is chaotic whose components no single mind can comprehend or control. America is process. And in so far as people have been "American"—as distinguished from being (as most of us, in at least some of our activities, have been) mere carriers of transplanted cultural traditions—the concern with process has been reflected in the work of their heads and hearts and hands.

Suggested Topics: 1. Are Americans "different"? 2. America's contributions to the world. 3. What America should learn from the rest of the world. 4. America and the arts. 5. The "tempo of life" here and abroad.